CRITICAL ISSUES IN CHINA'S GROWTH AND DEVELOPMENT

The Chinese Economy Series

This series examines the immense importance of China within the global economy. Books in the series view the Chinese economy in many ways, such as: a transition economy, a bridge between the developing and developed nations, a vital member of the WTO, and even as a potential rival to the US.

Providing readers with high quality monographs and edited volumes by authors from the East and West, this series is a truly global forum on one of the world's key economies.

Series Editors

Aimin Chen, Indiana State University, USA
Shunfeng Song, University of Nevada-Reno, USA

Recent Titles in the Series

The Efficiency of China's Stock Market
Shiguang Ma
ISBN 0 7546 4241 0

Technology and Knowledge Transfer in China
Richard Li-Hua
ISBN 0 7546 3928 2

Urbanization and Social Welfare in China
Edited by Aimin Chen, Gordon G. Liu and Kevin H. Zhang
ISBN 0 7546 3313 6

Urban Transformation in China
Edited by Aimin Chen, Gordon G. Liu and Kevin H. Zhang
ISBN 0 7546 3312 8

China's Economic Development and Democratization
Yanlai Wang
ISBN 0 7546 3620 8

Critical Issues in China's Growth and Development

Edited by
YUM K. KWAN and EDEN S.H. YU
City University of Hong Kong

ASHGATE

Published by
Ashgate Publishing Limited
Gower House
Croft Road
Aldershot
Hampshire GU11 3HR
England

Ashgate Publishing Company
Suite 420
101 Cherry Street
Burlington, VT 05401-4405
USA

Ashgate website: http://www.ashgate.com

British Library Cataloguing in Publication Data
Critical issues in China's growth and development. - (The Chinese economy series)
1.China - Economic conditions - 1976-2000 - Congresses
I.Title II.Kwan, Yum K. III.Yu, Eden S. H. IV.Chow, Gregory C. (Gregory Chi-chong), 1929-
338.9'51'009045

Library of Congress Cataloging-in-Publication Data
Critical issues in China's growth and development / by Yum K. Kwan and Eden S.H. Yu, [editors].
p. cm. -- (The Chinese economy series)
Includes bibliographical references and index.
ISBN 0-7546-4270
1. China--Economic policy. 2. China --Economic conditions. 3. Economic development--Social aspects--China. I. Kwan, Yum K. (Yum-Keung) II. Yu, Eden Siu-hung. III. Series.

HC427.95.C75 2004
330.951--dc22

2004018316

ISBN 0 7546 4270 4

Printed and bound by Athenaeum Press, Ltd.,
Gateshead, Tyne & Wear.

Contents

List of Contributors *vii*
Editors' Introduction *ix*

PART I: ECONOMIC GROWTH

1 Higher Education in China: A Growth Paradox?
Belton M. Fleisher 3

2 Taxation and Economic Growth in China
Roger H. Gordon and Wei Li 22

3 How Size Matters to Future Chinese Growth: Some Trade–Theoretic Considerations
Henry Wan Jr. 41

4 Product Innovation, Capital Accumulation, and Endogenous Growth
Heng–fu Zou 66

PART II: FOREIGN DIRECT INVESTMENT AND TRADE

5 Regional Attributes, Public Inputs and Tax Competition for FDI in China
Chi–Chur Chao, Win–Lin Chou and Eden S.H. Yu 83

6 An Econometric Estimation of Locational Choices of Foreign Direct Investment: The Case of Hong Kong and U.S. Firms in China
K.C. Fung, Hitomi Iizaka, Chelsea C. Lin and Alan Siu 97

7 Revealed Comparative Advantages and Intra–regional Trade of the World's Three Major Regions: 1980–1995
Leonard K. Cheng, Siu Fai Leung and Zihui Ma 108

PART III: INTERNATIONAL FINANCE

8 Trade, Financial Linkages and Contagion of Currency Crises
Lawrence J. Lau and Isabel K. Yan 133

9 Exchange Rate Dynamics: Where is the Saddle Path?
Yin–Wong Cheung, Javier Gardeazabal and Jesús Vázquez 201

10 How Well Has the Currency Board Performed? Evidence from Hong Kong
Yum K. Kwan and Francis T. Lui 217

PART IV: SOCIOECONOMIC ISSUES

11 A Modified Harris–Todaro Model of Rural–Urban Migration for China
Derek Laing, Chuhwan Park and Ping Wang 245

12 The 'Banker Effect' on Chinese Stock Pricing
Yuan Shu and Guoqiang Bin 265

13 China's Food Economy and Its Implications for the Rest of the World 276
Ninghui Li

Index *303*

List of Contributors

Guoqiang Bin is a Ph.D. candidate at Lingnan (University) College, Zhongshan University, China.

Chi–Chur Chao is Professor in Economics at the Chinese University of Hong Kong.

Leonard K. Cheng is Professor and Head of Economics at the Hong Kong University of Science and Technology.

Yin–Wong Cheung is Professor of Economics at University of California, Santa Cruz,USA.

Win–Lin Chou is Professor in Economics at the Chinese University of Hong Kong.

Belton M. Fleisher is Professor of Economics at Ohio State University, USA.

K.C. Fung is Professor of Economics at University of California, Santa Cruz, USA.

Javier Gardeazabal is Associate Professor at the University of the Basque Country, Spain.

Roger H. Gordon is Professor of Economics at University of California, San Diego, USA, and Research Associate of the National Bureau of Economic Research and the Centre for Economic Policy Research.

Hitomi Iizaka is a Research Associate at the Department of Economics, University of California, Santa Cruz, USA.

Yum K. Kwan is Associate Professor of Economics at the City University of Hong Kong.

Derek Laing is Associate Professor of Economics at the Pennsylvania State University, USA.

Lawrence J. Lau is Kwoh–Ting Li Professor of Economic Development and Senior Fellow of the Hoover Institution at Stanford University, USA.

Siu Fai Leung is Associate Professor of Economics at the Hong Kong University of Science and Technology.

Ninghui Li is Associate Professor at Institute of Agricultural Economics, Chinese Academy of Agricultural Sciences, China.

Wei Li is Associate Professor of Business Administration at the Darden Graduate School of Business at the University of Virginia, USA.

Chelsea C. Lin is Assistant Professor of Economics at National Dong Hwa University, Taiwan.

Francis T. Lui is Professor of Economics and Director of the Center for Economic Development at the Hong Kong University of Science and Technology.

Zihui Ma is a Ph.D. candidate at the Hong Kong University of Science and Technology.

Chuhwan Park is a researcher at Electronics and Telecommunication Research Institute in Seoul, Korea.

Yuan Shu is Professor of Economics and President of Lingnan (University) College, Zhongshan University, China.

Alan Siu is Associate Professor of Economics at the University of Hong Kong.

Jesús Vázquez is Associate Professor at the University of the Basque Country, Spain.

Henry Wan Jr. is Professor of Economics at Cornell University, USA.

Ping Wang is Professor and Chair of Economics at Vanderbilt University, Research Associate of the National Bureau of Economic Research, and Vice President of the East Asian Research Institute, USA.

Isabel K. Yan is Assistant Professor of Economics at the City University of Hong Kong.

Eden S.H. Yu is Chair Professor of Economics at the City University of Hong Kong.

Heng-fu Zou is Professor of Economics at Peking University and Wuhan University, China, and Senior Research Economist of the World Bank.

Editors' Introduction

This book consists of 13 chapters selected from a total of 44 papers presented at the International Conference in Honour of Professor Gregory Chow on 'China and the World Economy.' The conference was organized by the City University of Hong Kong, and took place June 14–16, 2002. A world renowned economist, Gregory Chow has made path–breaking contributions in econometrics, dynamic economics, and the Chinese economy. Since the gradual shift from a predominantly central planned economy to a market based economy in the late 1970s, China has experienced unprecedented economic growth. To contribute to understanding current rapid economic growth and development, this book examines a number of critical issues in the following four areas: economic growth, foreign direct investment (FDI) and trade, international finance, and socioeconomic issues. These topics constitute the main themes of the four parts of the book.

Part I consists of four chapters which investigate, respectively, how higher education, tax reforms, the size of the Chinese market, and access to advanced technology affect the rate of China's economic growth. In the first chapter, Belton M. Fleisher examines the impact of China's higher education on its economic growth. Fleisher presents statistical evidence of the positive contribution of a relatively small proportion of university graduates on China's economic transformation. However, he argues that China's potential for further growth could be hampered by a lack of sufficient university graduates. Furthermore, Fleisher points out that it would be desirable for China to improve resource allocation for higher education.

In Chapter 2, Roger H. Gordon and Wei Li examine the positive role of the tax system in China's recent breathtaking economic transformation. The early tax reform and resultant fiscal decentralization in the 1980s facilitated local governments' collection of profit tax from small and new firms, leading to strong local government support for firm entry. While this tax policy led to a high growth rate, it also generated many tax distortions that grew in importance over time. The reform of the tax system in the 1990s, shifting away from corporate taxes and tariffs towards a value–added tax, substantially reduced these tax distortions while still preserving many of the incentives encouraging entry and growth.

In Chapter 3, *How Size Matters to Future Chinese Growth: Some Trade–Theoretic Considerations*, Henry Wan Jr. explores the ramifications for China's economic potential of the facts that China is the world's largest in population and second largest in total real output. He shows analytically that size matters from a variety of perspectives, including factor proportions, terms of trade, economies of scale, market power and policy coordination. He explains the recent strong performance of China's economy and predicts its future economic prospects in light of the importance of a nation's size.

In Chapter 4, Heng–fu Zou presents a model of endogenous economic growth integrating product innovation and physical capital accumulation. He examines the long–run relationship between product development and capital formation. Following the line of research by Romer and by Grossman and Helpman, Zou further distinguishes the role of product development and capital accumulation in endogenous growth. He demonstrates how these two factors can determine long–run growth rates. Zou also explores the effect of international technology transfers from a developed country to a developing economy. He shows that the rate of capital accumulation in the less–developed country is partially related to the rate of product development in the developed nation.

Part II consists of three chapters which address the following three interesting questions. What are the attributes of a region in China that can attract foreign investment? What are the main determinants of locational choices by Hong Kong and U.S. firms for their direct investments in China? And what influences the extra–regional trade and intra–regional trade of the world's three major regions?

In Chapter 5 on regional attributes, public inputs and tax competition for foreign investment in China, Chi–Chur Chao, Win–Lin Chou and Eden S.H. Yu examine the determinants of inward foreign direct investment (FDI) into various regions of China. Although the growth rate of the Chinese economy is remarkable, it is very uneven across regions. Why would foreign firms invest in only a few areas in China? Chao, Chou and Yu construct a theoretical model, incorporating region–specific (geographical location, human capital, regional GNP etc) and economy–common factors (tax incentives and preferential treatment), to explain regional competition for FDI. A panel data set is used to estimate the determinants of FDI inflows into China for the period of 1985–2000. Their findings reveal that tax competition is not effective in attracting FDI.

Chapter 6 *An Econometric Estimation of Locational Choices of Foreign Direct Investment: The Case of Hong Kong and U.S. Firms in China*, by K.C. Fung, Hitomi Iizaka, Chelsea C. Lin and Alan Siu, examines the locational choices of Hong Kong and U.S. direct investment in China for the period from 1990 to 1999. They consider the implications of regional GDP, local labor costs, and regional labor quality for FDI. Their empirical results reveal some similarities and differences in the significance of these factors. Local GDP in China significantly influences investment inflows from both origins. Nonetheless, investment from Hong Kong is more sensitive to local labor costs, whereas U.S investment is more sensitive to the quality of labor.

In Chapter 7, Leonard K. Cheng, Siu Fai Leung and Zihui Ma investigate the extra– and intra–regional trade of the world's three major regions: the Asian Pacific Rim economies (APRE), the European Union (EU), and the North American Free Trade Area (NAFTA) for the period 1980–1995. Utilizing the concept of Revealed Comparative Advantage, they show that all three regions have a comparative advantage, relative to the rest of the world, in technology intensive products in addition to having comparative disadvantage in natural resource intensive products. Two models are tested for intraregional trade. Based on the empirical results, the authors reject a proportional–spending model, and argue that a gravity model provides a better account of the intra–regional trade intensities of the EU and NAFTA.

Part III deals with several emerging issues of international finance. The three chapters in this part address the following questions. What is the role of trade and financial linkages in the contagion of financial crises during the 1990s? How valid is the overshooting hypothesis of Dornbusch? How well has Hong Kong's currency board performed?

In Chapter 8 on trade, financial linkage and contagion of currency crises, Lawrence J. Lau and Isabel K. Yan examine the role played by international trade and financial linkages in the 1994 Mexican and 1997 Asian crises. They construct a new index of trade competitiveness among countries. On the basis of this index, they find that trade has become increasingly competitive in the last decade. This index is useful in identifying countries vulnerable to crisis contagion.

Chapter 9, *Exchange Rate Dynamics: Where is the Saddle Path?* by Yin–Wong Cheung, Javier Gardeazabal and Jesús Vázquez, offers an alternative perspective on the validity of the well–known overshooting hypothesis of Dornbusch. These authors show that the saddle–path dynamics inherited in the standard Dornbusch overshooting model and the cointegration between exchange rates and prices do not co–exist. They also verify that the Johansen procedure has the ability to discriminate between saddle–path dynamics and cointegration. Their empirical example suggests that the empirical data they examined may not exhibit saddle–path dynamics.

In Chapter 10, Yum K. Kwan and Francis T. Lui deploy the structural vector autoregressive model to evaluate the empirical performance of the currency board system used by Hong Kong since the early 1980s. They argue that Hong Kong's stable fiscal policy plays a key role for the apparent success of the currency board regime. Furthermore, the currency board can explain about two–thirds of the reduction in output and inflation volatility.

The three chapters in Part IV tackle a host of critical socioeconomic issues in connection with China's rapid economic transformation over the last two decades. The issues are related to the efficacy of the household registration rule, the relationship between bankers' behaviour and share prices, and the implications of China's agricultural policy for its food supply and welfare.

In Chapter 11, Derek Laing, Chuhwan Park and Ping Wang develop a Harris–Todaro framework of rural–urban migration in China. They explore the impact of the household registration rule on migration and urban employment. They argue that enforcing the registration rule to discourage illegal inter–regional migration could lead to a higher job finding rate and a lower urban unemployment rate. Their finding will provoke some controversy among academics.

In Chapter 12, *The 'Banker Effect' on Chinese Stock Pricing*, Yuan Shu and Guoqiang Bin construct a model to analyze pricing in the Chinese stock market. They examine the dynamic relationships among 'stock banker' behaviour, stock price, and corporate performance. Their main finding is that stock pricing can be significantly influenced by bankers' behaviour, while there is no significant relationship between share concentration and corporate performance.

In the final chapter, *China's Food Economy and Its Implications for the Rest of the World*, Ninghui Li utilizes a computable general equilibrium (CGE) approach to examine the impact of China's agricultural policy on its national food provision and the effect of changes in foreign market conditions upon the supply of and demand for food in China. By linking China's Agricultural Policy Simulation Model (CAPSiM) with the Global Trade Analysis Project (GTAP) model, Li provides a projection of China's import and export of major agricultural products up to 2020 and the welfare gain or loss under various scenarios.

This volume provides a useful handbook for readers to gain a good understanding of various critical issues in China's international trade and economic development. The papers included pay tribute to Gregory Chow, who recently retired from Princeton University after a distinguished half–century academic career. Professor Chow has played a pivotal role in cultivating a generation of younger and active economists from China, trained in modern economics, now spreading all over the world.

The editors would like to acknowledge the support of the following institutions in co–organizing the international conference which resulted in the papers selected for this volume: Chinese Economics Association in North America (CEANA); Chinese Economists Society (CES); Institute of Economics, Academia Sinica of Taiwan; Lingnan (University) College at Zhongshan University of China; Lingnan University of Hong Kong; and the School of Economics at Renmin University of China. Our thanks also go to the Department of Economics and Finance and the Research Center for International Economics of the City University of Hong Kong for organizing the conference. Last but not least, we would also like to thank the authors who presented their work at the conference, the reviewers for their assistance in the selection of papers for this volume, and the able assistance of Liling Feng, Eric Lam, Ryan Man, Keiko Shinohara and Kevin Yuen. Without their effort, this book would not have become a reality.

PART I
ECONOMIC GROWTH

Chapter 1

Higher Education in China: A Growth Paradox?

Belton M. Fleisher[1]

Introduction

It is commonplace to assign education an important role in economic growth. Mankiw (2001, p. 253) asserts that in general, 'Education—investment in human capital—is at least as important as investment in physical capital for a country's long–run economic success.' Barro and Sala–i–Martin (1999, chapter 12) in their exhaustive empirical analysis of cross–country differences in growth rates, report significant effects of schooling on economic growth, and they note that the proportion of population with secondary and higher education is the most significant correlate of growth rates, *cet. par.* Hanushek and Kimko (2000) note that in a broad cross section of countries, direct measures of labor–force quality as measured by scientific and mathematics test scores have a large and significant relationship to economic growth rates. Bils and Klenow (2000), while more reserved in their attribution of a causal relationship, recognize a modest impact of schooling on growth rates in an international cross section. Kreuger and Lindahl (2001, p. 1130), in their meta–analysis of literature on effect of schooling on growth, find that evidence supports a positive effect of initial level of education on growth among low–productivity countries. In both neoclassical and endogenous growth paradigms, education—particularly higher education—has an important role in determining productivity and its growth. Indeed, we are here today to honor someone who, in both word (e.g. Chow, 2002, chapter 21) and deed has demonstrated his wholehearted belief in the power of education to promote social well–being and who has applied his knowledge and belief in China's behalf.

Low education level, indeed illiteracy, was a major problem for China's economic development during its first steps toward industrialization (under foreign entrepreneurship) in the 1920s (Spence, 1991); in the early post–revolution period of the 1950s, continued illiteracy among urban workers and lack of education among industry leaders contributed to low productivity, wasted investment, and poor execution of economic plans and directives (Spence, 1991; Naughton, 1995). Given the desire to follow Soviet–style industrialization, the Chinese Communist Party adopted a policy of investing in basic social needs, i.e., elementary health and basic education (Naughton, 1995, p. 27), but China did not follow the Soviet pattern in promoting higher education to support its industrialization policies.

Table 1.1 Higher education and economic growth rates for selected countries

Country	*GNP/Capita 1993 Dollars*	*Annual Growth GNP/Capita 1980–93 (%)*	*Gross Enrollment Ratio in Higher Education (%)*[b]		*Total Public Spending on Education as per cent of GNP 1992*[c]
			1980	1993	
China	490	8.2 (7.7)[a]	1	2	2.1
India	300	3.0	4	8	3.7
Korea (Republic)	7,660	8.2	16	51	4.2
Malaysia	3,140	3.5	4	7	5.5
Thailand	2,110	6.4	13	19	4.0
Hong Kong	18,060	5.4	5	20	2.9
Japan	31,490	3.4	29	32	4.7
Former USSR	2,340	−1.0	22	45	8.2
United States	24,740	1.7	56	72	5.7

a Figure in parentheses is for 1978–91 and is modified to account for over reporting. See Wang and Meng (2001).

b Gross enrollment ratio is the number of all post–secondary students divided by university–going age group. The second column contains data for the 1993 or for the following dates: India 1992, Hong Kong 1991, United States 1990.

c This represents spending on all education levels.

Source: World Bank (1997, p.6).

Mao's fear of the political power of an educated elite, evidenced by repression of intellectuals in the Hundred–Flowers movement (Spence, 1991, pp. 571–573) and Cultural Revolution, led to deterioration in the stock of higher–education human capital. Between the mid–1960s and 1976, the proportion of technicians in the industrial labor force declined from 4 per cent to 2.6 per cent (Naughton, 1995, p. 39); moreover, there was dramatic compression of the wage premium paid to college graduates (Fleisher and Wang, 2003b). Naughton (1995, p. 132) reports that according to the 1985 Industrial Census only 11.5 per cent of the top three–to–ten managers in each enterprise surveyed had a college education. Indeed, well less than half of enterprise leaders had even a high–school education. Given a broad concurrence on the critical role of higher education in determining a nation's

Table 1.2 The level of schooling, particularly higher education, is important for GDP/capita

Province	*GDP/Cap 1995 Yuan*	*Prop College Grads 1987*
Beijing	13073	0.066
Tianjin	10308	0.034
Hebei	4444	0.0065
Shanxi	3569	0.0071
InnerMon	3013	0.015
Liaoning	6380	0.016
Jilin	4414	0.012
Heilongjiang	5465	0.046
Shanghai	18943	0.011
Jiangsu	7299	0.0062
Zhejiang	8074	0.0064
Anhui	3357	0.0085
Fujian	6965	0.0061
Jiangxi	3080	0.0062
Shandong	5758	0.0057
Henan	3313	0.00378
Hubei	4162	0.00913
Guangdong	7973	0.0055
Guangxi	3543	0.0037
Hainan	5225	0.0051
Sichuan	3201	0.0041
Guizhou	1853	0.011
Yunnan	3044	0.013
Shaanxi	2843	0.011
Gansu	2288	0.0057
Qinghai	3430	0.0038
Ningxia	3328	0.0099
Xinjiang	4319	0.0055

Source: China Regional Statistical Yearbook (1978–95); State Statistical Bureau (1987).

economic progress, China's experience since reform is, on its face, a puzzle, or to put it more favorably, even more remarkable than may appear from its growth record alone.[2]

Table 1.1 contains a nonrandom but not atypical sample of countries with developing and advanced economies, and China's experience appears to belie

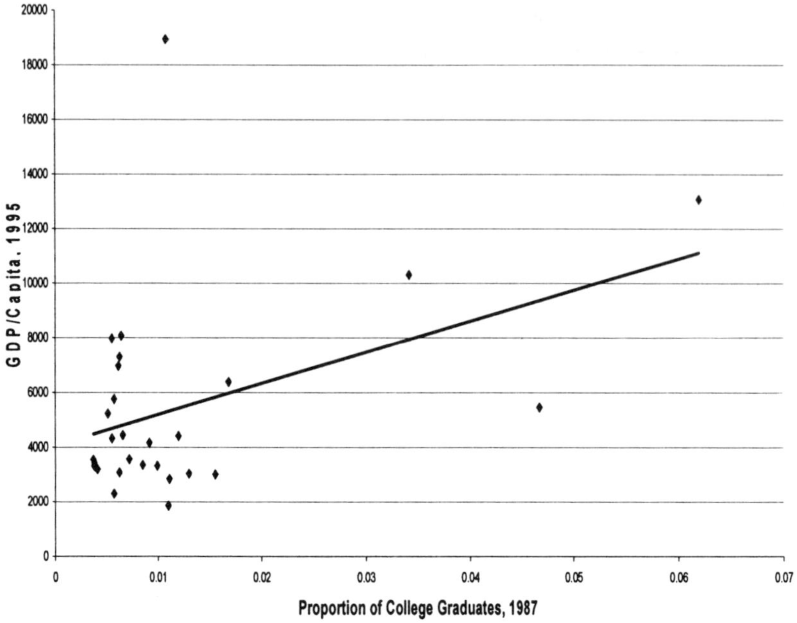

Figure 1.1 Provincial GDP per capita and proportion of college graduates

Source: State Statistical Bureau (1998).

one's belief in the power of investment in human capital to promote growth. Even when adjusting for over reporting of real growth during much of the reform era (Rawski, 2001; Wang and Meng, 2001), China exhibited one of the world's, and Asia's, highest real growth rates while devoting the smallest proportion of its GNP to education and claiming the lowest enrollment ratio in institutes of higher education among its college–age population.[3] Does China's experience refute the received wisdom that higher education is a necessary condition for economic progress, or does its exceptional growth record suggest that its potential for even higher growth has been limited by an undersupply of college graduates?

In this chapter I argue for the second interpretation and survey evidence supporting my belief that with more resources devoted to investment in the higher education of its human resources, China will achieve even more rapid economic progress than it has to date. I also explore the impact of China's education policies on regional, sectoral, and personal income disparities. The remainder of the chapter proceeds as follows. The following section presents evidence of the impact of education—particularly higher education—on China's economic growth. If China has achieved exceptional economic progress since reform with such a small

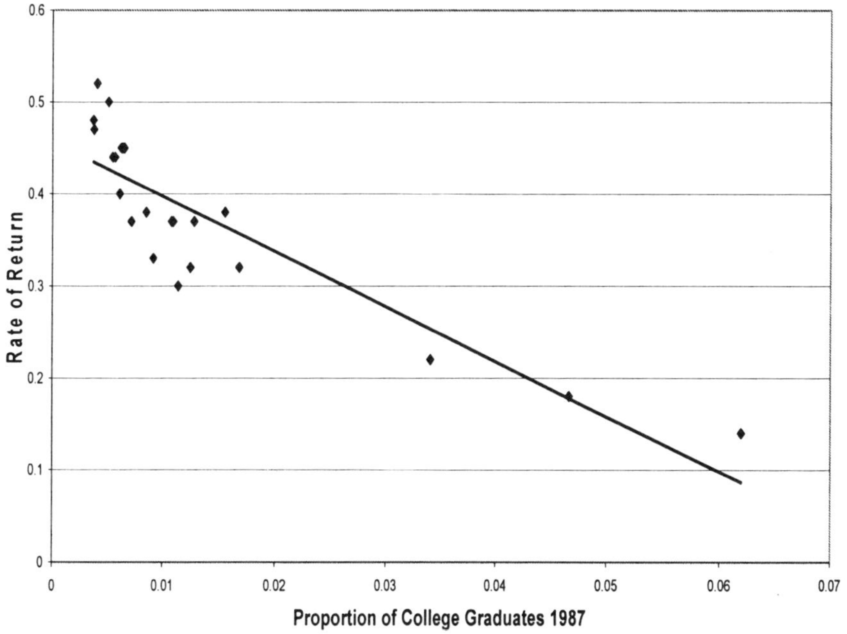

Figure 1.2 Rate of return to higher education

Source: Fleisher and Chen (1997), State Statistical Bureau, 1998.

proportion of college graduates, is it because they do not contribute much to production? The evidence suggests otherwise. This section also treats the impact of higher education on per–capita GDP and economic growth across regions. To what extent are the widening gaps between the coastal and interior provinces exacerbated by the geographical distribution of educational resources? Are educational resources allocated to where the payoff is highest? Following this, we summarize evidence of the impact of schooling on production at the enterprise level. The next section is an overview of research on the impact of schooling on personal income. We explore the relationship between pay and workers' marginal product, education and interregional migration, and how education helps workers cope with shocks resulting from economic reform and decline of the state sector.

Does education raise GDP and foster economic growth in China?

One possible explanation of China's seemingly paradoxical growth record is that higher education simply does not pay off in China. The evidence contradicts this hypothesis. Table 1.1 and Figure 1.1 illustrate a pronounced positive cross–provincial relationship between 1995 per–capita GDP and the 1987 proportion of college graduates across Chinese provinces. Of course, this simple positive relationship begs the question of reverse causation between schooling and income, as does a positive correlation between growth and education. However, I believe that a substantial body of both macroeconomic and microeconomic research points to a positive causation running from schooling to growth.

Studies using aggregate data

Fleisher and Chen (1997) use panel–estimation techniques to estimate total factor productivity (TFP) across 25 provinces for the period 1978–93. (Excluded provinces have insufficient data.) They then relate TFP and TFP growth to the following explanatory variables: coastal location, vintage of the physical capital stock, investment in housing, the annual flow of new university graduates in the population, and a measure of transportation infrastructure. They find that both TFP and TFP growth are positively and significantly related to the higher–education proportion and that the relationship is robust to level– and first–difference specifications of the time–series regression. Based on the contribution of higher educational attainment to TFP growth, they estimate marginal rates of return to additional investment in higher education across the provinces in their panel. The mean estimated rate of return for coastal provinces (corrected for out–migration of college graduates) is 34 per cent and that for noncoastal provinces is 40 per cent, both of which are higher than marginal rates of return they estimate for investment in transportation infrastructure. The relationship between rates of return to higher education and the proportion of college graduates in each province in 1987 is shown in Figure 1.2. Provinces with higher proportions of college graduates (and higher GDP/capita) tend to have lower marginal returns (although still high in an absolute sense) than lower–income provinces with lower proportions of college graduates in their populations.[4]

In my opinion, neither Fleisher and Chen's results nor those of studies discussed below are seriously compromised by the possibility of reverse–causation emphasized by Bils and Klenow (2000). Bils and Klenow's elegant argument and empirical investigation assumes individual wealth maximization in a regime of freedom of choice and forward–looking behavior that is difficult to apply to the Chinese populations' educational decisions in the 1970s and 1980s. An implication of Fleisher and Chen's research is that attempts to attenuate the widening gap between interior and coastal per–capita income by fostering investment in physical capital are severely hampered by lack of attention to the productivity–enhancing effects of investment in higher education.

A number of more recent papers report evidence of a significant positive relationship between higher levels of education and GDP and GDP growth using aggregate data at the national and provincial level. Démurger (2001) uses a panel of 24 provinces (excluding municipalities) over the period 1984–1998 to estimate a positive, significant, and robust relationship between the proportion of population with secondary– or higher education and per–capita growth, holding constant a number of 'usual suspect' variables, including measures of infrastructure capital. Chen and Feng (2000) estimate a cross–sectional growth equation for 29 Chinese provinces covering the period 1978–1989. Explanatory variables include initial real GDP per capita, the initial level of the higher–education (above secondary) enrollment rate, and variables representing fertility, inflation, trade openness, importance of state ownership, degree of industrialization, and the share of investment in GDP. They find that the higher–education enrollment rate has a statistically significant and substantial relationship to provincial economic growth rates. The estimate is robust to the inclusion of alternative additional explanatory variables.

While not estimating the impact of schooling directly, Wang and Yao (2002) use growth accounting methods to introduce education into the aggregate production function for China and find human capital contributed significantly to economic growth over the entire period 1952–99. In the pre–reform period, when China overcame widespread illiteracy, Wang and Yao report that investment in human capital accounted for almost half of per–capita GDP growth through 1977. From 1978 through 1999, investment in education contributed somewhat more than 10 per cent to overall per–capita growth. Their estimates are robust to alternative assumptions on physical–capital depreciation rates and factor shares. Note that in the growth–accounting context, education is treated as a factor of production rather than as contributing to total factor productivity (Krueger and Lindahl, 2001).

Studies using micro data

Research based on micro data provinces valuable and substantive evidence on the contribution of higher education to production, although there is relatively little data on schooling of workers at the firm level in China. Fleisher, Dong, and Liu (1996) estimate production functions for a sample of 30 government–owned enterprises in the paper industry, using data for the years 1985, 1987, and 1990. They estimate the marginal product of production workers with less than secondary–school education to be 10,399 yuan in 1990 prices and for production workers with at least a secondary–school diploma to be 19,700 yuan. For managers and engineers who had not received degrees from a four–year college or university, the estimated marginal product is negligible, whereas for those who had successfully completed four years of college or university, the estimated marginal product is extraordinary, nearly 2,000,000 yuan per year. The authors note that while this figure may at first seem implausible, it implies that adding one additional college–trained manager or engineer is estimated to have raised output by 0.756 per cent, a not so terribly shocking addition in an environment where professional training is very scarce.[5]

In research based on a sample of 442 urban enterprises of all major types of ownership collected in the second half of 1992 for the year 1991 Fleisher and Wang (2003a) divide the labor force into two groups: production workers and

Table 1.3 Rates of return to college education in urban china[a]

Dependent Variable and Year Acquired First Job				
Earnings, All	Hourly Wage, All	Hourly Wage, Before 1980	Hourly Wage, 1980–87	Hourly Wage, 1988–95
4.5%	6.8%	5.8%	9.2%	9.5%

[a] Rates of return are calculated as the 10th root of the ratio of college graduates' earnings or wage rate relative to elementary school graduates, based on multiple–regression estimates.

Source: Li (2003), tables 3 and 4.

technical/administrative staff. Their estimated production function yields estimates of the average marginal product of labor to be 131,970 yuan for technical/administrative workers and 2,008 yuan for production workers. Unfortunately there is insufficient information in these data to estimate the marginal rate of return to schooling in production directly; however a back–of–the envelope calculation based on the assumption that technical/administrative workers have on average 7 more years of schooling than production workers implies that the average rate of return to an additional year of schooling in this range is 82 per cent! In the same paper, they use data from a panel survey of 200 large rural enterprises (mostly TVE's) for the years 1984 to 1990.[6] While not reported explicitly in the paper, the estimated output elasticities for technical/administrative workers and production workers imply an average ratio of marginal products of about 4. Using the same assumptions as for the urban sample implies an average rate of return to and additional year of schooling to be approximately 22 per cent. While not as astoundingly (some might say outrageously) large as derived from the urban sample, this is still a large return to investment. Investigation of reasons underlying the difference between the likely effect of higher education on production in rural versus urban enterprises would be a fascinating topic for further study.

Schooling does affect output in China

We do not have a single 'best' estimate of the impact of higher education on output in China, but evidence from both aggregate and disaggregate data, across regions, rural and urban sectors, and across various ownership types consistently supports the hypothesis that the impact on production is significant and substantial. What are the likely sources of this relationship? They are to be found in the myriad ways that highly–skilled and talented individuals increase productivity both directly, and perhaps more importantly, indirectly through the allocation of resources and adopting and adapting of new technology as cited widely in the growth literature.

That pay in China commensurate with such productivity would have been inconceivable during the pre–reform and early reform period should not be surprising in an economy where enterprise leaders were not rewarded monetarily for winning business 'tournaments' (Lazear and Rosen, 1981).

Schooling and income in China

In the last section we explored the paradox of China's high rate of economic growth despite its relatively low proportion of college graduates, who are indeed productive in the Chinese economy. A second anomaly is that despite substantial evidence that education is highly productive, the fortunate few with college degrees have not appeared to benefit proportionately from their acquired knowledge and skills. They may be smart (and productive), but they have not been getting rich, either in absolute or relative terms. Clearly, education 'pays', but the claimants for education's rewards do not appear to have been those who embody investment in human capital.

Schooling and wages

From reform into the early 1990s, wage differences by level of skill, occupation, and/or schooling remained very narrow, implying that returns to higher education were quite low in comparison with those in other industrialized and industrializing countries,[7] including the Russian Federation (Nesterova and Sabirianova, 2002) and those in some smaller transition economies, such as the Czech Republic (Munich, Svejnar, and Terrell, 2002), Slovenia (Orazem and Vodopivec, 1995), and Bulgaria (Jones and Ilayperuma, 1994). Although returns to higher education in the Russian Republic have also been very low, this can in large part be attributed to the extraordinarily high proportion of college graduates in Russia, which is certainly not the case in China, as indicated in table 1.1.[8]

One might expect that low personal returns to schooling mainly affected employees in enterprises where wage scales were determined by the wage grid that prevailed under central planning (Knight and Song, 1991), but in fact the low relative pay of workers with higher levels of education has been observed in enterprises of all ownership types and appears to have persisted longer than might be expected based on the record in eastern European transition economies.

Recent research suggests that reform and marketization may finally be contributing to an increase in the relative wages of educated workers, although the evidence is not universal. Li (2001) reports that the return to schooling, particularly higher education, has indeed increased. Li's research involves three major departures from earlier studies: (1) he uses data from the urban sample of the 1995 China Household Income Project (CHIP–95) conducted in 1996 and based on a sample of 6,928 households and 21,688 individuals; (2) the CHIP–95 data include information on work hours, which are negatively correlated with hourly pay, leading to negative bias in estimated returns when weekly or monthly income is the dependent variable; (3) the CHIP–95 data contain more accurate information on actual work experience than previous surveys. A fourth feature differentiating Li's work from earlier research on private returns to schooling in China is estimation according to year of first job, before 1980, 1980–87, and 1988–1995. Individuals whose first job occurred prior to 1980 clearly have schooling of an older 'vintage' and are more likely to have been affected by educational biases of the Cultural Revolution. Li asserts (reasonably) that year of first job is likely to reflect the 'grandfathering' of wage differentials inherent in the old wage grid. In a society where interfirm mobility has been severely limited by well–known economic and political constraints, it has surely been relatively more difficult for older workers to take advantage of opportunities offered by economic reform. Li's econometric results indicate that overall returns to schooling in China remain low, on average, but that returns to college graduates are higher than returns to lower levels of education.[9] In other words, there is evidence that the relative scarcity of college graduates has begun to pay off in terms of earnings; these higher relative earnings may now be providing greater incentives for people to obtain higher education.

Some of Li's empirical results are summarized in table 1.3. Notice that hen hourly wage is used as the measure of earnings, the rate of return is about half again as high as when monthly earnings is used. The rate of return to the cohort of college graduates whose first job was before 1980 is less than 2/3 that of the most recent cohort, and the latter is a respectable 9.5 per cent, much higher than found in earlier studies, but still not 'high' by international standards. Li also finds that the rate of return for the entire population of college graduates who have private–sector jobs was 9.3 per cent, while for those who had jobs in state–owned enterprises it was 7.1 per cent. In Gansu, where barely more than 1/3 of school–aged children entered senior middle school and 2 per cent were college graduates (1996–97 average), Li reports that the rate of return to persons with college degrees was 9.9 per cent; in Guangdong, where 57 per cent of school–aged children entered senior middle school and 4 per cent of the population were college graduates, the rate of return was only 3.6 per cent (Li, 2001, China Statistical Yearbook 1996, 1997, and China Statistics Publisher, 1996). While the gap between Gansu and Guangdong conforms to the difference in the relative scarcity of college graduates between the two provinces, the very low figure for Guangdong is surprising, given that Guangdong province is presumably a hotbed of economic development and other evidence that returns in the private sector outweigh those in the state sector. In a study using even more recent data than Li (2003), Park, Song, Zhang, and Zhao (2003) report that the return to college education in urban China exceeded 10% in 1999.

Schooling and resource allocation: The household perspective

Despite evidence that the wages of highly educated workers have begun to more closely match their contribution to production and to growth, it appears that a significant gap remains, both in absolute and relative terms. An explanation of this gap is China's ongoing transition from planned to market economy, but it is the transition itself that offers many opportunities for educated workers that may elude their less–advantaged counterparts.

Yang (2002) explores the allocation of resources between farm and nonfarm production in a sample of households in Sichuan province over the period 1986–1995. This is a particularly interesting period in the evolution of China's economic reform, because in 1983 government policies limiting the freedom of rural workers to leave agricultural employment were gradually loosened (Yang, 2002). Yang explores how effectively households reallocated their human and physical resources between agricultural and nonfarm activities (that is, toward employment in township and village enterprises). The measure of effectiveness is household profit, defined to be gross household income less direct expenditure on inputs, e.g., seeds, fertilizer, fuel, and other items. Yang reports that households in which at least one member had a high school or college education allocated 17.7 per cent more capital to nonfarm uses than did those in which the highest education was only primary school. A similar pattern was found for labor allocation. The total effect on household profits is summarized as follows: 'If the highest level of education is raised from primary to high school, the family earnings would increase by 6.13 per cent.'

Given the statistically significant impact of schooling on rural household net income, which Yang reports comes primarily from the allocative effect of education—the ability to deal with economic change and disequilibria (Schultz, 1975, Welch, 1970), how important is the effect of schooling on income in economic terms? Can such empirical results be related to the large effects of higher education on production and growth reported in preceding sections? At first glance, the economic impact reported by Yang is not very impressive in terms of economic magnitude. After all, the opportunity cost of sending a child through secondary and higher education is not trivial, and a 6 per cent increase in household income (which in Yang's sample averaged 653 yuan per year in 1986 prices) is not a very large sum. For a yardstick, consider the following simple calculation, to achieve a marginal rate of return of 10 per cent on 10 years of additional education using the simplest human–capital investment model requires that the income of a college graduate be 2.6 times that of a primary–school graduate.

I believe that a key to the puzzle of the small economic magnitude of the impact of higher education on farm household income is to consider the small scale of Chinese rural households' economic operations. If we were hypothetically to enlarge the household by tenfold, is it unrealistic to project that the same individual with a high–school or college diploma could not still achieve a 6 per cent increase in household income, but one that would be ten times greater in absolute value? Looked at from the point of view of unexploited scale economies, the empirical evidence on the statistically significant but economically small impact of higher education on rural household income may make sense when compared to the economically large effects of higher education on provincial economic growth reported by Fleisher and Chen (1997) and the very large effect in the Chinese paper industry reported by Fleisher, Dong, and Liu (1996). For example, an enlightened (read educated) village or county official who helps achieve a better allocation of local or regional resources through more efficient regulation of property rights, trade flows, etc., could contribute a large economic impact even if it is modest in percentage terms. Similarly, a single additional well–trained engineer or manager of a large firm may effect a modest proportional increase in efficiency, again achieving a large 'bang for the yuan.'

Schooling and resource allocation: The labor–market perspective

From another perspective on the allocative role of education, Zhang, Huang, and Rozelle (ZHR, 2002) have explored the labor–supply behavior of a panel of 310 individuals in 109 families observed in four villages of Jiangsu province in the years 1988, 1992, and 1996. This period encompasses the macroeconomic slowdown of 1989 and 1990 and the recovery of the mid–1990s. ZHR's econometric results show that between 1988 and 1996, education became an important determinant of whether an individual was able to obtain an off–farm job, while where one lived (i.e. in which village) sharply declined in importance. By 1996, an additional year of education increased the probability of finding off–farm work by 14 per cent, *cet. par.* They also report evidence that individuals with higher levels of schooling were better able to acquire or re–acquire an off–farm job as the economy recovered from recession between 1992 and 1996.

ZHR report a marked increase in the relationship between schooling and wages over the time of their surveys. While they estimate no impact of schooling on wages in 1988 and 1992, by 1996, they estimate the marginal rate of return to completing the 7th grade to be 9 per cent, much higher than reported in earlier studies. ZHR report that the marginal personal rate of return to schooling falls as attained education rises, in contrast to Li (2001), but their sample includes very few who have graduated from high school or above; moreover their sample is geographically and sectorally narrow.

Urban labor markets have experienced not only aggregate economic shocks, but also the shock of restructuring state–owned enterprises. While inefficient use of human and physical resources have historically held back China's economic growth, the benefits of reform and global competition cannot be fully realized or equitably distributed if workers who are laid off under *xia gang* do not find productive and rewarding new jobs. Appleton, Knight, Song, and Xia (AKSX, 2002) study the efficiency and distributional impact of urban workforce (defined to include only workers with urban *hukou*) retrenchment using a nationally representative urban household survey conducted by the Chinese Academy of Social Sciences in 1999. They find that not only is the probability of being laid off significantly and negatively related to years of schooling, but also among those workers who have suffered *xia gang*, the probable length of joblessness falls significantly as years of schooling increase. Other variables constant, the risk of being laid off in any period of time fell by 0.76 per cent for each additional year of schooling, and, for laid–off workers, the probability of being reemployed in a given period of time rose by 6 per cent per year of additional schooling.

Additional calculations from AKSX's results provide further insight into the important of schooling in helping workers deal with economic change. The sample consists of 4000 households from thirteen cities in six provinces, enlarged by 503 households with members who had experienced layoff in the five–year period following the end of 1994. Of the 6929 workers in the sample, 1159 had experienced layoff; and 433 of these, or 37 per cent, were employed at the time of the survey. Clearly the reemployment prospects for *xia gang* workers are dim. Average years of schooling of the sample are approximately 11 years. Consider the experience of two laid–off workers, one with 12 years of schooling, the other with only six years, but identical in all other respects including family composition and years of work experience. The probability that the worker with only six years of schooling would have been employed at the time of the survey is approximately 26 per cent, while the probability for the worker with 12 years of schooling is approximately 40 per cent. Moreover, the worker with 12 years of schooling had a lower risk of being laid off in the first place.

Another aspect of resource allocation from the labor–market perspective is migration. Legal restrictions on population movement, enforced by the need for *hukou* to obtain urban social and economic benefits, sharply curtail interregional and urban–rural migration in the presence of immense differences in earning and income opportunities. (For a brief description of the economic and institutional background of migration restrictions and the concomitant sectoral income disparities, see Zhao, 1999.) Johnson (2003) uses data from the 1990 and 2000 population censuses to estimate provincial population gains and losses from migration. He reports that 15 provinces experienced net out migration and 16 net in migration (including the four urban provinces of Beijing, Chongqing, Shanghai, and Tianjin). Guangdong province far outdistanced any others in terms of absolute and proportional magnitude of loss or gain, with a population increase of 15 million, 25 per cent, attributed to in migration. All the other provinces experienced in– or out migration of far smaller proportion, and, compared to the United States in the late 1990s, where interregional economic disparities are surely smaller than in China, interregional migration in China is 'small' (2003).

Labor–force movement does occur, however, and without it many urban menial jobs would go unfilled. There are also workers with higher educational attainment among migrants—even among the so–called 'floating population', according to a study of rural migrants to Shanghai reported by Roberts (2001). Roberts' study is based on a 1993 sample of over 54,000 'floating' residents of Shanghai, defined to be individuals without a Shanghai *hukou*. Among them, slightly more than 60 per cent are categorized as rural laborers, 22 per cent as 'social' migrants (e.g. migrating to join other family members), and about 18 per cent as 'other', two–thirds of whom held nonagricultural *hukou* and 42 per cent of whom had education of at least some high school. Even within the rural–labor category, over 7 per cent were in the 'higher' education group, and among those with at least some high school, the most likely employer was a state–owned or collectively–owned enterprise.

Zhao (1999) reports that in a 1995 household survey conducted in Sichuan province, rural nonfarm nonmigrant workers had higher schooling levels than did those who had migrated out of their local areas, even though they contributed less to household incomes than comparable workers who migrated. Zhao infers that the uncertainty of employment without *hukou*, transportation, lodging, and psychic costs of migration outweighed immediate economic gains. Zhao's results may not

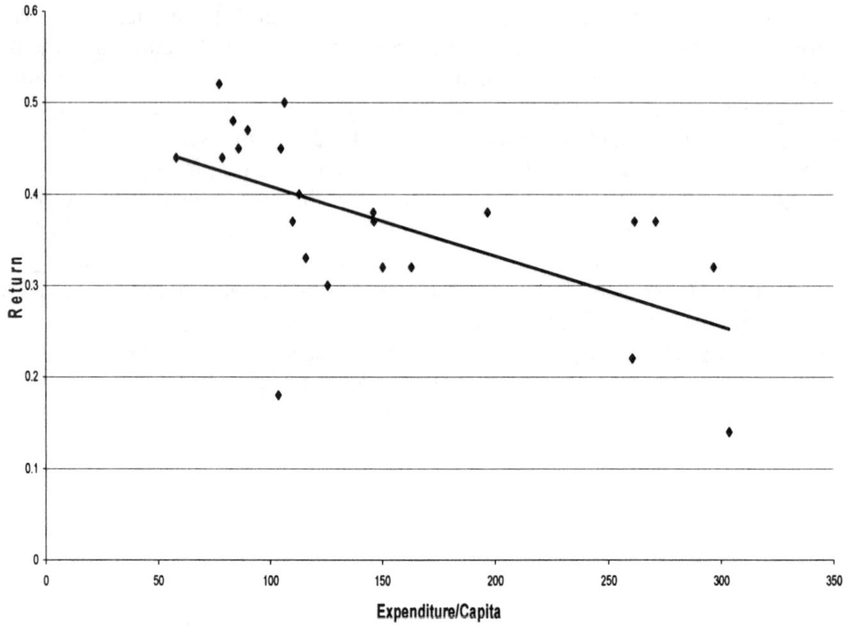

Figure 1.3 Provincial returns to schooling and expenditure per capita

Source: China Statistical Publisher (1998), Fleisher and Chen (1997).

apply to all of China, though, as she (1995 and 1999) does report that higher levels of schooling significantly increased the probability of obtaining a permanent *hukou* for migrants to Beijing. Consistent with Zhao's research, Zhu (2002) finds, based on a 1993 survey in Hubei province that the effect of education on the income level of migrants was less than for nonmigrants.

Conclusion

The importance of investment in higher education for China's economic growth is supported by an impressive body of evidence. (See also Chow, 2002.) It contributes directly to worker productivity and, perhaps more importantly in China's transitional economy, through its contribution to the ability of managers and officials to deal with change and disequilibria. Its impact appears to be greatest at the level where decision–makers can influence larger–scale operations. There is some evidence that the government recognizes the importance of higher education, and in 1998 through 2000 new enrollments in institutes of higher education

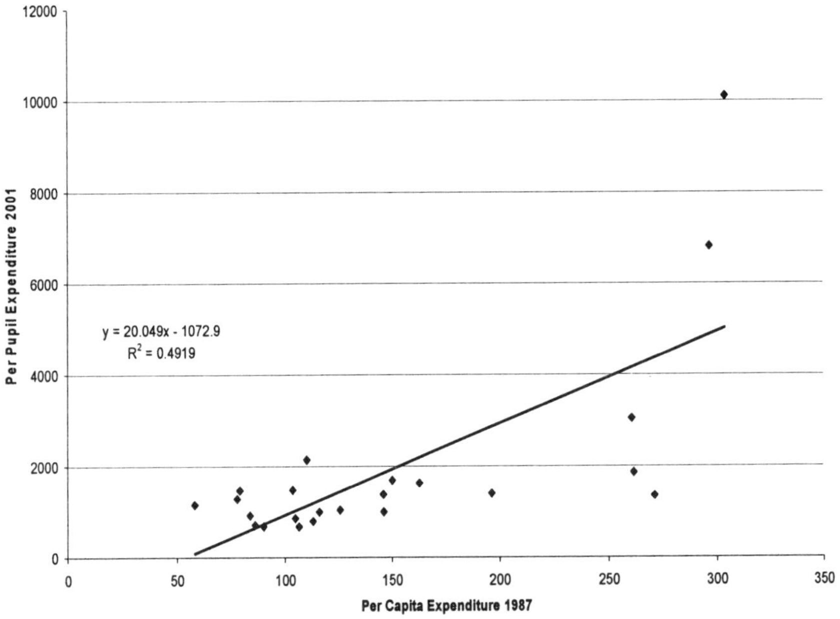

Figure 1.4 Provincial schooling expenditure 1987 and 2001

Source: China Statistical Publisher (1998), Fleisher and Chen (1997), Heckman (2003b).

increased markedly, with public spending on education reaching over 3 per cent of GDP in 2001 (Heckman, 2003b). Total spending has increased more, due to the response of private spending to the perceived benefits of education in terms of income and general living standards (Heckman, 2003b).

Hopefully, much of this increased expenditure is being directed toward areas where its productivity is highest. China will grow even more rapidly if it adopts more effective policies toward higher education. One important area is in the geographical allocation of education resources. The relationships illustrated in Figures 1.3 and 1.4 show that government educational expenditures have been directed toward provinces where the rate of return is lowest instead of where they would contribute most to China's economic growth.[10] This was true in the 1980s and remains so today. This perverse allocation has important policy implications for policies aimed at reducing widening regional economic inequality: Redirection of educational resources toward areas where they are most valuable would also complement efforts to encourage investment in physical capital. Additionally, policies to develop social infrastructure in less–favored regions will not only increase the productivity of private investment, but will also make it more attractive for college–trained workers to live away from the traditionally preferred locations.

Notes

1 I have benefited from comments at the First Sino–US International Conference on Public Administration, Renmin University of China, June 17, 2002, Beijing and the faculty–graduate student seminar of the China Center for Economic Research at Peking University. I would like to thank explicitly Alan Debrauw, Masanori Hashimoto, Fuchun Jin, Joseph Kaboski, Hao Li, Justin Y Lin, Hajime Miyazaki, Xiaojun Wang, Bruce Weinberg, and Yaohui Zhao for their helpful comments on an earlier draft.

2 Wang and Yao (forthcoming) contains a succinct quantitative outline of the evolution of China's education since 1949.

3 China does not have a relatively high proportion of secondary–school graduates, either. In 1997, the ratio of graduates from the top level of secondary school to the number of college graduates among the population age 6 and over was 3.8, while the ratio of the over–25 population of India, Japan, and the former Soviet Union whose highest level of schooling was the last year of secondary school to those who were college graduates was about 5.5, 2.1, and 13.5, respectively (Statistical Yearbook of China 1998, tables Appendix 3–17 and 20–7.)

4 This negative relationship is consistent with a simple declining marginal efficiency of capital in the presence of variation in the supply of funds.

5 It has been pointed out to the author that under planning, managers and engineers were appointed to positions in state enterprises for various reasons that are likely to be correlated with firm size. Whether the omission of variables reflecting these reasons results in a positively biased estimate of the marginal product of college–graduate engineers and managers is far from clear. The very nature of the regression estimation holds constant firm size as measured by raw materials and physical capital. A possible source of unobserved variable bias would be that the 'best' managers and engineers were assigned to the 'best', or most productive firms. In the cited study of the paper industry, variables thought to be correlated with productivity, e.g. level of ownership and location in Shanghai are included as regressors. Moreover, there is no reason a priori to suppose that the best personnel would have been assigned to enterprises that were doing particularly well, other things equal, just the opposite is as likely, or more likely, to be true. Indeed, I have anecdotal evidence supporting this view. In 1989, an acquaintance with a bachelor's degree from a major Chinese university mentioned to me that he had been assigned the task of helping to salvage a rural enterprise that was plagued with inefficiency and losses.

6 For a fuller description of the urban and rural samples, see Fleisher and Wang (2001).

7 For references see Fleisher and Wang (2001).

8 Graduates of 4–year universities in China in the population 16 years of age and older was less than 1% in 1997 (Statistical Yearbook of China, 1998).

9 The relatively high rate of return to higher schooling levels is also reported in Krueger and Lindahl (2001). In a related study, Li and Luo (2003) find that measurement error and omitted ability bias have resulted in estimates of the overall

return to schooling that are far lower than the true return. Their study does not report rates of return by educational level or region, however.

10 As noted above, interprovincial migration in China does not appear to create a sufficiently large 'brain drain' so that local investments in higher education by interior provinces would simply generate benefits for coastal provinces. From a more global perspective, there would seem to be sufficient international migration barriers for Chinese citizens to enable China to reap the rewards of subsidizing higher education. I thank Alan Debrauw for emphasizing this point. Anecdotal evidence suggests that when nations acquire a sufficient number of highly educated workers, the rewards to education can be obtained through changes in comparative advantage and international trade. An example is the outplacement of computer programming tasks by United States software developers to India. This is a topic that requires much more research.

References

Appleton, S., Knight, J., Song, L. and Xia, O. (2002), 'Labor Retrenchment in China: Determinants and Consequences', *China Economic Review* **13**(2,3), pp. 252–275.

Barro, R.J. and Sala–i–Martin, X. (1999), *Economic Growth*, Cambridge, MA: MIT Press.

Bils, M. and Klenow, P.J. (2000), 'Does Schooling Cause Growth?', *American Economic Review* **90**(5), pp. 1160–1183.

Chen, B. and Yi, F. (2000), 'Determinants of Economic Growth in China: Private Enterprise, Education, and Openness', *China Economic Review* **11**(1), pp. 1–15.

China Statistics Publisher (1996), *China's Regional Economy 1978–1995*, Beijing.

Chow, G.C. (2002), *China's Economic Transformation*, Malden, MA and Oxford, UK: Blackwell Publishers.

DeBrauw (2002), 'Three Essays on Migration, Education, and Household Development in Rural China', unpublished Ph.D. dissertation, Department of Agricultural and Resource Economics, University of California, Davis.

Démurger, S. (2001), 'Infrastructure and Economic Growth: An Explanation for Regional Disparities in China', *Journal of Comparative Economics* **29**(1), 95–117.

Fleisher, B.M. and Chen, J. (1997), 'The Coast–Noncoast Income Gap, Productivity, and Regional Economic Policy in China', *Journal of Comparative Economics* **25**(2), pp. 220–236.

Fleisher, B.M., Dong, K. and Liu, Y. (1996), 'Education, Enterprise Organization, and Productivity in the Chinese Paper Industry', *Economic Development and Cultural Change* **44**(3), pp. 471–487.

Fleisher, B.M. and Wang, X. (2001), 'Efficiency Wages and Work Incentives in Urban and Rural China', *Journal of Comparative Economics* **29**(4), pp. 645–662.

Fleisher, B.M. and Wang, X. (2003a), 'Skill Differentials, Return to Schooling and Market Segmentation in a Transition Economy: The Case of Mainland China', *Journal of Development Economics* (in press).

Fleisher, B.M. and Wang, X. (2003b), 'Returns to Schooling in China Under Planning and Reform', Working Paper, Department of Economics, Ohio State University, http://economics.sbs.ohio–state.edu/Fleisher/working_papers/Fleisher–Wang.doc.

Heckman, J.J. (2003a), 'China's Investment in Human Capital', *Economic Development and Cultural Change* **51**(4), pp. 795–804.

Heckman, J.J. (2003b), 'China's Investment in Human Capital', Working Paper, Department of Economics, University of Chicago.

Hanushek, E.A. and Kimko, D.D. (2000), 'Schooling, Labor–Force Quality, and the Growth of Nations', *American Economic Review* **90**(5), pp. 1184–1208.

Huang, J. and Rozelle, S. (1996), 'Technological Change: Rediscovering the Engine of Productivity Growth in China's Rural Economy', *Journal of Development Economics* **49**(2), pp. 337–369.

Johnson, D.G. (2003), 'Provincial Migration in China in the 1990s', *China Economic Review* **14**(1), pp. 22–31.

Jones, D.C. and Ilayperuma, K. (1994), 'Wage Determination under Plan and Early Transition: Evidence from Bulgaria', Working Paper No. 94/7, Department of Economics, Hamilton College.

Knight, J. and Song, L. (1991), 'The Determinants of Urban Income Inequality in China', *Oxford Bulletin of Economics and Statistics* **53**(2), pp. 123–154.

Kreuger, A.B. and Lindahl, M. (2001), 'Education for Growth: Why and For Whom?', *Journal of Economic Literature* **39**(4), pp. 1101–1136.

Lazear, E.P. and Rosen, S. (1981), 'Rank–Order Tournaments as Optimal Labor Contracts', *Journal of Political Economy* **89**(5), pp. 841–864.

Li, H. (2003), 'Economic Transition and Returns to Education in China', *Economics of Education Review* **22**(3), pp. 317–328.

Li, H. and Yi, L. (2003), 'Is the Return to Schooling Really Low in Urban China?', *Pacific Economic Review*, in press.

Li, T. and Zhang, J. (1998), 'Returns to Education under Collective and Household Farming in China', *Journal of Development Economics* **56**(2), pp. 307–335.

Mankiw, G.N. (2001), *Principles of Macroeconomics 2nd Edition,* Orlando, FL: Harcourt College Publishers

Munich, D., Svejnar, J. and Terrell, K. (2002), 'Returns to Human Capital under the Communist Wage Grid and During the Transition to a Market Economy', Working Paper 272a, Ann Arbor, MI; William Davidson Institute.

Naughton, B. (1995), *Growing Out of the Plan*, Cambridge: Cambridge University Press.

Nesterova, D. and Sabirianova, K.Z. (1998), 'Investment in Human Capital under Economic Transformation in Russia', Economic Education and Research Consortium Economic Research Program, Working Paper Series No. 99/04, http://www.eerc.ru/publications/workpapers/WP_99–04E.pdf.

Orazem, P. and Vodopivec, M. (1995), 'Winners and losers in the Transition: Returns to Education, Experience, and Gender in Slovenia', *The World Bank Review* **9**(2), pp. 201–230.

Park, A., Song, X., Zhang, J. and Zhao, Y. (2003), 'The Growth of Wage Inequality in Urban China, 1988 to 1999', unpublished paper, Ann Arbor, Mi: Department of Economics.

Rawski, T.G. (2001), 'What is Happening to China's GDP Statistics?', *China Economic Review* **12**(4), pp. 347–302.

Roberts, K.D. (2001), 'The Determinants of Job Choice by Rural Labor Migrants to Shanghai', *China Economic Review* **12**(1), pp. 15–39.

Schultz, T.W. (1975), 'The Value of Ability to Deal with Disequilibrium', *Journal of Economic Literature* **13**(2), 827–846.

Schultz, P.T. (1988), 'Education Investment and Returns', in H. Chenery and T.N. Srinivasan (ed.), *Handbook of Development Economics* vol. 1, Amsterdam: North Holland, pp. 543–630.

Spence, J. (1991), *The Search for Modern China*, New York: W. W. Norton & Co.

State Statistical Bureau (1998 and other years), *China Statistical Yearbook*, Beijing: China Statistical Information and Consultancy Center.

Wang, X. and Lian M. (2001), 'A Reevaluation of China's Economic Growth', *China Economic Review* **12**(4), pp. 338–345.

Wang, Y. and Yao, Y. (2002), 'Sources of China's Economic Growth 1952–99: Incorporating Human Capital Accumulation', *China Economic Review* **14**(1), pp. 32–52.

Welch, F. (1970), 'Education in Production', *Journal of Political Economy* **38**(1), pp. 35–59.

World Bank (1997), *China Higher Education Reform*, Washington DC: The World Bank.

Yang, D.T. (2002), 'Education and Allocative Efficiency: Household Income Growth during Rural Reforms in China', *Journal of Development Economics* (in press).

Zhang, L., Huang, J. and Rozelle, S. (2002), 'Employment, Recessions, and the Role of Education in China', *China Economic Review* **13**(2,3), pp. 313–328.

Zhao, Y. (1995), 'Labor Mobility, Labor Migration and Returns to Schooling in Rural China', Ph. D. dissertation, University of Chicago.

Zhao, Y. (1999), 'Labor Migration and Earnings Differences: The Case of Rural China', *Economic Development and Cultural Change* **47**(4), pp. 767–782.

Zhu, N. (2002), 'Impact of Income Gap on Migration Decisions in China', *China Economic Review* **13**(2,3), pp. 213–230.

Chapter 2

Taxation and Economic Growth in China

Roger H. Gordon and Wei Li [1]

Introduction

China's economic transformation during the past twenty years has been breath–taking. As of the early 1980s, China was one of the poorest countries in the world. The economy was almost entirely state–owned. Virtually all allocation decisions were made through the government planning ministries. Goods were largely rationed, prices were only an accounting convention, and the economy was largely closed.

Since then, per capita GDP has grown by a factor of at least five.[2] The country has largely shifted to a market economy, most industries are highly competitive, and international trade with the rest of the world is large and growing. There is now a vibrant private sector, rapid FDI, and a thriving stock market. While the state–owned sector still constitutes 52% of industrial value–added and 18% of gross industrial output (as of June 2002), these fractions continue to drop steadily.

What explains this dramatic success of the Chinese economic reforms to date? Many answers can be and have been explored.[3] The objective of this chapter is to focus in particular on the role of the tax system in the development process.

Fifteen years ago, as discussed in more detail in the next section, the Chinese tax system was typical of those in the poorest countries. The main source of tax revenue for the national government was taxes (and dividends) collected from large capital–intensive firms, which were almost entirely owned by the national government. Statutory profits tax rates were very high, and there were many supplementary taxes and fees in addition.

Two other important sources of revenue were high tariffs on imports and high seignorage due to a rapid growth in the money supply. In spite of the high tax rates, however, revenue collection was not that high, partly because only a small part of the economy was subject to these taxes.[4] In addition, the rate of evasion on these taxes was high, and due to high rates of corruption many payments never showed up in reported government revenue.

All of these characteristics are common among the poorest countries. Table 2.1 compares the sources of tax revenue in China between 1985 and 1999 with the average figures from comparable and richer countries reported in Burgess and Stern (1993). Table 2.2 compares seignorage in China between 1986 and 1999 with that from comparable and richer countries.

Table 2.1 Tax revenue by type: a comparison between China and the rest of the world

A. China			Income Taxes				Domestic Taxes				
Year	GNP per Capita (1987 USD)	Total tax	Total	Individual*	Corporate**	Other	Total	Excise	General Sales, Turnover, VAT	Of which VAT	Agricutural taxes	Customs Duties
1985	$314	22.77%	7.76%		7.76%		11.10%		10.64%	1.65%	0.47%	2.29%
1986	$285	20.49%	6.79%		6.79%		10.63%		10.19%	2.28%	0.44%	1.49%
1987	$297	17.89%	5.56%		5.56%		9.53%		9.11%	2.12%	0.42%	1.19%
1988	$352	16.01%	4.53%		4.53%		8.96%		8.46%	2.57%	0.49%	1.04%
1989	$374	16.13%	4.14%		4.14%		9.07%		8.57%	2.55%	0.50%	1.07%
1990	$306	15.21%	3.86%		3.86%		8.54%		8.07%	2.16%	0.47%	0.86%
1991	$305	13.83%	3.38%		3.38%		7.82%		7.40%	1.88%	0.42%	0.87%
1992	$350	12.38%	2.71%		2.71%		8.17%		7.73%	2.65%	0.45%	0.80%
1993	$425	12.29%	1.96%		1.96%		8.65%		8.28%	3.12%	0.36%	0.74%
1994	$368	10.96%	1.52%		1.52%		7.91%	1.04%	6.37%	4.94%	0.50%	0.58%
1995	$460	10.33%	1.73%	0.22%	1.50%		7.33%	0.93%	5.93%	4.45%	0.48%	0.50%
1996	$520	10.18%	1.43%		1.43%		7.37%	0.91%	5.92%	4.36%	0.54%	0.44%
1997	$556	11.06%	1.64%	0.35%	1.29%		7.63%	0.91%	6.19%	4.41%	0.53%	0.43%
1998	$580	11.82%	1.18%		1.18%		8.19%	1.04%	6.64%	4.63%	0.51%	0.40%
1999	$585	13.04%	1.50%	0.51%	0.99%		8.30%	1.00%	6.78%	4.74%	0.52%	0.69%
B: International Comparison: world averages by income brackets (source: Burgess and Stern, 1993)												
Income range: GNP/capita (1987 USD)	Average GNP/capita (1987 USD)										(Other)	
$<360	$239	14.02%	3.46%	1.36%	2.19%	0.19%	4.55%	1.66%	2.44%		0.46%	5.30%
$360-749	$517	19.66%	5.74%	2.53%	2.92%	0.21%	4.74%	1.95%	2.30%		0.49%	7.58%
$750-1619	$1,127	18.62%	5.98%	2.18%	4.08%	0.30%	6.06%	2.64%	2.68%		0.74%	4.64%
$1620-6000	$2,996	19.79%	6.81%	2.14%	3.80%	0.84%	5.41%	1.99%	2.40%		1.02%	3.12%
All Developing	$1,241	18.05%	5.51%	2.08%	3.29%	0.40%	5.21%	2.07%	2.46%		0.68%	5.13%
$>6000	$13,477	31.21%	10.96%	8.45%	2.37%	0.14%	9.43%	3.02%	5.58%		0.83%	0.72%

* Data on individual income tax are availale on a few years only. Source: http://english.peopledaily.com.cn/200101/11/eng20010111_60146.html.

** Income taxes paid by state-owned and collective enterprises only.

Table 2.2 Seignorage as a proportion of GDP

Year	Argentina	Brazil	Chile	China	India	Indonesia	Malaysia	Thailand	Japan	U.S.
1985	13.44%	–	43.99%	–	2.89%	1.08%	0.88%	0.66%	0.35%	0.50%
1986	2.22%	–	13.52%	5.65%	2.20%	1.39%	0.54%	0.80%	0.73%	0.78%
1987	3.96%	–	4.69%	3.31%	2.54%	0.72%	0.69%	1.75%	0.82%	0.26%
1988	8.41%	–	1.01%	6.05%	2.22%	–0.47%	1.42%	1.21%	1.25%	0.30%
1989	31.07%	–	–0.70%	5.95%	2.46%	1.46%	2.92%	1.33%	1.32%	0.22%
1990	8.56%	13.05%	16.52%	8.49%	1.85%	0.90%	3.00%	1.44%	0.79%	0.48%
1991	3.37%	11.36%	8.63%	7.80%	2.48%	0.18%	2.07%	1.05%	–0.15	0.20%
1992	1.56%	16.03%	7.67%	5.50%	1.16%	1.52%	3.17%	1.41%	–0.39	0.48%
1993	1.72%	20.11%	4.82%	12.98%	2.81%	0.46%	1.83%	1.33%	0.56%	0.52%
1994	0.52%	19.04%	7.02%	10.03%	2.95%	1.30%	5.56%	1.23%	0.30%	0.50%
1995	–0.97%	0.86%	4.73%	6.73%	1.77%	0.98%	4.54%	1.90%	0.81%	0.27%
1996	0.11%	1.29%	5.37%	9.66%	1.30%	1.97%	9.50%	1.24%	0.92%	0.28%
1997	0.68%	2.06%	5.67%	6.38%	1.48%	2.43%	7.22%	1.55%	0.84%	0.47%
1998	0.14%	–0.83%	–1.36%	1.14%	1.60%	3.84%	–12.27%	–0.51%	0.45%	0.36%
1999	0.05%	0.49%	3.26%	3.02%	1.44%	1.99%	12.55%	5.96%	5.09%	1.20%
Average	4.99%	8.35%	8.32%	6.62%	2.08%	1.32%	2.91%	1.49%	0.91%	0.45%
Average annual inflation rate	503.39%	595.23%	14.29%	8.72%	8.90%	11.87%	1.14%	3.07%	4.01%	3.28%

Note: Seignorage is measured by the increase in reserve money this year over the previous year.

Source: IMF International Finance Statistics.

As argued in a later section, such a tax structure with very high tax rates on a narrow tax base can create large efficiency costs for the economy, discouraging investment and production in the large capital–intensive firms that are subject to high 'under–the–table' and 'over–the–table' tax payments, shifting production instead to the rest of the economy. Offsetting this pressure, however, the heavy dependence of the government on a small sector in the economy can induce the government to favor these heavily taxed sectors through its control of bank loans and regulations restricting entry of competing firms and competing imports.

The net effect, in most developing countries, appears to be that the government largely succeeds in stifling the entry and development of firms that are more difficult to tax and that compete with the existing large firms that do contribute tax revenue to the government. The result can be a stagnant and largely closed economy, dominated by large firms, with little innovation and little competition.

Yet fifteen years later, as also seen in Tables 2.1 and 2.2, the tax structure in China has changed substantially. The latest figures not only show a growth in tax revenue as a fraction of GDP, but also show an important shift away from corporate taxes, tariffs and seignorage towards a value–added tax. In addition, state control over the banking system has largely ended; the national government now collects taxes from small as well as large firms and private as well as state–owned firms. While not yet typical of the tax structure in developed economies, the changes are still dramatic.

Why has China made such strides in restructuring its tax system? Was this restructuring in fact effective in improving economic incentives? Is this restructuring simply a by–product of its rapid development generally, or has the design of its tax system played an important role supporting this development?

Our description above characterized the national tax system. In a subsequent section, we focus on a key, and unusual, additional aspect of the Chinese fiscal system. China has been very unusual in granting substantial fiscal autonomy to regional and local governments. Starting in 1980, China allowed local governments to collect and retain taxes from any firms they set up within their jurisdiction, enabling the government as a whole to collect revenue from a sector that is effectively untaxed in most poorer countries. The result was strong local government support for firm entry, leading to a rapid rate of entry and intense competition in most industries. While this fiscal decentralization led to rapid entry and growth of smaller firms, which proved to be the key success of the initial Chinese reforms, we describe in this section a variety of economic distortions that arose as part of this fiscal decentralization.

Perhaps in response to these remaining pressures, the national government shifted policy in 1994. As described in more detail later, it adopted a modern accounting system in July 1993, in February 1994 it instituted a major banking reform that effectively ended day to day government oversight of specific lending decisions, while in January it enacted a major change in the structure of the tax system. In particular, it lowered the income tax rate from 55% to 33%, and enacted a new value–added tax at 17% on most goods and services and a reduced rate of 13% on agricultural products and inputs, energy and minerals. The national government, through the newly founded National Tax Bureau, took over responsibility for collecting VAT, excise taxes, and income taxes from enterprises controlled by the national government. Local governments, through Local Tax Bureaus, were given responsibility for collecting business taxes (turnover taxes on services and sales of intangible assets and real estate properties), income taxes from individuals and from local firms, agricultural taxes, and property taxes. In general, the new tax system assigned taxes that are harder to collect to local governments, which presumably had an information advantage over the national government.

We then argue that these reforms were intimately linked. Publicly available and verifiable information on firm earnings is essential in enabling the national government to administer a broad–based tax system. Such information can come from accurate accounting statements, from bank records, and from receipts from all sales and purchases. Without such records, a firm can easily hide its transactions from the tax authorities, and any tax inspector who does trace down income can hide this information from the rest of the government, collecting side payments from the firm instead. The banking and accounting reforms, as well as the enactment of requirements that firms maintain receipts for all sales and purchases, appear to have been essential prerequisites for the transformation of the Chinese tax system. While, not surprisingly, these reforms were not that successful immediately in enabling the national government to monitor the income and value–added of firms, progress is being made.

In theory, how would these reforms affect the incentives of both firms and different levels of the government? If this updated tax system proves to be workable, existing firms should now face much less distorted investment incentives. At least as importantly, national government officials should also face much more neutral incentives when exercising any remaining controls over the allocation of resources within the economy. Given the drop in the income tax rate and the shift in most excise tax revenue to the national government, local officials may also face less distorted incentives.[5]

The above steps in the development of China's tax system therefore appear to be major steps in the development of the economy more generally. The success of the fiscal decentralization during the 1980s, in particular, was dramatic. The more recent reforms also have the potential to provide a net improvement in economic efficiency, perhaps at the cost though of slower economic growth.

Chinese tax structure, 1985–1993

China's shift towards market allocations in industry began around 1984–5. As under the planning system, the government still required firms to deliver a specified number of units of output to the government at a preset price and in exchange delivered so many units of each of the required inputs, also at a preset price.

As of 1984–5, however, firms were given the discretion to sell any residual output in the market, and to buy supplementary inputs as needed in the market.[6] In addition, the allocation of planned goods became less tightly controlled, so that firms could sometimes receive (and be required to make) side payments to assure delivery of these goods (Li, 2001a, 2001b).

Accompanying this decentralization of decision–making, the government introduced turnover taxes on goods (product tax) and services (business tax) and a profits tax on firms. Statutory tax rates were set quite high. With only a few exceptions, turnover taxes on most goods and services were assessed ad valorem on reported value of the sales, with rates ranging from 3% on salt, 20% on beer and TV sets, to 65% on grade–A cigarettes. Accounting profits were subject to a 55% tax rate. In addition, depreciation allowances were transferred to the government, to be reallocated as the government saw fit. While interest payments were deductible, interest rates were very low so that these deductions were not large.

Given the high tax rates and the additional payment of depreciation deductions to the government, tax payments in theory should have been very high. However, financial accounts were still relatively new, giving the firm substantial flexibility to understate sales revenue and profits. The traditional reporting from firms to the government focused on detailed information about physical quantities of inputs and outputs, not financial flows. With the 'dual–pricing' system, where the values of some inputs/outputs were based on planned prices and others based on market prices, the government would find it very hard to monitor the reported financial figures given the traditional information on quantities.

Tax inspectors of course would attempt to document the firm's sales revenue and accounting profits, in order to enforce the tax system. Given the lack of any outside information, however, this simply created the problem of monitoring the monitors. Given the information otherwise available to the government about quantities of inputs and outputs, a tax inspector would have substantial flexibility in choosing what revenue and financial profits figures to report for the firm after an audit. The apparent result commonly was bargaining and under–the–table payments between the firm and the tax inspectors, while reported revenue and profits remained low.

Facing such widespread evasion under the tax system, by 1987–88 the national government shifted to use of a 'contract responsibility system' to collect revenue from firms. Rather than trying to monitor the firm's sales and profits year by year, the government instead signed a contract with each firm specifying the firm's tax payments over the next several (commonly five) years. Some contracts also imposed investment or other requirements on firms. In some of these contracts, tax payments were entirely set ex ante. In others, there was a base payment with a supplementary tax imposed equal to some percent of any profits earned above some level.

By 1988, however, after many of these contracts were signed, China experienced a growing inflation rate, reducing the real value of these preset tax obligations. In addition, monitoring of firm sales and profits remained very difficult, so that tax payments continued to stagnate.

As in other poorer countries, the national government collected these taxes almost entirely from large capital–intensive (and in China state–owned) firms, where monitoring was less difficult. In most poorer countries, smaller firms largely escape these turnover and profits taxes entirely, since they operate in a cash economy and therefore leave no paper trail. Here, China took a different approach and decentralized oversight of the taxation of smaller firms to regional and local governments. While these local governments did succeed in collecting substantial revenue from these smaller firms, as discussed in the following section, the national government received very little of this revenue.

One other unusually successful source of revenue during this period in China was seignorage as seen in Table 2.2. Many developing countries (e.g., Argentina, Brazil and Chile in the 1980s and early 1990s) also collected substantial seignorage revenue, suffering in exchange a resulting high inflation rate. During this period, however, China was shifting from a planned economy that did not make more than symbolic use of money[7] to one where money did play a central role in transactions. This allowed a substantial increase in the money supply with relatively modest inflation.[8] However, this transition to a monetary economy was largely complete within a decade, so that any further use of seignorage carried an increasing risk of inflation.

As seen in Tables 2.1 and 2.2, government revenue (not counting seignorage) as a fraction of GDP declined steadily during this period. While the fraction of GDP collected in tax revenue remained comparable to that collected in other developing countries, the resulting budgetary constraints on the government limited its ability to finance needed investments in infrastructure, education, etc.

Consequences of this tax structure

Given the high tax rates that existed under the income tax in place as of 1985, based on the statutory tax structure alone Chinese firms would have faced highly distorted investment incentives, if investment decisions were made at the firm level.[9] Consider, for example, the decision by the firm to invest some of its own funds in additional capital. Denote the value of the marginal product of capital by f_K, the true economic depreciation rate by d, and the opportunity cost of funds for the firm by r.[10] Income taxes alone due on this investment, assuming that depreciation deductions in fact equal the true rate of depreciation, equal $0.55(f_K - d) + d$. The firm then breaks even as long as $f_K - d - (0.55(f_K - d) + d) \geq r$, or if $f_K - d \geq 2.2(r + d)$. If the depreciation rate, for example, were 10%, then even if the opportunity cost of funds were only 10%, the required rate of return on the capital, net of depreciation, would have been 44%. Compared to an average rate of return on capital in the U.S. of around 10%,[11] this required rate of return is extremely high. Supplementary taxes would raise it further.

Based on the tax law alone, therefore, very little investment should have occurred in these large firms. Without offsetting policies, the expected outcome would be a major shift in resources out of this highly taxed sector into other sectors that were not in practice subject to these taxes from the national government. The result would then have been very little tax revenue, and an economy artificially induced to consist mainly of firms that are small enough to avoid detection and oversight by the tax authorities.

In fact, however, investment rates in the large capital–intensive firms were substantial. Given the heavy dependence of the national government on tax revenue (and dividend payments) from these firms, it actively intervened to offset the effects of these large tax distortions on the investment rate. To begin with, the government internalized the high tax rates by actively directing large–scale investments to priority sectors and firms. To the extent that investment decisions were increasingly decentralized to firm managers, the government compensated for the high tax rates through providing cheap credit or even grants to finance desired investment projects in these firms. With cheap enough credit, firms could still be induced to go ahead with a project, in spite of the high tax rates.[12]

In order to induce a large firm to invest, in spite of the high tax rate it faces, the effective interest rate on a bank loan would need to be very low, perhaps even requiring that only a fraction of the initial principle be repaid. While the firm then breaks even on the investment project, the government–owned bank would likely lose revenue on net, due to the frequency with which loans are not fully repaid. The government, however, receives both turnover and income tax revenue from the firm on the resulting return from the investment. Therefore, bank loans should be attractive to the government as long as the combined return from additional taxes as well as any loan repayments covers the opportunity cost of the funds.[13] If the loan repayment terms are set so that the firm breaks even, then the government and the government controlled banks are the ones who are affected at the margin by the investment. As a result, allocation decisions for these firms largely remained under the control of the central government, though inevitably were made based on poor information.

Since these large firms were state–owned, the government could also use its control over managerial incentives to provide extra compensation in proportion to the firm's tax payments, to induce managers to focus on pretax rather than after–tax profits when deciding whether to invest.[14] To the extent this succeeds, the interest rate charged on bank loans could be higher. When these large firms were at a comparative disadvantage relative to competing firms abroad, the government could protect them through use of tariff and nontariff barriers. If and when these firms acquired a comparative advantage and started to export, however, then the government had an incentive to encourage more exports than would arise with free markets, again in order to expand the size of this taxed sector relative to the rest of the economy.[15]

Since revenue to the national government depended heavily on the profits of these large firms, the 'private' incentives faced by the national government would be to keep these profits high. It could do this for example by helping these firms maintain low wage rates and high consumer prices. Wage levels in fact were largely set by the national government, and the government aided industries to coordinate their consumer prices, in effect facilitating monopoly pricing. Imports were subject to high tariff rates, so that they provided comparable revenue to goods produced domestically.

The national government would also have an incentive to restrict competition from smaller firms, since this competition would not only divert profits to a sector not as easily subject to national taxation, but would also lower profits generally.

Without entry, experimentation and innovation would be stifled. This does seem to characterize government behavior in many poorer countries. As discussed in the next section, the situation in China was more complex. While the national government often did attempt to stifle the activities of smaller firms, it simultaneously created incentives for local governments to encourage this activity.

Fiscal decentralization during 1985–1993

The above description omits a key feature of the Chinese economic structure during this period—fiscal decentralization.[16] Starting in 1980, the Chinese national government started to transfer oversight and control of the vast majority of small and medium–sized state–owned enterprises to local governments, mostly at the municipal level. At the same time, the national government signed contracts with all regional and local governments, allowing them to collect turnover and income taxes and supplementary fees from these smaller firms under their control, and to keep the resulting revenue net of preset and so 'largely' lump–sum payments to the national government based on the contract signed with the national government.[17] In exchange, local governments had the responsibility to finance a wide range of local public goods.

In addition, local governments were given control of the allocation of loans from local banks. The funds available to these banks came in part from local deposits and in part from funds transferred from the national bank.

These elements of the Chinese fiscal system during this period were very unusual, and proved to be highly successful. Local governments proved to be much more effective than national governments elsewhere in monitoring and collecting revenue from these smaller firms. Since they effectively 'owned' these firms, and had representatives from the local government working within the firms, there were many sources of information to use in monitoring taxable sales and income.

Since the tax rates in theory were the same on small and large firms, these local firms also faced sufficiently high effective tax rates that investment would have been very limited if decisions were made by the firm, facing market interest rates and market prices. Local governments, however, also provided cheap loans and grants to these smaller firms, to assure that investment levels were at the level desired by the local government. If the interest rate and supplementary tax rates were in fact set so that these firms break even on additional investment, then the local government would be the only one affected by additional investment. It also had full control over the allocation of funds—control and ownership coincided.

In addition, local governments operated in a competitive environment, unlike the national government. While both centrally controlled and locally controlled firms grew and improved in productivity, the firms financed through local governments, many of them classified as collectives or township and village enterprises, were the clear success of this stage of the Chinese reform. Faster growth by these firms steadily reduced the share of gross industrial output by state–owned firms from over 74% in 1980 to 18% in June 2002. This success seems to have been directly due to the innovative decision to decentralize control over the administrative supervision, the allocation of credit, and the taxation of smaller firms to regional and local governments.

This success did not come without problems, however. There were many. To begin with, the incentives faced by national and local governments on the allocation of credit were in sharp conflict, with the national government gaining tax revenue from funding the large firms, and local governments gaining by funding smaller ones. The changing political influence of local vs. national governments, rather than relative rates of return, then played a key role in the allocation of funds.[18]

In addition, each local government gained tax revenue from investments in its jurisdiction, but not from investments in other jurisdictions. In theory, there would be an interest rate on loans between different jurisdictions which would allow jurisdictions to mutually gain from an efficient flow of funds. With interest rates set administratively at very low levels, however, and without a legal system to enforce such contracts, such a flow of funds did not seem to occur, resulting in an inefficient allocation of investment across jurisdictions. Similarly, local governments received no revenue from firms controlled by the national government, so had no incentive to loan money to these firms.

The allocation of investment within a jurisdiction also appeared to be inefficient. Effective tax rates varied by industry, being particularly high for example for cigarettes, alcoholic beverages and for many consumer durables, where excise tax rates were high. The local government could then collect much more in tax revenue from investments in these industries than from investments in other local firms. Rather than industries facing higher tax rates shrinking in size relative to more lightly taxed industries, they expanded based on the extra funding provided by the local banks under the control of the local government.[19]

A good example is the development of China's refrigerator industry described in detail in Liu and Jiang (1997). China had a small refrigerator industry in 1978 with 20 producers and an annual production of only 28,000 units. The turnover tax introduced in 1983 on refrigerators was set at 20%. The industry's gross margin was high. A government study found that the 1987 ex–factory price of refrigerators (including the turnover tax) was between 130% to 190% of the average production cost. Not surprisingly, local governments invested heavily in this industry, often using loans from banks under their control to finance capacity construction and expansion. By 1985, the number of refrigerator producers had risen to 115, and production to 1.45 million units. In 1999, China produced 12 million units, making it one of the largest refrigerator producers in the world. But most producers were making losses after paying indirect taxes.

Similar issues arose with respect to private vs. township and village enterprises (TVE's). TVE's were firms set up and officially owned by the local governments. As owners, the local government appointed the managers, and could assign other local government employees to oversight positions within the firm. As a result, the local government could easily monitor the firm's profits. In principle, the local government had no such authority over private firms, making it much harder to monitor and tax their profits. To the extent the local government could collect taxes more easily from TVE's than from private firms, however, it had an incentive to discourage competition from private firms undermining the profits of TVE's, and it also had an incentive to focus local bank lending on TVE's whose profits could be effectively monitored by the local government. In practice, though, 'private' firms did often find ways to work out a modus vivendi with local governments, perhaps through sharing ownership, appointing local representatives to positions within the firm, precommitting to a certain level of tax payment, etc.[20] While such bargaining inevitably made entry more complicated than in a developed economy, the private sector did gradually expand, and at an increasing rate. By 1999, it produced 62% of the gross output in the nonstate sector.

In addition, tax revenue depended on local production, not local consumption. With effective tax rates varying by industry, local governments were not willing to allow unrestricted trade with other jurisdictions. In particular, they had a fiscal incentive to prevent imports of goods where local production was heavily taxed, and an incentive to encourage exports of these heavily taxed local goods.[21] While in theory contracts could be designed between local governments that would allow for production of heavily taxed goods to be concentrated in the firms with the lowest production costs, in practice these contracts did not quickly develop. Instead, local governments protected local firms facing high tax rates from competition from goods produced in other jurisdictions. The result was a proliferation of inefficiently small firms in industries where tax rates were relatively high. For example, while the minimum efficient scale in annual refrigerator production was estimated to be about 200,000 units per firm, the average production of Chinese firms was only 12,592 units in 1985 Liu and Jiang (1997).

A tax system based on local production is also vulnerable to tax competition. Individual entrepreneurs, who contemplate negotiating with a local government to open up a new TVE or private firm, have a choice about which local government to approach. Competition among local governments should force down the effective net tax rate (taxes paid relative to subsidies provided, for example, through cheap credit) to the point where the local government breaks even by accepting the new firm, collecting no net revenue from the firm. As the economy became more sophisticated, increasingly the initiative for new firms came from individuals who had this discretion about where to set up business, implying a decline in the ability of local governments to collect revenue from firms in their jurisdiction.

Another problem was that local governments had an incentive to lend more funds than they had, since any extra loans to local firms provided substantial extra tax payments as well as interest payments sufficient to repay depositors (or the central bank) on the funds they provided. As a result, some local banks tried to pay an interest rate on deposits above the rate set administratively by the national government,[22] though the national government worked hard to prevent such behavior. In addition, local governments often loaned more funds than they had, on the expectation that the national government would bail them out by providing supplementary funds. In practice, this expectation seemed to be justified while the national government could threaten never to provide such supplementary funding again, this threat was not 'time–consistent'. The result was an expansion in credit beyond what could be funded through existing deposits and tax revenue, resulting in an expansion in the money supply and in the inflation rate beyond that intended by the national government.

The net result of these competitive pressures was rapid entry, falling profit rates as the monopoly power of state–owned firms were undermined, and a very rapid rate of economic growth and of productivity growth. The continuing fall in government revenue as a fraction of GDP, however, imposed very costly constraints on the local as well as national governments, limiting needed expenditures on education, infrastructure, and other government services.

Policy reforms since 1994

In 1994, there were a series of major policy reforms. To begin with, the government phased out the dual–track system by eliminating any allocation through the plan. Massive entry by local firms and private firms into various sectors had succeeded in creating a very competitive product market. As market–clearing prices became the only prices for most goods and services, financial flows became more informative for economic decision–making and for tax purposes than physical quantities. As a result, the government in 1994 shifted from the previous accounting system, which had focused on carefully documenting quantities of inputs and outputs but had been less careful in monitoring financial flows, to one that closely followed the form of income and balance sheet statements used in developed economies. The hope, with this reform, presumably was that the resulting accounting reports from outside auditors would provide much more valuable information to the government about the state of the economy generally, but also the size of taxable sales, value–added and profits earned by each firm.

In addition, the government enacted a major reform of the banking sector. Until then, the banks were largely arms of the government planning ministries, allocating funds approved by these ministries and relying on the ministries to cover any resulting accounting losses they might experience. Following the reform, the day–to–day links between the banks and the government were largely broken. Banks were supposed to operate on standard commercial principles, making loans based on their prospect of being repaid. By this period, real interest rates had risen dramatically compared to their levels in the 1980s, and were plausibly market clearing.

Finally, the government enacted a major reform of the tax system, replacing the contract system with fengshuizhi or the system of separate taxation. To begin with, the new system redefined the revenue sources of national and local governments. Local taxes continued to include the profits taxes and remittances from local firms, a turnover tax on services (other than railroad transportation, banking and insurance), property taxes, personal income taxes, and stamp duties, while national taxes included customs duties, value–added taxes on imports, excise taxes, and profits taxes and remittances from national firms. The new value–added tax on industrial production, the largest source of tax revenue, was shared between the national government (75%) and local governments (25%). The enforcement of taxes was divided between the National Tax Bureau and Local Tax Bureaus. The

Local Tax Bureaus collected local taxes, while the National Tax Bureau collected national taxes and shared taxes.

In addition, the profits tax rate was reduced from 55% to 33%, so was now comparable or even lower than the rates in effect in the major developed economies. The value–added tax rate was set at 17% on most goods and at a reduced rate of 13% on agricultural products and inputs, energy and minerals. Such rates are very much comparable to those in place within the E.U. To help in the enforcement of this tax, firms were required to keep receipts on all transactions, both purchases and sales. In principle, cross–checking of receipts would provide the government an additional source of information and oversight over these firms. Since the tax base for a value–added tax simply depends on the sum of receipts for sales, with a credit for any VAT already paid as reported on the receipts for purchases, monitoring these receipts was sufficient to monitor the value–added tax base.[23]

Assessment of 1994 reforms

Several separate reforms happened to occur at the same time. Our presumption is that these reforms were in fact closely interconnected. Only with the elimination of dual prices on goods and services could financial accounts provide meaningful information on the state of the economy and the size of the tax base. Through the adoption of the new accounting system and the higher resulting quality of information about firm sales and purchases, the national governments potentially saw enough improvement in its ability to monitor market transactions by all firms that it could take over the assessment of value–added and excise taxes from local governments and end the fiscal contract system in favor of a tax system more in line with international practices. Only with a reduction in the effective profits tax rate could the government consider abandoning the implicit offsetting subsidies to interest rates that had previously been used to maintain a reasonable investment rate. In addition, the creation of a competitive market–oriented banking system should generate growing productivity in the financial sector, making it more attractive for firms to make greater use of banks as financial intermediaries for their transactions. Since use of banks generates a paper trail, it establishes a record of transactions available to the tax authorities. Greater use of banks therefore increases the potential tax base. Finally, the requirement that firms keep receipts for all transactions, while linked directly to the VAT, also helps in documenting sales and purchases of inputs that enter into the profits tax base as well.

As seen in Table 2.3, the share of central government revenue rose sharply in 1994 as the central government claimed the bulk of the VAT. The aggregate numbers did show some initial problems with the reforms, however, as consolidated tax revenue fell in 1994 and 1995.[24] Since exports were exempt under the VAT, firms initially reported huge levels of exports, inconsistent with the amounts reported at the border and enough to wipe out all VAT liabilities. Similarly, there were stories of firms surreptitiously acquiring books of receipts that they could use to create fictional credits for purchases on goods where in fact no VAT

Table 2.3 Government revenue

	Government revenue as a proportion of GDP			*Central gov't share of total revenue*
Year	*Consolidated*	*Central*	*Local*	
1980	25.67%	6.30%	19.38%	24.52%
1981	24.18%	6.40%	17.78%	26.46%
1982	22.90%	6.55%	16.35%	28.61%
1983	23.03%	8.26%	14.78%	35.85%
1984	22.91%	9.28%	13.63%	40.51%
1985	22.36%	8.59%	13.78%	38.39%
1986	20.80%	7.63%	13.17%	36.68%
1987	18.39%	6.15%	12.23%	33.48%
1988	15.79%	5.19%	10.60%	32.87%
1989	15.76%	4.86%	10.90%	30.86%
1990	15.84%	5.35%	10.48%	33.79%
1991	14.57%	4.34%	10.23%	29.79%
1992	13.08%	3.68%	9.40%	28.12%
1993	12.56%	2.76%	9.79%	22.02%
1994	11.16%	6.22%	4.94%	55.70%
1995	10.67%	5.57%	5.11%	52.17%
1996	10.91%	5.39%	5.52%	49.42%
1997	11.62%	5.68%	5.94%	48.86%
1998	12.61%	6.24%	6.36%	49.53%
1999	13.97%	7.14%	6.83%	51.11%

was paid. How well the operation of the system has improved over time is hard to judge from a distance, though we do see revenue from the VAT growing at a rate faster than the GDP growth rate.

These reforms, while dramatic, were only some of the major policy changes that occurred during the late 1990s. During this period, China successfully negotiated to become a member of the WTO, resulting in a substantial fall in tariff rates. Previously, the government faced a strong fiscal incentive to use tariffs to protect large state–owned firms from competition from imports. With the shift towards reliance primarily on the VAT, where the tax rate is relatively equal on all sectors, the national government has more neutral incentives, facilitating this reduction in tariff rates.

In addition, during the last few years, China has been experiencing a deflation, in sharp contrast to the inflationary pressures present during most of the 1980s. Given that nominal interest rates are still set administratively, and have not changed much over time, this shift from inflation to deflation is the main reason why real interest rates are now closer to market–clearing levels, facilitating the shift to a commercial banking sector. That tax revenue continued to grow during this period in spite of the fall in tariff and seignorage revenue shows the importance of the changes enacted in the tax system.

If these combined reforms in the accounting, banking, and tax systems did in fact work as intended, to what degree would they have reduced or eliminated the various distortions and pressures described above that arose under the previous tax system? The design of tax reform did seem to respond to several of the pressures that existed under the previous tax system. For example, under the previous system, local governments favored industries that paid high excise tax rates. After the reform, this excise tax revenue instead goes to the national government, making local government incentives more neutral. For the national government, the value–added tax becomes a primary source of revenue. This tax should be far easier to enforce than the previous income tax, given the use of receipts to document all revenue and deductions. Reflecting this, the national government took on responsibility for collecting the VAT not just for the large state–owned firms, but for all firms, large and small, state–owned and private. As a result, at least based on the VAT the national government has no reason to favor one sector over another. While profits tax revenue from small firms still goes to local governments, leaving some incentive for the national government to favor large firms,[25] the reduction in the profits tax rate causes this bias to be less than it had been.

Local governments maintained control over the income tax on local firms, where they should still have much greater ability to monitor profits. In addition, local governments continue to receive revenue from those taxes, such as the property tax and the personal income tax, that should be particularly sensitive to the economic climate created by the local government. These taxes as a result create clear economic pressures on local governments to develop a favorable economic climate.[26]

Note, however, that the reduction in reliance on the profits tax, where revenue from local firms goes to local governments, and the increase in reliance on a VAT, where the bulk of the tax revenue goes to the national government, implies in itself a shift in tax revenue from local governments to the national government. Table 2.3 shows that the change was dramatic in 1994, increasing the central government share of revenue from 22% to 56%. This shift in revenue in itself could result in more support for large firms and less for small firms.

In addition, the reduction in the profits tax rate to the level seen in other countries, and the shift to an accounting measure of profits more in line with those in the developed economies imply that any distortion to a firm's investment incentives should also be in line with those in developed economies. As a result, allowing bank loans to be made on a commercial basis and allowing interest rates to rise to market–clearing levels again is in line with what happens elsewhere. Too little investment may occur, but these losses could well be of second–order importance relative to the gains from shifting decision–making on investments from the government to firms, where information about potential returns should be far better.

The shift to a commercial banking sector, however, in theory puts strong limits on the extent to which any level of government can favor one sector over another.

In theory, banks would no longer be expected to favor large firms over small firms, and heavily taxed firms over lightly taxed firms. Instead, they should base credit decisions simply on the likelihood of repayment.

Given the relatively underdeveloped state of the banking system, however, banks may not yet be that effective in evaluating credit risks, particularly for smaller firms. Given the resulting lemons problem, credit rationing should become a much larger problem than it had been when smaller firms were under the close monitoring and control of local governments. Without such easy access to credit, entry will become much harder and smaller firms will likely grow less quickly than before.

A number of other countries have dealt with this problem by developing industrial groups, e.g. keiretsu or chaebols, in which banks have an ownership stake in industrial firms, and as partial owners can monitor them closely in order to judge the value of further investments in these firms. This cross–ownership structure parallels that of the local government and the TVE's prior to the 1994 reforms, but occurs entirely through the private sector. Our expectation is that this type of industrial grouping is likely to develop as well in China, at least at this stage of its economic development, in order to replicate some of the advantages of the economic institutions prior to the 1994 reforms but without direct government participation in the process.

Such industrial groups may be reasonably effective at allocating credit among members of the group. It would remain difficult, however, for potential entrants to obtain credit, unless they can form a joint venture with an existing industrial group.

In addition, however, these tax reforms more directly discourage firm entry. Previously, entry was largely financed by funds under the control of the local government, and returns from any investment largely accrued to the local government. After the reforms, new firms are much more likely to be self–financed. If the entering firm fails, the entrepreneur can well bear all of the losses.[27] If it succeeds, it is subject to both profits and value–added taxes. As emphasized in Cullen and Gordon (2002), this asymmetric treatment of losses and profits under the tax system can strongly discourage entry. Developed economies normally lessen this tax distortion by making initial losses deductible from personal taxable income. The personal income tax plays little role in China to date, however.

In addition, with better publicly available information from accounting reports and bank records, tax assessors have less discretion when reporting findings from a tax audit. Therefore, the room for corruption among tax officials should have been reduced as well, if there is sufficient outside oversight of the accounting reports.

Summary

As of the mid–1980s, the national government in China had a fiscal structure very similar to that in most developing countries, relying primarily on profits taxes on large capital–intensive firms, tariffs, and seignorage. Given such heavy reliance on a narrow sector of the economy, governments in these economies are under strong fiscal pressure to protect the profits of these large firms from competition from small firms and from imports. Without much entry and with little competition, these economies commonly stagnate.

Yet the Chinese economy has grown at a remarkable rate. Our hypothesis is that a key explanation for the differing outcome in China was the fiscal decentralization that was adopted in China at the very beginning of the reform period. Under this fiscal decentralization, local governments could collect profits taxes from small firms and new entrants, and could allocate credit to these firms. In practice, they did have enough sources of information to collect revenue effectively from these firms. As a result, they had a strong fiscal incentive to encourage entry and productivity growth in these firms, so as to increase future taxable profits.

While this fiscal innovation did generate very rapid growth initially, it created its own problems. For example, tax competition undermined the tax base, and local governments had an incentive to protect local firms facing high tax rates, while the national government still had a competing incentive to protect large firms.

Since 1994, there have been a series of reforms in the tax law, in accounting procedures, in banking, and in tariff rates, that have led China to have a fiscal structure much more similar to that in developed economies. While this system may not be quite as supportive of entry and growth as the previous system, it should deal well with many of the problems that arose under the previous system.

Notes

1 This chapter was written for the Conference on China and the World Economy, in honor of Gregory Chow, that took place in Hong Kong during June 14–16, 2002. It is literally true that without Gregory's help this chapter would not have been written, since the two of us met at the Economics Training Program in Beijing in the fall of 1986, a program that Gregory set up and administered. More broadly, we have been inspired by Gregory's own work to make careful use of existing economic insights derived from market economies to better understand why the Chinese economy has evolved as it has. We started developing ideas for this chapter when Roger Gordon visited the University of Virginia as a Batten Fellow at the Darden Graduate School of Business Administration. We gratefully acknowledge the financial support from the Batten Institute.

2 Unless we state otherwise, the data we use in this chapter are drawn from Datastream and the online database published by National Bureau of Statistics of China at http://www.stats.gov.cn.

3 For comprehensive and in–depth analyses of China's dramatic economic transformation, see Chow (1985a, 1985b, 1993, 1994, 2002).

4 Eighty percent of the population worked in agriculture, where taxation was much more difficult. Prior to the late 1970s, the national government collected implicit agricultural taxes using price scissors underpricing of agricultural products relative to industrial products manufactured by state–owned firms to channel taxable surpluses to the state–owned sector. To protect this tax base, the national government monopolized the procurement of agricultural products, prohibiting peasants from directly selling grain in free markets. By the early 1980s, however, agricultural reforms gradually raised procurement prices and reduced the implicit taxes on peasants. By the mid 1990s, the government had raised procurement prices for grain

above both domestic and international market prices, providing implicit subsidies to peasants.

5 However, new entry may be less attractive than before, since the private entrepreneur bears all the potential costs, but still faces relatively high tax rates on potential gains.

6 Allocation decisions were decentralized step by step, however. The government still controlled the allocation of bank loans, an issue we return to below. The assignment of workers to firms also remained heavily controlled by the government.

7 A common aphorism was that 'money was neither necessary nor sufficient to purchase goods'. Instead, allocations were commonly arranged through the distribution of rationing permits.

8 For more discussion on the relationship between money and price level in China, see Chow (1987).

9 While actual tax payments were not that high, avoidance of statutory tax payments was likely to have been largely offset by under–the–table payments. In theory, a tax inspector could hold out for close to the tax liability he could legally impose on the firm, in exchange for reporting less to the government.

10 This opportunity cost equals the rate of return that the firm's managers would require for foregoing use of the funds now in exchange for a presumed use of the extra revenue in the future generated by the new investment. This required rate of return could be high in part due to the uncertainty about their claim on any future profits, e.g. due to short–term managerial contract, as well as due to uncertainty about the size of these future profits.

11 See, for example, Feldstein and Summers (1977).

12 The loans from banks controlled by the national government went almost exclusively to firms whose tax payments went to the national government.

13 For further exploration of this issue, see Gordon (2003).

14 For further discussion, see Gordon, Bai and Li (1999).

15 This may be part of the explanation for the high export rates of the Asian Tigers, where government support may have led to even larger exports than would have occurred with free markets.

16 For more discussion, see Li (1997).

17 These payments were typically fixed for a five year period, but could change during later periods, providing some implicit revenue sharing with the national government.

18 For example, following the Tiananmen crackdown in 1989, the central government asserted control more forcefully. As a result, over a million nonstate firms were forced to shut down.

19 Such overexpansion suggests that the local governments cared more about their tax revenue than about the remaining after–tax profits of local firms.

20 For further discussion, see Li (1996).

21 According to a news digest published on www.chinabeer.com (accessed on May 19, 2002), many localities impose a 0.20 yuan per bottle tariff on non–local beers. In some instances, retailers were ordered not to carry non–local brands.

22 See Park (forthcoming) for further discussion.

23 Monitoring profits in contrast remained much more complicated, for example requiring extensive record keeping on the dates and purchase prices of all capital and inventories.

24 The fall in tax revenue was more than compensated by the sharp increase in seignorage in the mid–1990s as seen in Table 2.2.

25 In 1997, at the 15th Party Congress, the Chinese leadership affirmed a new policy towards state–owned enterprises. Summarized by the slogan, 'grasping the big ones and letting go the small ones', this policy permitted smaller state–owned firms to be

either privatized, combined into Chaebol–type enterprise groups led by large state–owned firms, or shut down. It signified the national government's preference towards large firms.

26 See Gordon and Wilson (2001) for further discussion.

27 New firms will inevitably have negative value–added initially. If this results in a tax rebate, then the government does share in the potential losses as well as profits. However, in practice, such rebates in the event of negative value–added are unusual. In addition, the firm can go bankrupt, implicitly sharing its losses with its creditors. Bankruptcy procedures are only now being clarified, however.

References

Burgess, R., and Stern, N. (1993), 'Taxation and Development', *Journal of Economic Literature* **31**, pp. 762–830.

Chow, G.C. (1985a), *The Chinese Economy*, Harper & Row Publishers, New York.

Chow, G.C. (1985b), 'A Model of Chinese National Income Determination', *Journal of Political Economy* **93**, pp. 782–792.

Chow, G.C. (1987), 'Money and Price Level Determination in China', *Journal of Comparative Economics* **11**, pp. 319–333.

Chow, G.C. (1993), 'Capital Formation and Economic Growth in China', *Quarterly Journal of Economics* **108**, pp. 809–842.

Chow, G.C. (1994), *Understanding China's Economy*, World Scientific Publishing Co., Singapore.

Chow, G.C. (2002), *China's Economic Transformation*, Blackwell Publishers, Oxford, UK.

Cullen, J.B., and Gordon, R.H. (2002), 'Taxes and Entrepreneurial Activity: Theory and Evidence for the U.S.', N.B.E.R. Working Paper No. 9015.

Feldstein, M.S., and Summers, L.J. (1977), 'Is the Rate of Profit Falling?', *Brookings Papers on Economic Activity*, pp. 211–227.

Gordon, R.H. (2003) 'Taxes and Privatization', in S. Cnossen and H. Sinn (eds.), *Public Finance and Public Policy in the New Century*, MIT Press, Cambridge.

Gordon, R.H., Bai, C. and Li, D.D. (1999), 'Efficiency Losses from Tax Distortions Vs. Government Control', *European Economic Review* **43**, pp. 1095–1103.

Gordon, R.H., and Wilson, J.D. (2001), 'Expenditure Competition', NBER Working Paper No. 8189.

Li, D.D. (1996), 'A Theory of Ambiguous Property Rights in Transition Economies: The Case of the Chinese Non–State Sector', *Journal of Comparative Economics* **23**, pp. 1–19.

Li, W. (1997), 'The Impact of Economic Reform on the Performance of Chinese State Enterprises, 19801989', *Journal of Political Economy* **105**, pp. 1080–1106.

Li, W. (2001a), 'Corruption and Resource Allocation: Evidence from China', University of Virginia.

Li, W. (2001b), 'Measuring Corruption: An Indirect Approach Using Chinese Enterprise Survey Data', University of Virginia.

Liu, S. and Jiang, X. (1997), 'Industrial Policy and Growth: A Study of Refrigerator Industry in China', in S. Zhang (ed.), *Case Studies in China's Institutional Change*, Shanghai People's Press, Shanghai.

Park, A. (forthcoming) 'Competition under Credit Rationing: Theory and Evidence from China', *Journal of Development Economics*.

Chapter 3

How Size Matters to Future Chinese Growth: Some Trade–Theoretic Considerations

Henry Wan Jr.[1]

Introduction

It is both a distinction and a challenge to contribute a chapter honoring Professor Gregory Chow, especially in this conference devoted to the Mainland Chinese economy. As a leading econometrician and a researcher with deep insight, Professor Chow himself has contributed greatly to this subject. In addition, there already exists a voluminous literature on the institutions and economic performance of China. As a novice to this area, I shall focus on some aspects that are closely related to my background and less studied by others.

Since the 1978 reform, the Chinese development has depended heavily on its 'openness' to the external markets. Such interactions with the trading world follow certain regularities. These are evident from the development experience of other economies which are in some fashion, similar to China. It is useful to question whether and how does China's size influence the interactions between China and the rest of the world.

Whenever the Chinese economy is being discussed, what first comes to one's mind is often its 'size' in area, population, or total output value. In research, we have to decide *what* exactly 'size' means, *how* that matters in analytic terms, and *whether* size poses special opportunities or challenges to China. These issues are important to policy making, like a navigation chart is to a pilot. Most such issues concern the relative strength of a country in international transactions. They may thus be studied from the trade–theoretic angle. A systematic survey of all these aspects should be useful for policy analysis.

We approach the matter from a variety of viewpoints: (a) the population size, and related to it, the aspect of factor proportions; (b) the issue of reciprocal demand, between a country and the rest of the world, and hence the terms of trade; (c) the economies of scale; (d) the strategic trade aspect, namely market power; and finally, (e) the co–ordination aspect, when in real life, decentralized decisions are made in 'incomplete markets'. We relate such discussions to the performance of the Chinese economy in its recent past as well as the economic prospects for its future.

Size and factor proportions

Today, China is the most highly populated nation. Its population of 1.24 billion in 1998 is almost five times as numerous as the American population of 275 million. Located largely in the temperate zone, these two countries are broadly comparable in territorial size. Yet within its territory, China is often less well endowed than America in its total amount of many kinds of natural resources. The following comparison in Table 3.1 is far from exhaustive. It serves only for illustration.

Comparison may also be made in terms of the endowments in standing timber, fresh water, iron ore, etc. Not only in per capita endowment of natural resources, but also in both physical and human capital, however measured, China is much less well endowed per capita than America today. In the history of trade theory, what qualifies as America's abundant factor of production has become the subject of the Leontief Paradox. However, in its trade with America, or most of the other countries, Chinese export is definitely labor intensive.

In principle, large economies need to trade less than small economies. Their endowments tend to be more balanced. Different regions may complement each other. But compared to other East Asian economies like Japan and Korea, the Mainland Chinese economy is no more self–sufficient in natural resources, in spite of its size in area. In many ways, the supposedly large size of China actually means abundant labor, coupled with the relative scarcity in various other resources, skilled manpower included.

For such a crowded country, the slowing down of its population growth rate is a desirable achievement. Soon, China would not be the most populous country. But it benefits the world as a whole more on environmental grounds, than it benefits China in terms of trade. Facing the same trading world, the terms of trade of every labor–abundant country must deteriorate in response to the unchecked population growth, whether in China or anywhere else. In trade theory, this is the lesson of the 'integrated equilibrium' for the trading world. In other labor–abundant countries, population growth has remained unchecked. Thus, fierce Chinese population control may delay global warming for the world, but will not save China from the worsening terms of trade against labor intensive products.

Soon the aging Chinese population, with its rising dependency ratio, will be at a competitive disadvantage relative to a labor–abundant country whose birth rate starts to drop later: its share of working age in the population will be larger than the Chinese. This will be even more true, if the child labor laws remain unenforced. As a remedy, China has to accumulate physical and human capital to change its comparative advantage, in a timely fashion, like Japan had been successfully doing.

Even in physical capital formation, one needs some perspective. For example, beyond some point, Chinese infrastructure construction must take account of some global limit for growth. A thought experiment should bring us some realism. Today, many industries have easily migrated across the Taiwan Strait. Any difference in production technology among the Chinese on both shores is marginal and temporary. Thus in the foreseeable future, the per capital output value in

Table 3.1 Comparative endowments: China and USA

	China	*USA*
Crude petroleum (million bbls.)	24,000	22,317
Coal reserve (million tons)	114,500	240,518
Farm land (thousand hectares)	166,902	393,471

Mainland China should reach Taiwan's level today and the consumption patterns may converge in short course. Today's person–to–motor vehicle ratio stands at 4.3 in Taiwan to 128 in the rest of China. By then, the expected motor vehicle ownership in China could be 288 million, which is more than 80% of the total American automobile ownership today (the vehicle/person ratio for the 275 million Americans being 1.3). Given the highly inelastic world supply and demand of petroleum,[2] such a prospect should be approached with some forethought.

Vehicles do not travel in a vacuum. Tomorrow's transportation is likely to be carried on roads built today. Americans presently travel on the highway system laid down in the Eisenhower years. Thus, when infrastructure is constructed in China nowadays, it is time to give thoughts to how the economy might look in 50 years. Hopefully such a vision is not based upon the hypothesis that a growing Chinese economy has no appreciable effect on Chinese import prices. (That is, the *small* country assumption in the trade theory literature). It is the unthinking urban sprawl that makes the energy demand difficult to control for the richer societies today.

It is worthwhile to note that the average income is much higher in Hong Kong than in Taiwan, but the person/vehicle ratio is only 13.1. This comparison shows that the energy demand of high income societies is far from inflexible. Thoughtful urban design today can make a great deal of difference tomorrow.

The question of reciprocal demand

What we have just discussed concerns factor proportions, on the supply side. Now we turn to the demand side. From the viewpoint of resources per capita, China today may not be that different from South Korea, in the early 1960s. Being populous is a relevant fact to China. Size is clearly a constraint here, not a strength. Now in the N–goods general equilibrium setting, modeling the demand of the (heterogeneous) 'rest of the world' analytically is not a simple task.[2] But even a less formal approach can be quite convincing.

Let us say, at time t, Korea has exported M units of some particular output. This means with a population of 46 million in 1998, on a per capita basis, Koreans have exported M/46,000,000 units of that good in question, and gained certain benefit from that transaction. This product may be textile, steel, automobile,

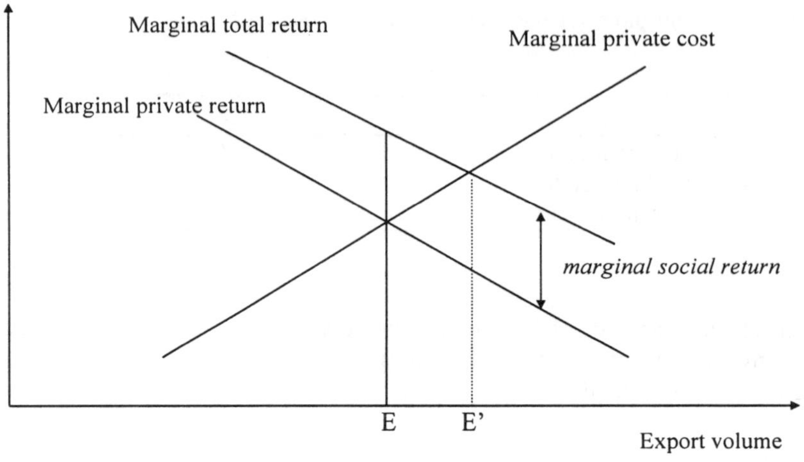

Figure 3.1 Export externalities

dynamic random memory chips (DRAMs), whatever. Now if China is to achieve the same effect by exporting M/46,000,000 units per person, the world market must absorb nearly 30M units, since the Chinese population is almost 27 times that of the Korean. Common sense predicts that this export goal is hard to meet, even if China can produce goods of the same quality but charges a much lower unit price. For example, if Korea has exported microwave ovens, but where can China get 27 times more new foreign customers? In the trade literature, this mental experiment may appear unfamiliar. But logically, this is just an extension of the theory of *immiserized growth*.

But the implication does not stop here. Exporting brings many benefits besides the static gains from trade, conventionally measured. It offers the opportunity for a developing economy to acquire technology (through customers' feedbacks) and experience unavailable at home.[4] It brings forth contact and reputation. It imposes discipline on inefficient domestic enterprises, demanding labor unions and sometimes corrupt government administrators, once it is recognized by the general public that export performance is in the national interest, not to be jeopardized for private gain. It motivates the society to accumulate the specific human capital for foreign trade. All these benefit the economy as a whole, rather than any particular trader or producer in the export business. For convenience, they shall be called collectively, 'trade externalities'. These are public goods with a non–rival nature, relevant to a country with any size. For example, labor mobility across firms facilitates the diffusion of best practices inside national borders. In conventional welfare analysis, the situation is shown in Figure 3.1. Thus, there is a cause for any State devoted to economic development to promote export activities, moving the equilibrium in Figure 3.1 from E to E'.

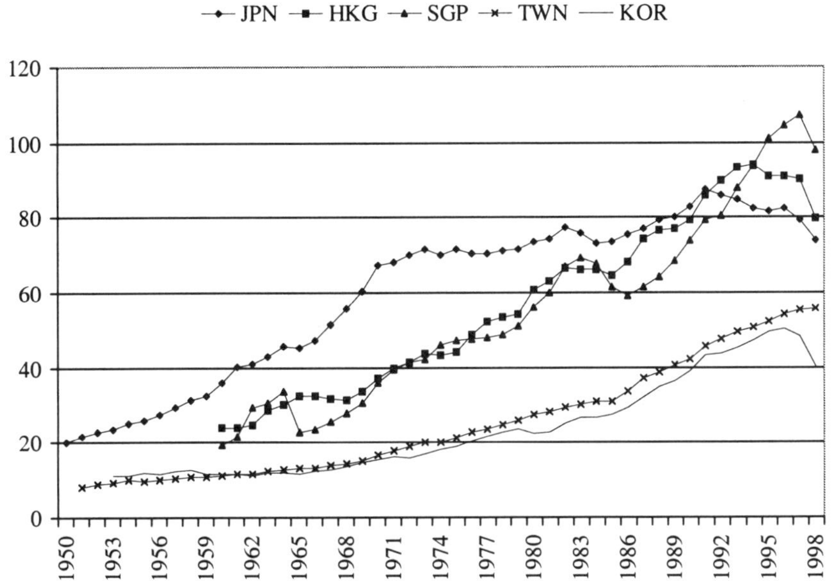

Figure 3.2 The East Asians catching up with the US

It is reasonable to believe that such external benefits from trade are particularly important for developing economies where current practices need improvement. This is also empirically verifiable. In the second half of the century, cross–Pacific trade blossomed between Japan and the four Newly Industrialized Economies (Korea, Taiwan, Hong Kong and Singapore) on one side and America on the other. There is no intrinsic reason that the static trading gain would benefit America less than America's trade partners. In contrast, the less developed East Asia has much more to gain from trade externalities than the developed America. Thus, the testable implication of trade externalities is that with expanded trade, East Asia would begin to catch up with America in this last half century, narrowing the differences in per capita real GDP.

We use data from the Penn World Table version 6.0 to plot the results in Figure 3.2, where each series of the Asian per capita real GDP is shown as a percent of the US data. The hypothesis of trade externality is not falsified by evidence.

One may question whether trade expansion is the key cause for catching up. We gain more insight from Figure 3.3, in which the series for Argentina is added. Clearly, Argentina was ahead of all the East Asia Five in the early 1950s but eventually fell behind all these five.

In fact, Argentina is not all that atypical among the developing economies. The real question is whether and by how much the catching up performance can be attributed to the openness of an economy. For verification, we use the series of the

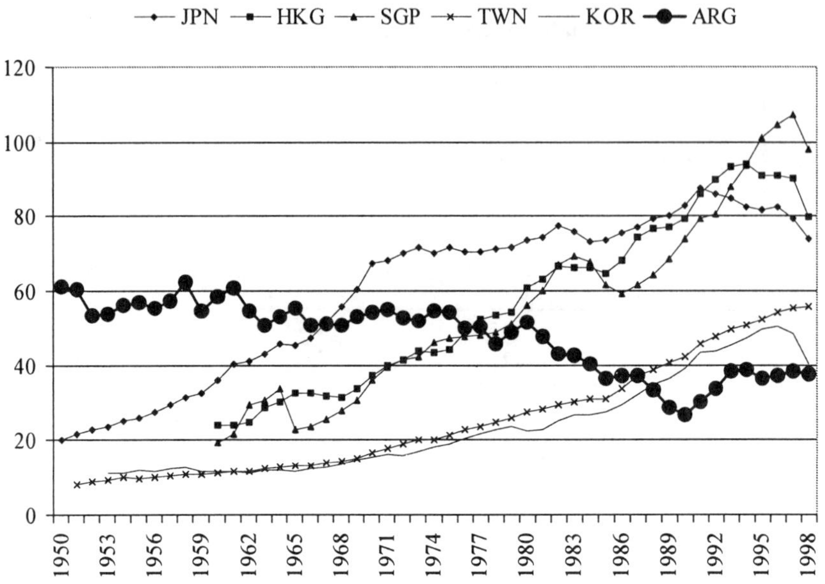

Figure 3.3 Argentina falls behind

'openness index' = (Export + Import)/GDP, available from the Penn World Table 6.0. The 'openness' for these six economies is depicted in Figure 3.4 for the years 1956, 1966, 1976, 1986 and 1996. Thus the hypothesis that openness facilitates catching up cannot be rejected. Argentina is the least open among the six, for all the five selected years, with the possible exception of 1996, where the Japanese economy is slightly less open. But by then Japan is an advanced industrialized economy, openness does not provide the trade externalities urgently in need.

From the viewpoint of the Mainland Chinese economy, what Figure 3.1 and Figures 3.2–3.4 convey is that openness benefits the catching up process. Since on the per capita basis, the conventional gains from export—a private returns—are likely to be small for China relative to say, Korea, it appears that the Chinese State should make effort to magnify the effect of the private returns for acquiring external benefits. This seems to be a *prima facie* call for export promotion.

On the other hand, our previous analysis of reciprocal demand indicates that the size factor works against the degree of Chinese openness. On a per capita basis, one cannot hope for Chinese exports to match what the other East Asian economies achieved earlier, unit for unit. Even though a straightforward approach to trade promotion cannot work very well, the State should amplify the private returns from trade for the sake of trade externalities.

Can such a policy work? History suggests yes, and Japan is a clear example. Facing severe dollar shortages in the 1950s, the entire Japanese society identified export as a top priority, under the slogan, 'export or starve'. Since then, to

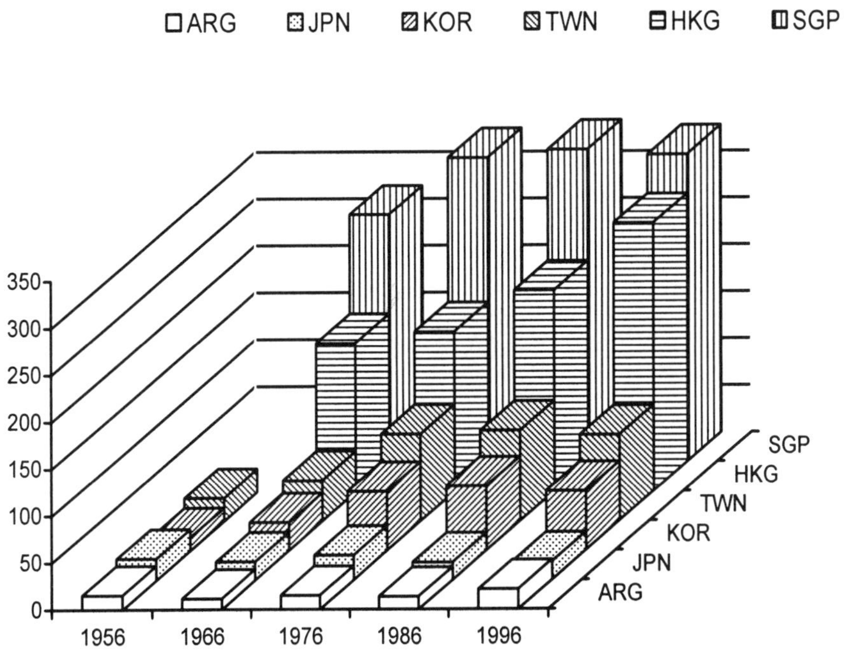

Figure 3.4 Openness index

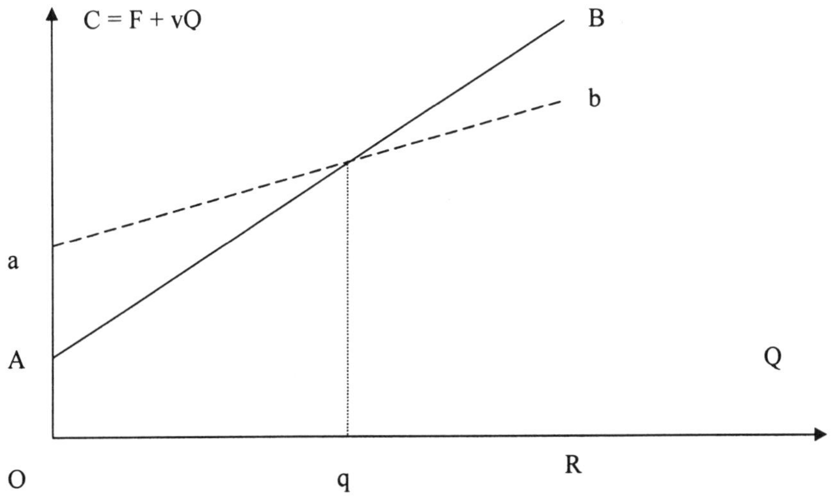

Figure 3.5 Economy of scale

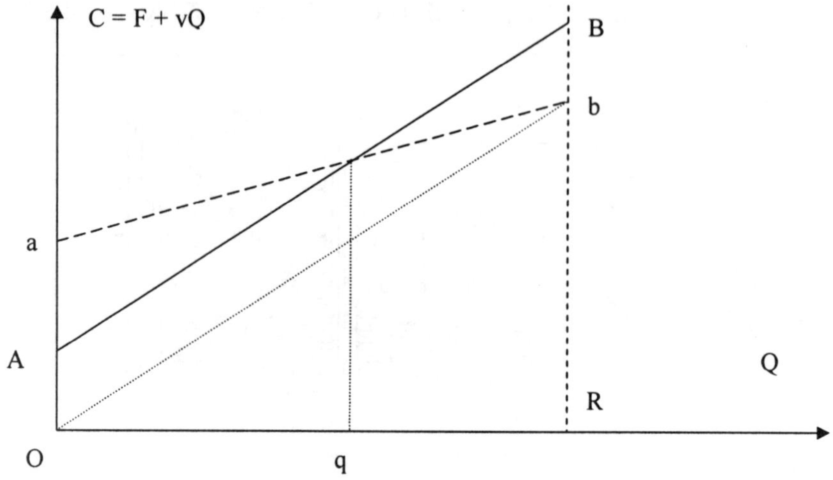

Figure 3.6 Sunk cost does not matter to the entrenched firm

ameliorate international trade friction, Japan has repeatedly accepted 'voluntary export restrictions'. Therefore, Japan has benefited from 'trade externalities' even though in terms of the openness index, Japan is far less open than Korea and Taiwan.

The point of avoiding trade friction is also relevant to China. Already China's Asian neighbors, Singapore included, are concerned that Chinese trade expansion would displace Southeast Asia economies in the export market and as a destination of direct foreign investment.[5] When necessary, the pursuit of both export promotion and voluntary export restraint by Japan seems to form a viable precedence.

Western historians often puzzle over the fact that just before Prince Henry of Portugal promoted the national capacity for navigation, in the hope of profiting from the China trade, Ming China had stopped the Chinese naval excursions into the South Seas. The above discussion should go far to solve that 'mystery'. For the Chinese, the asymmetry in size between China and its trading partners had diluted the static trading gain, and hence government interest.

Of course, by hindsight, the development of ocean shipping has contributed to the subsequent rise of the West, and trade externalities were overlooked by China in the Ming dynasty.

The supply side once more—increasing returns

Leaving population size aside, we now consider 'size' in total gross national product (GDP). In terms of purchasing power parity, China ranks second in the world, between America and Japan. In nominal GDP, the Chinese economy is still larger than every developing country (having surpassed Brazil during the last decade), and is only smaller than America, Japan, Germany, France, the United Kingdom and Italy.[6] The sizeable difference between these two measures has grown in the last decade, and is relatively unusual in the world. This is to be addressed later.

We are now considering the issue of absolute size in productive operations rather than the size relative to other countries. Since industrialization is such an important aspect in development, and industrial production often exhibits internal or external scale economies, 'big push' has been a favorite concept in the literature of growth and development. Can China get much advantage from this angle? The answer seems to be yes, in principle, but not necessarily all that much. A simplified diagram in Figure 3.5 illustrates the point.

Figure 3.5 is the simplest model where up to some level, R, the total production cost of a certain product can be divided into two components: one proportional to the units produced, the other a constant. Two types of technology are depicted: the solid line is less costly up to the break even point q; the dotted line represents an alternative process that is more efficient above the critical point q.

Now for a country engaging in trade, what matters most is maximizing the per capita value–added, whatever the product mix. There are four reasons why the presence of economies of scale does not imply that country size confers national economic advantage. First of all, an economy can produce high–value niche products, with a worldwide demand below the point q in Figure 3.5. The advantage of mass production associated with the cost curve ab is simply out of place. Second, even small economies can enjoy major world market shares of goods they export. For example, Singapore can satisfy a significant portion of the world demand for computer hard drives. Large country size is not needed. Third, the efficiency of increasing returns may benefit all consumers of such a product with no special advantage for the country producing it.[7]

Finally, Figure 3.6 illustrates an example where the market demand is at a particular volume R, with the price equal to the average cost of the entrant firm (with a higher fixed cost but a lower variable cost), as well as the variable cost of the entrenched firm.

$$[v + F/R]_{\text{entrant}} = p = [v]_{\text{entrenched}}$$

Under the reasonable assumption that all fixed cost is sunk cost, the entrenched firm has nothing more to lose at this equilibrium, and the entrant firm can never make any positive profit. This seems to describe well the situation facing such industries like shipbuilding, automobile, and steel making, etc. In the world market, all these industries have developed excess capacities. Those producers with large market share may reap zero or negative economic benefit: the non–positive profit margin is precisely what serves as the barrier to entry.

Such a scenario prevails in a world experiencing rapid technological change. Economic obsolescence is a constant threat to industries with large fixed equipment, that is, the industries with significant internal increasing returns. Of

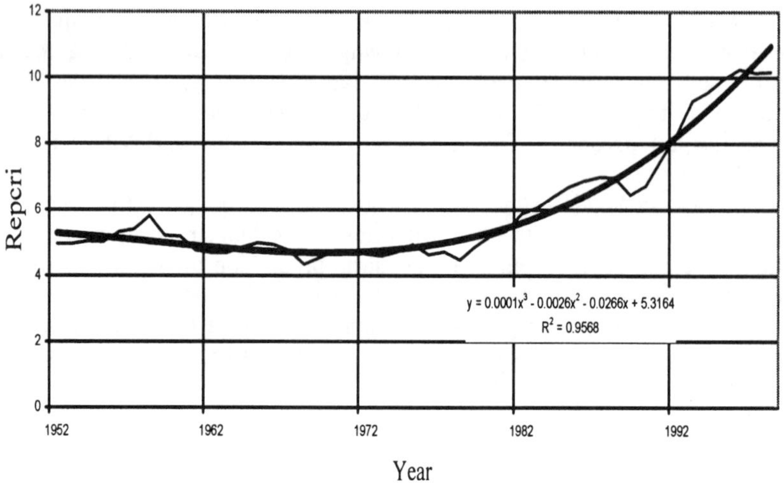

Figure 3.7 The relative per capita real income (REPCRI) of China

course, external increasing returns to scale are also very important. But, with the rise of global supply chains, such externalities become cross–national in nature. Thus, country size loses much of its importance. In fact, Ernst (2001) questions the South Korean strategy to specialize in DRAMs with massive capital spending, without mastering first the high–end technology.

The perspective of 'strategic trade theory'

In trade negotiations more than in other aspects, size may provide China the clear advantage of wielding significant bargaining power,[8] because of what the Chinese market already is, also because of what it can easily become. The critical questions are what is the nature of such power, and how should it be deployed.

Market power comes from what a country can promise to buy, or offer to sell. What China exports today is based upon a large pool of hardy, intelligent labor, ready and eager to learn. In comparison with what is available in Korea and Japan, their formal training and industrial skill can improve, and also need improvement. Unlike Mideast oil producers, China has nothing irreplaceable to withhold from the world market. In the final analysis, it is the size of China's domestic market that is particularly appealing. To any trade partners of modest size, to capture a sizeable share of this large potential market is advantageous. This is because there are economies of scale in marketing just as in production. The crucial question for China is what to bargain for from these relatively smaller partners? More succinctly, where does China's long term national economic interest lie? Knowing

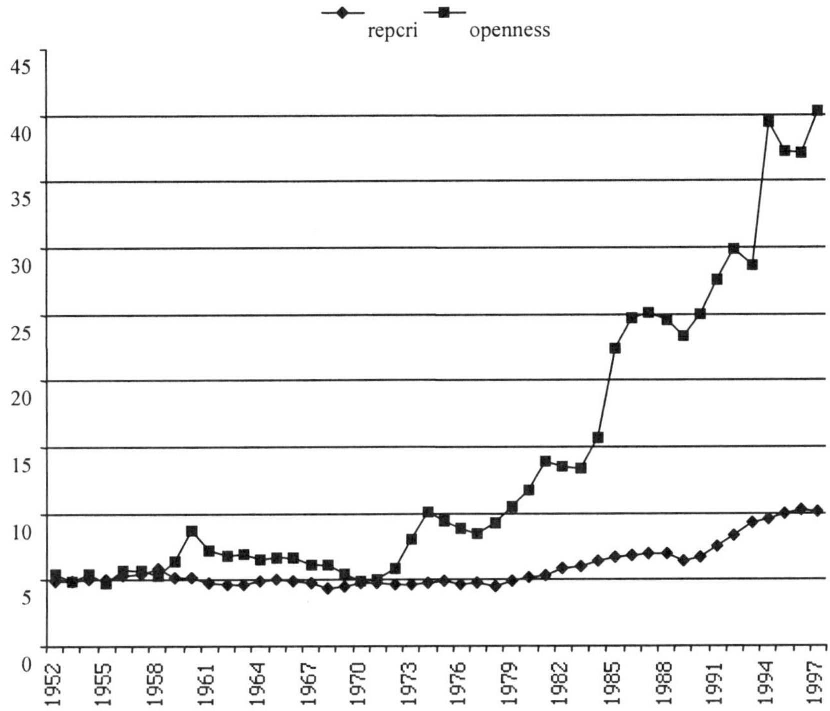

Figure 3.8 The relative per capita real income (REPCRI) and openness index of China

well which way the economy can grow is the prerequisite of getting there. Our previous analysis suggests that China should not bargain with these small trading partners for market access, just to acquire static trading gain. On per capita basis, the benefit cannot be very significant, in any case. It is far more important to bargain for market openings which facilitate skill accumulation. That will allow Chinese to receive more reward for what they already produce, from the world market. More will be said on this important but complex topic.

Size, marketization and future growth

The economy of China forms a class by itself. Prior to 1978, it was a command economy with relatively sluggish growth, leaving intact the income gap between itself and the advanced economies. Among all Communist economies, China is one of the first to embark on market reform. Decentralization improved the system performance. Its cautious opening to the world market has introduced more advanced technology from abroad. This has allowed productivity to rise with only

Table 3.2 Catching–up Regression, China, 1952–98

Dependent variable: Growth rate of REPCRI

	Coefficient	*t–value*	
Intercept	0.106	1.86	–
REPCRI	–0.027	–1.90	–
Openness	0.005	2.33	–
Adj. R Square	–	–	0.093
Observations	–	–	46

Note: REPCRI = relative per capita real income

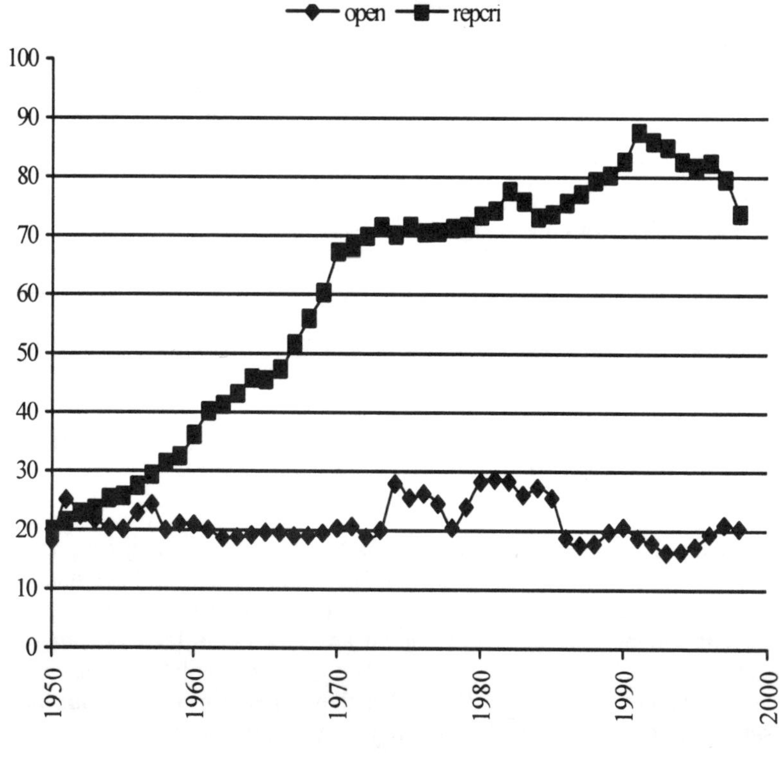

Figure 3.9 The relative per capita real income (REPCRI) and openness index of Japan

modest indigenous R & D Under the reformed system, the process of catching up resembles the workings of a private ownership economies. Emulation is a contact game. Contact depends upon trade and foreign investment. The catching up process slows down as the remaining technology gap begins to close.

As a transition economy, this gradualist approach has allowed China to score considerable growth but avoid gross instability, with its political system preserved

Table 3.3 Catching–up regression, Japan, 1950–98

Dependent variable: Growth rate of REPCRI

	Coefficient	*t–value*	
Intercept	0.155	4.004	–
REPCRI	–0.002	–4.663	–
Openness	–0.001	–0.513	–
Adj. R Square	–	–	0.358
Observations	–	–	38

Note: REPCRI = relative per capita real income

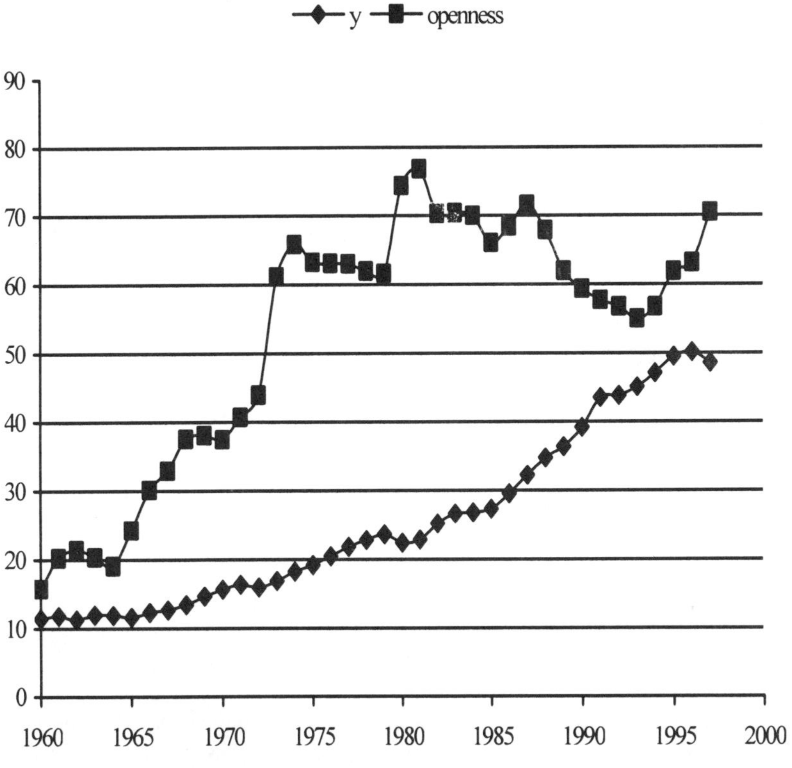

Figure 3.10 The relative per capita real income (REPCRI) and openness index of Korea

up to this day. The institutional transformation entails a sequence of devolution of decision power. When each round of deregulation begins, local decision makers in government units and the state owned enterprises seize newly gained power for rapid expansion. In a world of incomplete markets, such exuberance intensifies coordination failure, and causes the economy to overheat. The inexperienced decision makers and inadequate laws and regulations soon open the doors to additional inefficiency, corruption and instability. With rising prices and material shortage threatening social stability, the central authority then tightens the rein, through credit squeeze or administrative measures. Stabilization then ushers in slower growth, until the government has regained the confidence to decentralize the system further. Such recurrent boom–bust cycles of reform often mask the process of the catching up process.

In this process of reform, the size of the country complicates the oversight task of the government.

In a nutshell, so far, the interplay of four elements has shaped Chinese growth:

(1) As a developing economy—provided certain conditions are met—the catching up process operates under appropriate conditions to narrow down the income gap from the advanced economies.
(2) Some levels of trade and foreign investment are essential to help technology acquisition from abroad and allow the catching up process to function.
(3) Because China was once a centrally planned economy, the Chinese reform has taken the form of a sequence of structural transformations through deregulation, and repeated boom–bust cycles.
(4) The size of the country makes it especially challenging to ameliorate those boom–bust cycles.

The performance of the economy in the recent past

Using the Penn World Table version 6.0, we plot the relative per capita real income (REPCRI) series for China over the period 1952–1998 in Figure 3.7. As we recall, this series is the ratio of per capita real GDP (measured on the basis of purchasing power parity by the Heston–Summers method) between a particular country and the USA. The convex parabolic trend might appear to fit the data well. But for reasons explained in the last section, such temporal interpolation is misleading, since it does not reflect the working of the four factors (1)–(4) discussed above.

Next, we plot REPCRI and the openness index of China against time, in Figure 3.8. Note that the openness index exceeded 10% only once in the 27 years before 1978, but in every one of those 19 years after 1979. It has reached 40% in 1997. Likewise, the relative per capita real income of the China has hovered around 5% of the American level, showing no trend in the first period, but risen more or less steadily to 10% by 1997. This reduces the income gap from America.

We run a regression of the catching up rate (the growth rate of REPCRI) against both the level of REPCRI and the openness index. The result is shown in Table 3.2. The rate of catching up depends positively upon the openness index (significant at the 2.5% level) and negatively upon the level of relative per capita real income.

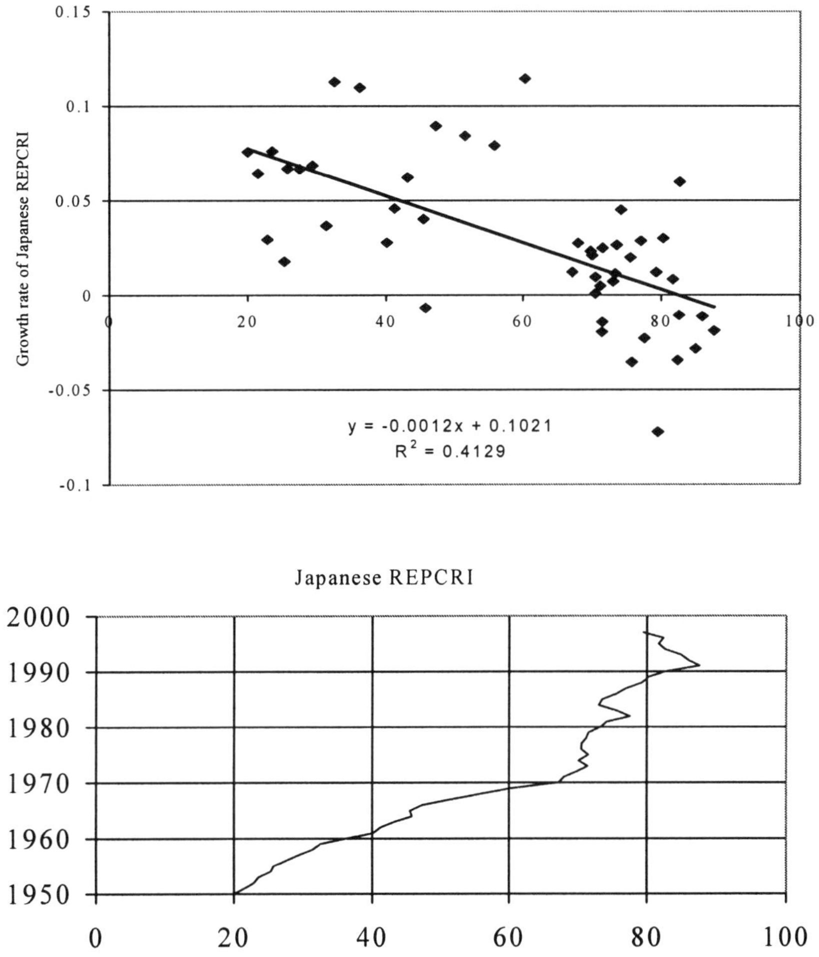

Figure 3.11 The Japanese economy settles at a 'limit gap'

For comparison, we plot the corresponding Japanese and Korean data in Figure 3.9 and Figure 3.10. Tables 3.3 and 3.4 display the regression results for those two countries.

Within these samples of observations, the openness index changes little for Japan throughout the entire period and fluctuates at a rather high level for Korea over much of the latter part of the observed period. Understandably, it is insignificant in explaining the Japanese catching up process and of marginal significance (at about 10%) for the Korean catching up.

The Japanese regression is highly significant both for the positive intercept and the negative REPCRI coefficient. For the Korean regression, the negative REPCRI

Table 3.4 Catching–up regression, Korea, 1960–98

Dependent variable: Growth rate of REPCRI

	Coefficient	*t–value*	
Intercept	0.027	1.048	-
REPCRI	–0.002	–2.046	-
Openness	0.001	1.707	-
Adj. R Square	-	-	0.064
Observations	-	-	38

Note: REPCRI = relative per capita real income

Table 3.5 Catching–up regression, China, 1979–88

Dependent variable: Growth rate of REPCRI

	Coefficient	*t–value*	
Intercept	0.277	2.999	-
REPCRI	–0.040	–2.700	-
Adj. R Square	-	-	0.411
Observations	-	-	10

Note: REPCRI = relative per capita real income

coefficient is significant at the 5% level. All these confirm the Gerschenkron hypothesis that the gap between the North and the South represents a technology backlog for the less developed country to emulate. The rate of gap–reduction slows down as the gap is reduced in size. Also as Kuznets (1982) stated and Coe, Helpman and Hoffmaister (1997) confirmed, openness is helpful for emulation.

For Japan, we can drop the openness index and plot out the scatter diagram between the catching up rate and the REPCRI in Figure 3.11, where the lower panel reproduces the time portrait of the REPCRI in a transposed form. This shows, the observed slowing down of the Japanese economy in the 1990s may well mean its catching up process with America has reached a steady state, with the Japanese per capita real income at about 80% of that of America (or a steady state value of the gap at 20%). For Korea, the openness index is far from settling down, so that nothing can be said yet about the steady state value of any Korean gap.

Can anything be said about the dynamics of China's catching up process? To this we now turn. Figure 3.12 displays the time portrait of the catching up rate of China.

The recent slowing down of the Chinese economic growth has attracted much attention, coming at a time when the Japanese economy has a period of negligible growth. Customarily, the Japanese difficulties are attributed to temporary setbacks and bad policy while the Chinese events invite doubts about the fundamental economic structure. A word on what is happening to the economy of China is in order.

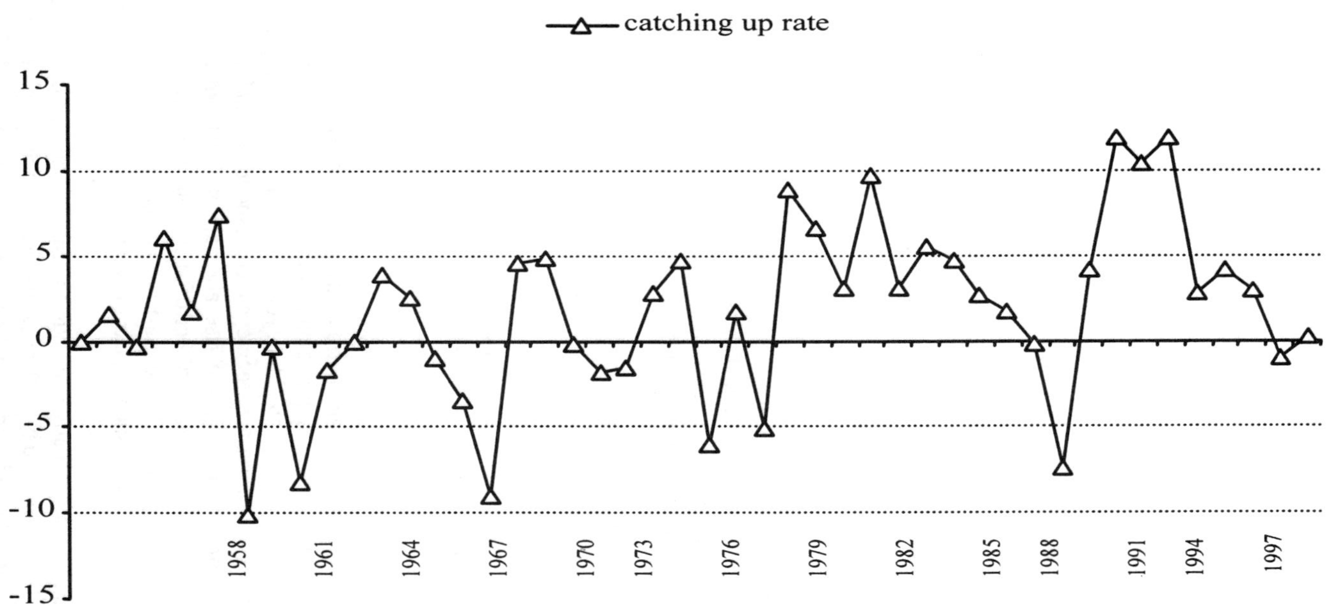

Figure 3.12 **Time portrait of the catching up rates for China**

Table 3.6 Catching–up regression, China 1989–97

Dependent variable: Growth rate of REPCRI

	Coefficient	*t–value*	
Intercept	0.258	3.345	–
REPCRI	–0.023	–2.695	–
Adj. R Square	–	–	–0.439
Observations	–	–	9

Note: REPCRI = relative per capita real income

In studying the recent past, we are interested in either the properties of a system (for example, how growth responds to openness) or its future outlook. For the latter purpose, some past record is to be excluded because of changed circumstances. For example, most major Chinese economic initiatives were carried out by mass mobilization, before 1978, but not once afterwards. The inclusion of a record that is no longer relevant only complicates the task of forecasting. We thus concentrate on the post–1978 reform period which can be further divided into two sub–periods: 1979–1988 and 1989–1997. We regress the catching up rate against the REPCRI, for each sub–period and the entire post–1978 reform period. The results are reported in Tables 3.5–3.7 and Figures 3.13–3.14.

The intercept and the slope coefficients are significant at the 3% level for both sub–periods, but not for the entire post–reform period. To test the null hypothesis,

H_0: there is no structural change,

we compute the statistic,

$$\begin{aligned} \text{F–ratio} &= \{(0.03815649 - 0.01924160)/2\}/[(0.01924169)/(18-4)] \\ &= 0.009456105/0.0012026056 \\ &= 7.863 > 6.51, \end{aligned}$$

so the null hypothesis is rejected at the 1% level.

The scatter plots for these two sub–periods are displayed as Figure 3.13 and Figure 3.14. What has taken place then is a pair of the 'boom–bust' reform cycles characteristic to the economy of China. The cyclical elements are strong, masking the catching up mechanism. Moreover, each cycle corresponds to such distinct and non–recurrent, institutional facts, like the rise and fall of the town and village industries. An analogy is the economic effect of such non–economic events like the World Wars in the 20th century. These must be accepted as exogenous shocks. Any attempt to ignore or to predict such shocks on an econometric basis will not be helpful.

But at the very least, two qualitative conclusions can be drawn. First, at least in part, the Japanese difficulties today reflect deep–seated technological realities, namely, Japan has joined the older industrial countries like Britain and Germany, living in a world of rapid technological innovations implemented in America. Any

Table 3.7 Catching–up regression, China, 1979–97

Dependent variable: Growth rate of REPCRI

	Coefficient	*t–value*	
Intercept	0.084	1.555	–
REPCRI	–0.006	–0.852	–
Adj. R Square	–	–	–0.016
Observations	–	–	18

Note: REPCRI = relative per capita real income

reform in Japan will help, but unless the worldwide technological leadership is fundamentally shifted (like the overtaking of Britain by America), its situation is not going to change much. Specifically, its real per capita income will advance with America, with some lag.

Second, in its catching up, China has much further to go, before reaching a status like Japan. The precise course of advance is decided by many institutional factors, not predictable by traditional economic means. Paraphrasing Mark Twain, the rumors about the loss of steam in the Chinese catching up is certainly exaggerated.

At the same time, one cannot be complacent about the future. The thought experiment regarding car ownership in China reaching the Taiwanese level is a sobering thought. In today's technology, if that event happens overnight, then global warming, or resource depletion or both, will become an immediate concern, to Chinese and non–Chinese alike, with severe trade friction a distinct possibility. Today, the rest of the world is concerned about what China will export, especially in the area of manufactured goods. By that time, their concern would be what China will import, perceived as wreaking havoc to every oil–importing economy. Such events must be anticipated way in advance.

It is worthwhile to note that the average income is much higher in Hong Kong than in Taiwan, but the person/vehicle ratio is only 13:1, that is, only about one third of the ratio for Taiwan. Of course, every economy has its own conditions. Still, this comparison shows that the energy demand of high income societies is far from immutable. Thoughtful urban and regional design for the Chinese Mainland now can make a great deal of difference in future days.

Some more immediate matters

Under the current institutions, the economic growth of China has attracted huge amount of foreign investment and enjoyed an export boom. In turn, such foreign investment and export operations have used China as an export platform. Through transfer prices or the management of global supply chains, much of such exports were conducted by the foreign owned or foreign managed firms, with a large portion of the financial rewards going to those foreign interests. Much of the market gained by China in recent years represents industries migrated from Hong Kong and Taiwan, with part of the fabrication process done in China, but with the

Table 3.8 Capability to market abroad

Per capita GDP	*Nominal (US $)*	*P.P.P. (US $)*	*Nominal/P.P.P.*
Chinese Mainland	860	3,070	28%
Hong Kong	25,200	24,350	103%
Japan	38,160	24,400	156%

other parts (typically the more profitable segments) carried out elsewhere. Suppose Hong Kong and Taiwan form significant parts of the 'industrial pipeline' for China, and the recent investment from these two places implies the imminent depletion of the mobile portions of industries there, common sense argues that the pace of growth for China would have to take a breather. In short, the pace of rapid growth of China over the last dozen years may be hard to keep up.

In some sense, the current level of openness of China has served its purpose, but it is not likely to stay in the long run.[9] As a general rule, openness decreases with size. Figure 3.15 compares the openness indicator of Japan, Korea, Taiwan, Argentina and China, over the decades. Initially, data confirms this negative association between population size and the openness index. Japan provides an example where high growth does not call for very high level of openness. China is now more open than Japan, according to the index we used.

On the other hand, there is also much scope for growth for China, even though its nature has received scant notice. Table 3.8 reports the 1997 real and nominal per capita GDP of Hong Kong, China and Japan, from which we can measure the capability of market abroad for these three economies.

Thus, for each unit of GDP, measured by its ability to meet domestic needs, Chinese on the Mainland can receive no more than 30% of its worth in the world market, but Chinese in Hong Kong can get more worth abroad. The ability of Japanese to translate their own ware into international value is more than five times of the ability of China.

Now from (a) the current value of the 'openness' index of 40%, and (b) the fact that trade of China is approximately balanced (but with some surplus), export counts about 20% of the Chinese GDP. Should China match Japan in its ability of get its 'money's worth' in exporting to the world market, then China can double its GDP, without increasing its physical volume of export. Today, Koreans export large volumes of their Hyundai automobile or Samsung mobile phone under their own brands. In contrast, a large portion of Chinese exports are sold to, or through, multinational firms in globalized supply chains.

Now these multinational systems are far from being monopolies and monopsonists. As oligopolies they compete fiercely against each other, seeking to

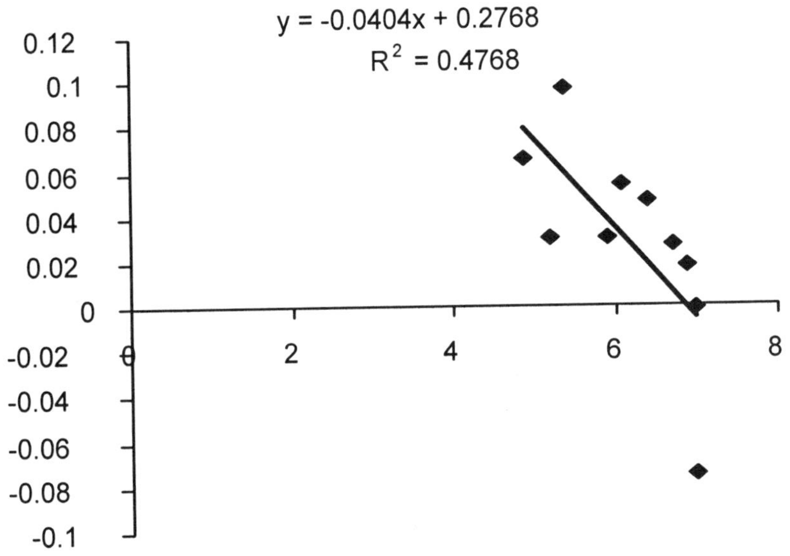

Figure 3.13 **Catching–up scatter, China, 1979–88**

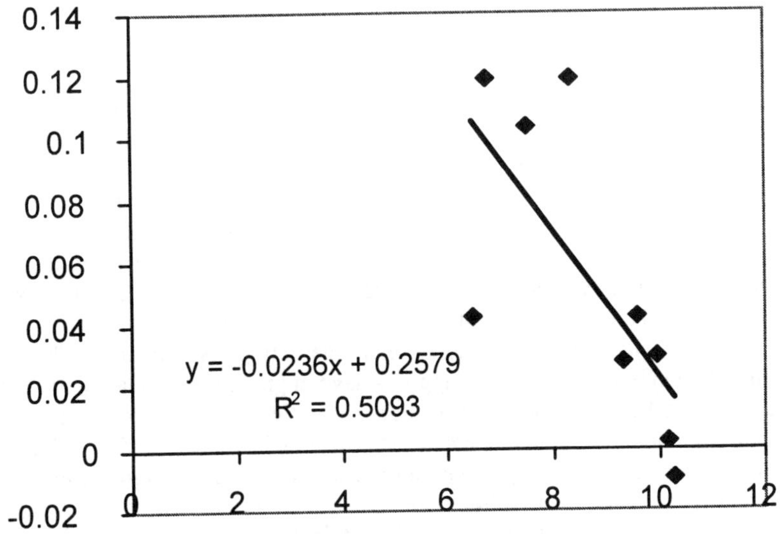

Figure 3.14 **Catching–up scatter, China, 1989–97**

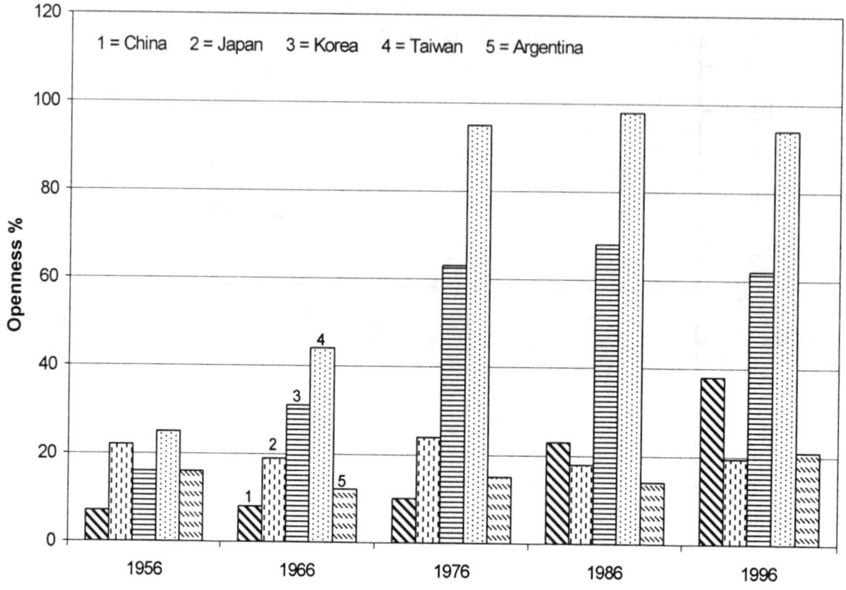

Figure 3.15 Openness: China in context

outflank rivals with supply sources of equal worth at the lowest cost, be it in China, Indonesia, Vietnam, or Lesotho. So by improving the 'worthiness' of their exports, Mainland Chinese exporters can win a far larger share of their goods' worth. This can be done, through better organization and stronger institutions, making product quality more stable or delivery time more punctual. Solid performance brings connections, then reputation and finally, in due time, reward. After all, that was how the Hong Kong Chinese gained their foothold on the world market, and they have not done badly now, according to Table 3.8. The force of the world market is certain and impartial, whether or not one deems it morally just.

For China, prowess for international marketing is valuable, but not indispensable. Once when Chinese suppliers have improved their quality or service on the world market, Chinese fabrication capacities would become highly in demand to the international managers of the rival supply chains. Additional growth can then be realized, not by exporting more of the same, but through better reward for essentially the same effort. Such bootstraps self–enrichment does not call for exporting physically more than today. No single foreign competitor of Chinese exports need be displaced from their current jobs. It will only mean a redistribution of the trade gains inside the supply chain.

Another main source for growth is through backward linkage. Today, the export industries of China depend heavily on manufactured imports from abroad, from machines, tools to parts, components and processed material. To make outputs competitive in the world market, such inputs must be of such high and reliable quality, and available just in time, so that they have to be procured abroad, at considerable cost. In fact, when a Taiwanese factory produced bicycles in Mainland China, initially 70% of the cost was for inputs from Japan and Taiwan. This was also the source of the earlier difficulties faced by the Beijing Jeep Corporation. Historically, the same type of problems was also present for Korea and Taiwan, until satellite industries there became mature. The local content of exports usually rises with the value–added for the exporting country and implies a lower 'openness' index.

Since Chinese customers have no 'economic chauvinism' (in fact, they have some preference for their imports over their import–substitutes), better earned Chinese means better clients for the non–Chinese. Certainly, such development–by–self improvement cannot be realized over night. Yet, judging by what the Chinese in Hong Kong have achieved, it is clearly within reach of the Mainland Chinese.

Returning to what is discussed in a previous section, here is where the long term Chinese economic interest is. The Chinese have considerable bargaining power inherent in their huge domestic market. It should be devoted to realize such capabilities, rather than to win market access of one good or another, for its own sake.

Postscript

Since the completion of the initial draft, two valuable sources have come to my notice.

First, a monograph on Immiserizing Growth: A Question of Changing Terms of Trade (*Pin Kun Hua Zeng Chang—Mao Yi Tiao Jian Bian Dong Zhong De Yi Wen*) by Ruzhong Wang (in Chinese ISBN7–80618–631–X) published by the Shanghai Academy of Social Science in 1999. This indicates the awareness of the issue of immiserizing growth in China.

Second, the statement of Professor Lawrence Lau, before the Congressional–Executive Commission on China on Sept. 23, 2003. Based upon a study by Fung and Lau in *Asian Economic Journal* 14, pp. 489–96, 2003, this testimony provides an in–depth analysis of the position of China in the American supply chain, which provides huge profit to multinational firms but very little contribution to the GDP of China, since the Chinese workers mostly only do assembly jobs.

Notes

1 I appreciate greatly the comments by S. Clemhout, the editorial assistance of Andrea Williams–Wan, as well as the technical help by Jaehun Chung, but I take full responsibility for all the deficiencies in this chapter. Thanks are also due to the patient expert help of Paulette S. Carlisle.

2 Or else the oil boycott would never be an effective weapon.

3 In view of the Sonnenschein–Mantel–Debreu Theorem. See MasColell et al. (1995) and others.

4 This is particularly true, if domestic consumers are too poor to demand high standards. The practice of stringent quality control will then be alien to the society. See Morawetz (1981).

5 See Tan (1997).

6 By the year 2000, China had a total nominal GDP larger than Italy, and next to only France.

7 See Helpman and Krugman (1985).

8 The degree of this advantage is relative. It is conditioned on the assumption that the size of one player in the market would not pose perceived threat to other players to form a countervailing coalition against it. The exclusion of Japan from GATT membership—until Americans sponsored Japan—after World War II is an example of how such interactions work. The more export and foreign investment are regarded by developing economies today as key instrument for development, the more they become anxious that Chinese development would not hinder their own development agenda. It is not well understood in these countries that the success of China in export and attracting foreign investment comes partly from China's role as the export platform for other Sinitic economies, namely, Hong Kong and Taiwan, a role they could not play with the same effectiveness in any case, due to cultural distances.

9 The Chinese population is 27 times of Korea, and its openness index is about 2/3 of Korea. In the long run per capita incomes may equalize between these two countries. After all, currently all Sinitic economies, save Mainland China, has higher GDP per capita than the Korean. But then, the Chinese trade will be 18 times of the Korean trade. Currently Korean trade is about 2.5% of the world trade, then the Chinese trade will be 45% of the world total. So 90% of the world trade will involve the Chinese. This prospect is clearly absurd.

References

Coe, D.T., Helpman, E. and Hoffmaister, A.W. (1997) 'North South Spillovers', *Economic Journal* **107**, pp. 134–49.

Ernst, D. (2001), 'Catching Up and Post–crisis Industrial Upgrading: Searching for New Sources of Growth in Korea's Electronics Industry', in F.C. Deyo, R.F. Doner, and E. Hershberg (eds.) *Economic governance and the challenge of flexibility in East Asia* Rowman & Littlefield, Lanham, MD.

Helpman, E., and Krugman, P.R. (1985) *Market Structure and Foreign Trade: Increasing Returns, Monopolistic Competition and the International Economy*, MIT Press, Cambridge, MA.

Kuznets, S. (1982), 'Modern Economic Growth and the Less Developed Countries' in K.T. Li and T.S. Yu (eds.), *Experience and Lessons of Economic Development in Taiwan*, Academia Sinica, Taipei.

MasCollel, A., Whinston, M.D. and Green, J.R. (1995), *Microeconomic Theory*, Oxford University Press, New York.

Morawetz, D. (1981), *Why the Emperor's New Clothes Are Not Made in Columbia: A Case Study in Latin American and East Asian Manufactured Exports*, Oxford University Press, Washington, DC.

Tan, K.Y. (1997) 'China and the ASEAN: Competitive Industrialization through Foreign Investment', in B. Naughton ed., *The China Circle, Economics and Technology in the PRC, Taiwan and Hong Kong,* Brookings Institution Press, Washington, DC.

Chapter 4

Product Innovation, Capital Accumulation, and Endogenous Growth

Heng–fu Zou

Introduction

This chapter integrates both product innovation and physical capital accumulation in a simple model of endogenous growth and examines the long–run relationship between product development and capital formation. It also studies the impact of international technology transfers and international trade on long–run capital accumulation.

This work can be regarded as a continuation of the line of research initiated by Romer (1990), Grossman and Helpman (1991), and Helpman (1992). In the Romer model, the innovative products are horizontally differentiated capital goods and are produced from the homogeneous final output. These differentiated capital goods are in turn employed to produce the final output. A different modeling strategy is adopted by Grossman and Helpman. In the Grossman–Helpman model, the innovative products are intermediate inputs into the production of a single, final good. But the final good can be either consumed by households or can be invested in the form of capital accumulation by firms. In both models, a similar, perhaps surprising, conclusion has been drawn: physical capital accumulation plays only a supporting role in the story of long–run growth because the primary sources of growth are a variety of factors such as the rate of time preference, the productivity of product innovation, and the elasticity of substitution across brands, 'while the investment rate adjusts so as to keep the rate of expansion of conventional capital in line with the growth rate of output' (Helpman, 1992). Some related approaches to the dynamics of innovation and long–run growth can be found in Stokey (1988, 1991a, 1991b), Aghion and Howitt (1992), Gort and Klepper (1992), and Stein (1997).

In this chapter, we intend to offer a different perspective on capital accumulation, product innovation, and output growth. In particular, we hope to distinguish the role of the marginal productivity of capital in determining the long–run rates of both product innovation and physical capital accumulation. In our model, all differentiated goods are produced using capital input, and can be consumed, or invested to increase capital stock, or used for product innovation. This modeling option has already been pointed out in Grossman and Helpman (1991), even though they choose to model capital as the homogeneous final good.

We should not argue about the plausibility of treating capital stock as the accumulated differentiated products, because in the real world capital does take many forms such as machinery, buildings, tools, and so on. In modeling capital as differentiated goods, our model agrees with the Romer (1990) model, but it differs from the Romer model in assuming that the final consumption in our model also consists of all differentiated goods instead of a single, homogeneous good as in the Romer model.

In this alternative framework, we will demonstrate how the long–run growth rates of capital accumulation and product innovation are determined. In particular we will show the roles of the productivity of the capital stock and the efficiency of product innovation process in determining the long–run rates. In addition, we extend the basic model to an open economy and show that trade in goods not only improves welfare, but also accelerates capital accumulation. Furthermore, for a developing country receiving technology transfers from a developed country such as in the North–South model, the rate of capital accumulation in the South is shown to be partly determined by the rate of product innovation in the North.

This chapter is organized as follows. The next section will set up the dynamic model with both capital accumulation and product innovation. The growth rates of different variables will be derived. Following this, we consider the effect of technology transfers from the developed country on product innovation and capital accumulation in the developing country. The next section extends the model to the case with international trade and shows the impact of trade on capital accumulation. We then conclude this chapter.

The model

The consumer preference is the standard Dixit–Stiglitz CES utility function, which has been used by Krugman (1979), Judd (1985), and Grossman and Helpman (1991) among many others in studying the dynamic process of product innovation:

$$(4.1)\quad U = \int_0^\infty e^{-\rho t}\left(\int_0^\infty c(n,t)^\theta \, dn\right)dt,$$

where $c(n, t)$ is the rate of consuming good n at time t, ρ is the time discount rate, and $0 < \theta < 1$. Here θ has the usual economic implication that the elasticity of substitution between any two goods is $(1 - \theta)^{-1}$.

At any time t, the available variety of goods in this economy is given by $[0, N(t)]$. New product can be obtained through costly product development:

$$(4.2)\quad \dot{N}(t) = R^\alpha,$$

where R is the spending on product development, and $0 < \alpha < 1$. Obviously, α measures the efficiency level of product innovation as a higher value of α yields more new variety with the same input R than a lower value of α.

The production functions for all goods are identical:

$$(4.3) \quad x(n,t) = \beta k(n,t),$$

where $x(n, t)$ is the output of good n at time t, $k(n, t)$ is the capital input to produce good n at time t, and β is the marginal productivity of capital at time t. In the context of endogenous growth, this constant return production function specified in (4.3) has been quite popular, see Barro (1990) and Rebelo (1991) for the arguments.

At time t, the total capital stock is given by $K(t)$:

$$(4.4) \quad K(t) = \int_0^\infty k(n,t)dn = \int_0^N k(n,t)dn\,.$$

In our model, both physical investment and product development utilize differentiated goods. For simplicity, we assume that all differentiated goods are perfect substitutes for these two purposes, even though they are imperfect substitutes in consumption. Since the utility function is symmetric in the variety of goods and since the marginal utility of each good is diminishing, the optimal consumption of each good at time t is the same: $c(n, t) = C(t)$ for all $n \subseteq [0, N]$. Thus we can write the discounted utility in (4.1) as

$$(4.1') \quad U = \int_0^\infty e^{-\rho t} N(t) C(t)^\theta dt\,.$$

Furthermore, due to identical consumption for each good and identical production function in (4.3), and due to the perfect substitutability across goods in physical investment and product development, the optimal output of each good at time t is also the same: $X(t) = x(n, t)$ for $n \subseteq [0, N]$ and

$$(4.3') \quad X(t) = \beta K(t) / N(t).$$

Therefore, all products that are not consumed can be either used for investment or for product development:

$$\dot{K}(t) = \int_0^N x(n,t)dn - \int_0^N c(n,t)dn - R - \delta K,$$

here δ is the rate of capital depreciation. Upon substituting $x(n, t) = X(t)$ and $c(n, t) = C(t)$ for all $n \subseteq [0, N]$

(4.5) $\dot{K}(t) = \beta K(t) - N(t)C(t) - R(t) - \delta K(t).$

Equation (4.5) says that the aggregate output is allocated among consumption, product innovation, the replacement of the depreciated capital, and new capital formation.

The optimization problem is to maximize (4.1') subject to the two dynamic constraints (4.5) and (4.2) with the initial values $K(0)$ and $N(0)$ given.

The current value Hamiltonian is:

(4.6)
$$H(K,C,N,R,\lambda,\omega) = N(t)C(t)^{\theta} + \lambda[\beta K(t) - N(t)C(t) - R(t) - \delta K(t)] + \omega R(t)^{\alpha}$$

where $\lambda(t)$ is the shadow price of capital, and $\omega(t)$ is the shadow price of product variety.

The first–order conditions necessary for optimization are:

(4.7) $\theta C(t)^{\theta-1} = \lambda(t),$

(4.8) $\alpha\omega(t)R(t)^{\alpha-1} = \lambda(t),$

(4.9) $(\beta - \delta - \rho) = -\dot{\lambda}(t)/\lambda(t),$

(4.10) $C(t)^{\theta} - \lambda(t)C(t) = \omega(t)\rho - \dot{\omega}(t),$

(4.11) $\dot{K}(t) = \beta K(t) - N(t)C(t) - R(t) - \delta K(t),$

(4.12) $\dot{N}(t) = R^{\alpha},$

and the transversality conditions:

$$\lim_{t\to\infty} \lambda(t)K(t)e^{-\rho t} = 0, \lim_{t\to\infty} \omega(t)N(t)e^{-\rho t} = 0.$$

Equation (4.7) implies that the marginal utility of consumption for every product and the shadow price of capital are equalized at all time. Equation (4.8) indicates that the allocation of resource for capital formation and product innovation is guided by the equality of their shadow price ratio to their marginal cost ratio: $\lambda(t)/\omega(t) = \alpha R^{1-\alpha}$. Equations (4.9) and (4.10) are the Euler conditions for the shadow prices of capital and innovation, respectively. Equation (4.11) restates the dynamic budget constraint (4.5), and equation (4.12) restates the technology generating new product variety, namely, equation (4.2).

Denote

$$g = -\dot{\lambda}(t) / \lambda(t).$$

From (4.9),

$$g = \beta - \delta - \rho.$$

For endogenous growth to be possible, g is assumed to be positive as usually done, e.g., Barro (1990) and Rebelo (1991). Then take log–differentiation in (4.7):

(4.13) $\dot{C}(t) / C(t) = g / (1 - \theta).$

Or

(4.13') $C(t) = C(0)e^{gt/(1-\theta)},$

where $C(0)$ is the initial consumption of every product, which is discussed in the appendix. Expression (4.13) says that the growth rate is positively related to the marginal productivity of capital β, negatively related to the time preference ρ, and positively related to the elasticity of substitution $(1 - \theta)^{-1}$.

Substituting (4.7) into (4.10):

$$(1 - \theta)C(t)^{\theta} / \omega(t) = \rho - \dot{\omega}(t) / \omega(t).$$

If we focus on a constant growth rate for the shadow price of product variety, the right–hand side of the above equation is constant. Then take log–differentiation on both sides:

(4.14) $\dot{\omega}(t) / \omega(t) = \theta \dot{C}(t) / C(t) = \theta g / (1 - \theta).$

Next, log–differentiate (4.8) and use (4.9) and (4.14):

(4.15) $\dot{R}(t) / R(t) = g / (1 - \theta)(1 - \alpha).$

Or

(4.15') $R(t) = R(0)e^{gt/(1-\theta)(1-\alpha)},$

and $R(0)$ is the initial spending on product innovation, and it is determined in the appendix together with the initial consumption $C(0)$. In equation (4.15), the growth rate of the product–development spending is an increasing function of the marginal productivity of capital β, the elasticity of substitution in consumption $(1-\theta)^{-1}$, the efficiency of innovation technology α, but it is a decreasing function of the time preference ρ.

With (4.12) and (4.15'), we can solve the variety of products available at time t given the initial variety $N(0)$:

$$(4.16)\quad \begin{aligned} N(t) &= [R^{\alpha}(0)(1-\theta)(1-\alpha)/\alpha g[e^{\alpha gt/(1-\theta)(1-\alpha)}-1]+N(0) \\ &= R(t)^{\alpha}[(1-\theta)(1-\alpha)/\alpha g]+A(0), \end{aligned}$$

where $A(0) = [N(0) - R^{\alpha}(0)(1-\theta)(1-\alpha)/\alpha g]$. If $R(0)$ is known, $A(0)$ is just a constant because $N(0)$ is given.

The growth rate of the variety of products is given by:

$$\dot{N}(t)/N(t) = \{[(1-\theta)(1-\alpha)/\alpha g]+A(0)R(t)^{-\alpha}\}^{-1}$$

Since $R(t)$ approaches infinity as time t goes to infinity, the long–run growth rate of the variety is:

$$(4.17)\quad \lim_{t\to\infty}\dot{N}(t)/N(t) = \alpha g/(1-\theta)(1-\alpha),$$

which is the product of the efficiency of product innovation, α, and the growth rate of product–development spending,

$$\dot{R}(t)/R(t).$$

With the solutions of consumption and product variety, we can calculate the discounted utility:

$$\begin{aligned} U &= \int_0^{\infty} N(t)C(t)^{\theta}e^{-\rho t}dt \\ &= \int_0^{\infty} R(0)^{\alpha}C(0)^{\theta}[(1-\theta)(1-\alpha)/\alpha g]e^{[-\rho+\theta g/(1-\theta)+\alpha g/(1-\theta)(1-\alpha)]t}dt \\ &\quad + \int_0^{\infty} C(0)^{\theta}A(0)e^{[-\rho+\theta g/(1-\theta)]t}dt. \end{aligned}$$

For the above expression to be bounded, the following condition is required:

$$\theta g/(1-\theta)+\alpha g/(1-\theta)(1-\alpha) < \rho.$$

Since $g = \beta - \delta - \rho > 0$, the condition above is the same as

$$(4.18)\quad (\beta-\delta)(\alpha+\theta-\alpha\theta) < \rho.$$

Condition (18) also implies that

(4.19) $g/(1-\theta)(1-\alpha) < (\beta-\delta)$.

Now to find the optimal path of capital accumulation, we substitute (4.13'). (4.15'), and (4.16) into (4.11) and solve:

$$K(t) = -[R(0)+C(0)R(0)^{\alpha}(1-\theta)(1-\alpha)/\alpha g] \cdot [g/(1-\theta)(1-\alpha)-(\beta-\delta)]^{-1} e^{gt/(1-\theta)(1-\alpha)} - A(0)C(0)[g/(1-\theta)-(\beta-\delta)]^{-1} e^{gt/(1-\theta)} + B(0)e^{(\beta-\delta)t} \quad (4.20)$$

where

$$B(0) = K(0)+[R(0)+C(0)R(0)^{\alpha}(1-\theta)(1-\alpha)/\alpha g] \cdot [g/(1-\theta)(1-\alpha)-(\beta-\delta)]^{-1} + A(0)C(0)[g/(1-\theta)-(\beta-\delta)]^{-1}.$$

For capital accumulation and product innovation, we want to make sure that the transversality conditions are satisfied. Using condition (4.19), we can easily show that

$$\lim_{t\to\infty} \omega(t)N(t)e^{-\rho t} = 0.$$

But for the capital stock,

$$\lim_{t\to\infty} \lambda(t)K(t)e^{-\rho t} = \lim_{t\to\infty} \theta C(0)^{\theta-1} K(t)e^{-(\beta-\delta)t} = \theta C(0)^{\theta-1} B(0).$$

Hence the transversality condition requires that

(4.21) $B(0) = 0$.

Substituting (4.21) into the capital–accumulation equation (4.20):

$$K(t) = -[R(0)+C(0)R(0)^{\alpha}(1-\theta)(1-\alpha)/\alpha g] \cdot [g/(1-\theta)(1-\alpha)-(\beta-\delta)]^{-1} e^{gt/(1-\theta)(1-\alpha)} - A(0)C(0)[g/(1-\theta)-(\beta-\delta)]^{-1} e^{gt/(1-\theta)}. \quad (4.22)$$

Since $g/(1-\theta)(1-\alpha) < (\beta-\delta)$ the first term on the right hand side of (22) is positive. Furthermore, since $g/(1-\theta)(1-\alpha) > g/(1-\theta)$ the first term will dominate the second term as time t goes to infinity, and the long–run growth rate of the capital stock is:

$$(4.23)\quad \lim_{t\to\infty} \dot{K}(t)/K(t) = g/(1-\theta)(1-\alpha).$$

Thus the long–run growth rate of capital is the same as the growth rate of product development spending. In particular, equation (23) implies that in the long run the preference, the innovation technology, and the productivity of capital jointly determine the growth rate of capital. This result is very different from the ones obtained by Romer (1990) and Helpman (1992) because the marginal productivity of capital plays no role in the determination of the long–run growth rate in their models.

In concluding this section, we make a general observation based on the expressions for the growth rates of the endogenous variables. Even though the growth rates for the endogenous variables are eventually constant, they differ in their magnitudes. In fact, the long–run growth rate of capital accumulation and the growth rate of product development spending are higher than the consumption growth rate:

$$(4.24)\quad g/(1-\theta)(1-\alpha) > g/(1-\theta)$$

for $0 < \alpha < 1$. The long–run growth rate of product variety is smaller than the long–run growth rate of the capital stock, but it may be higher or lower than the rate of consumption growth depending on whether $\alpha/(1-\alpha)$ is larger or smaller than one.

Effects of technology transfers

Technology transfers have recently received considerable attention since Krugman (1979) has formally modeled them in a North–South product–cycle model; see Dollar (1986, 1987). Here we extend our model to the case of exogenous technology transfers from the North to the South. Think the country in our model as the South. As in Krugman (1979), the South receives technology transfers from the North in the following way: at any time t, it obtains part of the know–how about how to produce the product variety in the developed world without incurring any cost:

$$(4.25)\quad \dot{N}(t) = R(t)^{\alpha} + \pi N^{*}(t).$$

In (4.25), $N^{*}(t)$ is the product variety known in the North, and $\pi(>0)$ is the rate of technology transfers.

With equation (4.25) replacing equation (4.2), the optimal conditions for consumption and product development spending are not altered. In particular, the growth rates are the same:

$$\dot{C}(t)/C(t) = g/(1-\theta),$$

and

$$\dot{R}(t)/R(t) = g/(1-\theta)(1-\alpha).$$

The important change is the dynamic equation for product innovation. Substitute $R(t)$ into $N(t)$ and solve for $N(t)$:

(4.26) $N(t) = A'(0) + [R^{\alpha}(0)(1-\theta)(1-\alpha)/\alpha g]e^{\alpha g t/(1-\theta)(1-\alpha)} + \int \pi N^{*}(t)dt.$

If the growth rate of product variety in the North is given by an exogenous rate γ: $\dot{N}^{*}/N^{*} = \gamma$, as in Krugman (1978), then

$$N(t) = A'(0) + [R^{\alpha}(0)(1-\theta)(1-\alpha)/\alpha g]e^{\alpha g t/(1-\theta)(1-\alpha)} + \pi N^{*}(0)e^{\gamma t}/\gamma.$$

where $A'(0) = N(0) - [R^{\alpha}(0)(1-\theta)(1-\alpha)] - \pi N^{*}(0)/\gamma$. If $\gamma > \alpha g/(1-\theta)(1-\alpha)$, then $N(t)$ will grow eventually at the rate of γ. If we imagine that over time the South can catch up with the efficiency levels of both capital and innovation in the North, then $\gamma > \alpha g/(1-\theta)(1-\alpha)$. In general the long–run growth rate is:

(4.27) $\lim_{t\to\infty} \dot{N}(t)/N(t) = \max[\alpha g/(1-\theta)(1-\alpha, \gamma].$

Again we want to make sure that the discounted utility is bounded. Substitute $C(t)$ and $N(t)$ into the objective function:

$$U = \int_0^{\infty} C(0)^{\theta} A'(0) e^{[-\rho+\theta g/(1-\theta)]t} dt$$
$$+ \int_0^{\infty} R(0)^{\alpha} C(0)^{\theta}[(1-\theta)(1-\alpha)/\alpha g] e^{[-\rho+\theta g/(1-\theta)+\alpha g/(1-\theta)(1-\alpha)]t} dt$$
$$+ \int_0^{\infty} [C(0)^{\theta}\pi/\gamma] e^{[-\rho+\theta g/(1-\theta)+\gamma]t} dt.$$

For the expression above to be bounded, the following condition is required:

(4.28) $\rho > \max[\gamma + \theta g/(1-\theta), \alpha g/(1-\theta)(1-\alpha) + \theta g/(1-\theta)].$

It is obvious that technology transfers can lead to more rapid product innovation in the developing country. But how do these transfers affect capital accumulation in the developing South? To answer this question, we solve for $K(t)$ in the budget constraint (11) with substitution for $C(t)$, $N(t)$, and $R(t)$:

$$(4.29)\quad \begin{aligned} K(t) = &-[R(0)+C(0)R(0)^{\alpha}(1-\theta)(1-\alpha)/\alpha g] \\ &\cdot[g/(1-\theta)(1-\alpha)-(\beta-\delta)]^{-1}e^{gt/(1-\theta)(1-\alpha)} \\ &-[C(0)N^{*}(0)\pi/\gamma][\gamma+g/(1-\theta)-(\beta-\delta)]^{-1}e^{[\gamma+g/(1-\theta)]t} \\ &-A^{'}(0)C(0)[g/(1-\theta)-(\beta-\delta)]^{-1}e^{gt/(1-\theta)}. \end{aligned}$$

As before, in deriving (4.29) we have used the transversality condition to impose the requirement:

$$(4.30)\quad \begin{aligned} B'(0) = &K(0) \\ &+[R(0)+C(0)R(0)^{\alpha}(1-\theta)(1-\alpha)/\alpha g][g/(1-\theta)(1-\alpha)-(\beta-\delta)]^{-1} \\ &+[C(0)N^{*}(0)\pi/\gamma][\gamma+g/(1-\theta)-(\beta-\delta)]^{-1} \\ &+A^{'}(0)C(0)[g/(1-\theta)-(\beta-\delta)]^{-1}=0. \end{aligned}$$

In examining (4.29), we note that the coefficient for $e^{[\gamma + g/(1 - \theta)]t}$ is always positive under the condition (28) because $[\gamma + g/(1 - \theta)] < \rho < (\beta - \delta)$ (recall that $g = \beta - \delta - \rho > 0$ or $\beta - \delta > \rho$). Therefore, the rate of product innovation in the developed North, γ, stimulates capital accumulation in the developing South. Not only this, the long run growth rate of capital also depends on the rate of product innovation in the developed North:

$$(4.31)\quad \lim_{t\to\infty}\dot{K}(t)/K(t)=\max[\gamma+g/(1-\theta),g/(1-\theta)(1-\alpha)]$$

that is to say, if $\gamma > \alpha g/(1 - \theta)(1 - \alpha)$, i.e., the rate of product innovation in the North is larger than the rate of product innovation in the South without technology transfers, then the long–run rate of capital accumulation in the South, not only the level of capital accumulation, is partly determined by the rate of product innovation in the North. In this case, the higher the rate of product innovation in the developed North, the higher the product innovation in the developing South, and the higher the long–run equilibrium growth rate of the capital stock in the developing South. Thus the link between capital accumulation in the developing country and technology transfers from the developed world is established in our model.

The economic intuition of this link is as follows. As technology transfers from the North accelerate product innovation in the South, more product variety will become available in the South, and more consumption demand for variety will be generated. To meet the rising consumption demand, the South will expand its capital stock and raise the production capacity. Thus technology transfers from the North lead to faster capital accumulation in the South.

Finally, to complete our solution, we need to determine the initial values $C(0)$ and $R(0)$. Schematically, we can just follow what we have done in the appendix and we omit this part here.

Effects of international trade

In this section, we want to show that foreign trade, even without technology transfers, can stimulate the rate of capital accumulation. This result applies to the developing country as well as to the developed country.

Assume that there are two countries in the world: the home country and the foreign country. The model we consider here is for, say, the home country. With foreign goods introduced into the model symmetrically as in Judd (1985), and Grossman and Helpman (1991), the objective function of the home country is modified to be:

$$(4.32)\quad \max U = \int_0^\infty e^{-\rho t}[N(t)+N^*(t)]C(t)^\theta dt,$$

subject to

$$(4.33)\quad \dot{K}(t) = \beta K(t) - [N(t)+N^*(t)]C(t) - R(t) - \delta K(t),$$

$$(4.34)\quad \dot{N}(t) = R(t)^\alpha,$$

where $N^*(t)$ is the number of product variety in the foreign country. In writing (4.32) and (4.33), we have assumed that all foreign goods prices are equal to one in terms of home goods. Since all goods are symmetric in the utility function, the consumption level of each good will be the same, namely, $C(t)$.

With these modifications, no change has been made on equations (4.7), (4.8), (4.9), and (4.12). Therefore, the growth rates for the consumption level of each good, the product–development spending, and the product variety remain the same as in section 2. Therefore we still have

$$(4.13)\quad \dot{C}(t)/C(t) = g/(1-\theta),$$

$$(4.15)\quad \dot{R}(t)/R(t) = g/(1-\theta)(1-\alpha),$$

$$(4.17)\quad \lim_{t\to\infty} \dot{N}(t)/N(t) = \alpha g/(1-\theta)(1-\alpha).$$

Thus, unlike the case of technology transfers, the growth rate of product variety is not affected by foreign trade even though the number of variety consumed in the home country increases by $N^*(t)$ at time t.

We still assume that the product variety in the foreign country grows at an exogenous rate ($\gamma = \dot{N}^*(t)/N^*(t)$) and the initial variety in the foreign country is $N^*(0)$. Then the discounted utility in the home country is

$$
\begin{aligned}
U &= \int_0^{\infty} C(0)^{\theta} A(0) e^{[-\rho+\theta g/(1-\theta)]t} dt \\
&+ \int_0^{\infty} R(0)^{\alpha} C(0)^{\theta} [(1-\theta)(1-\alpha)/\alpha g] e^{[-\rho+\theta g/(1-\theta)+\alpha g/(1-\theta)(1-\alpha)]t} dt \\
&+ \int_0^{\infty} [C(0)^{\theta} N^*(0)] e^{[-\rho+\theta g/(1-\theta)+\gamma]t} dt.
\end{aligned}
$$

The last term in this expression represents the welfare gain from consuming the foreign variety of products. Again, for this discounted utility to be bounded, the following condition is required:

$$(4.28) \quad \rho > \max[\gamma + \theta g/(1-\theta), \alpha g/(1-\theta)(1-\alpha) + \theta g/(1-\theta)].$$

To see the impact of trade on capital accumulation in the home country, we solve (4.33):

$$
(4.35) \quad
\begin{aligned}
K(t) &= -[R(0) + C(0)R(0)^{\alpha}(1-\theta)(1-\alpha)/\alpha g] \\
&\cdot [g/(1-\theta)(1-\alpha) - (\beta-\delta)]^{-1} e^{gt/(1-\theta)(1-\alpha)} \\
&- [C(0)N^*(0)][\gamma + g/(1-\theta) - (\beta-\delta)]^{-1} e^{[\gamma+g/(1-\theta)]t} \\
&- A(0)C(0)[g/(1-\theta) - (\beta-\delta)]^{-1} e^{gt/(1-\theta)}.
\end{aligned}
$$

The imposition of the transversality condition on the capital stock gives rise to:

$$
(4.36) \quad
\begin{aligned}
B''(0) &= K(0) \\
&+ [R(0) + C(0)R(0)^{\alpha}(1-\theta)(1-\alpha)/\alpha g][g/(1-\theta)(1-\alpha) - (\beta-\delta)]^{-1} \\
&+ [C(0)N^*(0)][\gamma + g/(1-\theta) - (\beta-\delta)]^{-1} \\
&+ A(0)C(0)[g/(1-\theta) - (\beta-\delta)]^{-1} = 0.
\end{aligned}
$$

In equation (4.35), we note that the coefficient for $e^{[\gamma + g/(1-\theta)]t}$ is again positive under the condition (4.28) because $[\gamma + g/(1-\theta)] < \rho < (\beta - \delta)$. Therefore, trade with the foreign country brings about more capital accumulation in the home country. Essentially, trade plays the role of technology transfers in stimulating capital accumulation in the home country. In the long run,

$$
(4.37) \quad
\begin{aligned}
\lim_{t\to\infty} \dot{K}(t)/K(t) &= \max[\gamma + g/(1-\theta), g/(1-\theta)(1-\alpha)] \\
&= \max[(\dot{N}^*/N^*) + g/(1-\theta), g/(1-\theta)(1-\alpha)].
\end{aligned}
$$

Thus, the growth rate of the capital stock in the home country is increasing with the growth rate of product variety available from the foreign country. To provide the economic intuition for this result, we note that the availability of foreign goods is always welfare–enhancing for the home country given the Dixit–Stiglitz consumer preference. But the rising consumption of the foreign goods needs to be financed through the exports of the home goods, which in turn call for the expansion of the capital stock in the home country in order to produce more home goods in exchange for more foreign goods.

Conclusion

This chapter has extended the Romer model and the Grossman–Helpman model to the case here in which consumption, investment, and product development use differentiated goods, while all goods are produced with capital. This simple framework has shown that the interaction among the productivity of capital, the efficiency in innovation and consumer preferences determine the long–run rates of both product innovation and capital accumulation. Thus the one–way causality from product innovation to capital accumulation in the Romer model and the Grossman–Helpman model has been revised to the two–way interaction in our model.

This simple framework has also been utilized to examine the effects of technology transfers and international trade on product innovation and capital accumulation in an open economy. Even though the stimulating impact of trade and technology transfers on capital accumulation and growth has observed empirically in many developing countries, our theoretical model has provided a strong argument in establishing the causality from technology transfers and trade to rapid capital accumulation and product innovation.

The simple model can also be extended to deal with other issues related to economic openness and growth in developing countries. In particular, we can consider how exports and technology imports in developing countries affect capital accumulation, consumption, and innovation in a two–gap model with both domestic technology (domestic capital) and foreign technology (foreign capital) (Zou, 1998a). In addition, in this model, we have assumed perfect competition in the world product market. If a developing country's exports have certain market power, intertemporal pricing of exports becomes an important issue for a developing country in determining the optimal paths of accumulation and innovation, and we have studied part of this issue in Zou (1998b).

Appendix: determination of the initial values

To complete our solutions to the dynamic paths of consumption, product development spending, innovation, and capital accumulation in section 2, we must determine the initial values of consumption $C(0)$ and product–development spending $R(0)$, given the initial values of two state variables $K(0)$ and $N(0)$. That can be done as follows.

We first note that condition (21), $B(0) = 0$, provides us a nonlinear relationship between $C(0)$ and $R(0)$ with $K(0)$ and $N(0)$ given.

Now differentiate the dynamic equation of capital accumulation (4.22) with respect to t and evaluate the derivative at $t = 0$:

$$\begin{aligned}\dot{K}(0) = &-[R(0) + C(0)R(0)^{\alpha}(1-\theta)(1-\alpha)/\alpha g] \\ &\cdot[g/(1-\theta)(1-\alpha)-(\beta-\delta)]^{-1}g/(1-\theta)(1-\alpha) \\ &- A(0)C(0)[g/(1-\theta)-(\beta-\delta)]^{-1}g/(1-\theta).\end{aligned}$$

Combining this initial investment equation with the dynamic budget constraint in (4.11) evaluated at $t = 0$:

$$\dot{K}(0) = \beta K(0) - N(0)C(0) - R(0) - \delta K(0),$$

we obtain another relationship between $C(0)$ and $R(0)$:

$$\begin{aligned}&-[R(0) + C(0)R(0)^{\alpha}(1-\theta)(1-\alpha)/\alpha g] \\ &\cdot[g/(1-\theta)(1-\alpha)-(\beta-\delta)]^{-1}g/(1-\theta)(1-\alpha) \\ &- A(0)C(0)[g/(1-\theta)-(\beta-\delta)]^{-1}g/(1-\theta) \\ &= \beta K(0) - N(0)C(0) - R(0) - \delta K(0).\end{aligned} \tag{4.38}$$

With $C(0)$ and $R(0)$ determined from equations (4.22) and (4.38), the optimal initial invest is given by the dynamic budget constraint (4.11) and the initial increase in product variety is given by

$$\dot{N}(0) = R(0)^{\alpha}.$$

References

Aghion, P. and Howitt, P. (1992), 'A Model of Growth Through Creative Destruction', *Econometrica* **60**, pp. 323–351.

Barro, R. (1990), 'Government Spending in a Simple Model of Endogenous Growth', *Journal of Political Economy* **98**, pp. S103–S125.

Dollar, D. (1986), 'Technological Innovation, Capital Mobility, and the Product Cycle in North–South Trade', *American Economic Review* **75**, pp. 177–190.

Dollar, D. (1987), 'Import Quota and the Product Cycle', *Quarterly Journal of Economics* **102**, pp. 615–632.

Gort, M. and Klepper, S. (1992), 'Time Paths in the Diffusion of Product Innovations', *Economic Journal* **92**, pp. 630–653.

Grossman, G. and Helpman, E. (1991), *Innovation and Growth in the Global Economy*. MIT Press.

Helpman, E. (1992), 'Endogenous Macroeconomic Growth Theory', *European Economic Review* **136**, pp. 237–267.

Judd, K. (1985), 'On the Performance of Patents', *Econometrica* **53**, pp. 567–586.

Krugman, P. (1979), 'A Model of Innovation, Technology Transfer, and the World Distribution of Income', *Journal of Political Economy* **87**, pp. 253–266.

Rebelo, S. (1991), 'Long Run Policy Analysis and Long Run Growth', *Journal Of Political Economy* **99**, pp. 500–521.

Romer, P. (1990), 'Endogenous Technology Change', *Journal of Political Economy* **98**, pp. S71–102.

Segerstrom, P.S. (1991), 'Innovation, Imitation, and Economic Growth', *Journal of Political Economy* **99**, pp. 807–827.

Stein, J. (1997), 'Waves of Creative Destruction: Firm–Specific Learning–by–Doing and the Dynamics of Innovation', *Review of Economic Studies* **64**, pp. 265–288.

Stokey, N. (1998), 'Learning by Doing and the Introduction of New Goods', *Journal of Political Economy* **96**, pp. 701–717.

Stokey, N. (1991a), 'Human Capital, Product Quality, and Growth', *Quarterly Journal of Economics* **106**, pp. 587–616.

Stokey, N. (1991b), 'The Volume and Composition of Trade Between Rich and Poor Countries', *Review of Economic Studies* **158**, pp. 63–80.

Zou, H. (1998a), 'Exports, Technology Imports, and Long–run Growth', Working Paper, Development Research Group, The World Bank.

Zou, H. (1998b), 'Export Externalities, Export Pricing, and Endogenous Growth', Working Paper, Development Research Group, The World Bank.

PART II
FOREIGN DIRECT INVESTMENT AND TRADE

Chapter 5

Regional Attributes, Public Inputs and Tax Competition for FDI in China

Chi–Chur Chao, Win–Lin Chou, and Eden S.H.Yu

Introduction

Since the adoption of the open door policy in 1978, the Chinese economy has grown remarkably. The growth rates have been, however, uneven across regions. On average, the GDP per capital in the coastal provinces grew at ten , while it was around eight in the central provinces and seven for the western region. Geographic location is apparently of importance for explaining the regional disparity in China's growth.[1] One factor that has contributed significantly to regional growth is foreign direct investment (FDI). In 2000, twelve fast–growing provinces, including the coastal regions, Fujian, Guangdong and Jiangsu, received about 87 percent of total FDI inflows to China. Attracting FDI to regions has become a top priority for provincial governments.

There are many factors that affect FDI inflows. In this chapter we follow Hines (1996) and group the determinants into two categories: region–specific and economy–common factors. For instance, geographical location, human capital and stages of regional development belong to the former, while tax incentives and preferential treatment belong to the latter. Using this classification, we can study theoretically and empirically the determinants of regional distribution of FDI in China.

In the next section a theoretical model incorporating region–specific and economy–common factors is constructed for explaining regional competition for FDI. In this model, capital is perfectly mobile between regions, but labor is not. Note that the assumption of labor immobility is consistent with China's household registration system (*hukou*). As region–specific attributes may be of vital importance in attracting FDI, economic–common factors such as tax policy cannot be ignored. Tax revenue from FDI can be utilized by local governments in providing public infrastructure, which contributes positively to the productivity of capital. To allure FDI, low tax rates tend to be offered by regional governments. This is the conventional argument for tax competition in FDI. However, if public inputs can raise the productivity of capital and hence the output level, high tax rates can be justified for generating more tax revenue. In this case, higher tax rates would not deter the inflows of FDI. So, do low tax rates allure FDI in China? This becomes an empirical question.

The sections following the theoretical model will provide an answer to this question. We use a panel data set to estimate FDI inflows in China for the period of 1985 to 2000. Two explanatory variables are: region–specific attributes and tax rate differentials. Since characteristics of regions influence stages of regional development, provincial GNP can be used to approximate region–specific attributes. After performing panel unit root and cointegration tests on provincial FDI, GNP and tax data, we estimate the long– and short–run effects of regional GNP and tax rate differentials on FDI by using error correction models. Our findings show that for China, the tax competition policy is not effective in attracting FDI. Instead, the region–specific factor captured by regional GNP is of importance in explaining the geographical location of FDI in China.

A theoretical model

This section presents a theoretical framework for determining FDI competition between regions in an economy. To simplify the analysis, we consider a one–good, two–region economy. For region 1, good Y is produced by using labor (L) and capital (K), along with public inputs (G) and region–specific factors (S): $Y = F(L, K, G, S)$. The production function exhibits constant returns to scale in labor and capital, and the productivities of these inputs are positively affected by public inputs and region–specific attributes.[2] Following Wilson (1986), capital is assumed to be regionally mobile but labor is not. To finance the public inputs, a tax (τ) on capital is imposed. The financing constraint of region one's government is therefore:

$$(5.1)\quad G = \tau K.$$

Similarly, the government of region two imposes a capital tax (τ^*) and provides public inputs (G^*), with the budget constraint:

$$(5.2)\quad G^* = \tau^* K^*,$$

where K^* is the amount of capital in region two. To simplify the analysis, it is assumed that capital in the economy ($\overline{K}$) is totally foreign–owned and fixed, i.e., $K + K^* = \overline{K}$.

Since capital is perfectly mobile, its after–tax rates of returns must be equalized between regions:

$$(5.3)\quad r - \tau = r^* - \tau^*,$$

where $r = F_K$ and $r^* = F_K^*$, denoting the values of the marginal product of capital in regions one and two, respectively. Note that the price of good Y is normalized to unity.

Equations (5.1)–(5.3), describing the production side of the economy, consist of three unknowns, K, G and G^*, with region–specific variables, S and S^*, and tax instruments, τ and τ^*. We consider first the impact of the region–specific factors on capital allocation. Solving (5.1)–(5.3), we obtain:

(5.4) $dK/dS = -F_{KS}/D > 0,$

where $F_{KS} > 0$ and $D = (F_{KK} + F_{KK}^*) + \tau F_{KG} + \tau^* F_{KG}^* < 0$ by the stability condition.[3] Equation (5.4) states that regional specific attributes, such as human capital, geographical location, etc., play a positive role in attracting foreign capital.

We turn next to the effect of capital tax on inflows of foreign capital. A higher capital tax raises its user cost, which lowers capital inflows to the region. However, if tax–revenue financed public inputs can raise the productivity of capital, the higher capital tax can actually allure foreign capital. These two conflicting forces make inflows of capital indeterminate. This can be seen by solving (5.1)–(5.3) to obtain:

(5.5) $dK/d\tau = (1 - KF_{KG})/D \lesseqgtr 0,$

where $F_{KG} > 0$ capturing the positive externality of public inputs on the productivity of capital. In the absence of the public inputs in the production function (i.e., $F_{KG} = F_{KG}^* = 0$), we have $dK/d\tau < 0$; the higher tax rate lowers the inflow of capital. In addition, the tax revenue effect is: $dG/d\tau = K[1 + (\tau/K)(dK/d\tau)] \lesseqgtr 0$, depending on the tax elasticity of capital. Nevertheless, in the presence of public inputs, we can have $dK/d\tau > 0$ from (5), if the positive externality of public inputs on the productivity of capital dominates. In this case, higher capital tax rates increase tax revenue: $dG/d\tau > 0$.

The above results can be summarized as the following: (proposition 1) in an economy with regionally mobile capital, an improvement in the region–specific investment environment attracts more foreign capital. Furthermore, higher capital taxes can still allure foreign capital if the productivity of capital can be raised through more provision of public inputs.

Since the presence of public inputs affects regional capital inflows, it is worthwhile to examine the optimal rate of capital tax. Suppose social welfare of the region depends positively on government's tax revenue and residents' private utility, and this can be expressed by the region's utility function: $U = U(G, C)$. Note that private utility is generated from consumption of good Y. The amount of consumption, C, is the production of good Y net of the payments to foreign capital, i.e., $C = F(K, L, G, S) - rK$. From (3) we have $rK = (r^* - \tau^* + \tau)K$, which is utilized in maximizing the region's utility function to obtain the optimality condition:

(5.6) $U_G/U_C = [K(1 + dr^*/d\tau) - F_G(dG/d\tau)]/K[1 + (\tau/K)(dK/d\tau)],$

where $dr^*/d\tau = F_{KK}^*(dK^*/d\tau) + F_{KG}^*(dG^*/d\tau) \gtrless 0$.

Consider first the special benchmark case in (6): capital is regionally immobile and public inputs are absent in the production function. It is immediate that $dK/d\tau = dr^*/d\tau = F_G = 0$, and hence (6) simplifies to $U_G = -U_C$. This yields the efficient capital tax rate as the marginal social benefit of taxation (U_G) just equals its marginal social cost ($-U_C$). The increase in regional welfare arising from an additional unit of government revenue from capital tax exactly offsets the decline in its utility due to an extra unit decrease in private consumption.

Next, consider two additional special cases of (6):

1. If capital is mobile between regions but public inputs do not affect the productivity of capital, then we have: $F_G = 0$, $dK/d\tau < 0$ and $dr^*/d\tau < 0$. Substituting these into (6), we obtain: $U_G/U_C > 1$ when the price elasticity of capital is elastic.[4] This implies that the marginal social benefit of taxation exceeds its marginal social cost. Because the demand for capital is elastic, a *lower* tax rate is needed for raising tax revenue so as to reduce U_G. Thus, tax competition for FDI is not efficient.
2. When public inputs affect the production of good Y but capital is regionally immobile, we have $F_G > 0$ and $dG/d\tau > 0$ but $dK/d\tau = dr^*/d\tau = 0$. From (6), we obtain: $U_G/U_C < 1$, implying that the marginal social benefit of taxation falls short of its marginal social cost. Since capital is not mobile, the tax base is fixed, *higher* tax rate is warranted for shifting foreign capital rents to domestic consumption, thereby lowering U_C.

Lastly, for the general case that public inputs affect the production of good Y and capital is mobile between regions, we have $U_G/U_C \gtrless 1$ in (6). Hence, the optimal tax rate on capital tends to be lower if the influence of capital mobility is stronger, whereas the tax rate is higher when the externality of the public inputs on the productivity of capital is larger.

The above discussions on tax competition for FDI can be stated as follows: (proposition 2) for an economy with regional tax competition for FDI, the higher the degree of inter–regional capital mobility, the lower the tax rates. In contrast, the greater the contribution of public inputs to the productivity of capital, the higher the tax rates.

Empirical analysis

The empirical model

We now turn to the empirical analysis of regional flows of FDI in China. It is proposed that the directional inflow of foreign capital to a region depends on the tax differential between a host region and its competitors. To facilitate the empirical investigation, we specify the following long–run demand relation for inflows of FDI (FDI_i) in the host region i:

(5.7) $FDI_{it} = \alpha_{0i} + \delta_i(\tau_{it} - \bar{\tau}_t) + \beta_i GDP_{it} + \varepsilon_{it}, i = 1,\ldots,N, t = 1,\ldots,T,$

where GNP_{it} represents the GNP in region i at time t, ε is an error term, N is the number of regions in a country, and T is the number of time–series observations. Note that τ_i is the tax rate in region i, and $\bar{\tau}$ expresses the average regional tax rate which is weighted by shares ω_i (i.e., $\bar{\tau} = \Sigma_i\omega_i\tau_i$).

Equation (7) is estimated by using a sample of panel data on 25 provinces[5] in China covering the period 1985 to 2000. The tax rate τ_i is not available and is estimated, on a provincial basis, by dividing the tax lump sum by total pre–tax profits, where the tax lump sum is obtained by subtracting gross after–tax profits of industrial enterprises in a province from total pre–tax profits.[6] In computing the weighted average regional tax rate $\bar{\tau}_i$, three alternative measures of the weights ω_i are used, namely, province i's share of total FDI, province i's share of total GNP, and the share of population in province i. We denote the alternative measures of $\bar{\tau}$ as $\bar{\tau}_f$, $\bar{\tau}_g$ and $\bar{\tau}_p$, and the corresponding tax differentials $(\tau_{it} - \bar{\tau}_t)$ as $d\tau_f$, $d\tau_g$ and $d\tau_p$.

The variables on FDI and GNP are measured in 1990 RMB yuan, and the tax rates are adjusted for inflation rates. In estimating equation (5.7), the FDI and GNP are expressed in per capita terms and logarithmic form. The names of the 25 provinces are listed in Appendix A. The main data for this study is obtained from various issues of the *China Statistical Yearbook* and provincial statistical yearbooks.

Panel unit root and panel cointegration tests

Before estimating equation (7), we need to confirm whether the variables, i.e., *FDI*, *GNP*, and tax rate differentials used in the equation are cointegrated. If they are cointegrated, it is reasonable and helpful to include income and tax differentials in the specification of the FDI demand function to describe changes in FDI inflows in the long run.

To determine a potentially cointegrated relationship, we first pre–test the variables *FDI*, *GNP* and the three alternative $d\tau$'s, for their order of integration, that is, to check whether the individual variables contain unit roots. If all the variables are stationary, the conventional ordinary least squares (OLS) estimation method can be used to estimate the relationship between these variables. But if at least one of the variables is found to be non–stationary, more care is required.

As Pantula, Gonzalez–Farias and Fuller (1994) have shown unit root tests based on the OLS estimator (such as the conventional ADF tests) are the least powerful. Thus, instead of using the ADF test, which is a pure time–series method, we conduct panel unit root tests[7] by pooling time–series observations across the 25 provinces. Since the panel unit root tests of Choi (2001) have been found to be more powerful than the tests previously proposed such as the IPS test, which has been widely used in international finance and macroeconomics, we will employ the

Table 5.1 Panel unit root test results[a]

Variable	P test	Z test	L test	IPS test	Critical values for IPS test
lnFDI	66.08	−1.14	−1.53	−1.85	−2.49
lnGNP	24.52	2.55	2.43	0.84	−1.84
$d\tau_f$[b]	132.8[c]	−6.21[c]	−6.73[c]	−2.69[c]	−2.49
$d\tau_g$[b]	153.5[c]	−7.11[c]	−8.02[c]	−2.82[c]	−2.49
$d\tau_p$[b]	151.2[c]	−7.33[c]	−7.91[c]	−2.83[c]	−2.49

[a] The lag order used for the DF–GLS test is chosen by the BIC lag selection method. The p–values for the DF–GLS test were calculated by using the simulation programs provided by Choi at T=50. A time trend is used in the test for all variables except ln*GNP*.

[b] $d\tau_f = (\tau - \overline{\tau}_f)$, $d\tau_g = (\tau - \overline{\tau}_g)$ and $d\tau_p = (\tau - \overline{\tau}_p)$, where τ = regional tax rate, $\overline{\tau}_f$ = weighted average regional tax rate with the provinces' share of total FDI as the weight, $\overline{\tau}_g$ = weighted average regional tax rate with the provinces' share of total GNP as the weight and $\overline{\tau}_p$ = weighted average regional tax rate with the provinces' share of population as the weight.

[c] Significant at the 5% level.

Choi procedure in this study. It is notable that the Choi tests allow for heterogeneous error variances across all groups. Since our sample is selected across 25 different provinces, it is likely to have heterogeneity in error variances. Nevertheless, the Choi tests we employ can account for the heterogeneity in our sample. The main idea of the Choi tests is to combine *p*–values from a univariate unit root test applied to each group in the panel data. The unit root tests employed in the construction of the combination tests are the DF–GLS tests proposed by Elliott, Rothenberg and Stock (1996). Briefly, for a sample of N regions (i = 1, 2,..., N) observed over T periods, the Choi test evaluates the null hypothesis that all the time series are unit–root non–stationary against the alternative that *at least* one of the time series is stationary. This alternative includes as a special case the alternative hypothesis considered in the IPS test. The null is tested with the following combination test statistics:

$$(5.8)\quad P = -2\sum_{i=1}^{N} \ln(p_i),$$

$$(5.9)\quad L = \sum_{i=1}^{N} \ln\left(\frac{p_i}{1-p_i}\right),$$

Table 5.2 Panel cointegration tests

Pedroni test:	
H_0 : No cointegration between lnFDI and lnGNP	(N= 25, T=15)
Panel v[a]	3.29[c]
Panel rho	0.01
Panel PP	–0.30
Panel ADF	–1.53[d]
Group rho	1.38
Group PP	–0.20
Group ADF	–1.56[d]
McCoskey–Kao test:	–
H_0: Cointegration exists between lnFDI and lnGNP	–
LM–DOLS[b]	0.23
LM–FM[b]	0.42

[a] See note 9 for details of Pedroni's test statistics. All Pedroni's test statistics, except the panel v test, use the left tail of the standard normal distribution to reject the null.

[b] DOLS and FM are the dynamic and fully modified OLS estimation methods, respectively. The 5% and 10% critical values are –1.65 and –1.28, respectively.

[c] Significant at the 5% level.

[d] Significant at the 10% level.

and

$$(5.10)\quad Z = \frac{1}{\sqrt{N}}\sum_{i=1}^{N}\Phi^{-1}(p_i),$$

where the p_i is the p–value from a unit root test for region i, and $\Phi(.)$ is the standard normal cumulative distribution function. (5.8) is called the inverse chi–square test statistic in meta–analysis,[8] (5.9) is the logit statistic, and (5.10) is the inverse normal statistic. The asymptotic distributions of these test statistics are given in Appendix B. Among the combination tests, Choi (2001) has shown that the Z test outperforms the other tests and is recommended for empirical applications.

We now apply these combination tests to the panel data of model (5.7). The results using Choi's combination tests are reported in Table 5.1. For the purpose of comparison, we also present the t–bar statistics of IPS in the same table. The combination tests and the t–bar test do not reject the unit–root null at the five percent level for FDI and GNP, suggesting they are non–stationary. Further panel unit root tests on these variables in their first difference indicate that they are

Table 5.3 Estimation of long–run income elasticities[a]

	OLS	DOLS	FM
lnGNP	3.33 (29.15[b]	2.66 (10.95)[b]	0.39 (1.88)[c]
R^2	0.69	0.72	0.01

[a] The dependent variable is ln*FDI*. Estimations are based on the pooled data 1986–2000 for 25 provinces in China. One lead and one lag of first differenced independent variables are used when applying the DOLS method. Figures in parentheses are t–values.

[b] Significant at the 1% level.

[c] Significant at the 5% level.

Table 5.4 Estimated error correction models using OLS method[a]

	(i)	(ii)	(iii)
ECM_{t-1}	-0.22	-0.22	-0.22
	(-5.96)[c]	(-5.96)[c]	(-5.96)[c]
$d\tau_f$[b]	-0.00001	-	-
	(-0.05)	-	-
$d\tau_g$[b]	-	-0.00001	-
	-	(-0.09)	-
$d\tau_p$[b]	-	-	-0.00002
	-	-	(-0.15)
Constant	-4.70	-4.70	-4.70
	(-5.69)[c]	(-5.69)[c]	(-5.69)[c]
R^2	0.09	0.09	0.09

[a] The dependent variable is Δln*FDI.* Equations are based on the pooled data from 1986 to 2000 for 25 provinces. Figures in parentheses are t–values. *ECM* is the cointegrated relationship estimated by the OLS method and reported in Table 5.3.

[b] $d\tau_f = (\tau - \overline{\tau}_f)$, $d\tau_g = (\tau - \overline{\tau}_g)$ and $d\tau_p = (\tau - \overline{\tau}_p)$, where τ = regional tax rate, $\overline{\tau}_f$ = weighted average regional tax rate with the provinces' share of total FDI as the weight, $\overline{\tau}_g$ = weighted average regional tax rate with the provinces' share of total GNP as the weight and $\overline{\tau}_p$ = weighted average regional tax rate with the provinces' share of population as the weight.

[c] Significant at the 1% level.

Table 5.5 Estimated error correction models using DOLS method[a]

	(i)	(ii)	(iii)
ECM_{t-1}	–0.23	–0.23	–0.23
	(–6.52)[c]	(–6.52)[c]	(–6.52)[c]
$d\tau_f$[b]	–0.00001	-	-
	(–0.06)	-	-
$d\tau_g$[b]	-	–0.00001	-
	-	(–0.10)	-
$d\tau_p$[b]	-	-	–0.00002
	-	-	(–0.16)
Constant	–3.90	–3.90	–3.90
	(–6.17)[c]	(–6.17)[c]	(–6.17)[c]
R^2	0.11	0.11	0.11

a The dependent variable is $\Delta\ln FDI$. Equations are based on the pooled data from 1986 to 2000 for 25 provinces. Figures in parentheses are t–values. *ECM* is the cointegrated relationship estimated by the DOLS method and reported in Table 5.3.

b $d\tau_f = (\tau - \overline{\tau}_f)$, $d\tau_g = (\tau - \overline{\tau}_g)$ and $d\tau_p = (\tau - \overline{\tau}_p)$, where τ = regional tax rate, $\overline{\tau}_f$ = weighted average regional tax rate with the provinces' share of total FDI as the weight, $\overline{\tau}_g$ = weighted average regional tax rate with the provinces' share of total GNP as the weight and $\overline{\tau}_p$ = weighted average regional tax rate with the provinces' share of population as the weight.

c Significant at the 1% level.

integrated of order one. As for the three tax differentials $d\tau$'s, the tests indicate that they are stationary.

We next turn to the panel cointegration tests. The recently developed panel cointegration tests by McCoskey and Kao (1998) and Pedroni (1997, 1999), that are shown to be more powerful than the conventional tests, are employed in this study. Noting that the tax differentials $d\tau$'s are stationary variables, they are excluded from the cointegration analysis. The estimated statistics of Pedroni tests[9] shown in Table 5.2 indicate that the null of no cointegration is rejected by three of the seven test statistics when testing the cointegration between FDI and income. In the meantime, the two LM statistics of the McCoskey–Kao test reported in Table 5.2 do not reject the null of 'cointegration'. Overall, five of the nine test statistics support the existence of the cointegration relationship between FDI and income in all 25 provinces, suggesting that income is useful in explaining the behavior of FDI inflows in the long run.

Modeling panel cointegrated regressions

On the basis of the existence of the cointegrated relationship found between FDI and GNP, we now proceed to estimate the cointegrated regressions in the form of $\ln FDI_t = \alpha_0 + \beta \ln GNP_t + \varepsilon_t$. The estimated coefficient $\hat{\beta}$ on GNP is the long–run income elasticity. The OLS estimate is biased due to endogeneity in GNP. To account for the problem of endogeneity bias, we employ two bias correction estimation methods, that is, the dynamic OLS (DOLS), and the fully modified (FM) OLS. Specifically, we use the DOLS method which includes lags and lead of the first differences of the right–hand side variables as additional explanatory variables to correct for the possible endogeneity bias and small sample bias. While the DOLS method is parametric, the FM method uses non–parametric correction terms in the estimation (see Kao and Chiang, 2000 for discussions on these methods). Table 5.3 shows the estimated long–run income elasticities based on the conventional OLS, DOLS and FM methods. On the basis of the estimated results, we can make the following observations:

First, the OLS method leads to spurious regressions and biased estimates. Affected by the presence of unit roots, the t–statistic does not have the conventional t–distribution. Hence little confidence can be placed on the OLS estimate reported in Table 5.3. Second, consistent with the findings of Kao and Chiang (2000), we show that the DOLS estimator outperforms the conventional OLS and the FM estimators.[10] Third, the conventional OLS method gives a larger income elasticity than the DOLS and FM methods. Fourth, the DOLS estimator is statistically significant at the one percent level, while the FM estimator is significant at the five percent level. In general, the estimates obtained from all methods support the argument that there is a significant impact of region–specific attributes on FDI.

Estimation of the error–correction models

As the tax differential variables ($d\tau$) are found to be stationary, they are excluded from the cointegrated regressions. To investigate whether they may affect the FDI inflows, we construct the error correction model by incorporating both the long–run relationship between variables, and the short–run dynamic behavior. In constructing such a model, we utilize both the long–run relationship between FDI and GNP shown in Table 5.3 and the tax differential variables that capture the short–run dynamics.

The panel error correction model is specified as follows:

$$\Delta \ln FDI_t = \lambda_1 + \lambda_2 d\tau_t + \gamma ECM_{t-1} + \sum_{j=1}^{p-1} \theta_j \Delta \ln GNP_{t-j} + \sum_{j=1}^{p-1} \delta \Delta \ln FDI_{t-j} + \mu_t \quad (5.11)$$

where the symbol Δ is the first difference operator, $d\tau_j$ are tax differential variables, and ECM_{t-1} (= $\ln FDI_{t-1} - \alpha - \beta \ln GNP_{t-1}$) is the error correction term. These terms show how the system converges to the long–run equilibrium, and the convergence is assured when γ is between zero and minus one. We construct three error correction terms using the OLS, DOLS and FM estimates of long–run elasticities reported in Table 5.3. We estimate and report three different error–correction models, and the estimated models are reported in Tables 5.4–5.6. Since all variables in (5.11) are stationary, these error correction models can be estimated by the OLS method. Upon inspecting the results in Tables 5.4–5.6, we can make the following observations:

First, the error correction term (ECM) coefficients are always negative and are statistically significant, suggesting that the regional GNP has a significant long–run effect on FDI inflows in all provinces. This evidence validates an equilibrium relationship among the variables. It implies that ignoring the cointegrating relations would result in model misspecification. The first–differenced GNP ($\Delta \ln GNP$) which captures the short–run income effect was found to be insignificant, hence was not included in the model. Second, the three tax rate differential variables: $d\tau_f$, $d\tau_g$, and $d\tau_p$ have a negative effect on FDI, and the resulting equations are numbered (i) to (iii), respectively, in Tables 5.4–5.6. However, none of them are significant. Third, the statistical fit (measured by R^2) of the equations in Table 5.5 is better than those in Tables 5.4 and 5.6. Diagnostic test statistics (not shown here) indicate no first order serial correlation problem in the models.

Conclusions

This chapter has examined the determinants for regional FDI distribution in an economy with public inputs. Public inputs, financed by the revenue from capital taxes, enhance the productivity of capital. Thus, preferential capital tax policies would not be a reason for alluring FDI, because low tax rates may not mean more provision for public inputs. Using a panel data set from China, our empirical study confirms this theoretical result: regional tax differentials have no impact on FDI inflows either in the long run or short run. Instead, FDI inflows are affected by regional–specific attributes measured by provincial income. This result echoes the finding by Cheng and Kwan (2000). They also find the regional market, measured by regional income, has a positive effect on FDI inflows in China. Therefore, the use of tax policy to attract FDI may not be as effective as expected by policy makers.

Appendix A

The list of 25 sample provinces/cities is as follows:

a. Provinces or cities in Eastern region: Beijing, Tianjin, Hebei, Shanxi, Liaoning, Jilin, Heilongjian, Shanghai, Jiangsu, Zhejiang, Anhui, Fujian, Jiangxi, Shandong, Henan, Hubei, Hunan and Guangdong.

b. Provinces in Western region: Guangxi, Guizhou, Yunnan, Shaanxi, Gansu, Sichuan and Chongqing.

Appendix B

The following is a summary of asymptotic distributions of combination tests.

Test procedure	Test statistics	Critical value distribution
Inversechi-square	$P = -2\sum_{i=1}^{N} \ln(p_i),$	Chi-square with 2N degrees of freedom.
Logit	$L = \sum_{i=1}^{N} \ln\left(\frac{p_i}{1-p_i}\right),$	Student's t with $5N$+4 degrees of freedom.
Inverse normal	$Z = \frac{1}{\sqrt{N}}\sum_{i=1}^{N} \Phi^{-1}(p_i),$	Standard normal.

Notes

1 See Bao, et al. (2002) for a detailed discussion.

2 See Barro (1990) for issues on public inputs in the production function.

3 Letting ρ be the differential of capital returns between regions, $\rho = F_K - \tau - (F_K^* - \tau^*)$, the adjustment process for the capital market is: $\dot{\rho} = \alpha\rho(K)$, where the dot over the variable denotes the time derivative. Stability of the system requires that $d\rho/dK < 0$. Solving (1)–(3), we obtain: $dK/d\rho = 1/D$. Hence, we need $D < 0$ for stability.

4 This requires that $(\tau/K)(dK/d\tau) < dr^*/d\tau < 0$, where $dr^*/d\tau = -F_{KK}^*(dK/d\tau)$. If $F_{KK}^*(= \partial r^*/\partial K^*) = F_{KK} = (\partial r/\partial K)$, then we can obtain: $1 < r/\tau < -(\partial K/\partial r)(r/K)$.

5 Four provinces, namely, Tibet, Qinghai, Ningxia and Xinjiang, are excluded from our sample due to the lack of FDI data.

6 Since the computed tax lump sum includes the tax on city maintenance and construction, consumption tax, resources tax and extra charges for education, which should be borne by the enterprises in selling products and providing industrial services (see the explanatory note in *China Statistical Yearbook 2001*, p. 462), the tax rate computed in this study includes the extra fees cited above. In 2000, our estimate for the regional tax rate ranged from 9.30 percent (Heilongjiang) to 71.5 percent (Yunnan), with a regional average of 35.5 .

7 Among the studies in testing panel unit roots are Levin and Lin (1992, 1993), Quah (1994), Im, Pesaran and Shin (2003, IPS test), and Choi (2001) to mention a few, while those in panel cointegration include Engle and Granger (1987), Pedroni (1997, 1999), McCoskey and Kao (1998), Kao and Chiang (2000), and Moon and Phillips (1999).

8 See Hedges and Olkin (1985) for a detailed discussion of meta–analysis.

9 Four of Pedroni's seven panel cointegration statistics are based on pooling along the within–dimension, and three based on pooling along the between–dimension. Within the first category, three of the four tests, namely, the panel variance (ν), panel rho, and panel PP, involve the use of non–parametric corrections, and the fourth is a parametric ADF–based test called the panel ADF test. In the second category, two of the three tests, namely, the group rho and group PP, use non–parametric corrections while the third, called group ADF test, is again an ADF–based test.

10 The Monte Carlo simulations in Kao and Chiang (2000) have shown that the OLS estimator has a non–negligible bias in finite samples, and the FM estimator does not improve over the OLS estimator in general. They suggest using the DOLS estimator in practice. Their simulations also find that OLS, FMOLS and DOLS estimators are asymptotically normally distributed. But, the asymptotic distribution of the OLS estimator is shown to have a non–zero mean.

References

Bao, S., Chang G.H., Sachs, J.D. and Woo, W.T. (2002), 'Geographic Factors and China's Regional Development under Market Reforms, 1978–1998', *China Economic Review* **13**, pp. 89–111.

Barro, R.J. (1990), 'Government Spending in a Simple Model of Endogenous Growth', *Journal of Political Economy* **98**, pp. S103–S125.

Cheng, L.K. and Kwan, Y.K. (2000), 'What Are the Determinants of the Location of Foreign Direct Investment? The Chinese Experience,' *Journal of International Economics* **51**, pp. 379–400.

Choi, I. (2001), 'Unit Root Tests for Panel Data', *Journal of International Money and Finance* **20**, pp. 249–272.

Elliott, G., Rothenberg, T.J. and Stock, J.H. (1996), 'Efficient Tests for an Autoregressive Unit Root', *Econometrica* **64**, pp. 813–836.

Hedges, L.V. and Olkin, I. (1985), *Statistical Methods for Meta–Analysis*, Orlando: Academic Press, Inc.

Hines, J.R.Jr. (1996), 'Altered States: Taxes and the Location of Foreign Direct Investment in America', *American Economic Review* **86**, pp. 1076–1094.

Im, K.S., Pesaran, M.H. and Shin, Y. (2003), 'Testing for Unit Roots in Heterogeneous Panels', *Journal of Econometrics* **115,** pp. 53–74.

Kao, C. and Chiang, M.H. (2000), 'On the Estimation and Inference of a Cointegrated Regression in Panel Data', Working paper, Center for Policy Research, Syracuse University.

Levin, A. and Lin, C.F. (1992), 'Unit Root Tests in Panel Data: Asymptotic and Finite Sample Properties,' Department of Economics, University of California at San Diego, Discussion Paper No. 92–93.

Levin, A. and Lin, C.F. (1993), 'Unit Root Tests in Panel Data: New Results,' Department of Economics, University of California at San Diego, Discussion Paper No. 93–56.

McCoskey, S. and Kao, C. (1998), 'A Residual–based Test for the Null of Cointegration in Panel Data,' *Econometric Reviews* **17**, pp. 57–84.

Moon, H.R. and Phillips, P.C.B. (1999), 'Maximum Likelihood Estimation in Panels with Incidental Trends', *Oxford Bulletin of Economics and Statistics* **61**, pp. 711–747.

Pantula, S.G., Gonzalez–Farias, G. and Fuller, W.A. (1994) 'A Comparison of Unit–Root Test Criteria', *Journal of Business and Economic Statistics* **12**, pp. 449–459.

Pedroni, P. (1997), 'Panel Cointegration: Asymptotic and Finite Sample Properties of Pooled Time Series Tests with An Application to the PPP Hypothesis, New Results', Working Paper, Department of Economics, Indiana University.

Pedroni, P. (1999), 'Critical Values for Cointegration Tests in Heterogeneous Panels with Multiple Regressors', *Oxford Bulletin of Economics and Statistics* **61**, pp. 653–670.

Quah, D. (1994), 'Exploiting Cross–Section Variations for Unit Root Inference in Dynamic Data', *Economics Letters* **44,** pp. 9–19.

Wilson, J.D. (1986), 'A Theory of Interregional Tax Competition', *Journal of Urban Economics* **19**, pp. 296–315.

Chapter 6

An Econometric Estimation of Locational Choices of Foreign Direct Investment: The Case of Hong Kong and U.S. Firms in China

K.C. Fung, Hitomi Iizaka, Chelsea C. Lin and Alan Siu

Introduction

In this chapter we would like to extend Gregory Chow's pioneering work on the study of the Chinese economy.[1] Specifically, we shall examine econometrically the locational choices of Hong Kong and U.S. firms investing in China.

China has high, sustained growth rates for the last twenty years. China has an average growth rate of around 10 percent since 1978. Along the coastal areas, the average growth rate is about 12 percent. It is widely believed that China's growth is at least due in part to the large amount of foreign direct investment (FDI). In fact, among developing countries, China is now the largest recipient of FDI in the world. Given the important role of FDI in China's growth, it is thus critical to examine further the characteristics of FDI in China.[2]

In particular, it is important to examine a regional breakdown of inward FDI since income inequality across provinces has been widening in China. If some of the poorer regions can attract more FDI, this will lessen the disparity in economic welfare between provinces in China and will lower the likelihood of large–scale social unrest. In this respect, the Chinese government has proactively initiated the 'Go West' policy, which encourages economic development in the less developed central and western regions.[3] It is our hope that our study examining econometrically the determinants of Hong Kong and U.S. direct investment in China can help in understanding how provinces can attract more foreign investment. For example, our study shows that a better quality of labor is particularly useful in attracting U.S. investments, while tax preferences related to the Special Economic Zones (SEZs) and lower labor costs can induce a larger amount of Hong Kong investments.

Direct investments in China from different sources tend to have different characteristics. If provinces in China are mainly concerned with technology transfer, they should pay more attention to what attracts investments from the United States. Hong Kong investments tend to be, by comparison, more labor–

intensive, so if regions are interested in increasing local employment, they should enact policies that will attract investment from Hong Kong.[4] Thus our study, which analyses the determinants of investments from Hong Kong and the United States in different regions in China, will add to our understanding in this important area.

In this chapter we will use a regional panel data set for the years 1990–1999 and attempt to investigate the relative importance of the determinants of U.S. and Hong Kong direct investment in China.[5] The remainder of the chapter is organized as follows. The next section discusses the panel regression model. We specify and provide a description of the various important determinants of U.S. and Hong Kong direct investments in various Chinese regions. After this, we discuss our estimation method. Next we report and analyze our panel regression results. The final section concludes.

Model specification

The analysis in this section is an attempt to assess the relative importance of factors in determining the flow of investment into each region of China from Hong Kong and the United States for the period 1990–1999.

We start with the basic model that is derived from a reduced form specification for demand for inward direct investment. Let FDI_{ij} be the foreign direct investment from country i to region j. Then, the relationship between FDI and its determinants can be written as $FDI_{ij} = f(X_{j,})$, where X_j is a vector of variables that captures the overall attractiveness of region j to FDIs. The variables included in this vector are assumed to be exclusively dependent on the regional characteristics of the host country.

The basic regression model above can be written as a linear specification of the following form:

$$\ln(FDI_{j,t}) = \alpha_j + \beta_1\ln(GDP_{j,t}) + \beta_2\ln(LAGWAGE_{j,(t-1)}) + \beta_3\ln(HE_{j,t}) + \beta_4(INFRA_{j,t}) + \beta_5(SEZ_{j,t}) + \beta_6\ln(OCC_{j,t}) + \beta_7\ln(ETDZ_{j,t})$$

where the subscript "j" and "t" stands for region j at year t and the variables used in this analysis are defined below.

$FDI_{i,t}$	: FDI from country i to region j at time t
$GDP_{j,t}$	: GDP of region j at time t
$LAGWAGE_{j,(t-1)}$	: Average wage of region j at time t–1
$HE_{j,t}$	: the ratio of number of students enrolled in higher education in region j to its population at time t
$INFRA_{j,t}$	: kilometers of both high quality roads and railway in region per square kilometer of land mass at time t
$SEZ_{j,t}$	: the number of Special Economic Zones in region j at time t
$OCC_{j,t}$	: the number of Open Coastal Cities in region j at time t
$ETDZ_{j,t}$	: the number of Economic and Technological Development Zones in region j at time t

Table 6.1 Panel regression results for Hong Kong direct investment in China, 1990–1999

Variable	*Coefficient*	*t–statistics*	*Level of Significance*
CONSTANT	12.47	6.72	1%
GDP	0.80	6.83	1%
LAGWAGE	-1.12	-6.26	1%
HE	0.54	3.22	1%
INFRA	0.37	2.80	1%
SEZ	1.70	5.50	1%
OCC	0.90	2.60	1%
ETDZ	0.15	0.53	-
d.f.	243	-	-
Adj. R Squared	0.71	-	-
LM test	2.15 (10%)	-	-

A great number of research papers has investigated the determinants of the locational choices of FDI.[6] The above variables have been identified as important factors in much of the existing literature. In particular, Cheng and Zhao (1995) and Cheng and Kwan (2000) examined the locational determinants of *aggregate* foreign direct investments in China. Our contribution here is that we separate out investments from Hong Kong and from the United States. We are thus able to compare and contrast the determinants of these two very important yet very different sources of direct investments. Furthermore, we expand our data set to a longer time series, covering 10 years of data, from 1990–1999.

In order to examine the importance of size of the local market, Gross Domestic Product (GDP) of each region is used in the analysis. The importance of market size has been confirmed in many empirical studies. For the foreign investors, the size of the host market, which represents the host country's economic condition and/or potential demand for their output, should be an important element in the FDI decision–makings. As the variable is used as an indicator for market potential for the products of foreign investors, the expected sign for the variable is positive. It is also expected that the more foreign investors target the local market (instead of exporting the produced goods), the larger the magnitude of the positive coefficient.

Since the cost of labor is a major component of the cost function of a firm, the wage variables are frequently tested in the literature. A high nominal wage in the host region, other things being equal, deters inward FDI. This must be particularly so for the firms which engage in labor–intensive production activities. Therefore, the expected sign for this variable is negative. However, regional wages may be high because of high local inflows of FDI. To avoid the potential simultaneity bias between investment and wages, we elect to use in our specification the nominal wage lagged one period.

Table 6.2 Panel regression results for U.S. direct investment in China, 1990–1999

Variable	*Coefficient*	*t–Statistics*	*Level of Significance*
CONSTANT	8.19	3.73	1%
GDP	1.04	6.43	1%
LAGWAGE	-0.69	-3.27	1%
HE	0.97	4.19	1%
INFRA	0.30	1.62	10%
SEZ	0.38	0.86	-
OCC	1.56	0.35	-
ETDZ	0.70	2.14	5%
d.f.	241	-	-
Adj. R Squared	0.71	-	-
LM test	30.39 (1%)	-	-

'HE' is included in the equation to capture the average level of human capital in each region. Although the expected sign of the variable is positive, the importance of this variable would be higher for technology– and capital–intensive industries than for labor–intensive industries.

The hypothesis that well–developed regions with superior transportation facilities are more attractive to foreign firms relative to others is examined by including the proxy, density of roadway and railway. A better index of infrastructure should attract more investments. Therefore, the expected sign here is positive.

The model also includes three policy variables to examine the effects of policy incentives to attract FDIs in China. These policy variables are the number of SEZs (Special Economic Zones), the number of OCCs (Open Coastal Cities), and the number of ETDZs (Economic and Technological Development Zones) in each region. In these areas, foreign firms are granted preferential tax and other favorable policies and can flexibly deal with foreign businesses. Foreign firms are expected to be lured by lower taxes and other related pro–FDI measures. The expected signs for all these policy variables are positive. The detailed explanation for the designation of each policy is given in Appendix A. The data sources are explained in Appendix B.

Panel regression estimation

The estimation used to analyze the model above is the *random effects* model. The formulation of the model can be specified as follows:

$$y_{it} = \alpha + \beta' x_{it} + \varepsilon_{it} + u_i$$

Table 6.3 Market destinations of goods produced by Hong Kong firms in China (in shares of values)

Market/Year	*1992*	*1993*	*1995*
China	35.4%	59.0%	53.6%
United States	14.1%	3.5%	7.9%
Hong Kong	13.2%	19.5%	12.8%
Japan	7.5%	3.0%	3.2%
Taiwan	12.1%	1.3%	1.8%
European Union	7.1%	2.5%	1.6%
Southeast Asia	3.5%	1.9%	6.0%
Others	7.1%	9.4%	13.0%

Source: Fung, Lau and Lee (2004).

where the disturbance term, ε_{it} is associated with both time and the cross sectional units, which are regions within China in this analysis, and u_i is the random disturbance that is associated with the ith region and is assumed to be constant through time. In another words, the region specific constant terms are assumed to be randomly distributed across cross–sectional units. The further assumption made for the model is as follows: $E[\varepsilon_{it}] = E[u_i] = 0$, $Var[\varepsilon_{it}] = \sigma^2_\varepsilon$, $Var[u_i] = \sigma^2_u$, $Cov[\varepsilon_{it}, u_j] = 0$ for all i, t, and j, $Cov[\varepsilon_{it}, \varepsilon_{js}] = 0$ if $t \neq s$ or $i \neq j$, $Cov[u_i, u_j] = 0$ if $i \neq j$.

The regression disturbance, w_{it}, can be written as; $w_{it} = \varepsilon_{it} + u_i$, the variance and covariance of all disturbances are; $Var[w^2_{it}] = \sigma^2 = \sigma^2_\varepsilon + \sigma^2_u$, and $Cov[w_{it}, w_{is}] = \sigma^2_u$.

Therefore, the disturbances in different periods are correlated for a given i, because of their common component, u_i. The efficient estimator, then, is generalized lease squares (GLS). The two–step estimators are computed by first running ordinary least squares (OLS) on the entire sample. Then, the variance components are estimated by using the residuals from the OLS. These estimated variances are then used in the second step to compute the parameters of the model.[7]

Estimation results

Estimation results of the model for Hong Kong and the United States are presented in Table 6.1 and 6.2, respectively.

To complement and help our interpretations of the econometric results, let us also present two 'stylized' characteristics of Hong Kong and U.S. direct investments based on independent surveys. First, according to Fung, Lau and Lee (2004), the type of industries that U.S. companies invest in tends to be more capital–intensive and technology–intensive. Second, in 1995, U.S. firms in China

Table 6.4 Market destinations of goods produced by U.S. firms in China (in shares of values)

Market/Year	*1992*	*1993*	*1995*
China	69.5%	82.5%	84.5%
United States	15.6%	9.6%	8.4%
Hong Kong	2.8%	2.5%	1.6%
Japan	1.9%	0.6%	0.5%
Taiwan	0.0%	0.0%	0.3%
European Union	3.6%	0.4%	0.2%
Southeast Asia	2.8%	0.8%	2.5%
Others	3.8%	3.6%	1.9%

Source: Fung, Lau and Lee (2004).

sold 84.5 percent of their goods produced in China in the domestic Chinese market, whereas Hong Kong firms in China sold 53.6 percent of their goods in China (Table 6.3 and 6.4). In other words, only 15.5 percent of the U.S. goods made in China are exported. For Hong Kong firms, 46.4 percent of their goods made in China are exported outside of China. Thus, in general, U.S. direct investments are aimed primarily at the Chinese domestic market. By comparison, Hong Kong firms do care about the Chinese market, but they also use China as a site for low–cost production and export a large share of their goods from China.

From Tables 6.1 and 6.2, our regression results show that the size of the nominal regional GDP is an important factor for both Hong Kong and U.S. investors. The coefficients for this variable are positive and statistically significant at the 1% level, confirming the hypothesis that the amount of FDI inflow is positively related to the host region's market size. However, the magnitude of the impact of the variable is about 29% larger for U.S. investments compared to those from Hong Kong. Table 6.1 and 6.2 indicate that a one–percent increase in regional GDP is associated with a 0.80 percentage increase in Hong Kong direct investment and 1.04 percentage increase in U.S. investment. One interpretation for this difference may be due to the different characteristics of U.S. and Hong Kong investments indicated in the above surveys. According to Table 6.3 and Table 6.4, U.S. firms tend to invest in China to penetrate the Chinese market, while for Hong Kong firms; they export a much larger share of their goods outside of China. The larger magnitude of the GDP coefficient for U.S. investment may be due to the higher U.S. emphasis on the local Chinese market than those from Hong Kong.

The lagged wage variable is also an important determinant in the analysis. The coefficients for both Hong Kong investments and U.S. investments are both significant at the 1% level. The evidence of a strong negative impact of the wage variable agrees with Cheng and Kwan's (2000) findings. Other than the constant term, the absolute value of the point estimate of the wage variable is the second largest for the Hong Kong regression among all the explanatory variables examined. Compared with the wage coefficient in the U.S. regression, it is also larger by approximately 62%. This seems to suggest that Hong Kong is much more sensitive to labor costs than those from the U.S. This difference can be understood by the fact that Hong Kong investment is more concentrated in labor–intensive industries, whereas U.S. investments tend to be more capital–intensive and technology–intensive (Fung, Lau and Lee 2004).

Unlike previous studies by Cheng and Zhao (1995), and Cheng and Kwan (2000) who use the aggregate amount of FDI as the endogenous variable, we find strong evidence of a positive effect of labor quality (captured by the variable HE) on both Hong Kong and U.S. direct investment. But the effect of the labor quality proxy is much less pronounced on Hong Kong investment — it is over 40% smaller than that for the U.S. investment.[8]

The above findings of a large significant negative impact of the lagged wage and a much smaller impact of the labor quality on Hong Kong direct investment may again reflect the difference in the characteristics of investment projects from Hong Kong and those from the United States. As discussed earlier, Hong Kong investment projects concentrate more in labor–intensive industries such as electrical appliances, food processing, footwear, textiles, and so on, where relatively lower level of skill is required. On the other hand, direct investment from the U.S. is largely concentrated in capital– and technology–intensive industries such as electrical equipment, chemicals, electronics, transportation equipment, and so on, where labor skill rather than just low labor cost is a much more significant factor in determining the profitability of their investments.

In addition, our panel regression also shows that the quality of regional infrastructure has a significant positive influence on direct investment inflow in China from both Hong Kong and from the United States. But the coefficient for the U.S. regression is found to be only significant at the 10% level. This again may be due to the fact that U.S. places more emphasis on the local market than Hong Kong. For Hong Kong investors, who send a larger share of their goods outside of China, a good highway is essential to allow their goods to reach a port or an airport for exports. By comparison, domestic Chinese distribution may need fewer miles of railroad and highways.

The effect of SEZ is positive for Hong Kong direct investment. Out of the three types of government policy variables, SEZ appears to be the most influential for Hong Kong direct investment. The explanatory variable OCC is also found to have significant positive effects in attracting investment from Hong Kong, although the magnitude of the impact of the variable is much smaller than that of the SEZ.[9] The results support the hypothesis that regions designated with SEZ and OCC confer advantages to these regions. By implementing tax and other policies favorable to foreign investors, SEZs and OCCs lower tax burdens on the foreign investors. They also signal an open economic environment where market reforms will continue to take place. Special Economic Zones are often said to have lost its competitive edges in attracting FDI as the policy of preferential tax treatment spread throughout China (from the south to the north and from the coastal areas to the interior), however this study shows unambiguously the significant positive effect of those areas in the case of attracting Hong Kong direct investment. On the other hand, for U.S. direct investment, the impacts of both SEZ and OCC are absent. In contrast, the variable ETDZ is significant at the 5 percent level for U.S. direct investment. ETDZs are areas designed for enhancing FDIs from foreign firms that are technologically advanced. They are often located in or near provincial capitals or transport hub cities. ETDZs may be more important for U.S. firms and not for Hong Kong firms because U.S. investments are more technology–intensive.

Conclusion

This chapter extends Chow's seminal work on the study of the Chinese economy. In particular, we examine the determinants of direct investment from Hong Kong and the United States in China, using a regional data set from 1990 to 1999. Using a random effects model, we found various similarities and differences in the importance and the magnitudes of the determinants of FDI among these two investment sources.

We show that the absolute level of GDP has a significant positive impact on inflows of direct investment from both Hong Kong and the United States. However, it is shown that U.S. investments are more sensitive to local market demand than Hong Kong investments. This may be explained by the fact that U.S. firms sell more to the domestic Chinese market, while Hong Kong firms tend to use China as a low–cost hub to manufacture goods for export to markets to countries outside China (Fung, Lau and Lee 2004).

Another major difference between the Hong Kong and U.S. investments appears in the significance of the average labor quality, measured by the proportion of the students enrolled in the higher education relative to the region's population. Direct investments from the United States are significantly influenced by regional labor quality, whereas the influence is weaker for the case of Hong Kong. In contrast, Hong Kong investments are much more sensitive to low labor costs than those from the United States. This may be because direct investments from Hong Kong are more concentrated in labor–intensive industries that only require relatively low labor skill. By comparison, U.S. investments are concentrated in technology–intensive and capital–intensive industries.

The hypothesis that a good quality of infrastructure is conductive to attract FDI is strongly supported for the cases of both Hong Kong and the United States, with Hong Kong investments being somewhat more sensitive to the infrastructure quality index.

Evidence is also found that regions with a higher number of Special Economic Zones and Open Coastal Cities which implement preferential treatments to foreign investors still have great advantages over other regions in attracting FDI. This positive effect appears to exert a larger influence on Hong Kong direct investment. On the other hand, U.S. investments (but not Hong Kong investments) are lured by regions with Economic and Technological Development Zones. The difference again may be due to the fact that U.S. investments are more technologically advanced compared to those from Hong Kong.

Appendix A: Policy designation

Special Economic Zones:

Shenzhen, Zhuhai, and Shantou in Guangdong; Xizmen in Fujian; Hainan.

Open Coastal Cities:

Dalian in Liaoning; Qinhuangdao in Hebei; Tianjin; Yantai and Quingdao in Shandong; Lianyungang and Nantong in Jiangsu; Shanghai; Ningbo and Wenzhou in Zhejiang; Fuzhou in Fujian; Guangzhou and Zhanjiang in Guangdong; Beihai in Guangxi.

Economic and Technological Development Zones:

Dalian, Yingkou and Shenyang in Liaoning; Qinhuangdao in Hebei; Tianjin; Yantai, Quingdao and Weihai in Shandong; Lianyunggang, Kunshan and Nantong in Jiangsu; Guangzhou and Zhanjiang in Guangdong; Ningbo in Zhejiang; Fuzhou, Rongqiao and Dongshan in Fujian; Minhang, Hongqiao and Caohejin in Shanghai; Wenzhou in Zhejiang; Harbin in Heilongjizng; Changchun in Jilin; Wuhu in Anhui; Wuhan in Hubei; Chongqing in Sichuan; Dayawan and Pnyu's Nansha in Guangdong; Xiaoshan and Hangzhou in Zhejiang, Beijing; Urumqi in Xinjiang.

Appendix B: Data sources

The following data taken from the Almanac of China Foreign Relations and Trade (various issues):

- contracted Hong Kong direct investment for 1993–1999
- contracted U.S. direct investment for 1993–1999

The following data are taken from the China Foreign Economic Statistical Yearbook 1994:

- contracted Hong Kong direct investment for 1990, 1991 and 1992
- contracted U.S. direct investment for 1990, 1991 and 1992

The following regional data for 1996–1999 are taken from the Statistical Yearbook of China, 1997 and 1998, and for 1990–1995, they are taken from China Regional Economy A Profile of 17 years of Reform and Opening–Up (1996): GDP, the number of students enrolled in the higher education, the number of students enrolled in the specialized secondary schools, the distance of roadway, the distance of railway, the average lagged nominal wage.

Notes

1 For example, see Chow (1994, 2002).
2 For an excellent study of the relationship between capital formation and economic growth in China, see Chow (1993).
3 For an examination of the recent economic reforms in China, see Chow (2000).
4 U.S. and Japanese direct investments for this period tend to be in more capital–intensive and technology–intensive industries compared to those from Taiwan and Hong Kong. For details, see Fung, Lau and Lee (2004).
5 For a comparative study of Japanese and U.S. trade with China, see Fung and Iizaka (1998).
6 Examples of such works are Lunn (1980), Kravis and Lipsey (1982), Owen (1982), Scaperlands and Balough (1983), Luger and Shetty (1985), Maki and Meredith (1986), Culem (1988), Wheeler and Mody (1991), Coughlin, Terza, and Arromdee (1991), Friedman, Gerlowski, and Silberman (1992), Woodward (1992), Smith and Florida (1993), Hines (1996). For the case of China, the studies include Cheng and Zhao (1995), Head and Ries (1996), and Cheng and Kwan (2000).
7 For a reference, see Chow (1983).
8 The possibility of dissimilar impact of labor quality on FDI from different country of origin was suggested in Cheng and Kwan (2000).
9 The importance of SEZ in a location decision of FDI is also confirmed by Cheng and Zhao (1995), and Cheng and Kwan (2000), using aggregate FDI data.

References

Cheng, L.K. and Kwan, Y.K. (2000), 'What Are the Determinants of the Location of Foreign Direct Investment? The Chinese Experience', *Journal of International Economics* **51**, pp. 379–400.

Cheng, L.K. and Zhao, H. (1995), 'Geographical Pattern of Foreign Direct Investment in China: Location, Factor Endowments, and Policy Incentives', Department of Economics, Hong Kong University of Science and Technology.

Chow, G. (1983), *Econometrics*, New York: McGraw–Hill Book Company.

Chow, G. (1993), 'Capital Formation and Economic Growth in China', *Quarterly Journal of Economics* **108**, pp. 809–842.

Chow, G. (1994), *Understanding China's Economy*, New Jersey: World Scientific Publishing Company.

Chow, G. (2000), 'China's Economic Reform at the Beginning of the 21st Century', mimeo, Princeton University.

Chow, G. (2002), *China's Economic Transformation*, Malden: Massachusetts, Blackwell Publishers.

Coughlin, C., Terza, J.V. and Arromdee, V. (1991), 'State Characteristics and the Location of Foreign Direct Investment Within the United States', *Review of Economics and Statistics* **73**, pp. 675–683.

Culem, C.G. (1988), 'The Locational Determinants of Direct Investments among Industrialized Countries', *European Economic Review* **132**, pp. 885–904.

Friedman, J., Fung, H., Gerlowski, D. and Silberman, J. (1992), 'What Attracts Foreign Multinational Corporations? Evidence from Branch Plant Location in the United States', *Journal of Regional Science* **32**, pp. 403–418.

Fung, K.C. and Iizaka, H. (1998), 'Japanese and U.S. Trade with China: A Comparative Analysis', *Review of Development Economics* **2**, pp. 181–190.

Fung, K.C., Lau, L.J. and Lee, J. (2004), *U.S. Direct Investment in China*, AEI Press: Washington D.C.

Head, K. and Ries, J. (1996), 'Inter–City Competition for Foreign Investment: Static and Dynamic Effects of China's Incentive Areas', *Journal of Urban Economics* **40**, pp. 38–60.

Hines, J. (1996), 'Altered States: Taxes and the Location of Foreign Direct Investment in America', *American Economic Review* **86**, pp. 1076–1094.

Kravis, I.B. and Lipsey, R.E. (1982), 'The Location of Overseas Production and Production for Export by US Multinational Firms', *Journal of International Economics* **12**, pp. 201–223.

Luger, M.I. and Shetty, S. (1985), 'Determinants of Foreign Plant Start–Ups in the United States: Lessons for Policymakers in the Southeast', *Vanderbilt Journal of Transnational Law* **18**(2), pp. 223–245.

Lunn, J.L. (1980), 'Determinants of US Direct Investment in the EEC', *European Economic Review* **13**, pp. 93–101.

Maki, D.R. and Meredith, L.N. (1986), 'Production Cost Differentials and Foreign Direct Investment: A Test of Two Models', *Applied Economics* **18**, pp. 1127–1134.

Ministry of Foreign Economic Relations and Trade (various), *Almanac of China's Foreign Economic Relations and Trade*, Ministry of Foreign Economic Relations and Trade.

Owen, R.F. (1982), 'Inter–industry Determinants of Foreign Direct Investment: A Canadian Perspective', in A.M. Rugman (eds), *New Theories of Multinational Enterprises*, Croom Helm, London.

Scaperlanda, A. and Baslough, R. (1983), 'Determinants of US Direct Investment in the EEC Revisited', *European Economic Review* **21**, pp. 381–390.

Smith, D. and Florida, R. (1994), 'Agglomeration and Industrial Location: An Econometric Analysis of Japanese Affiliated Manufacturing Establishments in Automotive–Related Industries', *Journal of Urban Economics* **36**, pp. 23–41.

Wheeler, C. and Mody, A. (1992), 'International Investment Location Decisions: The Case of U.S. Firms', *Journal of International Economics* **33**, pp. 57–76.

Woodward, D. (1992), 'Locational Determinants of Japanese Manufacturing Startups in the United States', *Southern Economic Journal* **58**, pp. 690–708.

Chapter 7

Revealed Comparative Advantages and Intra–regional Trade of the World's Three Major Regions: 1980–1995

Leonard K. Cheng, Siu Fai Leung, and Zihui Ma[1]

Introduction

In this chapter we investigate empirically extra–regional trade and intra–regional trade for the world's three major trade regions, namely, the Asian Pacific Rim economies (APRE), the European Union (EU), and the North American Free Trade Area (NAFTA) for the period of 1980–1995. For extra–regional trade, we calculate and compare the Revealed Comparative Advantage (RCA) indices for these three regions and study how they changed over time. For intra–regional trade, we study the ratio of intra–regional exports to regional GDP and the ratio of intra–regional exports to total exports. We compare the ratios for the three regions and examine how well the intra–regional trade can be accounted by a proportional–spending model and a gravity model.

Since its introduction by Bela Balassa in the sixties, the concept of RCA has been applied widely to study an economy's or a group of economies' actual trade pattern and (by inference) its underlying comparative advantage and disadvantage. Most studies using the indices of RCA are concerned about the direction and magnitude of the comparative advantage of an economy or a group of economies in certain products or product groups vis–a–vis their selected trading partners or all trading partners.[2] Some of them use the RCA indices to analyze the impact on the exports of specific products or product groups to particular markets as a result of trade liberalization or preferential trade policy measures.[3] To the best of our knowledge, RCA indices have not yet been applied to the case where each of the major regions or trade groups is treated as a single unit of analysis, i.e., intra–regional trade is netted out of the regions' exports and the world's total exports.[4]

The EU comprises 15 Western European economies, i.e., Austria, Belgium, Denmark, Finland, France, Germany, Greece, Ireland, Italy, Luxembourg, the Netherlands, Portugal, Spain, Sweden, and the United Kingdom. NAFTA comprises three North American economies, namely, Canada, Mexico, and the United States. In this chapter, we take the third region to be APRE which is comprised of 14 economies along the Asian Pacific Rim, namely, Australia, Brunei, China, Hong Kong, Indonesia, Japan, Malaysia, New Zealand, New Guinea, the Philippines, Singapore, South Korea, Taiwan, and Thailand. Since APRE is not a formal trade bloc, we also consider a subset of APRE, namely, the East Asian Economies (EAE) that include China, Hong Kong, Japan, South Korea, and Taiwan, to be the third trade region. In calculating the RCA indices, economies not included in the three regions are treated as separate entities.

While the RCA indices measure extra-regional trade, we also study intra-regional trade by calculating the amount of exports among the economies within each region. Again, the third region is taken to be either APRE or EAE. In order to compare the intra-regional trade among the three regions, we measure the exports relative to either the regions' GDP or total exports. In addition to studying the evolution of the three regions' intra-regional trade over time, we examine whether the trade figures can be explained by a proportional-spending model and a gravity model.

The plan of the chapter is as follows. The next section discusses the four product categories adopted by us in the calculation of extra-regional exports, export-based RCA indices, and intra-regional exports. Following this, we report our findings about the three regions' comparative advantages and disadvantages in these four product categories from 1980 to 1995 and compares these findings with the related literature. The next section examines the differences in the regions' shares in intra-regional trade against their respective GDP shares. Penultimately, we discuss how well the intra-regional trade can be accounted by gross regional product (GRP) and other variables. The last section offers some concluding remarks.

Commodity aggregation system

The commodity trade statistics used for our analysis are compiled by the International Trade Division of Statistics Canada based on trade statistics submitted by individual economies to the United Nations.[5] We analyze the export statistics by adopting a commodity aggregation system developed by Krause (1982) but updated by us in order to conform to SITC Revision 2.[6] Commodity exports by each region are aggregated into four product categories, namely, (1) natural resource intensive products, (2) unskilled labor intensive products, (3) technology intensive products, and (4) human capital intensive products.

Changes in the relative importance of the four product groups in total world trade from 1980 to 1995 are shown in Table 7.1. The share of natural resource intensive products in world exports declined from over 50% in 1980 to slightly above 25% by 1995. In contrast, the shares of the other three product groups trended upward over time. The share of unskilled labor intensive products rose from 7.5% in 1980 to about 12.5% by 1995. The share of technology intensive products rose from 21.8% in 1980 to 36.6% by 1995. The increase in human capital intensive products was more modest. It rose from 15.4% in 1980 to 18.7% by 1995. Since the four categories do not exhaust the entire SITC products, the shares of the four product groups do not sum up to unity.

Krause's aggregation system has been used, among others, by Krause (1987) himself, Carolan, Singh and Talati (1998), and Cheng and Leung (1999). It is

Table 7.1 Shares of exports in total world exports (%) by products when the regions are APRE, EU, and NAFTA

Year	*Natural resource intensive products*	*Unskilled labor intensive products*	*Human capital intensive products*	*Technology intensive products*
1980	50.20	7.53	15.42	21.83
1981	47.98	8.24	16.41	22.93
1982	44.97	9.01	16.76	24.44
1983	43.58	9.50	16.23	25.49
1984	42.52	9.73	16.77	26.57
1985	37.91	10.08	18.04	28.67
1986	32.22	10.72	19.80	31.21
1987	31.64	11.43	19.62	31.14
1988	28.90	11.03	19.19	32.30
1989	30.80	11.49	19.04	32.86
1990	31.97	11.67	18.62	32.52
1991	29.76	12.12	18.75	34.55
1992	27.65	12.96	19.39	34.93
1993	26.07	13.30	19.71	35.65
1994	25.29	13.45	19.79	36.84
1995	25.64	12.50	18.69	36.59

Source: Statistics Canada, *World Trade Database 1980–1995.*

conceptually similar to that of Balassa and Noland (1989) who adopted a total of five product categories:

(1) Unskilled labor–intensive commodities.
(2) Natural resource–intensive commodities.
(3) Human capital–intensive commodities.
(4) R&D–intensive commodities.
(5) Physical capital–intensive commodities.

The main difference is that Krause's system does not contain the last category of Balassa and Noland, who already pointed out (p. 187) that '... as physical capital becomes more mobile internationally it ceases to be a source of comparative advantage.'

In their study, Richardson and Zhang (2001) aggregated the commodities into primary products (SITC 1–4) and manufactures (SITC 5–8). Among manufactures chemicals (SITC 5) and manufactured materials (SITC 6) are regarded as standardized manufactures whereas machinery and equipment (SITC 7) and finished manufactures (SITC 8) are regarded as differentiated manufactures. In addition, based on multiple–digit SITC codes, they also divided some of the manufactures into producer goods and consumer goods. As such, their aggregation system is quite different from ours.

Comparative advantage or disadvantage

The RCA index we use is more precisely known as the 'export revealed comparative advantage' (XRCA) index. Like other such indices, it is defined as the ratio of two ratios. The numerator ratio is the share of a given product category's export in a region's total exports, while the denominator ratio is the share of the world's total export of the product category in the world's total exports of all products. Mathematically, the XRCA of the mth region in the nth product category is

$$(7.1) \quad XRCA_{mn} = \frac{\dfrac{x_{mn}}{\sum_{n=1}^{N} x_{mn}}}{\dfrac{\sum_{m=1}^{M} x_{mn}}{\sum_{m=1}^{M}\sum_{n=1}^{N} x_{mn}}},$$

where x_{mn} = value of the mth region's export in the nth product category, $m = 1, 2, \ldots, M$, $n = 1, 2, \ldots, N$, M = total number of regions, and N = total number of product categories. An XRCA index greater than unity is taken to 'reveal' that the region has a 'comparative advantage' in the production of that product category, whereas an index smaller than unity is taken to 'reveal' that the region has a 'comparative disadvantage.' The larger is the absolute magnitude of XRCA, the greater is the comparative advantage or disadvantage, whichever the case may be.

Even though the relationship between the XRCA index and standard trade models has not been satisfactorily established,[7] this index and other related indices have been employed frequently since their introduction by Balassa because they do provide useful measures of the patterns of trade. Perhaps more importantly, there are no better indices of an economy's underlying real comparative advantage and disadvantage.

A number of papers have studied the empirical properties of the XRCA. A recent study by Hinloopen and Van Marrewijk (2001) of the XRCA of 12 EU members, based on their exports to Japan in 99 industries from 1992 to 1996, has shown that there was a positive correlation between XRCA exceeding unity (and other positive integers) and positive net exports, thus providing an empirical foundation for using XRCA in the presence of two–way trade. In addition, they show that the empirical cumulative distribution function of the index's magnitude was stable over time. Their finding that only about one third of industries had an index larger than unity is consistent with the theory of specialization, which would predict that a country is a net exporter in a small number of industries to the rest of the world but a net importer in many other industries. Their finding that EU's mean of the index across all industries was much larger than unity and sensitive to outliers is not an indictment against the index, but an indication that an export–share–weighted average may be a more meaningful measure than a simple arithmetic mean.

Hinloopen and Van Marrewijk have also found that the distribution of XRCA differed considerably across countries, thus making comparisons of the index between countries problematic. Even though trade theory alone does not predict the relationship between XRCA between countries, it would be helpful to identify empirically the effect of aggregating narrowly defined industries into more broadly defined industries, and aggregating countries into bigger regions.

In this section, we report the XRCA indices of APRE (or EAE), EU, and NAFTA in natural resource intensive products, unskilled labor intensive products, technology intensive products, and human capital intensive products. As far as we are aware of, this is the first study of its kind.

Comparative advantages and disadvantages of APRE, EAE, EU, and NAFTA

The XRCA indices of APRE, EU, and NAFTA in the four product categories from 1980 to 1995 are depicted in Figures 7.1–7.4. In addition, the XRCA indices of EAE and Japan are presented in the same figures assuming that EU and NAFTA remained as trade blocs. Replacing APRE by EAE or Japan has no effect on EU and NAFTA's numerator ratio of the XRCA index given in equation (7.1), but has an effect on the denominator ratio in the same equation. As a result, the XRCA indices for EU and NAFTA corresponding to EAE or Japan are different from those presented in Figures 7.1–7.4. However, the differences are very small and thus not presented to avoid cluttering.

Figure 7.1 shows that while APRE, EAE, and EU had a clear comparative disadvantage in natural resource intensive products throughout the entire period, NAFTA had a much smaller comparative disadvantage and in 1987 and 1988 even had a slight comparative advantage. APRE's index was 0.44 in 1980 but gradually declined to 0.33 by 1995. EAE's index remained within a narrow range of 0.14–0.17 throughout the entire period. EU's index also stood at 0.44 in 1980 but gradually increased to 0.61 by 1995. NAFTA's index stood at 0.81 in 1980 and continued to rise to reach 1.1 in 1988, fell back gradually to 0.89 by 1991, but recovered to 0.96 by 1995.

Figure 7.2 shows that NAFTA had a comparative disadvantage in unskilled labor intensive products but APRE and EAE had a comparative advantage in the same products throughout the entire period. In contrast, EU enjoyed a comparative advantage in these products until 1990, after which it had a comparative disadvantage. More specifically, NAFTA's index was 0.65 in 1980, fell to 0.39 by 1987, but

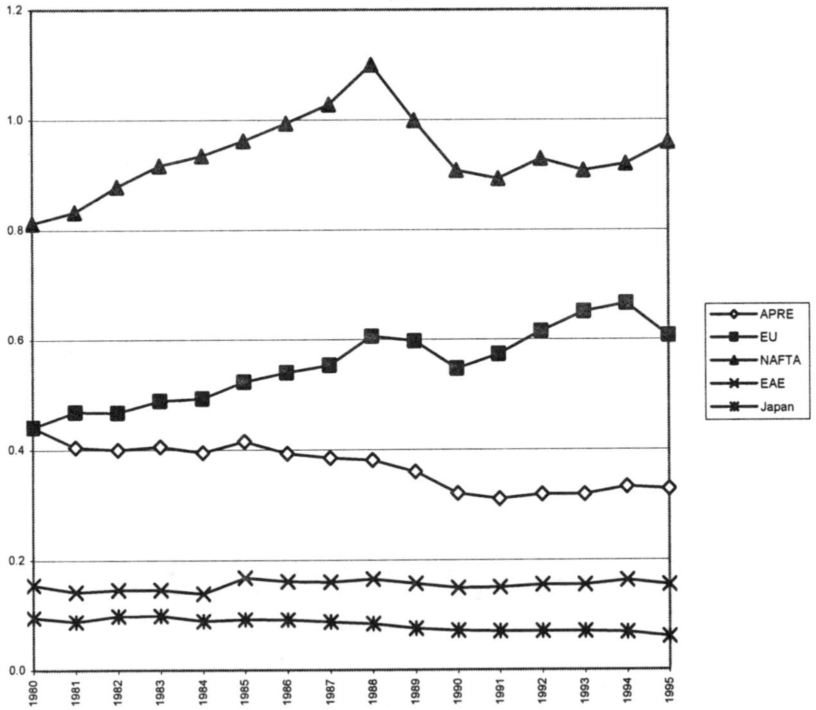

Figure 7.1 Evolution of comparative advantage of natural resource intensive products: 1980–1995

recovered to 0.46 by 1995. EU's index fell from 1.26 in 1980 to 0.81 in 1993 but recovered slightly to 0.85 in 1995. Even though APRE and EAE continued to enjoy a comparative advantage throughout the entire period, the former's index fell from 2.51 in 1980 almost without interruption to 1.70 by 1995 whereas the latter's index fell from 2.86 in 1980 to 1.66 by 1995.

As shown in Figure 7.3, while NAFTA had a comparative disadvantage in human capital intensive products, EU, APRE and EAE had a comparative advantage in the same products throughout the entire period. NAFTA's index deteriorated from 0.77 in 1980 to 0.47 in 1985 but subsequently improved to 0.74 by 1995. EU's index declined gradually from 1.75 in 1980 to 1.30 by 1995, whereas APRE's index declined from 2.07 in 1980 to 1.25 by 1995 and EAE's index declined from 2.62 in 1980 to 1.46 by 1995.

Figure 7.4 shows all four regions enjoyed a comparative advantage in technology intensive products, but APRE's and EAE's comparative advantages were substantially smaller than that of NAFTA. EU was ahead of both APRE and EAE until 1994 and 1993, respectively. NAFTA's index declined from 1.79 in 1980 to 1.40

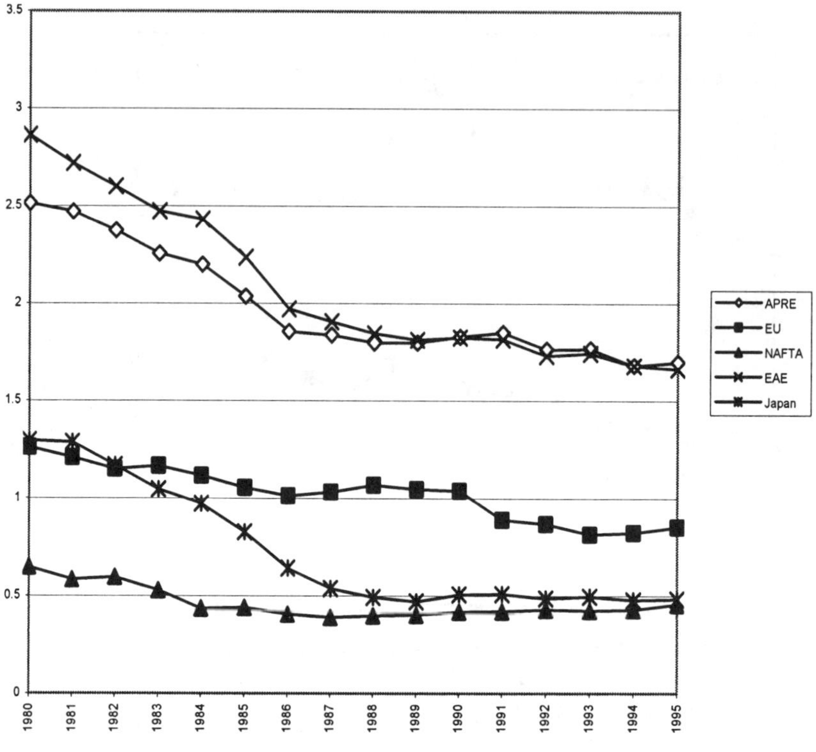

Figure 7.2 Evolution of comparative advantage of unskilled labour intensive products: 1980–1995

by 1995; EU's index declined from 1.71 in 1980 to 1.15 by 1995. APRE's index started out in 1980 at 1.00 (i.e., with neither comparative advantage nor comparative disadvantage) but managed to gain a slight comparative advantage of 1.18 by 1995. EAE's index started at 1.25 in 1980, fluctuated slightly in between but settled at 1.23 in 1995.

These changes of the regions' comparative advantages in technology intensive products are consistent with a generally held impression about the world's technological leaders and imitators during the sample period. First, the US was the world's technological leader, to be followed by Japan and EU. Second, members of APRE other than Japan were not known for their technological prowess. Third, South Korea, Taiwan, and Singapore managed to gradually narrow the technological gaps between them and the technological leaders during this period.

Figures 7.3 and 7.4 show that the comparative advantage of technology intensive products is not necessarily positively correlated with that of human capital intensive products. For instance, while EAE (and Japan alone) had an advantage in both products, NAFTA had an advantage in technology intensive products but a disadvantage in human capital intensive products. In addition, while APRE's comparative advantage in human capital intensive products was decreasing over the period, its advantage in technology intensive products showed a positive trend.

There are three differences between the XRCA indices of APRE and those of EAE. First, until 1990 EAE's comparative advantage in unskilled labor intensive products was slightly more substantial than that of APRE. Second, throughout the entire period EAE's comparative advantages in both technology intensive products and human capital intensive products were more substantial than those of APRE. Third, EAE's comparative disadvantage in natural resource intensive products was much more apparent than that of APRE. These differences are to be expected because EAE consists of member economies of APRE that are more abundant in human capital but scarcer in natural resources. The insignificant difference between their comparative advantages in unskilled labor intensive products is a reflection of the fact that China, a member of EAE, is as abundant in unskilled labor as the less developed non–EAE members of APRE.

We should caution the interpretation of the XRCA indices. They are calculated from the actual export statistics of the three regions and the remaining economies in the world are treated as separate entities. As such, they may reflect the regions' underlying 'real' comparative advantages and disadvantages, but they may also reflect the regions' success or failure in deploying their resources efficiently. Moreover, changes in the indices over time may reflect their success or failure in upgrading their respective production technology and building up their human capital.

Related literature

It is not easy to relate the above findings about comparative advantages and disadvantages of the world's three major trade regions to the literature because, as far as we are aware of, there are no prior studies on the subject. Nevertheless, it might still be useful to summarize the available related findings. Focusing on Japan and the US's comparative advantages between 1967 and 1985, Balassa and Noland (1989, p.186) discovered 'the transformation of Japan's comparative advantage from unskilled labor–intensive to human capital– and R&D–intensive manufactured goods, with its position with regard to physical capital–intensive products being approximately maintained over time.'

Japan's comparative advantages are also given in Figures 7.1–7.4 if EU and NAFTA were the only two trade blocs in the world. One can see that Japan's comparative disadvantage in natural resource intensive products, already very large between 1980 and 1985, continued to be magnified in the subsequent decade. Its unskilled labor intensive products had a slight comparative advantage until 1984 but by 1995 it had a significant comparative disadvantage of 0.48. Its comparative advantage in human capital intensive products, which at 3.12 was most pronounced in 1980, continued to fall throughout the entire period to 1.69 by 1995. In contrast,

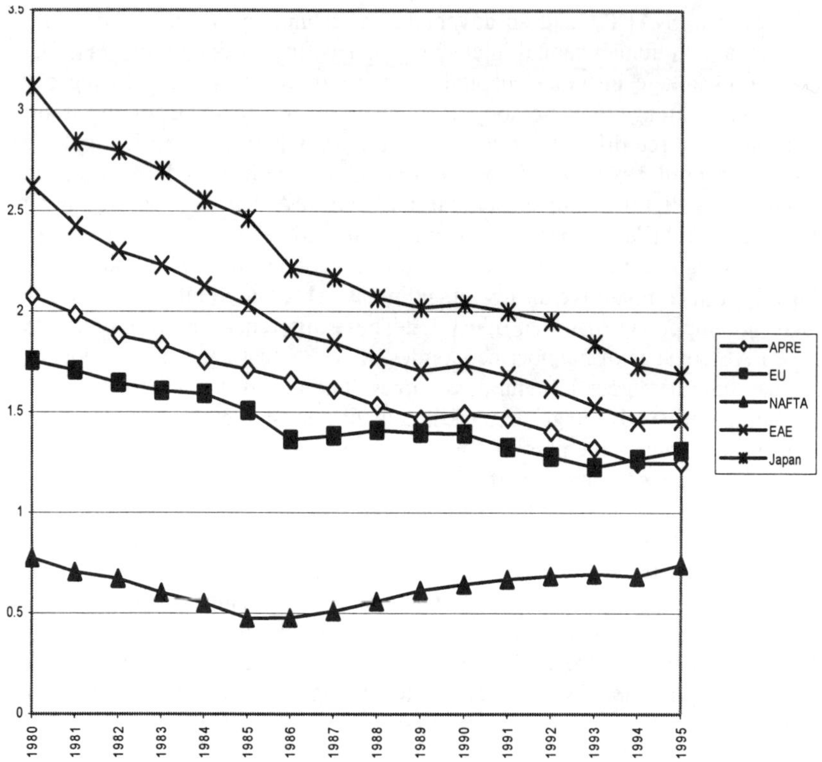

Figure 7.3 Evolution of comparative advantage of human capital intensive products: 1980–1995

its comparative advantage in technology intensive products remained relatively stable during the same period, fluctuating only narrowly between 1.6 in 1984 and 1.44 in 1993.

According to Balassa and Noland (1989, p.186), 'in the United States the principal change involved increased specialization in R&D–intensive products while the strong US disadvantage in unskilled labour–intensive products and its relative advantages in human capital– and physical capital–intensive products changed little over time.' In addition, 'the US could be expected to maintain its specialization in natural resource–intensive products.'

If the comparative advantage and disadvantage of the US were approximated by those of NAFTA (given the US' dominant role in NAFTA) when Japan is treated as the third region, then the results presented in Figures 7.1–7.4 are rather unexpected in light of Balassa and Noland's earlier findings. First, during the entire period the US had a comparative advantage in technology intensive products alone, but had a comparative disadvantage in the other three product groups. Second, like the EU, the US' comparative advantage in technology intensive products was falling rather than rising.

Richardson and Zhang (2001) focused on the comparative advantage and disadvantage of the US vis–a–vis different groups of trading partners. Their findings (on p. 196) indicate that 'the United States has comparative advantage in differentiated producer goods (e.g., capital equipment) in all regions—though it is less marked in Japan—and comparative disadvantage (except for chemicals) in standardized producer goods (e.g., metals) and consumer goods of all sorts.' In addition, there is 'the familiar US comparative advantage with the rest of the world in primary products (except fuels) and in manufactured chemicals, and the familiar mixed pattern across other manufactures. In these other manufactures, the United States performs best in machinery and equipment, but shows comparative disadvantage in manufactured materials and finished manufactures.' (p.201).[8]

Intra–regional and extra–regional trade

It is well known (e.g., see Frenkel (1997, p.21)) that, other things being equal, a larger region will have a larger share of intra–regional trade. One way to capture the importance of intra–regional trade while adjusting for the size of the regions is to compare their intra–regional trade/regional GDP ratios. Another way is to look at the intra–regional trade/total trade ratio.

Intra–regional exports and gross regional product

The ratios of the regions' intra–regional exports to their respective gross regional product (GRP) are given in Table 7.2. As one can see, EU's intra–regional trade/GRP ratio was the highest among the three regions. It fluctuated between 13.6% and 16.1% during the entire period. It was 3 to 4.7 times the NAFTA ratio and 1.7 to 3 times the APRE ratio.

APRE's ratio of intra–regional trade to GRP fluctuated between 6% and 7% from 1980 to 1989 with the exception of 1986 and 1987, when the ratio was at 5.2% and 5.6%, respectively. Beginning in 1990, the ratio increased almost without interruption and by 1995 it reached almost 9%.

NAFTA's ratio of intra–regional trade to GRP fluctuated between 3% and 3.5% from 1980 to 1991, but gradually increased to 5% by 1995. In comparison, NAFTA's ratio was only about half of the APRE ratio throughout the entire period.

Surprisingly, EAE's ratio of intra–regional exports to regional GRP throughout the period was rather close to that of NAFTA. From 1980 to 1983, NAFTA's ratio was higher than that of EAE but the opposite was true from 1984 to 1995.

Intra–regional exports and total exports

Now let us consider another measure of the intensity of intra–regional trade, namely the ratio of intra–regional exports to total exports to the world (to be denoted by INTRA). This measure is regarded as superior to the ratio of intra–

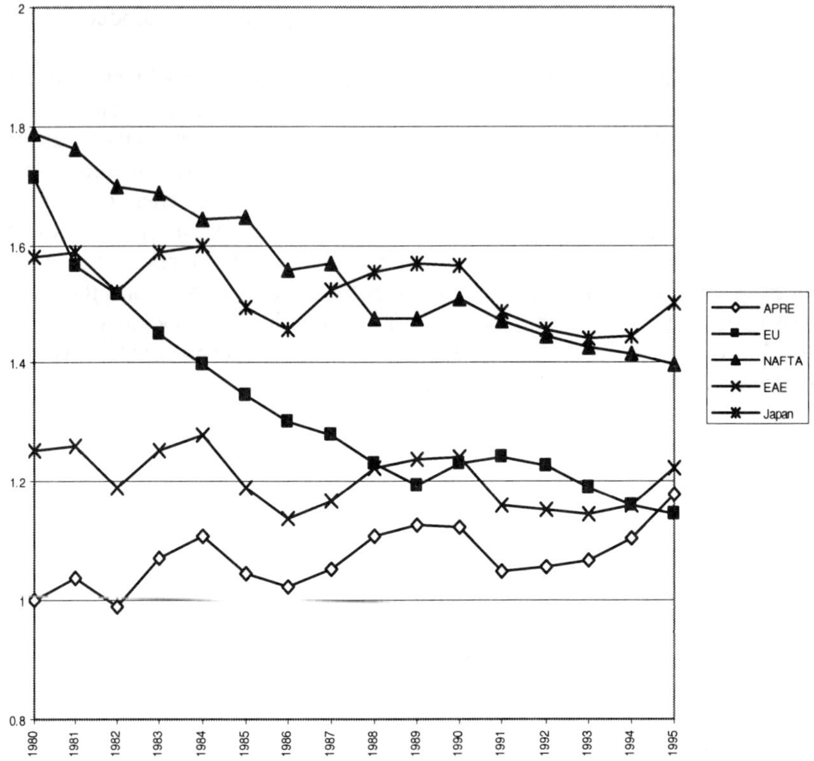

Figure 7.4 Evolution of comparative advantage of technology intensive products: 1980–1995

regional exports to GRP because it takes out the influence of both size and openness (Frenkel (1997, p.27)), not just the influence of size as measured by GRP.

The share of each region's intra–regional exports in total exports is given in the middle panel in Table 2. APRE's share increased almost with no interruption from 6.3% in 1980 to 13.8% by 1995. The magnitude of the growth of EAE's share was even more remarkable: it jumped from 2.1% in 1980 to 6.7% in 1995. In comparison, EU and NAFTA's shares grew more modestly. NAFTA's share grew from 5.5% in 1980 to 8.1% in 1985 and 8–8.5% during 1993–1995, but declined between 1986 and 1992.

EU's share was in the low 20% up to 1985, rose to the high 20% during 1989–1992, but stabilized at 25% during 1993–95. This share was significantly larger than those of APRE and NAFTA. In 1980 it was about 3.5–4 times those of the other two regions; in 1995 it was close to two times the share of APRE and three times the share of NAFTA. One explanation of this substantial difference between EU and the other two regions is that EU is comprised of many small countries.

Trade between different states in the US, the dominant economy in NAFTA, is by definition internal trade and thus not recorded as exports at all.

Extra–regional exports and GRP

The ratios of the three regions' extra–regional exports (i.e., exports to economies outside of their own respective regions) to their respective GRP are given in the third panel in Table 7.2. Unlike the case of intra–regional exports, the ratios of extra–regional exports to GRP of APRE and EU were quite similar. APRE's ratio varied between 8.3% and 11.0% whereas EU's ratio varied between 7.3% and 11.4%. For both regions, their ratios were higher during 1981–1985, but lower during 1986–1995. NAFTA's ratio was significantly lower than both APRE and EU. It varied between 4.1% and 6.6%.

The ratio for EAE was slightly larger than that for APRE. That is to be expected because APRE contains EAE as a proper subset. Other than the slight difference in magnitude, the two ratios tended to move in the same direction over the period.

Determinants of intra–regional trade: two related benchmarks

What accounts for the variations in intra–regional trade intensity (i.e., the ratio of intra–regional exports to total exports) as summarized in Table 7.2? We shall develop two related benchmarks using GDP and other variables that have been shown to affect bilateral trade (Frenkel, 1997; Frenkel and Rose, 2000). We shall compare the actual intra–regional trade intensity against these two benchmarks to see how close it is to the benchmarks.

The first benchmark is derived under the assumptions that there are no geographical, cultural, and political distances between any pair of economies and that demand for their products is symmetrical. That is to say, an economy's import from any other economy is proportional to the share of that other economy's GDP in Gross World Product (GWP). Under these conditions, the theoretical value of INTRA is derived as equation (A2) in Appendix II. If we substitute the three regions' (with a choice between APRE and EAE) shares in GWP, the number of their members, and the GDP shares of other economies in the world into this equation, then we can obtain the predicted values of INTRA.

The GDP shares may be based on nominal gross product as measured according to exchange rates or real gross product as measured according to purchasing power parity. The first two panels in Table 7.3 present the predicted values of INTRA using these two gross products in the calculations.[9] A comparison of the actual values of INTRA as contained in Table 7.2 with their predicted counterparts as contained in Table 7.3 reveals that the actual values are significantly larger than the predicted values. That is to say, regardless of whether equation (A2) is expressed in terms of nominal or real world product shares, the equation is grossly inadequate in explaining the three regions' actual intra–regional trade intensity.

Table 7.2 Intra–regional and extra–regional export

	Intra–regional exports/gross regional product (%)				*Intra–regional exports/total exports (INTRA (%))*				*Extra–regional exports/gross regional product (%)*			
Year	EAE	APRE	EU	NAFTA	EAE	APRE	EU	NAFTA	EAE	APRE	EU	NAFTA
1980	2.88	7.01	13.57	3.38	2.14	6.31	22.68	5.52	11.79	10.83	8.87	6.56
1981	2.97	6.92	13.60	3.32	2.42	6.90	20.48	6.27	12.48	10.86	10.19	6.00
1982	2.83	7.01	13.98	3.03	2.32	7.28	21.36	6.05	12.93	10.76	10.24	5.83
1983	2.84	6.41	14.20	3.13	2.60	7.43	21.71	6.94	12.19	10.18	10.06	4.92
1984	3.44	6.83	15.11	3.43	3.15	7.98	20.95	7.97	13.03	10.96	10.92	4.59
1985	3.74	6.55	16.09	3.35	3.48	7.99	22.52	8.06	12.98	10.58	11.36	4.12
1986	3.11	5.21	14.48	3.04	3.64	7.61	25.61	7.02	11.41	9.66	9.12	4.11
1987	3.37	5.58	14.40	3.25	4.07	8.23	26.97	6.89	10.76	9.34	8.24	4.28
1988	3.77	6.11	14.96	3.44	4.85	9.39	27.33	6.96	10.03	8.86	8.20	4.91
1989	3.78	6.52	15.65	3.42	4.66	9.73	27.19	6.98	10.47	9.08	8.42	5.10
1990	4.24	7.29	15.06	3.57	4.70	9.91	28.67	6.83	10.95	9.32	7.68	5.20
1991	4.47	7.58	14.60	3.54	5.47	11.22	28.64	6.83	10.54	9.00	7.36	5.32
1992	4.74	7.75	14.19	4.00	5.91	11.70	28.12	7.51	10.41	8.97	7.28	5.28
1993	4.48	7.44	14.31	4.16	6.29	12.60	25.07	7.98	9.69	8.35	9.14	5.01
1994	4.84	8.18	14.91	4.64	6.64	13.48	25.12	8.50	9.69	8.34	9.29	5.16
1995	5.23	8.92	15.37	5.02	6.73	13.76	24.99	7.95	9.90	8.44	9.78	6.06

Sources: Statistical Canada, *World Trade Database 1980–1995*; International Monetary Fund, *International Financial Statistics*, various issues.

Table 7.3 Predicted values of INTRA (%)

	Based on nominal gross product				*Based on real gross product*				*Based on the gravity equation of bilateral exports*			
Year	EAE	APRE	EU	NAFTA	EAE	APRE	EU	NAFTA	EAE	APRE	EU	NAFTA
1980	0.96	1.94	9.17	2.70	1.29	2.70	4.19	2.22	1.54	3.03	19.32	5.29
1981	1.00	2.13	6.74	3.53	1.32	2.83	3.96	2.36	1.69	3.44	16.61	6.52
1982	0.98	2.23	6.34	2.87	1.38	2.94	4.02	2.15	1.78	3.76	16.68	6.48
1983	1.09	2.51	5.76	3.08	1.46	3.12	3.93	2.05	1.98	4.19	16.53	7.28
1984	1.13	2.66	4.95	3.42	1.57	3.25	3.74	2.11	2.05	4.33	14.78	7.69
1985	1.12	2.89	5.01	3.54	1.74	3.46	3.65	2.07	2.08	4.48	15.11	7.96
1986	1.26	3.15	6.92	2.54	1.73	3.41	3.78	1.99	2.45	5.05	21.4	7.47
1987	1.39	3.29	8.24	2.37	1.81	3.57	3.80	1.99	2.69	5.33	24.35	7.25
1988	1.67	3.63	8.13	2.46	1.92	3.76	3.81	1.99	3.12	5.92	24.57	7.57
1989	1.76	3.79	7.67	2.76	2.01	3.97	3.89	2.05	3.34	6.3	23.47	8.08
1990	1.47	3.33	9.65	2.58	2.16	4.34	4.21	2.13	3.04	5.93	27.79	7.72
1991	1.73	3.79	10.03	2.68	2.15	4.50	4.29	2.20	3.45	6.62	29.05	7.96
1992	1.92	4.16	10.60	2.62	1.75	4.11	4.20	2.33	3.75	7.16	30.36	7.71
1993	2.52	5.38	8.47	2.77	-	-	-	-	4.43	8.37	26.24	7.8
1994	2.66	5.73	9.01	2.81	-	-	-	-	4.33	8.33	26.67	7.38
1995	3.00	6.40	10.52	2.30	-	-	-	-	4.35	8.32	27.29	6.22

Note: Real Gross Product is measured by purchasing power parity.
GNP figures for the Soviet Union were unavailable beginning in 1990. It is assumed that the Soviet Union's share in real gross world product from 1990 to 1992 was identical to its average share between 1980 and 1989, namely, 10%.

Sources: Statistical Canada, World Trade Database 1980–1995; International Monetary Fund, International Financial Statistics, various issues; Penn World Table 5.6.

Table 7.4 Regression results for a model of bilateral trade (t–statistics in parentheses)

Regressors	*Estimated Coefficients*
Constant	–7.433
	(–19.133)
Log(Product of GDP)	0.697
	(–70.86)
Log(Product of GDP per capita)	–0.026
	(–2.573)
Log(Distance)	–0.57
	(–23.627)
Common Language	1.245
	(–23.483)
Common Land Border	0.365
	(–5.937)
Adjusted R–Square	0.782

The significant discrepancy between the actual and predicted values of intra–regional trade intensity may be due to many factors. For instance, (a) distances and transport costs that favor intra–regional exports; (b) biases in preferences that favor products produced within each region; and (c) trade policies that favor intra–regional trade. To account for the influence of factors found to be important determinants of intra–regional trade, we estimate a model of bilateral trade along the lines of Frenkel (1997) and Frenkel and Rose (2000). Using data on bilateral exports as provided in Statistics Canada's world trade database and the panel data set of individual economies provided by Frenkel and Rose, we estimate an extended gravity model of bilateral trade using the following equation.

$$(7.2)\quad \log(\text{Bilateral Trade}_{ij}) = \beta_0 + \beta_1 \log(GDP_i \times GDP_j) + \beta_2(GDP_i \text{ per capita} \times GDP_j \text{ per capita}) + \beta_3 \log(\text{distance}_{ij}) + \beta_4 \text{Common Language} + \beta_5 \text{Common Land Border}$$

The variables are measured as follows: GDP is in thousands of US dollars, GDP per capita is in US dollars per person, and distance is in miles. Common Language is a dummy variable that equals 1 if the two countries use the same language, 0 otherwise. Common Land Border is a dummy variable that equals 1 if the two countries share a common border, 0 otherwise. Notice that the observed intra–regional trade intensity may also be due to policies in favor of regional integration (e.g., regional trade agreements and institutions). However, we have only included the non–policy variables in the above equation to see how well they can explain the

Table 7.5 Average deviation of predicted values from actual values of INTRA (%)

EAE	32.47
APRE	41.01
EU	14.02
NAFTA	8.16
EAE + EU + NAFTA	10.71
APRE + EU + NAFTA	15.22

observed intra–regional trade intensity without bringing in policy variables. Frenkel (1997) has studied the role of policy variables in explaining intra–regional trade intensity.

The estimation result of the above equation is given in Table 7.4 All the estimated coefficients are highly statistically significant. The model seems to be successful in accounting for variations in bilateral trade. Using the estimated equation, the predicted values of INTRA are given in the third panel in Table 7.3 A comparison of the actual values of INTRA as contained in Table 7.2 with their predicted counterparts as contained in Table 7.3 reveals that the predicted values based on the gravity equation are much closer to those based on the gross products. Moreover, even though the predicted values of APRE and EAE's intra–regional trade intensity still fall short of their actual values, the predicted values of NAFTA exceed their actual values in 10 out of 16 years; the predicted values of EU exceed their actual values from 1991 to 1995.

To assess the goodness of fit of the predicted values, we calculate the average percentage deviation of these values from the actual values, i.e.,

$$\Sigma \left| (\text{predicted value} - \text{actual value})/\text{actual value} \right| \div \text{number of observations.}$$

The average deviations of the predicted values from the actual values of INTRA for the regions separately and together are given in Table 7.5. The average deviations are extremely small for NAFTA, small for EU, larger and very large for EAE and APRE respectively. It seems that the gravity model with those variables included in equation (7.2) is quite adequate in accounting for the observed shares of intra–regional trade in total trade in NAFTA and EU, but less satisfactory in accounting for the observed shares in EAE and APRE. More specifically, in the cases of EAE and APRE the gravity model systematically under–predicts these shares.

To examine the gravity model in a more rigorous way, we employ the Wilcoxon–Mann–Whitney rank–sum test to check for each trade region whether the predicted values from the model are statistically different from the actual values. The rank–sum test is a nonparametric test for the equality of two distributions. For each trade region, the null hypothesis is that the distribution of the predicted values of INTRA based on the gravity model (the third panel in Table 7.3) is the same as the distribution of the actual values (the second panel in Table 7.2). For EAE and APRE, the p–values of the rank–sum tests are 0.003364 and 0.00007, respectively; hence the tests overwhelmingly reject the null hypothesis for each of these two regions. For EU and NAFTA, the p–values are 0.129 and 0.299, respectively; thus the rank–sum tests do not reject the null hypothesis at conventional levels of significance for both regions. In other words, the hypothesis that the predicted values and the actual values are derived from the same distribution cannot be rejected for EU and NAFTA. Thus, the gravity model offers a decent account for the INTRA values for EU and NAFTA but not for EAE and APRE.

Conclusions

This chapter presents a first attempt to understand some empirical aspects of extra–regional trade and intra–regional trade for the world's three major trade regions. In contrast to the literature, we treat each region as a unit of analysis. For extra–regional trade, we find some distinct differences among the XRCA indices for the three regions as well as their evolution over time. For intra–regional trade, we have limited success in explaining the regions' intra–regional trade intensities. In particular, the gravity model of bilateral trade tends to under–predict the intra–regional trade intensities of APRE and EAE. A more in–depth analysis is needed to understand the failure of the gravity model in the case of APRE and EAE. Possibilities include omitted variables and alternative specification of equation (7.2). The inclusion of trade policy may not be a good candidate, however, because APRE and EAE did not pursue more active policies to encourage intra–regional trade than EU or NAFTA. This is a puzzle to be resolved.

Appendix I: International Commodity Trade Classification System (based on SITC Revision 2)

Natural Resource Intensive Products

Commodity	SITC Rev. 2	
Food and live animals, chiefly for food	0	
Beverages and tobacco	1	
Beverages		11
Tobacco		12

Crude materials, except fuel	2, except 266, 267, and 269	
Mineral Fuels, lubricants, and related materials	3	
Coal		32
Cruel petroleum and petroleum products		333, 334
Gas, natural and manufactured		34
Electric current		35
Animal and vegetable oils	4	
Manufactured goods classified chiefly by material	6	
Leather		61
Cork and wood manufactures		63
Mineral manufactures		661–663
Pearls, precious and semi–precious stones		667
Pig iron		671, 672
Nonferrous metals		68

Unskilled Labour Intensive Products

Commodity	SITC Rev. 2	
Manufactured goods classified chiefly by material	6	
Textile yarn, fabrics, and textile products		651–657
Glass and pottery		664–666
Machinery and transport equipment	7	
Ships		793
Mis. Manufactured goods	8	
Furniture		82
Clothing		84
Footwear		85
Mis. Consumer goods		81, 83, 893, 895, 899
Toys		894
Commodities not classified by kind	9	
Armored vehicles and firearms		951

Technology Intensive Products

Commodity	SITC Rev. 2	
Chemicals and related products, n.e.s.	5, except 53 and 55	
Machinery and transport equipment	7	
Power generating machinery and equipment		71
Machinery specialized for particular industries		72
Metal working machinery		73
General industrial machinery and equipment		741–744
Office machines and auto. data processing equip		75
Telecommunications equipment and parts		764
Electrical machinery, apparatus, and appliances		771–774, 776, 778
Aircraft		792
Mis. Manufactured goods	8	
Scientific instruments		87
Optical equipment		881–884

Human Capital Intensive Products

Commodity	SITC Rev. 2	
Chemicals and related products, n.e.s.	5	
Dyes and paints		53
Perfumes and cleaning materials		55
Manufactured goods classified chiefly by material	6	
Rubber		62
Paper		64
Steel		673–679
Manufactures of metals		69
Machinery and transport equipment	7	
Non–electrical machines, tools, and parts		745,749
Television		761
Radio		762

Household electrical and non–electrical apparatus		775
Road vehicles		78
Trains		791
Mis. Manufactured goods	8	
Watches and clocks		885
Printed matters		892
Jewelry		896, 897
Musical instruments		898

Appendix II: The share of intra–regional exports in total exports and the share of regional GDP in GWP

In this appendix we derive the share of intra–regional exports in total exports in terms of the share of regional GDP in GWP. The critical assumption underlying our derivation is that consumers in the world will spend a fraction of his/her income on an economy's products that is directly proportional to the economy's share of GDP in GWP. That is to say, there is symmetric production differentiation among all economies, preferences are homothetic, and there are zero transport costs between any pair of economies.

We consider a world comprising four regions, three major regions APRE, EU, and NAFTA (to be indexed by *a*, *e* and *n*, respectively) plus the Rest of the World (to be indexed by *r*). Let y_{ji} be the GDP of the ith economy in region j, $j = a, e, n, r$; $i = 1,2,\ldots,m_j$; m_j = total number of economies in region j. Then,

$$\text{APRE's GDP} = \sum_{i=1}^{m_a} y_{ai},$$

$$\text{EU's GDP} = \sum_{i=1}^{m_e} y_{ei},$$

$$\text{NAFTA's GDP} = \sum_{i=1}^{m_n} y_{ni},$$

$$\text{ROW's GDP} = \sum_{i=1}^{m_r} y_{ri}, \text{ and}$$

$$\text{GWP} = \ Y = \sum_{i=1}^{m_e} y_{ei} + \sum_{i=1}^{m_a} y_{ai} + \sum_{i=1}^{m_n} y_{ni} + \sum_{i=1}^{m_r} y_{ri}.$$

Let s_j ($j = a, e, n, r$) denote region j's share of GDP in GWP, then

$$s_j = \sum_{i=1}^{m_j} \frac{y_{ji}}{Y},$$

and

$$s_a + s_e + s_n + s_r = 1.$$

Assuming that the qth economy in region p spends $(y_{ji}/Y)y_{pq}$ on goods produced by the ith economy in region j, where $q \neq i$, then intra–APRE exports is

$$\sum_{i=1}^{m_a} \sum_{q=1,q\neq i}^{m_a} \left(\frac{y_{aq}}{Y}\right) y_{ai} = \sum_{i=1}^{m_a}\sum_{q=1}^{m_a}\left(\frac{y_{aq}}{Y}\right) y_{ai} - \sum_{i=1}^{m_a}\left(\frac{y_{ai}^2}{Y}\right) = s_a \sum_{q=1}^{m_a} y_{ai} - \sum_{i=1}^{m_a} \frac{y_{ai}^2}{Y}.$$

On the other hand, APRE's exports to other economies is

$$\sum_{i=1}^{m_a}\left(\frac{y_{aq}}{Y}\right)\left(\sum_{i=1}^{m_e} y_{ei} + \sum_{i=1}^{m_n} y_{ni} + \sum_{i=1}^{m_r} y_{ri}\right) = s_a\left(\sum_{i=1}^{m_e} y_{ei} + \sum_{i=1}^{m_n} y_{ni} + \sum_{i=1}^{m_r} y_{ri}\right).$$

Thus, the sum of intra–APRE exports and APRE's exports to the world is

$$s_a Y - \sum_{i=1}^{m_a} \frac{y_{ai}^2}{Y}.$$

As a result, total exports is

$$Y - \left(\sum_{i=1}^{m_a} \frac{y_{ai}^2}{Y} + \sum_{i=1}^{m_e} \frac{y_{ei}^2}{Y} + \sum_{i=1}^{m_n} \frac{y_{ni}^2}{Y} + \sum_{i=1}^{m_r} \frac{y_{ri}^2}{Y}\right).$$

Let $INTRA_j$ denote the ratio of region j's intra–regional exports to total exports, then

$$\text{(A7.1)} \quad INTRA_j = \frac{s_j^2 - \sum_{i=1}^{m_j}\left(\frac{y_{ji}}{Y}\right)^2}{1 - \left[\sum_{i=1}^{m_a}\left(\frac{y_{ai}}{Y}\right)^2 + \sum_{i=1}^{m_e}\left(\frac{y_{ei}}{Y}\right)^2 + \sum_{i=1}^{m_n}\left(\frac{y_{ni}}{Y}\right)^2 + \sum_{i=1}^{m_r}\left(\frac{y_{ri}}{Y}\right)^2\right]}$$

If we make the simplifying assumption that the economies within each region are identical, then $y_{j1} = y_{j2} = \ldots = y_{jm_j} = y_j$ for each j. In this case, region j's GDP is $m_j y_j$,

$$GWP = Y = m_a y_a + m_e y_e + m_n y_n + m_r y_r,$$

$$s_j = \frac{m_j y_j}{Y},$$

and (A7.1) can be simplified to

$$\text{(A7.2)} \quad INTRA_j = \frac{s_j^2\left(1 - \dfrac{1}{m_j}\right)}{1 - \left[\dfrac{(s_a)^2}{m_a} + \dfrac{(s_e)^2}{m_e} + \dfrac{(s_n)^2}{m_n} + \dfrac{(s_r)^2}{m_r}\right]}.$$

Notes

1 We are grateful to Jeffrey Frenkel and Andrew Rose for their generosity in letting us use their panel data set on factors that affect bilateral trade. Corresponding Author: Professor Leonard Cheng, Department of Economics, Hong Kong University of Science and Technology, Clear Water Bay, Kowloon, Hong Kong. Tel: 2358–7621. Fax: 2358–4786. Email: leonard@ust.hk.

2 Among others, these studies include Balassa (1965), Balassa and Noland (1989), Hutchinson and Schumacher (1994), Richardson and Zhang (2001), and United Nations (1986).

3 For instance, Hutchinson and Schumacher (1994) attempted to measure the impact of the NAFTA agreement on the exports of different products exported by the Central American and Caribbean Basin economies to the U.S. and Mexico.

4 Richardson and Zhang (2001, p.197) point out that "only a few researchers have calculated RCA indexes by regional groupings of a country's trading partners." They calculated the US' RCA indices vis–a–vis different regional groupings, but did not treat those groupings as units of analysis in the sense that intra–regional trade would be netted from the regions' exports and from the world's total exports. Cheng and Leung (1999) calculated the RCA of APEC by eliminating intra–APEC trade. However, while APEC (which includes NAFTA as a subset) was treated as a single unit, the same was not done for EU.

5 The database is contained in a CD–ROM entitled *World Trade Database 1980–95*.

6 A description of this aggregation system in terms of the Standard International Trade Classification (Revision 2) is given in Appendix I.

7 See Hutchinson and Schumacher (1994, p.134) and Richardson and Zhang (2001, p.197).

8 The 'rest of the world' in Richardson and Zhang (2001) consists of 38 selected countries.

9 When the shares of GRP in GWP are based on nominal gross product, NAFTA's share rose from 30.3% in 1980 to 38.5% in 1985, but declined gradually to 31.8% by 1995. APRE's share stood at 16.8% in 1980 but increased steadily to 30.9% by 1995. As a subset of APRE, EAE's share in GWP was 3–5.5% below that of APRE's during the period. EU's share fluctuated between 22.4% and 32.6%. By

1995 the three regions were roughly equal in their GDP shares. When the shares of GRP in GWP are based on real gross product according to purchasing power parity, during the period between 1980 and 1992 NAFTA's share fluctuated narrowly between 25.2% and 26.7% while EU's share fluctuated narrowly between 19.8% and 21.5%. In contrast, APRE's share grew steadily from 18.4% in 1980 to 23.1% by 1992; EAE's share also grew steadily from 14.2% in 1980 to 17.6% by 1992.

References

Balassa, B. (1965), 'Trade Liberalization and "Revealed" Comparative Advantage', *Manchester School of Economic and Social Studies* **33**(5), pp.99–123.

Balassa, B. and Noland, M. (1989), 'The Changing Comparative Advantage of Japan and the United States', *Journal of the Japanese and International Economy* **3**, pp.174–188.

Carolan, T., Singh, N. and Talati, C. (1998). 'The Composition of US–East Asia Trade and Changing Comparative Advantage', *Journal of Development Economics* **57**, pp.361–389.

Cheng, L.K. and Leung, S.F. (1999), *Aspects of Market Integration in APEC: Trade, Foreign Direct Investment and Labor Migration*, APEC Secretariat, Singapore.

Frenkel, J.A. (1997), *Regional Trading Blocs in the World Economic System*, Institute for International Economics Washington, D.C.

Frenkel, J.A., and Rose, A. (2000), 'An Estimate of the Effect of Currency Unions on Trade and Growth', Working Paper.

Hillman, A.L. (1980), 'Observations on the Relation between "Revealed Comparative Advantage" and Comparative Advantage as Indicated by Pre–Trade Relative Prices', *Weltwirschaftliches Archiv* **116**(2), pp.315–321.

Hinloopen, J. and Van Marrewijk C. (2001), 'On the Empirical Distribution of the Balassa Index', *Weltwirschaftliches Archiv* **137**(1), pp.1–35.

Hutchinson, G.A. and Schumacher, U. (1994), 'NAFTA's Threat to Central American and Caribbean Basin Exports: A Revealed Comparative Advantage Approach', *Journal of Interamerican Studies and World Affairs* **36**(1), pp.127–148.

Krause, L.B. (1982), *U.S. Economic Policy toward the Association of Southeast Asian Nations*, Brookings Institution, Washington, D.C.

Krause, L.B. (1987), 'The Structure of Trade in Manufactured Goods in the East and Southeast Asian Region', in I. Bradford, Jr. and H. Branson (eds), *Trade and Structural Change in Pacific Asia*, NBER Conference Report, Chicago, University of Chicago Press, pp.205–225.

Richardson, J.D. and Zhang, C. (2001), 'Revealing Comparative Advantage: Chaotic or Coherent Patterns across Time and Sector and U.S. Trading Partner?', in M. Blomstrom and L. S. Goldberg (eds), *Topics in Empirical International Economics*, NBER Conference Report, Chicago, University of Chicago Press, pp.195–228.

United Nations, Industrial Development Organization (1986), *International Comparative Advantage in Manufacturing*, Vienna, Austria, United Nations.

World Bank (1995), *World Tables 1995*, Baltimore, MD, The Johns Hopkins University Press.

PART III
INTERNATIONAL FINANCE

Chapter 8

Trade, Financial Linkages and Contagion of Currency Crises

Lawrence J. Lau and Isabel K. Yan

Introduction

Contagion of currency and financial crises has been a great concern for policymakers and investors in the emerging countries because of the painful domino effects felt in these countries in the last decade. Following the Mexican devaluation of December 1994, Argentina suffered a crisis of investor confidence and, as a result, its economy slumped. The Asian Crisis of 1997 also wreaked havoc on emerging markets near and far. On July 2 1997, the value of the Thai baht dropped as much as 20 percent and the Thai government had to request "technical assistance" from the IMF. This crisis quickly spread through a number of Southeast Asian economies. On July 8 1997, Malaysia's Central Bank had to intervene to defend ringgit. Shortly after that, on July 11 1997, the Philippine peso was devalued. Indonesia had to widen its trading band for the rupiah in order to discourage speculators. Singapore also felt the pinch. On July 24 1997, the Singapore dollar began a gradual decline. On August 14 1997, Indonesia abandoned the rupiah's trading band and allowed the currency to float freely, triggering a plunge in the currency. On Oct 23 1997, Hong Kong's stock index fell 10.4 percent after the bank lending rate skyrocketed to 300 percent as a result of the monetary authority's effort to fend off speculative attacks on Hong Kong Dollar. At the same time, the South Korean Won began to weaken. On Nov 17 1997, the Bank of Korea abandoned its effort to prop up the value of the won, allowing it to fall below 1,000 against the dollar. The spillovers continued into 1998. On January 22 1998, Indonesia's currency plunged to an all–time–low, 12,000 rupiah against the dollar. On August 6 1998, the Asian markets plummeted as Hong Kong and China stepped in to defend their currencies against the attack. The Russian crisis of 1998 also exerted enormous pressure on the exchange rates and financial markets of other countries. The pressure quickly spread from one corner of the globe to the other. It forced the collapse of the Brazilian Real and brought about economic instability. The 1998 Russian Crisis pushed up Latin borrowing spreads 700 basis point to about 1,100, causing painful episodes of instability in Latin America (Mazmi, 2001).

A number of stylized facts related to the contagion of currency crises were

Table 8.1 (a) Exports of various Asian and Latin American economies to different regions in 1994

From \ To	Asia (Excluding Japan)	Latin America	EU	US	Japan
Latin American Countries					
Argentina	8.48%	**37.43%**	24.82%	10.59%	2.71%
Bolivia	0.65%	11.76%	25.85%	**26.87%**	0.17%
Brazil	10.36%	9.36%	**27.97%**	20.56%	5.90%
Chile	15.62%	10.56%	**24.21%**	17.21%	17.78%
Colombia	1.59%	10.31%	30.31%	**36.31%**	3.91%
Mexico	0.69%	1.84%	4.51%	**85.32%**	1.62%
Uruguay	8.77%	**31.42%**	21.22%	6.25%	1.08%
Venezuela	0.51%	14.02%	8.84%	**51.02%**	1.69%
European and EU Countries					
Denmark	4.87%	1.41%	**63.25%**	5.49%	4.13%
Finland	8.04%	1.45%	**58.47%**	7.19%	2.09%
France	6.25%	2.03%	**61.29%**	6.80%	1.90%
Germany	7.78%	2.77%	**57.57%**	7.95%	2.64%
Italy	7.13%	3.13%	**57.22%**	7.76%	2.13%
Spain	4.25%	4.15%	**70.57%**	4.93%	1.35%
Sweden	7.87%	2.00%	**56.28%**	8.62%	2.87%
UK	8.96%	1.78%	**53.25%**	13.02%	2.25%
Asian Countries					
China, Mainland	**40.27%**	0.97%	12.76%	17.72%	17.78%
Hong Kong	**45.62%**	1.29%	15.14%	23.24%	5.57%
India	20.36%	1.14%	**27.48%**	19.26%	7.95%
Indonesia	**33.68%**	0.92%	15.01%	14.55%	27.29%
Japan	**40.08%**	2.33%	15.48%	30.03%	-
South Korea	**32.05%**	3.03%	11.23%	21.32%	14.03%
Philippines	22.69%	0.53%	17.50%	**38.55%**	15.04%
Taiwan	-	-	-	26.15%	10.98%
Thailand	**34.12%**	0.65%	15.53%	20.90%	16.95%

Sources: *Direction of Trade* of the IMF and *Statistical Yearbook of the Republic of China*.

observed in the past decade. Firstly, contagion or spillover effects are often more regional than global (Glick and Rose, 1998). Secondly, the Russian default resulted in skyrocketing sovereign spreads in far–away Latin American countries even though Russia had few trade linkages with Latin America. Similarly, the economy of Argentina was hit hard after the 1994 Mexican crisis—a fact that is puzzling because Mexico and Argentina have only limited

Table 8.1 (b) Exports of various Asian and Latin American economies to different regions in 1997

From \ To	Asia (Excluding Japan)	Latin America	EU	US	Japan
Latin American Countries					
Argentina	11.00%	**46.57%**	15.71%	7.83%	2.19%
Bolivia	0.24%	**28.12%**	24.58%	20.73%	0.33%
Brazil	8.49%	10.25%	**26.99%**	17.45%	5.69%
Chile	18.24%	14.00%	**24.36%**	15.92%	15.72%
Colombia	1.22%	17.54%	22.68%	**37.90%**	3.14%
Mexico	0.97%	2.80%	3.64%	**85.60%**	1.05%
Uruguay	9.00%	**40.50%**	18.90%	5.98%	1.05%
Venezuela	0.58%	12.32%	6.04%	**47.24%**	0.97%
European and EU Countries					
Denmark	4.96%	1.25%	**63.54%**	4.58%	3.32%
Finland	10.07%	2.07%	**52.72%**	7.03%	1.93%
France	7.39%	2.43%	**60.57%**	6.29%	1.66%
Germany	7.49%	3.69%	**55.51%**	8.63%	2.31%
Italy	7.20%	4.67%	**54.64%**	7.93%	1.99%
Spain	3.77%	4.95%	**69.56%**	4.44%	1.05%
Sweden	8.16%	3.02%	**53.68%**	8.30%	2.93%
UK	8.61%	2.34%	**50.75%**	12.52%	2.46%
Asian Countries					
China, Mainland	**39.62%**	1.65%	13.05%	17.90%	17.40%
Hong Kong	**47.33%**	1.66%	14.73%	21.80%	6.08%
India	23.68%	2.01%	**25.14%**	19.37%	5.60%
Indonesia	**36.71%**	1.34%	15.16%	13.39%	23.36%
Japan	**42.16%**	2.82%	15.62%	28.12%	-
South Korea	**38.66%**	3.86%	11.14%	15.82%	10.84%
Philippines	26.15%	0.46%	18.01%	**35.10%**	16.63%
Taiwan	-	-	-	**24.21%**	9.58%
Thailand	**37.70%**	0.96%	15.97%	19.38%	15.17%

Sources: *Direction of Trade* of the IMF and *Statistical Yearbook of the Republic of China*.

direct and indirect trade linkages. What are the transmission channels by which the negative impacts of crises and turmoil are spread to other economies? The channels of transmission most widely studied in the literature fall mainly into following categories: direct and indirect trade linkages, financial linkages, asymmetric information and herding behaviors.

Table 8.1 (c) Exports of various Asian and Latin American economies to different regions in 2001

From \ To	Asia (Excluding Japan)	Latin America	EU	US	Japan
Latin American Countries					
Argentina	12.66%	**43.69%**	16.24%	10.30%	1.26%
Bolivia	1.16%	**52.18%**	10.31%	13.86%	0.20%
Brazil	8.44%	10.17%	**25.25%**	23.18%	3.70%
Chile	13.50%	17.58%	**24.71%**	18.46%	11.92%
Colombia	1.09%	21.68%	13.95%	**43.45%**	1.34%
Mexico	1.56%	1.78%	4.01%	**82.14%**	1.24%
Uruguay	6.56%	**32.34%**	15.30%	8.79%	1.67%
Venezuela	1.25%	8.77%	6.40%	**42.53%**	0.64%
European and EU Countries					
Denmark	4.38%	1.25%	**64.48%**	6.96%	3.50%
Finland	8.26%	2.57%	**53.14%**	9.76%	1.87%
France	5.71%	2.60%	**60.54%**	8.63%	1.53%
Germany	6.35%	3.04%	**55.21%**	10.57%	2.05%
Italy	5.92%	3.87%	**53.80%**	9.75%	1.75%
Spain	2.74%	5.05%	**69.01%**	4.63%	1.01%
Sweden	7.60%	3.90%	**51.95%**	11.26%	2.71%
UK	6.96%	1.80%	**54.42%**	15.94%	1.99%
Asian Countries					
China, Mainland	**32.92%**	2.12%	15.39%	20.42%	16.89%
Hong Kong	**48.59%**	1.50%	14.46%	22.34%	5.93%
India	**24.39%**	2.90%	24.14%	21.10%	4.53%
Indonesia	**38.33%**	1.42%	13.78%	15.35%	20.95%
Japan	**40.08%**	2.35%	15.99%	30.42%	-
South Korea	**35.49%**	4.06%	13.14%	20.93%	11.02%
Philippines	**34.36%**	0.79%	17.27%	28.24%	15.67%
Taiwan	-	-	-	22.51%	10.38%
Thailand	**35.40%**	1.30%	16.13%	20.34%	15.30%

Sources: *Direction of Trade* of the IMF and *Statistical Yearbook of the Republic of China.*

The trade linkage hypothesis is supported by the empirical findings of Eichengreen, Rose and Wyplosz (1997), Glick and Rose (1998) and Forbes (2001). The strong regional pattern of exports (as indicated in Table 8.1(a)–Table 8.1(c)) also helps to explain why contagion or spillover effects are mostly regional. Nevertheless, there are a number of limitations in the studies of trade linkages in the literature.

Table 8.2 (a) Composition of exports of various Asian and Latin American economies

Country	Industries	1995	1996	1997	1998	1999
Argentina	Total Export (million USD)	20213	23453	25423	25573	19881
	Food and Live Animals	**36.96%**	**38.29%**	**38.50%**	**36.70%**	**38.58%**
	Beverages and Tobacco	1.27%	1.26%	1.36%	1.27%	1.62%
	Crude Materials, inedible	10.21%	8.96%	5.37%	7.62%	9.65%
	Fuels, Lubricants, etc.	11.03%	13.96%	13.61%	10.23%	10.00%
	Animals,Veg.Oils,Fats,Wax	6.52%	6.33%	6.25%	8.32%	6.95%
	Chemicals Reltd. Prod. Nes.	6.12%	5.75%	6.02%	6.54%	6.97%
	Manufactured Goods	13.12%	12.05%	11.21%	10.60%	10.68%
	Machines, Transport Equip.	10.63%	10.48%	14.72%	15.76%	12.55%
	Misc Manufactured Articles	2.97%	2.36%	2.48%	2.35%	2.32%
	Goods Not Classified	1.17%	0.55%	0.48%	0.61%	0.68%
Brazil	Total Export (million USD)	45950	47537	51881	50923	46280
	Food and Live Animals	20.66%	22.42%	**21.30%**	20.42%	21.65%
	Beverages and Tobacco	2.12%	2.71%	2.76%	2.72%	2.07%
	Crude Materials, inedible	17.15%	16.65%	17.87%	18.12%	18.16%
	Fuels, Lubricants, etc.	0.76%	0.80%	0.70%	0.77%	1.11%
	Animals,Veg.Oils,Fats,Wax	2.02%	2.02%	1.66%	1.01%	0.47%
	Chemicals Reltd. Prod. Nes.	6.50%	6.71%	6.50%	6.32%	6.13%
	Manufactured Goods	**25.56%**	**22.67%**	20.67%	19.58%	19.79%
	Machines, Transport Equip.	17.04%	18.01%	20.72%	**23.74%**	**22.32%**
	Misc Manufactured Articles	6.73%	6.62%	6.24%	5.97%	6.28%
	Goods Not Classified	1.46%	1.39%	1.59%	1.35%	2.01%
Chile	Total Export (million USD)	15418	16214	16439	14868	15406
	Food and Live Animals	25.87%	27.08%	26.03%	29.66%	27.98%
	Beverages and Tobacco	1.38%	2.09%	2.90%	3.99%	3.83%
	Crude Materials, inedible	32.28%	27.41%	27.25%	24.17%	27.33%
	Fuels, Lubricants, etc.	0.43%	0.28%	0.30%	0.37%	0.53%
	Animals,Veg.Oils,Fats,Wax	0.59%	0.54%	0.15%	0.10%	0.18%
	Chemicals Reltd. Prod. Nes.	3.70%	3.72%	5.27%	5.29%	4.94%
	Manufactured Goods	**30.54%**	**31.12%**	**32.62%**	**30.47%**	**29.58%**
	Machines, Transport Equip.	1.60%	4.39%	2.36%	2.64%	2.58%
	Misc Manufactured Articles	2.37%	2.27%	2.29%	2.36%	1.91%
	Goods Not Classified	1.26%	1.10%	0.83%	0.94%	1.15%
Mainland China	Total Export (million USD)	221582	244239	274495	277061	306084
	Food and Live Animals	4.47%	4.51%	4.24%	4.01%	3.76%
	Beverages and Tobacco	0.44%	0.46%	0.33%	0.33%	0.27%
	Crude Materials, inedible	2.42%	2.17%	2.00%	1.70%	1.57%
	Fuels, Lubricants, etc.	2.39%	2.54%	2.47%	1.76%	1.48%
	Animals,Veg.Oils,Fats,Wax	0.10%	0.09%	0.14%	0.07%	0.03%
	Chemicals Reltd. Prod. Nes.	3.95%	3.70%	3.67%	3.45%	3.16%
	Manufactured Goods	15.44%	13.52%	13.64%	12.88%	12.56%
	Machines, Transport Equip.	23.13%	24.86%	26.39%	28.89%	30.47%
	Misc Manufactured Articles	**47.17%**	**47.62%**	**46.57%**	**46.33%**	**46.04%**
	Goods Not Classified	1.26%	1.10%	0.83%	0.94%	1.15%

Table 8.2 (b) Composition of exports of various Asian and Latin American economies

Country	Industries	1995	1996	1997	1998	1999
Colombia	Total Export (million USD)	10589	11096	12238	11971	12317
	Food and Live Animals	**36.91%**	**30.07%**	**33.34%**	**33.31%**	25.09%
	Beverages and Tobacco	0.27%	0.27%	0.22%	0.22%	0.24%
	Crude Materials, inedible	6.06%	6.34%	5.70%	5.56%	5.20%
	Fuels, Lubricants, etc.	24.70%	32.39%	30.80%	30.09%	**39.93%**
	Animals,Veg.Oils,Fats,Wax	0.14%	0.22%	0.27%	0.19%	0.23%
	Chemicals Reltd. Prod. Nes.	7.14%	7.76%	8.17%	7.94%	7.85%
	Manufactured Goods	10.45%	9.20%	8.48%	8.55%	8.31%
	Machines, Transport Equip.	2.63%	2.74%	3.53%	3.52%	2.46%
	Misc Manufactured Articles	8.46%	7.15%	7.23%	8.34%	7.20%
	Goods Not Classified	3.23%	3.87%	2.26%	2.31%	3.49%
India	Total Export (million USD)	30372	34810	36369	35622	35084
	Food and Live Animals	12.69%	17.08%	13.91%	14.64%	12.09%
	Beverages and Tobacco	0.24%	0.38%	0.58%	0.54%	0.46%
	Crude Materials, inedible	6.27%	6.62%	7.21%	6.39%	5.78%
	Fuels, Lubricants, etc.	1.77%	1.58%	1.40%	0.52%	0.30%
	Animals,Veg.Oils,Fats,Wax	0.77%	0.69%	0.59%	0.61%	0.69%
	Chemicals Reltd. Prod. Nes.	7.04%	7.84%	8.84%	9.00%	9.19%
	Manufactured Goods	**39.77%**	**36.18%**	**37.77%**	**38.30%**	**40.50%**
	Machines, Transport Equip.	7.44%	8.15%	8.75%	7.94%	7.97%
	Misc Manufactured Articles	23.61%	21.11%	20.45%	21.66%	22.45%
	Goods Not Classified	0.40%	0.38%	0.49%	0.40%	0.58%
Indonesia	Total Export (million USD)	44097	49526	51903	48980	50117
	Food and Live Animals	8.97%	8.38%	8.57%	9.26%	8.06%
	Beverages and Tobacco	0.28%	0.27%	0.37%	0.38%	0.34%
	Crude Materials, inedible	12.33%	11.34%	10.25%	9.96%	9.16%
	Fuels, Lubricants, etc.	**25.54%**	**27.14%**	**25.35%**	19.03%	**21.56%**
	Animals,Veg.Oils,Fats,Wax	2.88%	3.11%	3.27%	3.46%	2.73%
	Chemicals Reltd. Prod. Nes.	3.34%	3.26%	3.56%	4.61%	4.15%
	Manufactured Goods	20.89%	18.99%	18.86%	19.75%	20.13%
	Machines, Transport Equip.	6.70%	8.70%	10.24%	12.48%	14.16%
	Misc Manufactured Articles	18.74%	18.47%	18.95%	**19.52%**	18.84%
	Goods Not Classified	0.31%	0.33%	0.58%	1.55%	0.86%
S.Korea	Total Export (million USD)	106460	109312	113039	112958	124662
	Food and Live Animals	2.30%	2.23%	2.03%	2.06%	2.00%
	Beverages and Tobacco	0.10%	0.14%	0.11%	0.11%	0.13%
	Crude Materials, inedible	1.57%	1.52%	1.62%	1.47%	1.20%
	Fuels, Lubricants, etc.	1.94%	2.72%	3.38%	3.43%	3.84%
	Animals,Veg.Oils,Fats,Wax	0.01%	0.01%	0.02%	0.02%	0.01%
	Chemicals Reltd. Prod. Nes.	7.82%	7.72%	8.46%	8.97%	7.50%
	Manufactured Goods	21.03%	20.94%	20.73%	22.01%	18.62%
	Machines, Transport Equip.	**51.31%**	**51.51%**	**51.09%**	**49.66%**	**55.39%**
	Misc Manufactured Articles	12.04%	10.56%	9.60%	9.31%	9.39%
	Goods Not Classified	1.87%	2.64%	2.95%	2.96%	1.92%

Table 8.2 (c) Composition of exports of various Asian and Latin American economies

Country	Industries	1995	1996	1997	1998	1999
Malaysia	Total Export (million USD)	79348	85237	87661	80235	85512
	Food and Live Animals	2.50%	2.34%	2.23%	2.11%	1.88%
	Beverages and Tobacco	0.09%	0.14%	0.18%	0.15%	0.18%
	Crude Materials, inedible	7.40%	6.13%	5.29%	3.88%	3.63%
	Fuels, Lubricants, etc.	6.66%	7.47%	7.19%	5.94%	5.49%
	Animals,Veg.Oils,Fats,Wax	6.10%	4.75%	4.51%	5.95%	3.68%
	Chemicals Reltd. Prod. Nes.	2.86%	3.04%	2.99%	3.13%	2.97%
	Manufactured Goods	7.55%	8.03%	7.95%	7.64%	7.61%
	Machines, Transport Equip.	**55.65%**	**57.19%**	**58.90%**	**60.12%**	**63.63%**
	Misc Manufactured Articles	9.77%	9.81%	9.76%	9.86%	9.35%
	Goods Not Classified	1.42%	1.10%	1.00%	1.21%	1.59%
Mexico	Total Export (million USD)	78085	91735	106480	115161	130668
	Food and Live Animals	6.62%	5.72%	5.30%	5.24%	4.59%
	Beverages and Tobacco	0.79%	0.86%	0.92%	0.96%	1.00%
	Crude Materials, inedible	2.51%	1.98%	1.71%	1.38%	1.13%
	Fuels, Lubricants, etc.	9.70%	9.51%	9.90%	5.93%	6.80%
	Animals,Veg.Oils,Fats,Wax	0.08%	0.07%	0.03%	0.05%	0.04%
	Chemicals Reltd. Prod. Nes.	4.45%	3.95%	3.65%	3.34%	2.94%
	Manufactured Goods	9.99%	9.42%	8.94%	8.74%	7.63%
	Machines, Transport Equip.	**50.25%**	**52.54%**	**52.63%**	**55.60%**	**56.93%**
	Misc Manufactured Articles	12.14%	12.64%	13.70%	15.25%	15.16%
	Goods Not Classified	3.47%	3.31%	3.22%	3.51%	3.78%
Philippines	Total Export (million USD)	18721	22971	28401	30805	34542
	Food and Live Animals	9.99%	8.07%	6.30%	5.92%	5.31%
	Beverages and Tobacco	0.37%	0.37%	0.35%	0.26%	0.29%
	Crude Materials, inedible	4.60%	3.41%	2.86%	2.09%	1.72%
	Fuels, Lubricants, etc.	1.29%	1.52%	0.96%	0.65%	0.58%
	Animals,Veg.Oils,Fats,Wax	4.36%	2.92%	1.94%	2.42%	1.29%
	Chemicals Reltd. Prod. Nes.	1.42%	1.14%	0.99%	0.84%	0.65%
	Manufactured Goods	6.42%	5.41%	4.32%	3.84%	4.00%
	Machines, Transport Equip.	**46.19%**	**56.28%**	**64.28%**	**66.17%**	**70.30%**
	Misc Manufactured Articles	24.03%	19.59%	16.48%	15.28%	13.85%
	Goods Not Classified	1.32%	1.30%	1.53%	2.53%	2.02%
Singapore	Total Export (million USD)	79694	86127	86140	76946	74457
	Food and Live Animals	1.39%	1.37%	1.36%	1.34%	1.25%
	Beverages and Tobacco	0.37%	0.27%	0.26%	0.20%	0.20%
	Crude Materials, inedible	1.53%	1.10%	0.99%	0.91%	0.68%
	Fuels, Lubricants, etc.	10.86%	12.11%	10.46%	8.36%	6.79%
	Animals,Veg.Oils,Fats,Wax	0.41%	0.28%	0.25%	0.33%	0.32%
	Chemicals Reltd. Prod. Nes.	5.72%	5.60%	6.61%	7.12%	7.73%
	Manufactured Goods	3.73%	3.53%	3.59%	3.50%	3.02%
	Machines, Transport Equip.	**67.27%**	**67.66%**	**68.06%**	**68.44%**	**69.84%**
	Misc Manufactured Articles	6.30%	5.57%	5.62%	6.18%	6.75%
	Goods Not Classified	2.44%	2.52%	2.80%	3.61%	3.42%

Table 8.2 (d) Composition of exports of various Asian and Latin American economies

Country	Industries	1995	1996	1997	1998	1999
Taiwan	Total Export (million USD)	122412	127259	129955	123801	132504
	Food and Live Animals	3.44%	3.14%	1.72%	1.50%	1.47%
	Beverages and Tobacco	0.07%	0.04%	0.04%	0.04%	0.04%
	Crude Materials, inedible	1.74%	1.52%	1.55%	1.33%	1.17%
	Fuels, Lubricants, etc.	0.19%	0.19%	0.34%	0.26%	0.20%
	Animals,Veg.Oils,Fats,Wax	0.03%	0.04%	0.02%	0.03%	0.03%
	Chemicals Reltd. Prod. Nes.	8.01%	7.47%	7.08%	6.81%	6.64%
	Manufactured Goods	21.53%	20.86%	21.00%	20.92%	18.89%
	Machines, Transport Equip.	**48.67%**	**51.27%**	**53.42%**	**54.38%**	**57.22%**
	Misc Manufactured Articles	15.29%	14.51%	13.73%	13.39%	12.78%
	Goods Not Classified	1.03%	0.96%	1.09%	1.34%	1.56%
Thailand	Total Export (million USD)	49922	54373	56617	53831	56677
	Food and Live Animals	19.45%	18.85%	16.74%	16.90%	15.30%
	Beverages and Tobacco	0.23%	0.34%	0.31%	0.21%	0.18%
	Crude Materials, inedible	6.51%	6.16%	5.34%	4.52%	3.84%
	Fuels, Lubricants, etc.	0.39%	0.92%	1.50%	1.03%	1.38%
	Animals,Veg.Oils,Fats,Wax	0.06%	0.05%	0.06%	0.08%	0.06%
	Chemicals Reltd. Prod. Nes.	2.82%	2.99%	3.57%	4.35%	4.35%
	Manufactured Goods	11.15%	10.90%	10.75%	10.93%	11.21%
	Machines, Transport Equip.	**39.08%**	**40.84%**	**43.19%**	**42.72%**	**44.33%**
	Misc Manufactured Articles	18.99%	17.46%	16.87%	17.63%	17.60%
	Goods Not Classified	1.30%	1.49%	1.65%	1.63%	1.75%
Uruguay	Total Export (million USD)	2463	2643	2957	3098	2397
	Food and Live Animals	**41.74%**	**45.21%**	**43.96%**	**46.13%**	**42.68%**
	Beverages and Tobacco	0.45%	0.91%	1.12%	2.03%	2.42%
	Crude Materials, inedible	13.93%	13.70%	14.14%	9.36%	10.93%
	Fuels, Lubricants, etc.	0.93%	1.02%	0.44%	0.87%	0.88%
	Animals,Veg.Oils,Fats,Wax	0.49%	0.61%	0.71%	0.74%	0.71%
	Chemicals Reltd. Prod. Nes.	7.59%	6.62%	6.59%	7.04%	8.14%
	Manufactured Goods	17.05%	16.57%	16.94%	14.98%	15.85%
	Machines, Transport Equip.	6.46%	4.09%	5.44%	8.13%	9.39%
	Misc Manufactured Articles	10.76%	9.84%	8.59%	8.23%	8.14%
	Goods Not Classified	0.61%	1.44%	2.06%	2.49%	0.88%
Venezuela	Total Export (million USD)	17866	21862	23332	17183	19081
	Food and Live Animals	2.21%	2.21%	2.14%	2.57%	2.57%
	Beverages and Tobacco	0.30%	0.37%	0.37%	0.41%	0.51%
	Crude Materials, inedible	3.65%	3.28%	3.27%	3.94%	3.44%
	Fuels, Lubricants, etc.	**70.20%**	**74.48%**	**73.62%**	**68.71%**	**75.13%**
	Animals,Veg.Oils,Fats,Wax	0.03%	0.02%	0.01%	0.02%	0.05%
	Chemicals Reltd. Prod. Nes.	5.78%	5.07%	5.16%	5.72%	4.37%
	Manufactured Goods	13.38%	10.96%	11.67%	13.09%	10.64%
	Machines, Transport Equip.	3.41%	2.74%	3.06%	4.29%	1.99%
	Misc Manufactured Articles	0.54%	0.39%	0.44%	0.59%	0.49%
	Goods Not Classified	0.50%	0.48%	0.29%	0.66%	0.81%

Table 8.3 (a) Percentage of exports in 1995 to different destinations

Country	Rank	Industry 0: Food and Live Animals		Industry 1: Beverages and Tobacco		Industry 2: Crude Materials, inedible	
Argentina	1st	Brazil	27.3%	Brazil	19.1%	Netherlands	11.4%
	2nd	Germany	8.6%	Paraguay	12.9%	Germany	10.9%
	3rd	USA	7.1%	Spain	10.9%	Spain	9.3%
	4th	Spain	5.6%	UK	9.8%	Italy	8.9%
	5th	Italy	5.3%	USA	9.4%	France	6.6%
	6th	Netherlands	5.2%	Japan	9.0%	Brazil	5.9%
	7th	UK	3.7%	Germany	7.0%	China	4.8%
	8th	Chile	3.5%	France	4.7%	Portugal	3.5%
	9th	Japan	3.2%	Uruguay	3.9%	Turkey	2.6%
	10th	France	2.8%	Chile	2.0%	Chile	2.5%
		Industry 3: Fuels and Lubricants, etc.		Industry 4: Animal,Veg.Oils,Fats, Wax		Industry 5: Chemical Reltd. Prod. Nes.	
	1st	Brazil	36.7%	Brazil	9.6%	Brazil	27.6%
	2nd	Chile	22.9%	Venezuela	9.4%	Chile	12.0%
	3rd	USA	18.2%	S.Afr.Cus.Un	9.3%	USA	10.4%
	4th	Puraguay	6.5%	Chile	7.9%	Uruguay	9.1%
	5th	Uruguay	5.0%	Mexico	6.4%	Paraguay	4.6%
	6th	Colombia	2.4%	India	3.6%	Italy	2.9%
	7th	Bolivia	1.8%	China	5.7%	Mexico	2.8%
	8th	Spain	1.2%	Turkey	5.4%	HK	2.7%
	9th	Peru	0.9%	Colombia	4.3%	Germany	2.7%
	10th	Italy	0.9%	Pakistan	4.2%	Spain	2.4%
		Industry 6: Manufactured Goods		Industry 7: Machines, Transport Equip.		Industry 8: Misc. Manufacture Article	
	1st	Brazil	20.6%	Brazil	71.0%	USA	34.4%
	2nd	USA	14.4%	USA	4.3%	Brazil	29.5%
	3rd	Chile	7.2%	Uruguay	4.0%	Uruguay	6.5%
	4th	Italy	7.1%	Chile	3.6%	Chile	5.5%
	5th	HK	6.1%	France	2.4%	Italy	4.3%
	6th	Uruguay	4.6%	Paraguay	2.2%	Paraguay	4.0%
	7th	Japan	4.0%	Spain	1.8%	Spain	2.3%
	8th	Paraguay	3.1%	Peru	1.0%	Peru	2.2%
	9th	Germany	2.7%	Venezuela	0.8%	Germany	1.8%
	10th	China	2.5%	UK	0.8%	Colombia	1.7%

Sources: *Trade Analysis System* of the United Nations. The re–export data is from the *World Trade Atlas* Database.

Firstly, with the exception of Forbes (2001), measures of trade linkages in the literature fail to take into account the composition of trade. The composition of trade is crucial in determining the extent of trade competition between a country and the initial crisis country. Two countries should be considered as strong trade competitors only when they are exporting similar products or services to the same destination countries. Table 8.2(a)–Table 8.2(d) show the composition of exports for various Asian and Latin American countries and Table 8.3(a)–Table 8.4(p) give the major export destinations of

Table 8.3 (b) Percentage of exports in 1995 to different destinations

Country	Rank	Industry 0: Food and Live Animals		Industry 1: Beverages and Tobacco		Industry 2: Crude Materials, inedible	
Brazil	1st	USA	12.1%	USA	15.4%	Japan	16.6%
	2nd	France	9.8%	Paraguay	12.8%	Germany	13.6%
	3rd	Germany	8.8%	Germany	12.8%	USA	11.6%
	4th	Netherlands	8.5%	UK	11.4%	France	7.1%
	5th	Japan	8.3%	Japan	7.6%	Italy	6.7%
	6th	Italy	6.3%	Netherlands	3.8%	Korea	5.0%
	7th	Spain	4.8%	Spain	3.1%	Netherlands	4.9%
	8th	UK	4.1%	Italy	2.8%	Spain	4.7%
	9th	Argentina	3.8%	Philippines	2.5%	Belgium–Lux	3.8%
	10th	Denmark	2.2%	Belgium–Lux	2.4%	UK	3.7%
		Industry 3: Fuels and Lubricants, etc.		Industry 4: Animal,Veg.Oils,Fats, Wax		Industry 5: Chemical Reltd. Prod. Nes.	
	1st	USA	40.9%	China	59.6%	Argentina	24.3%
	2nd	Argentina	13.7%	Pakistan	7.6%	USA	14.3%
	3rd	Paraguay	9.7%	India	3.7%	Japan	9.3%
	4th	Uruguay	7.7%	USA	3.6%	Chile	4.6%
	5th	Canada	6.9%	Netherlands	2.7%	Germany	4.0%
	6th	Italy	3.7%	Japan	2.1%	Paraguay	3.4%
	7th	Colombia	3.4%	Turkey	2.1%	Uruguay	2.9%
	8th	Germany	2.0%	Korea	1.6%	Netherlands	2.3%
	9th	Indonesia	1.7%	Germany	1.4%	Colombia	2.3%
	10th	Spain	1.7%	Singapore	1.4%	France	2.2%
		Industry 6: Manufactured Goods		Industry 7: Machines, Transport Equip.		Industry 8: Misc. Manufacture Articles	
	1st	USA	22.8%	USA	26.1%	USA	50.7%
	2nd	Japan	11.4%	Argentina	19.7%	Germany	6.6%
	3rd	Argentina	8.6%	Chile	6.2%	Argentina	6.5%
	4th	Korea	5.9%	Germany	6.1%	UK	5.3%
	5th	Germany	5.0%	Italy	4.1%	Frnace	3.1%
	6th	Italy	3.6%	Uruguay	3.1%	Singapore	2.4%
	7th	Chile	3.5%	Paraguay	2.7%	Netherlands	2.3%
	8th	UK	2.9%	Peru	2.7%	Chile	2.1%
	9th	Thailand	2.2%	UK	2.3%	Canada	2.0%
	10th	Canada	1.8%	Colombia	2.0%	Uruguay	1.7%

Sources: *Trade Analysis System* of the United Nations. The re–export data is from the *World Trade Atlas* Database.

various Asian and Latin American countries in 1995 and 1999 respectively. Table 8.2(a)–Table 8.2(d) indicate that the Southeast Asian countries have a very similar export structure. In the Southeast Asia, Machine and Transport Equipments (SITC category 7) is the most important category of exports for South Korea, Malaysia, the Philippines, Singapore, Taiwan and Thailand. For Mainland China, export of machine and transport equipment is second only to that of the category of miscellaneous manufactured articles. During the last

Table 8.3 (c) Percentage of exports in 1995 to different destinations

Country	Rank	Industry 0: Food and Live Animals		Industry 1: Beverages and Tobacco		Industry 2: Crude Materials, inedible	
Chile	1st	Japan	22.4%	USA	28.3%	Japan	35.4%
	2nd	USA	22.4%	UK	13.7%	Germany	10.0%
	3rd	Brazil	6.1%	Canada	9.4%	USA	8.0%
	4th	Germany	5.6%	Japan	5.2%	Korea	7.9%
	5th	Nether.	5.1%	Denmark	4.2%	Brazil	6.8%
	6th	Spain	3.8%	Paraguay	3.8%	Spain	3.8%
	7th	UK	3.0%	Argentina	3.3%	China	3.5%
	8th	Canada	2.9%	Sweden	3.3%	UK	2.7%
	9th	France	2.8%	Germany	2.8%	Italy	2.4%
	10th	Argentina	2.4%	Norway	2.4%	France	2.2%
		Industry 3: Fuels and Lubricants, etc.		Industry 4: Animal,Veg.Oils,Fats, Wax		Industry 5: Chemical Reltd. Prod. Nes.	
	1st	USA	40.9%	Nether.	24.2%	USA	22.6%
	2nd	Argentina	21.2%	Norway	18.7%	Nether.	17.0%
	3rd	El Salvador	10.6%	Mexico	15.4%	Germany	7.0%
	4th	Bolivia	9.1%	Japan	12.1%	Peru	6.5%
	5th	Peru	9.1%	Germany	8.8%	Argentina	5.8%
	6th	Paraguay	3.0%	UK	7.7%	Spain	5.6%
	7th	Ecuador	1.5%	S.Afr.	3.3%	Japan	3.2%
	8th	Brazil	1.5%	Argentina	1.1%	Bolivia	3.0%
	9th	Belgium	1.5%	Ecuador	1.1%	Ecuador	3.0%
	10th	Mexico	0.0%	China	1.1%	Mexico	2.6%
		Industry 6: Manufactured Goods		Industry 7: Machines, Transport Equip.		Industry 8: Misc. Manufacture Articles	
	1st	France	12.7%	Argentina	33.7%	USA	28.2%
	2nd	Japan	10.7%	Peru	14.2%	Brazil	21.1%
	3rd	USA	9.9%	Colombia	10.6%	Agentina	18.1%
	4th	Italy	9.4%	Brazil	6.1%	Peru	6.8%
	5th	Brazil	8.7%	Bolivia	4.5%	Paraguay	4.7%
	6th	Germany	7.9%	Paraguay	4.1%	Bolivia	3.6%
	7th	Singapore	6.2%	USA	3.7%	Ecuador	3.0%
	8th	Indonesia	4.1%	Israel	3.7%	Mexico	1.9%
	9th	Argentina	4.0%	Ecuador	2.8%	Uruguay	1.6%
	10th	UK	3.8%	UK	2.8%	Germany	1.6%

Sources: *Trade Analysis System* of the United Nations. The re–export data is from the *World Trade Atlas* Database.

decade, South Korea, Malaysia, the Philippines, Singapore, Taiwan and Thailand have all been major exporters of electronic microcircuit and micro–assemblies products. Out of the 1075 4–digit SITC categories, electronic microcircuit and micro–assemblies products alone accounted for 12.7 percent of South Korea's total export, 15 percent of Malaysia's total export, 3 percent of Philippines's total export, 11 percent of Singapore's total export, 7.9 percent of Taiwan's total export and 4.7 percent of Thailand's total exports in 1997. In addition, in the machines and transport equipments industry, the US was the

Table 8.3 (d) Percentage of exports in 1995 to different destinations

Country	Rank	Industry 0: Food and Live Animals		Industry 1: Beverages and Tobacco		Industry 2: Crude Materials, inedible	
China	1st	Japan	46.8%	HK (for re–export)	64.9% (15.29%)	Japan	29.6%
	2nd	HK (for re–export)	17.8% (4.45%)	Singapore	13.4%	HK (for re–export)	12.2% (12.0%)
	3rd	USA	6.7%	Indonesia	5.0%	Korea	10.3%
	4th	Korea	4.3%	Japan	3.7%	USA	7.5%
	5th	Germany	3.7%	Macau	2.2%	Germany	6.2%
	6th	Singapore	3.3%	USA	1.5%	Italy	5.1%
	7th	France	2.1%	Germany	1.4%	Nether.	3.6%
	8th	Malaysia	1.9%	UK	1.0%	Indonesia	2.6%
	9th	Indonesia	1.3%	Philippines	0.8%	Thailand	2.2%
	10th	Canada	1.1%	Egypt	0.7%	India	2.2%
		Industry 3: Fuels and Lubricants, etc.		Industry 4: Animal,Veg.Oils,Fats, Wax		Industry 5: Chemical Reltd. Prod. Nes.	
	1st	Japan	40.4%	HK (for re–export)	80.0% (45.88%)	HK (for re–export)	18.5% (8.49%)
	2nd	Korea	16.2%	Japan	5.2%	Japan	14.5%
	3rd	HK (for re–export)	10.8% (0.27%)	Korea	3.5%	USA	10.7%
	4th	USA	9.3%	Germany	1.7%	Korea	7.0%
	5th	Singapore	4.1%	USA	1.3%	Germany	6.4%
	6th	India	2.5%	India	1.3%	Indonesia	3.2%
	7th	Italy	1.7%	Italy	1.3%	Thailand	3.1%
	8th	France	1.5%	Malaysia	0.9%	India	3.0%
	9th	Indonesia	1.4%	Singapore	0.9%	Italy	2.8%
	10th	Brazil	1.3%	UK	0.4%	UK	2.7%
		Industry 6: Manufactured Goods		Industry 7: Machines, Transport Equip.		Industry 8: Misc. Manufacture Articles	
	1st	HK (for re–export)	30.2% (12.23%)	HK (for re–export)	36.8% (30.83%)	HK (for re–export)	33.3% (25.12%)
	2nd	Japan	15.0%	USA	24.4%	USA	27.2%
	3rd	USA	13.5%	Japan	9.1%	Japan	15.7%
	4th	Korea	9.4%	Germany	5.8%	Germany	5.2%
	5th	Germany	4.1%	Singapore	3.2%	France	2.6%
	6th	Singapore	3.0%	France	2.5%	Canada	1.8%
	7th	Thailand	2.8%	Italy	1.6%	Italy	1.6%
	8th	Italy	2.0%	Korea	1.5%	Astralia	1.5%
	9th	Malaysia	1.8%	Canada	1.4%	UK	1.3%
	10th	UK	1.5%	UK	1.4%	Spain	0.9%

Sources: *Trade Analysis System* of the United Nations. The re–export data is from the *World Trade Atlas* Database.

most important export destination for all of the Southeast Asian countries in 1997. Because the Southeast Asian countries share a similar export structure and export destinations, there is a high risk of contagion of currency crises due

Table 8.3 (e) Percentage of exports in 1995 to different destinations

Country	Rank	Industry 0: Food and Live Animals		Industry 1: Beverages and Tobacco		Industry 2: Crude Materials, inedible	
Colombia	1st	Germany	26.0%	Spain	24.1%	USA	62.1%
	2nd	USA	23.2%	USA	17.2%	UK	6.9%
	3rd	Japan	7.0%	Venezuela	10.3%	Canada	3.9%
	4th	France	4.5%	France	10.3%	Germany	3.4%
	5th	Venezuela	4.0%	Ecuador	6.9%	Nether.	2.6%
	6th	Spain	3.7%	Algeria	6.9%	Venezuela	2.3%
	7th	Canada	3.6%	Germany	3.4%	Japan	2.2%
	8th	Nether.	3.5%	Belgium	3.4%	Spain	1.7%
	9th	Italy	3.3%	Paraguay	3.4%	Peru	1.7%
	10th	Sweden	2.3%	Peru	3.4%	France	1.4%
		Industry 3: Fuels and Lubricants, etc.		Industry 4: Animal,Veg.Oils,Fats, Wax		Industry 5: Chemical Reltd. Prod. Nes.	
	1st	USA	60.8%	Mexico	26.7%	Venezuela	26.7%
	2nd	Peru	12.3%	Venezuela	26.7%	Peru	15.7%
	3rd	UK	4.7%	USA	20.0%	Ecuador	14.7%
	4th	Nether.	3.9%	Honduras	13.3%	Chile	12.3%
	5th	Canada	3.6%	UK	0.0%	USA	9.3%
	6th	France	2.5%	Nether.	0.0%	Brazil	3.7%
	7th	Costa Rica	1.8%	Germany	0.0%	Mexico	2.6%
	8th	Germany	1.8%	Peru	0.0%	Costa Rica	2.2%
	9th	Portugal	1.6%	France	0.0%	Guatemala	1.9%
	10th	Spain	1.3%	Ecuador	0.0%	Panama	1.7%
		Industry 6: Manufactured Goods		Industry 7: Machines, Transport Equip.		Industry 8: Misc. Manufacture Articles	
	1st	USA	23.2%	Venezuela	38.8%	USA	52.5%
	2nd	Venezuela	15.8%	Ecuador	20.5%	Venezuela	16.5%
	3rd	Japan	10.3%	Peru	7.9%	Ecuador	5.1%
	4th	Ecuador	9.2%	USA	5.0%	Peru	3.3%
	5th	Peru	5.1%	UK	3.6%	Germany	3.1%
	6th	Finland	4.6%	Mexico	3.6%	Mexico	2.9%
	7th	France	4.4%	Costa Rica	2.2%	Brazil	2.7%
	8th	Germany	3.4%	Israel	2.2%	Chile	2.1%
	9th	Belgium	3.0%	Brazil	1.4%	Argentina	1.7%
	10th	Spain	2.6%	Panama	1.4%	Panama	1.3%

Sources: *Trade Analysis System* of the United Nations. The re-export data is from the *World Trade Atlas* Database.

to competitive devaluation.

In Latin America, however, the structure of export is more diverse. While Mexico's most important export products are transportation vehicles, which fall into the category of machines and transport equipment, Argentina's and Uruguay's most important exports are bovine related products, which fall into the category of food and live animals. For Brazil, non–roasted coffee in the category of food and live animals and non–agglomerated iron ore in the category of manufactured goods are the most important exports during the

Table 8.3 (f) Percentage of exports in 1995 to different destinations

Country	Rank	Industry 0: Food and Live Animals		Industry 1: Beverages and Tobacco		Industry 2: Crude Materials, inedible	
India	1st	Japan	18.0%	UK	29.2%	Japan	31.1%
	2nd	USA	11.6%	Germany	9.7%	USA	10.4%
	3rd	Saudi Ara.	6.3%	Saudi Ara.	8.3%	Italy	9.6%
	4th	UK	6.0%	USA	6.9%	China	9.3%
	5th	Italy	4.4%	Belgium	6.9%	Korea	4.7%
	6th	Indonesia	4.3%	Nether.	5.6%	Germany	4.3%
	7th	Malaysia	4.2%	Banglad.	2.8%	Indonesia	2.7%
	8th	Germany	3.9%	Poland	2.8%	UK	2.5%
	9th	Banglad.	3.6%	France	2.8%	Nether.	2.4%
	10th	Thailand	3.2%	Argentina	2.8%	Pakistan	2.2%
		Industry 3: Fuels and Lubricants, etc.		Industry 4: Animal,Veg.Oils,Fats, Wax		Industry 5: Chemical Reltd. Prod. Nes.	
	1st	Korea	39.0%	France	20.0%	USA	12.2%
	2nd	Japan	19.7%	USA	15.7%	Italy	7.2%
	3rd	USA	8.7%	China	12.3%	UK	6.5%
	4th	France	7.4%	Japan	10.6%	HK	6.1%
	5th	Banglad.	5.0%	Germany	8.5%	Germany	6.0%
	6th	UK	3.7%	Brazil	7.2%	Korea	4.2%
	7th	Singapore	3.2%	Italy	5.1%	Thailand	4.0%
	8th	Brazil	2.6%	Thailand	4.7%	Singapore	3.9%
	9th	Turkey	2.2%	Nether.	2.1%	France	3.6%
	10th	China	1.7%	UK	2.1%	Indonesia	3.4%
		Industry 6: Manufactured Goods		Industry 7: Machines, Transport Equip.		Industry 8: Misc. Manufacture Articles	
	1st	USA	22.4%	USA	15.0%	USA	27.8%
	2nd	HK	12.3%	UK	11.7%	Germany	17.2%
	3rd	Japan	9.9%	Singapore	9.8%	UK	11.9%
	4th	Belgium	7.7%	Germany	6.5%	France	7.0%
	5th	Germany	6.0%	Banglad.	4.4%	Italy	4.9%
	6th	UK	5.6%	Malaysia	4.1%	Nether.	3.5%
	7th	Italy	3.5%	Tanzania	3.0%	Japan	2.9%
	8th	Singapore	2.9%	HK	2.8%	Canada	2.6%
	9th	Thailand	2.8%	Nether.	2.7%	Swtiz.	2.0%
	10th	France	2.2%	Indonesia	2.7%	Australia	1.7%

Sources: *Trade Analysis System* of the United Nations. The re–export data is from the *World Trade Atlas* Database.

periods of 1995–1996 and 1997–1999 respectively. For Chile and Venezuela, the most important exports are copper and aluminum products respectively, both of which are included in the category of manufactured goods.

Even though trade competition is less severe in Latin America than in Southeast Asia, trade linkage is still an important channel of contagion in the region because intra–regional trade is very important for the Latin American countries. For instance, Brazil is a major export destination for both Argentina and Uruguay. In 1999, exports to Brazil accounted for 26 percent and 44.3

Table 8.3 (g) Percentage of exports in 1995 to different destinations

Country	Rank	Industry 0: Food and Live Animals		Industry 1: Beverages and Tobacco		Industry 2: Crude Materials, inedible	
Indonesia	1st	Japan	38.3%	USA	14.5%	Japan	31.6%
	2nd	USA	14.8%	Belgium	12.9%	USA	20.3%
	3rd	HK	6.1%	Spain	12.9%	Korea	10.8%
	4th	Germany	5.4%	Germany	12.1%	Philip.	4.4%
	5th	Malaysia	5.1%	Nether.	12.1%	China	4.1%
	6th	Nether.	3.6%	UK	7.3%	Spain	3.6%
	7th	Korea	3.1%	Malaysia	7.3%	Italy	3.1%
	8th	UK	2.7%	Denmark	4.0%	Germany	2.9%
	9th	China	2.1%	France	3.2%	Malaysia	2.2%
	10th	France	2.0%	Switz.	2.4%	Canada	1.7%
		Industry 3: Fuels and Lubricants, etc.		Industry 4: Animal,Veg.Oils,Fats, Wax		Industry 5: Chemical Reltd. Prod. Nes.	
	1st	Japan	60.7%	Nether.	17.5%	China	12.1%
	2nd	Korea	15.1%	Germany	16.9%	Japan	11.7%
	3rd	China	6.7%	India	6.5%	HK	11.0%
	4th	USA	6.5%	Italy	6.5%	Thailand	9.7%
	5th	Australia	3.4%	China	5.5%	Malaysia	8.9%
	6th	Italy	1.3%	spain	5.4%	India	8.1%
	7th	India	1.1%	Kenya	4.8%	Korea	7.8%
	8th	Thailand	1.0%	Belgium	4.8%	Philip.	7.1%
	9th	HK	0.7%	UK	4.1%	USA	4.7%
	10th	New Zeal.	0.7%	Japan	3.7%	Germany	2.4%
		Industry 6: Manufactured Goods		Industry 7: Machines, Transport Equip.		Industry 8: Misc. Manufacture Articles	
	1st	Japan	26.5%	USA	42.8%	USA	37.8%
	2nd	USA	10.6%	Japan	13.6%	Japan	12.8%
	3rd	HK	9.5%	Malaysia	7.6%	Germany	10.0%
	4th	China	7.5%	Germany	4.4%	UK	7.6%
	5th	Korea	7.2%	HK	3.9%	France	5.3%
	6th	UK	4.8%	France	3.8%	Nether.	3.9%
	7th	Germany	4.2%	UK	3.6%	Italy	3.4%
	8th	Malaysia	4.0%	Nether.	2.4%	Spain	2.0%
	9th	Australia	2.5%	Spain	2.4%	Canada	1.9%
	10th	Thailand	2.4%	Thailand	2.2%	Australia	1.6%

Sources: *Trade Analysis System* of the United Nations. The re–export data is from the *World Trade Atlas* Database.

percent of Argentina's and Uruguay's exports in the food and live animals industry—the most important export industry for both countries. Income effect that arises from close, direct trade linkages is a source of contagion during currency crises.

Secondly, contrary to the symmetry assumption that underlies the trade linkage measures of Eichengreen, Rose and Wyplosz (1997), trade competition between two countries need not be symmetric because the importance of the trade sector may be very different for the two countries which have different

Table 8.3 (h) Percentage of exports in 1995 to different destinations

Country	Rank	Industry 0: Food and Live Animals		Industry 1: Beverages and Tobacco		Industry 2: Crude Materials, inedible	
S.Korea	1st	Japan	69.3%	Japan	40.8%	China	30.6%
	2nd	HK	7.8%	HK	34.0%	Japan	20.9%
	3rd	USA	6.5%	USA	11.7%	HK	10.7%
	4th	China	2.6%	UK	3.9%	USA	10.1%
	5th	Thailand	2.2%	Greece	1.9%	Indonesia	7.4%
	6th	Spain	2.0%	Germany	1.9%	Pakistan	2.7%
	7th	Singapore	1.5%	Indonesia	1.9%	India	2.7%
	8th	Indonesia	1.1%	Singapore	1.0%	Thailand	1.5%
	9th	Canada	0.9%	Russian	0.0%	UK	1.1%
	10th	Australia	0.7%	Turkey	0.0%	Germany	1.1%
		Industry 3: Fuels and Lubricants, etc.		Industry 4: Animal,Veg.Oils,Fats, Wax		Industry 5: Chemical Reltd. Prod. Nes.	
	1st	Japan	46.1%	Japand	20.0%	China	28.3%
	2nd	China	19.1%	Thailand	20.0%	HK	14.3%
	3rd	HK	12.7%	Nether.	20.%	Japan	10.3%
	4th	USA	8.3%	China	10.0%	Indonesia	6.1%
	5th	Thailand	6.3%	USA	10.0%	USA	5.7%
	6th	Singapore	2.3%	Indonesia	10.0%	Thailand	5.6%
	7th	Malaysia	1.8%	Russian	0.0%	India	3.4%
	8th	Philippines	1.1%	HK	0.0%	Philip.	3.1%
	9th	Indonesia	1.0%	Kenya	0.0%	Malaysia	2.7%
	10th	India	0.5%	Malaysia	0.0%	UK	2.0%
		Industry 6: Manufactured Goods		Industry 7: Machines, Transport Equip.		Industry 8: Misc. Manufacture Articles	
	1st	China	19.8%	USA	30.9%	USA	34.2%
	2nd	Japan	18.1%	Japan	10.8%	Japan	28.9%
	3rd	USA	15.6%	Singapore	8.0%	Germany	5.3%
	4th	Indonesia	10.7%	Germany	7.2%	China	4.2%
	5th	Thailand	4.7%	HK	4.9%	HK	3.6%
	6th	Singapore	3.1%	China	4.3%	Canada	3.4%
	7th	Malaysia	2.6%	Malaysia	3.7%	UK	2.7%
	8th	Germany	2.5%	UK	3.0%	France	2.3%
	9th	Australia	2.0%	Canada	2.8%	Singapore	1.5%
	10th	Philip.	1.9%	France	2.4%	Nether.	1.3%

Sources: *Trade Analysis System* of the United Nations. The re-export data is from the *World Trade Atlas* Database.

degrees of openness and different economic size. For example, the competition facing the Mainland China from Singapore needs not be the same as the competition facing Singapore from the Mainland China because of the asymmetry in the importance of the export sector in the two countries.

To improve upon the measures of trade competition in the literature, this chapter introduces a new measure of trade competition that takes into account both the composition and destinations of exports of various Asian and Latin American countries without making the assumption of symmetric trade

Table 8.3 (i) Percentage of exports in 1995 to different destinations

Country	Rank	Industry 0: Food and Live Animals		Industry 1: Beverages and Tobacco		Industry 2: Crude Materials, inedible	
Malaysia	1st	Singapore	42.6%	Singapore	45.9%	Japan	28.6%
	2nd	Japan	9.3%	HK	41.9%	Korea	10.3%
	3rd	HK	8.0%	Indonesia	2.7%	Singapore	10.0%
	4th	Nether.	5.6%	USA	1.4%	Thailand	9.6%
	5th	USA	4.7%	France	1.4%	USA	5.3%
	6th	Germany	4.0%	China	1.4%	China	4.8%
	7th	UK	3.9%	UK	1.4%	Germany	4.0%
	8th	Australia	3.0%	Nether.	1.4%	Nether.	2.4%
	9th	China	2.1%	Oman	1.4%	HK	2.3%
	10th	Italy	2.0%	Thailand	0.0%	India	2.3%
		Industry 3: Fuels and Lubricants, etc.		Industry 4: Animal,Veg.Oils,Fats, Wax		Industry 5: Chemical Reltd. Prod. Nes.	
	1st	Japan	45.8%	Pakistan	18.8%	Singapore	15.7%
	2nd	Singapore	17.4%	China	15.1%	Japan	13.8%
	3rd	Thailand	13.7%	India	10.1%	USA	11.4%
	4th	Korea	10.7%	Singapore	9.7%	HK	11.1%
	5th	Indonesia	2.9%	Japan	6.3%	Korea	10.4%
	6th	India	1.9%	Egypt	3.9%	Thailand	6.1%
	7th	China	1.9%	Turkey	3.3%	China	5.5%
	8th	Australia	1.7%	Korea	2.8%	Indnonesia	4.1%
	9th	USA	1.5%	USA	2.8%	Nether.	3.8%
	10th	New Zeal.	1.2%	Australia	2.5%	Australia	3.5%
		Industry 6: Manufactured Goods		Industry 7: Machines, Transport Equip.		Industry 8: Misc. Manufacture Articles	
	1st	Singapore	24.4%	USA	31.6%	USA	30.7%
	2nd	Japan	16.3%	Singapore	27.89%	Singapore	28.7%
	3rd	HK	10.3%	Japan	7.9%	Japan	9.2%
	4th	USA	8.0%	HK	5.1%	Germany	5.6%
	5th	China	7.8%	Germany	4.6%	UK	4.7%
	6th	Korea	5.1%	UK	3.3%	France	3.2%
	7th	Thailand	3.8%	Thailand	3.1%	HK	2.2%
	8th	UK	3.1%	France	2.22%	Thailand	1.8%
	9th	Germany	2.6%	Canada	2.0%	Canada	1.6%
	10th	Indonesia	2.4%	Korea	1.4%	Australia	1.6%

Sources: *Trade Analysis System* of the United Nations. The re-export data is from the *World Trade Atlas* Database.

competition between any two countries.

The empirical studies of trade competition as well as the evidence on the strong regional patterns of trade all support the trade linkages hypothesis and help to explain why contagion or spillover effects are mostly regional. However, the trade linkage hypothesis cannot account for those cases in which countries that are not closely tied to the initial crisis country through trade have still been vulnerable to contagion or spillover—cases like that of Argentina in relation to Mexico and Indonesia to Thailand. This suggests that additional

Table 8.3 (j) Percentage of exports in 1995 to different destinations

Country	Rank	Industry 0: Food and Live Animals		Industry 1: Beverages and Tobacco		Industry 2: Crude Materials, inedible	
Mexico	1st	USA	77.8%	USA	71.5%	USA	60.6%
	2nd	Japan	4.8%	Canada	3.7%	Japan	9.8%
	3rd	Canada	3.7%	Japan	2.8%	China	4.3%
	4th	France	1.6%	Germany	2.6%	Canada	1.8%
	5th	Spain	1.4%	France	2.3%	Korea	1.8%
	6th	Italy	1.4%	Brazil	1.8%	Germany	1.7%
	7th	Germany	0.9%	Italy	1.6%	Brazil	1.6%
	8th	Algeria	0.8%	Spain	1.5%	Belgium	1.3%
	9th	Korea	0.8%	Belgium	1.5%	Argentina	1.2%
	10th	UK	0.8%	Denmark	1.3%	Chile	1.2%
		Industry 3: Fuels and Lubricants, etc.		Industry 4: Animal,Veg.Oils,Fats, Wax		Industry 5: Chemical Reltd. Prod. Nes.	
	1st	USA	79.2%	USA	76.3%	USA	38.9%
	2nd	Japan	8.1%	Cuba	8.5%	Brazil	5.3%
	3rd	Spain	7.0%	Uurguay	5.1%	Colombia	4.6%
	4th	Netherlands	1.2%	Japan	1.7%	Netherlands	4.0%
	5th	Dominican RP	1.1%	UK	1.7%	Argentina	3.4%
	6th	Canada	0.8%	Germany	1.7%	Chile	3.3%
	7th	Belgium-Lux	0.5%	Panama	1.7%	Venezuela	2.7%
	8th	Cuba	0.4%	Venezuela	0.0%	Belgium-Lux	2.6%
	9th	Jamaica	0.3%	Br.Virgin Is.	0.0%	Guatemala	2.4%
	10th	Portugal	0.2%	Guatemala	0.0%	Cuba	2.2%
		Industry 6: Manufactured Goods		Industry 7: Machines, Transport Equip.		Industry 8: Misc. Manufacture Articles	
	1st	USA	71.8%	USA	89.12%	USA	92.44%
	2nd	Venezuela	1.82%	Canada	3.45%	Canada	0.63%
	3rd	Chile	1.7%	Brazil	0.92%	Brazil	0.6%
	4th	UK	1.67%	Chile	0.78%	UK	0.49%
	5th	Belgium-Lux	1.68%	Germany	0.58%	Germany	0.45%
	6th	Canada	1.38%	Argentina	0.51%	Spain	0.41%
	7th	Japan	1.19%	France	0.43%	Japan	0.41%
	8th	Guatemala	1.16%	Venezuela	0.36%	Colombia	0.37%
	9th	Brazil	1.14%	Colombia	0.32%	Chile	0.36%
	10th	Germany	1.08%	Japan	0.28%	Guatemala	0.28%

Sources: *Trade Analysis System* of the United Nations. The re-export data is from the *World Trade Atlas* Database.

channels are involved. With the growing importance of the financial sector around the globe, financial linkages are naturally other channels of contagion that have received much attention in the literature. The financial linkages examined in the literature include common international creditors (competition for international funds) (Rijckeghem and Weder, 1999), cross–country hedging and portfolio rebalancing (Schinasi and Smith, 1999) and international

Table 8.3 (k) Percentage of exports in 1995 to different destinations

Country	Rank	Industry 0: Food and Live Animals		Industry 1: Beverages and Tobacco		Industry 2: Crude Materials, inedible	
Philippines	1st	Japan	40.9%	HK	40.6%	Japan	61.4%
	2nd	USA	2.18%	France	11.6%	Germany	7.2%
	3rd	Korea	6.6%	Egypt	8.7%	China	4.9%
	4th	HK	5.6%	Japan	7.2%	USA	4.8%
	5th	Germany	2.9%	USA	5.8%	UK	4.2%
	6th	Nether.	2.8%	Germany	5.8%	Korea	3.4%
	7th	Saudi Ara.	2.5%	Saudi Ara.	5.8%	HK	2.8%
	8th	Sanada	1.8%	Spain	4.3%	Malaysia	2.2%
	9th	Singapore	1.8%	UK	2.9%	France	2.0%
	10th	China	1.7%	Algeria	2.9%	Singapore	1.7%
		Industry 3: Fuels and Lubricants, etc.		Industry 4: Animal,Veg.Oils,Fats, Wax		Industry 5: Chemical Reltd. Prod. Nes.	
	1st	China	47.7%	USA	40.3%	HK	16.9%
	2nd	Japan	32.0%	Germany	15.2%	Japan	16.5%
	3rd	Singapore	6.6%	Nether.	10.6%	USA	15.0%
	4th	HK	5.8%	Belgium	5.4%	Thailand	11.7%
	5th	Korea	2.9%	Malaysia	3.4%	Indonesia	6.4%
	6th	Malaysia	2.9%	Korea	3.2%	Australia	5.3%
	7th	Mauritius	1.7%	Italy	2.7%	China	3.4%
	8th	Thailand	0.4%	France	2.4%	Korea	3.0%
	9th	Indonesia	0.4%	Mexico	2.3%	Singapore	3.0%
	10th	Australia	0.0%	Indonesia	2.3%	UK	3.0%
		Industry 6: Manufactured Goods		Industry 7: Machines, Transport Equip.		Industry 8: Misc. Manufacture Articles	
	1st	Japan	20.2%	USA	39.8%	USA	62.1%
	2nd	USA	19.1%	Japan	15.4%	Japan	9.2%
	3rd	Korea	17.2%	Singapore	10.1%	Germany	6.8%
	4th	Thailand	6.2%	HK	5.5%	UK	3.6%
	5th	HK	5.6%	Thailand	5.3%	France	3.4%
	6th	Singapore	5.2%	Germany	4.9%	Canada	2.6%
	7th	Germany	4.7%	Malaysia	3.9%	HK	2.2%
	8th	China	3.4%	UK	3.2%	Italy	1.2%
	9th	Malaysia	2.7%	Korea	2.1%	Nether.	1.1%
	10th	UK	2.5%	Canada	2.1%	Belgium	0.8%

Sources: *Trade Analysis System* of the United Nations. The re-export data is from the *World Trade Atlas* Database.

liquidity constraints (Goldfajn and Valdĕs, 1997; Calvo, 1999).

Table 8.5 (a) and Table 8.5 (c) indicate that there is a strong regional pattern in international lending. While US banks have had an extensive exposure to Latin America, Japanese banks have had an extensive exposure to Asia. This regional pattern provides an additional explanation for the stylized fact that contagion or spillover effects are often regional. This chapter employs three measures to measure the effect of common creditors. These measures include the fund competition indexes of Rijckeghem and Weder (1999), the

Table 8.3 (I) Percentage of exports in 1995 to different destinations

Country	Rank	Industry 0: Food and Live Animals		Industry 1: Beverages and Tobacco		Industry 2: Crude Materials, inedible	
Singapore	1st	Japan	23.0%	HK	76.3%	Brazil	12.6%
	2nd	HK	16.6%	Malaysia	7.9%	Indonesia	10.9%
	3rd	USA	11.3%	Japan	5.8%	Japan	10.5%
	4th	UK	5.2%	Saudi Ara.	2.1%	UK	7.3%
	5th	Malaysia	4.9%	Philip.	1.7%	HK	5.9%
	6th	Australia	4.7%	Indonesia	1.0%	India	5.57%
	7th	Philip.	4.7%	Spain	1.0%	Malaysia	4.5%
	8th	Thailand	4.2%	UK	0.7%	China	3.9%
	9th	Nether.	3.3%	USA	0.7%	Belgium	3.9%
	10th	Indonesia	2.1%	Nether.	0.7%	Canada	3.8%
		Industry 3: Fuels and Lubricants, etc.		Industry 4: Animal,Veg.Oils,Fats, Wax		Industry 5: Chemical Reltd. Prod. Nes.	
	1st	HK	24.4%	China	15.4%	Malaysia	12.3%
	2nd	Malaysia	14.7%	HK	15.4%	USA	12.2%
	3rd	China	14.1%	Indonesia	7.1%	HK	12.2%
	4th	Thailand	13.6%	Japan	6.5%	Indonesia	11.0%
	5th	Japan	9.5%	Kenya	4.3%	China	7.8%
	6th	Indonesia	9.4%	Egypt	4.3%	Thailand	7.5%
	7th	Korea	3.5%	Thailand	3.7%	Japan	6.3%
	8th	Austrailia	3.0%	India	3.7%	Philip.	5.1%
	9th	Philip.	27%	USA	3.7%	India	3.7%
	10th	Banglad.	2.6%	Saudi Ara.	3.7%	UK	3.6%
		Industry 6: Manufactured Goods		Industry 7: Machines, Transport Equip.		Industry 8: Misc. Manufacture Articles	
	1st	Malaysia	23.5%	USA	30.3%	USA	23.7%
	2nd	HK	14.2%	HK	10.9%	UK	13.7%
	3rd	Thailand	11.1%	Malaysia	10.8%	HK	11.9%
	4th	China	6.2%	Japan	835%	Malaysia	8.9%
	5th	Indonesia	4.7%	Germany	4.7%	Jpan	8.6%
	6th	Japan	4.6%	UK	4.3%	Thailand	3.9%
	7th	Germany	3.5%	Thailand	3.7%	Germany	3.5%
	8th	Philip.	3.4%	France	3.1%	Australia	3.0%
	9th	USA	3.3%	Korea	2.7%	Korea	3.0%
	10th	UK	3.1%	China	2.6%	Indonesia	2.6%

Sources: *Trade Analysis System* of the United Nations. The re-export data is from the *World Trade Atlas* Database.

common creditor indicators of Kaminsky and Reinhart (1998) and the indicators of Caramazza, Ricci and Salgado (2000), which measure the relative importance of common creditors and common borrowers.

On the other hand, cross–country hedging and portfolio rebalancing together with liquidity constraint explains why a shock in a country can trigger net sales of risky assets by international investors in other markets, even though the two markets have few trade ties and few direct financial linkages. We formulate in this chapter a GARCH model to measure the extent to which

Table 8.3 (m) Percentage of exports in 1995 to different destinations

Country	Rank	Industry 0: Food and Live Animals		Industry 1: Beverages and Tobacco		Industry 2: Crude Materials, inedible	
Taiwan	1st	Japan	75.8%	HK	42.4%	Japan	24.3%
	2nd	USA	7.2%	Australia	15.3%	China	21.3%
	3rd	Singapore	3.2%	Singapore	10.6%	HK	16.4%
	4th	HK	3.2%	Japan	9.4%	USA	5.7%
	5th	Thailand	3.1%	UK	9.4%	Korea	5.4%
	6th	Malaysia	1.6%	USA	8.2%	Indonesia	4.7%
	7th	Indonesia	1.0%	Jirea	2.4%	Malaysia	3.8%
	8th	China	0.9%	Germany	1.2%	Thailand	3.2%
	9th	Philip.	0.6%	Indonesia	1.2%	Philip.	3.1%
	10th	Canada	0.5%	Czech	0.0%	Germany	1.9%
		Industry 3: Fuels and Lubricants, etc.		Industry 4: Animal,Veg.Oils,Fats, Wax		Industry 5: Chemical Reltd. Prod. Nes.	
	1st	Korea	18.2%	HK	20.6%	China	27.9%
	2nd	S.Afr.	12.3%	Korea	14.7%	HK	25.8%
	3rd	China	11.0%	YSA	11.8%	Singapore	7.8%
	4th	HK	10.2%	China	8.8%	Japan	5.7%
	5th	Japan	8.9%	Thailand	8.8%	Thailand	4.4%
	6th	Singapore	7.2%	Indonesia	8.8%	USA	4.3%
	7th	Philip.	7.2%	India	8.8%	Malaysia	4.1%
	8th	Thailand	6.8%	Japan	5.9%	Indonesia	3.2%
	9th	Australia	5.9%	Malaysia	2.9%	Korea	2.1%
	10th	Indonesia	4.7%	Singapore	2.9%	Philip.	1.8%
		Industry 6: Manufactured Goods		Industry 7: Machines, Transport Equip.		Industry 8: Misc. Manufacture Articles	
	1st	HK	22.5%	USA	28.9%	USA	41.1%
	2nd	China	20.1%	HK	10.7%	Japan	13.6%
	3rd	USA	15.2%	Japan	9.0%	HK	6.9%
	4th	Haoab	7.1%	China	8.7%	China	5.4%
	5th	Malaysia	3.7%	Germany	6.0%	Germany	5.0%
	6th	Thailand	3.2%	Singapore	4.9%	UK	3.0%
	7th	Jirea	3.0%	Malaysia	6.5%	Singapore	2.5%
	8th	Germany	2.9%	Thailand	2.8%	Canada	2.4%
	9th	Singapore	2.8%	UK	2.7%	France	2.3%
	10th	Indonesia	2.2%	Nether.	2.3%	Australia	1.6%

Sources: *Trade Analysis System* of the United Nations. The re-export data is from the *World Trade Atlas* Database.

volatility in the financial market of a given country can spillover to other countries through the channels of either cross–country hedging and portfolio rebalancing or of international liquidity constraint. The GARCH model is based on Edwards' model of 1998a and 1998b. In order to measure more precisely the volatility spillovers from the initial crisis countries, the Edwards model is augmented with two variables that control for the common exogenous shocks from the US and Japan.

The chapter is organized as follows: the first section gives an introduction.

Table 8.3 (n) Percentage of exports in 1995 to different destinations

Country	Rank	Industry 0: Food and Live Animals		Industry 1: Beverages and Tobacco		Industry 2: Crude Materials, inedible	
Thailand	1st	Japan	28.5%	USA	16.2%	Japan	36.1%
	2nd	USA	18.6%	Indonesia	12.0%	USA	13.7%
	3rd	China	7.6%	Singapore	12.0%	China	9.0%
	4th	HK	5.4%	Germany	9.4%	Malaysia	6.5%
	5th	Malaysia	4.0%	UK	7.7%	Korea	5.9%
	6th	Indonesia	3.3%	Japan	7.7%	France	3.6%
	7th	Singapore	3.1%	Egypt	4.3%	Singapore	3.4%
	8th	Germany	3.1%	France	3.4%	Germany	2.7%
	9th	Korea	2.7%	Philip.	2.6%	Italy	2.6%
	10th	Nether.	2.5%	Nether.	2.6%	HK	2.6%
		Industry 3: Fuels and Lubricants, etc.		Industry 4: Animal,Veg.Oils,Fats, Wax		Industry 5: Chemical Reltd. Prod. Nes.	
	1st	Singapore	37.8%	Japan	37.5%	HK	18.2%
	2nd	Korea	36.7%	Malaysia	9.4%	Japan	16.7%
	3rd	Japan	8.2%	Korea	9.4%	China	12.8%
	4th	USA	5.1%	China	9.4%	Indonesia	11.7%
	5th	China	4.1%	Aingapore	9.4%	Malaysia	8.3%
	6th	Malaysia	3.6%	Indonesia	6.3%	Singapore	5.4%
	7th	Australia	2.0%	Australia	3.1%	USA	4.4%
	8th	HK	1.5%	USA	3.1%	Philip.	3.0%
	9th	Philip.	0.5%	Philip.	3.1%	Pakistan	2.6%
	10th	Indonesia	0.5%	Italy	3.1%	Australia	2.2%
		Industry 6: Manufactured Goods		Industry 7: Machines, Transport Equip.		Industry 8: Misc. Manufacture Articles	
	1st	USA	17.0%	Singapore	26.7%	USA	36.1%
	2nd	HK	13.5%	USA	25.8%	Japan	18.6%
	3rd	Japan	13.4%	Japan	15.5%	Germany	8.2%
	4th	Singapore	7.3%	Malaysia	5.1%	France	5.7%
	5th	Belgium	7.0%	Germany	4.1%	UK	5.1%
	6th	Bermany	4.0%	HK	3.9%	HK	3.6%
	7th	China	3.89%	UK	3.5%	Switz	2.5%
	8th	Malaysia	3.7%	Nether.	2.2%	Singapore	2.4%
	9th	UK	3.6%	France	1.7%	Nether.	1.8%
	10th	Australia	2.6%	Korea	1.2%	Canada	1.8%

Sources: *Trade Analysis System* of the United Nations. The re-export data is from the *World Trade Atlas* Database.

The next section defines the term fundamental–based contagion, as distinguished from true contagion. After this, we discuss in detail the channels of trade and financial linkages. The next section describes the various indexes and the GARCH model that have been constructed to measure trade and financial linkages between countries. The final section concludes. The data description is provided in the appendix.

Table 8.3 (o) Percentage of exports in 1995 to different destinations

Country	Rank	Industry 0: Food and Live Animals		Industry 1: Beverages and Tobacco		Industry 2: Crude Materials, inedible	
Uruguay	1st	Brazil	49.5%	Brazil	54.5%	China	20.7%
	2nd	UK	6.9%	Paraguay	18.2%	Germany	10.8%
	3rd	Israel	5.6%	Argentina	18.2%	Brazil	10.5%
	4th	USA	5.1%	Chile	9.1%	Italy	8.7%
	5th	Germany	4.6%	-	-	Spain	5.8%
	6th	Nether.	4.4%	-	-	HK	5.5%
	7th	Argentina	3.5%	-	-	UK	4.4%
	8th	Spain	3.2%	-	-	USA	4.4%
	9th	Italy	2.1%	-	-	Colombia	4.4%
	10th	Peru	1.8%	-	-	Turkey	3.2%
		Industry 3: Fuels and Lubricants, etc.		Industry 4: Animal,Veg.Oils,Fats, Wax		Industry 5: Chemical Reltd. Prod. Nes.	
	1st	Argentina	87.0%	Brazil	83.3%	Brazil	56.7%
	2nd	Brazil	8.7%	Italy	8.3%	Argentina	19.3%
	3rd	Bolivia	4.3%	Argentina	0.0%	Paraguay	5.9%
	4th	-	-	Spain	0.0%	Ecuador	3.2%
	5th	-	-	Nether.	0.0%	S.Afr.	1.6%
	6th	-	-	Israel	0.0%	Spain	1.6%
	7th	-	-	Colombia	0.0%	Chile	1.6%
	8th	-	-	Banglad.	0.0%	Bolivia	1.6%
	9th	-	-	Algeria	0.0%	Japan	1.1%
	10th	-	-	France	0.0%	Venezuela	1.1%
		Industry 6: Manufactured Goods		Industry 7: Machines, Transport Equip.		Industry 8: Misc. Manufacture Articles	
	1st	Brazil	32.4%	Argentina	49.7%	Brazil	47.2%
	2nd	Argentina	13.8%	Brazil	43.4%	Agrentina	18.9%
	3rd	USA	13.3%	Paraguay	1.3%	USA	15.5%
	4th	HK	6.2%	France	0.6%	Germany	4.9%
	5th	Germany	4.8%	USA	0.6%	Chile	3.4%
	6th	Italy	4.0%	Chile	0.6%	Paraguay	1.5%
	7th	Canada	2.9%	Venezuela	0.6%	Sweden	1.1%
	8th	FRance	2.4%	Italy	0.6%	Switz.	0.8%
	9th	UK	%2.4	UK	0.0%	Mexico	0.8%
	10th	Chile	1.7%	Mexico	0.0%	Japan	0.8%

Sources: *Trade Analysis System* of the United Nations. The re-export data is from the *World Trade Atlas* Database.

Definitions of contagion

As of Calvo and Reinhart (1996), contagion can be divided into two types: fundamentals–based contagion and true contagion. Fundamentals–based contagion arises when an infected country is linked to another via trade, finance or common exogenous shocks. Borde, Mizrach and Schwartz (1995) find that most of the high correlation among stock prices in emerging markets can be attributed to fundamentals, either in–country fundamentals or a sharing of external fundamentals.

Table 8.3 (p) Percentage of exports in 1995 to different destinations

Country	Rank	Industry 0: Food and Live Animals		Industry 1: Beverages and Tobacco		Industry 2: Crude Materials, inedible	
Venezuela	1st	Colombia	40.3%	Colombia	50.9%	USA	37.1%
	2nd	USA	28.1%	Brazil	11.3%	UK	14.7%
	3rd	Spain	5.1%	USA	9.4%	Brazil	5.5%
	4th	Germany	4.3%	Spain	9.4%	Colombia	5.2%
	5th	Italy	3.5%	Peru	7.5%	Italy	4.6%
	6th	Nether.	2.3%	Ecuador	3.8%	Nether.	4.4%
	7th	France	2.0%	Mexico	1.9%	Denmark	4.3%
	8th	Brazil	2.0%	Italy	1.9%	Japan	3.7%
	9th	Japan	1.5%	Chile	1.9%	Trinidad	2.9%
	10th	UK	1.5%	Argentina	1.9%	Mexico	2.8%
		Industry 3: Fuels and Lubricants, etc.		Industry 4: Animal,Veg.Oils,Fats, Wax		Industry 5: Chemical Reltd. Prod. Nes.	
	1st	USA	70.2%	Japan	40.0%	USA	26.3%
	2nd	Brazil	5.8%	USA	40.0%	Colombia	21.3%
	3rd	Germany	3.6%	Germany	20.0%	Peru	9.8%
	4th	Canada	3.4%	-	-	Chile	7.1%
	5th	Nether.	1.8%	-	-	Brazil	5.9%
	6th	Colombia	1.6%	-	-	Mexico	4.8%
	7th	Peru	1.4%	-	-	France	3.9%
	8th	UK	1.3%	-	-	Italy	3.3%
	9th	Costa Rica	1.2%	-	-	Ecuador	2.3%
	10th	Sweden	1.1%	-	-	Nether.	2.3%
		Industry 6: Manufactured Goods		Industry 7: Machines, Transport Equip.		Industry 8: Misc. Manufacture Articles	
	1st	USA	30.7%	Colombia	50.1%	USA	39.6%
	2nd	Colombia	17.4%	USA	25.6%	Colombia	28.1%
	3rd	Japan	15.3%	Ecuador	13.0%	Mexico	4.2%
	4th	Mexico	4.6%	UK	2.0%	Ecuador	3.1%
	5th	Peru	3.9%	Germany	1.1%	Peru	3.1%
	6th	Ecuador	3.0%	Brazil	1.0%	Panama	2.1%
	7th	Germany	2.6%	Spain	0.8%	Nether.	2.1%
	8th	Korea	2.1%	Mexico	0.7%	Chile	2.1%
	9th	Brazil	2.0%	Peru	0.7%	Brazil	2.1%
	10th	Costa Rica	1.9%	Nether.	0.7%	Spain	2.1%

Sources: *Trade Analysis System* of the United Nations. The re-export data is from the *World Trade Atlas* Database.

True contagion is defined as contagion that cannot be accounted for by the fundamentals. It remains even after all channels of potential interconnection have been controlled for. Most often, true contagion is associated with herding behavior on the part of investors. Frankel and Schmukler (1998) also call this type of contagion 'herding behavior contagion'. Herding behavior can be a result of information asymmetries among investors, cross–market hedging or multiple equilibria in the asset market. This 'true contagion' definition is used widely in the

Table 8.4 (a) Percentage of exports in 1999 to different destinations

Country	Rank	Industry 0: Food and Live Animals		Industry 1: Beverages and Tobacco		Industry 2: Crude Materials, inedible	
Argentina	1st	Brazil	26.0%	USA	24.5%	Brazil	13.1%
	2nd	Spain	9.8%	Paraguay	13.6%	China	11.0%
	3rd	USA	8.6%	UK	10.8%	Germany	10.5%
	4th	Germany	6.8%	Japan	9.6%	Nether.	9.7%
	5th	Italy	6.3%	Germany	8.0%	Sapin	7.7%
	6th	Nether.	4.4%	Uruguay	2.8%	Japan	6.8%
	7th	Belgium	3.5%	France	3.4%	USA	5.3%
	8th	France	3.4%	Brazil	2.8%	France	4.5%
	9th	Japan	3.4%	Nether.	2.8%	Korea	3.8%
	10th	Denmark	2.6%	Canada	1.9%	Italy	3.5%
		Industry 3: Fuels and Lubricants, etc.		Industry 4: Animal,Veg.Oils,Fats, Wax		Industry 5: Chemical Reltd. Prod. Nes.	
	1st	USA	41.6%	China	13.4%	Brazil	42.4%
	2nd	Brazil	36.5%	Pakistan	9.2%	Uruguay	13.1%
	3rd	Paraguay	9.9%	Brazil	8.8%	USA	10.7%
	4th	Uruguay	5.6%	Venezuela	7.7%	Mexico	3.8%
	5th	New Zealand	2.4%	Nether.	7.0%	Germany	3.0%
	6th	Thailand	1.0%	Egypt	6.2%	Peru	2.7%
	7th	Japan	0.6%	Russian	5.8%	Italy	2.5%
	8th	Nether.	0.6%	S. Afr.	5.6%	Colombia	2.5%
	9th	Ghana	0.5%	Algeria	5.3%	Paraguay	1.8%
	10th	Peru	0.3%	Malaysia	3.3%	UK	1.7%
		Industry 6: Manufactured Goods		Industry 7: Machines, Transport Equip.		Industry 8: Misc. Manufacture Articles	
	1st	USA	26.8%	Brazil	71.7%	USA	35.3%
	2nd	Brazil	23.9%	Uruguay	4.9%	Brazil	27.3%
	3rd	Uruguay	6.6%	USA	4.6%	Uruguay	14.7%
	4th	Italy	5.2%	Italy	3.8%	Spain	3.7%
	5th	HK	4.5%	Spain	2.6%	Mexico	3.7%
	6th	China	4.1%	Germany	2.3%	Colombia	2.2%
	7th	Japan	3.7%	Mexico	1.6%	Peru	1.9%
	8th	Spain	3.7%	France	1.6%	Italy	1.7%
	9th	Canada	1.9%	Paraguay	0.8%	UK	1.5%
	10th	Singapore	1.3%	Belgium	0.6%	Venezuela	1.3%

Sources: *Trade Analysis System* of the United Nations. The re-export data is from the *World Trade Atlas* Database.

contagion literature, which includes the work of Eichengreen, Rose and Wyplosz (1997) as well as Forbes and Rigobon (1999, 2000).

Masson gives a more detail classification of the contagion effect (1998, 1999). His classification is based on the causes of the exchange rates movements in the currency markets:

(1) Fundamental based movements: movements due to country specific events.

Table 8.4 (b) Percentage of exports in 1999 to different destinations

Country	Rank	Industry 0: Food and Live Animals		Industry 1: Beverages and Tobacco		Industry 2: Crude Materials, inedible	
Brazil	1st	USA	13.9%	USA	15.6%	Japan	13.3%
	2nd	Germany	9.7%	Germany	14.0%	USA	12.9%
	3rd	Nether.	7.9%	UK	10.5%	Germany	12.6%
	4th	France	7.7%	Russian	8.1%	China	7.1%
	5th	Japan	6.6%	Japan	7.5%	Italy	6.9%
	6th	Russian	6.0%	Paraguay	6.4%	Spain	6.2%
	7th	Belgium	4.5%	Poland	4.4%	France	5.4%
	8th	UK	4.4%	Nether.	4.1%	Nether.	5.2%
	9th	Argentina	3.8%	Spain	2.8%	Belgium	4.9%
	10th	Spain	3.6%	Switz.	2.1%	Korea	4.9%
		Industry 3: Fuels and Lubricants, etc.		Industry 4: Animal,Veg.Oils,Fats, Wax		Industry 5: Chemical Reltd. Prod. Nes.	
	1st	USA	62.4%	China	28.1%	Argentina	28.5%
	2nd	Argentina	7.8%	Egypt	9.7%	USA	18.3%
	3rd	Canada	6.4%	USA	7.8%	Japan	6.3%
	4th	Thailand	5.0%	HK	6.9%	Italy	5.5%
	5th	Colombia	4.5%	Nether.	5.5%	Germany	3.7%
	6th	Italy	4.1%	Japan	5.5%	Berlgium	2.7%
	7th	Paraguay	2.3%	Malaysia	5.1%	Korea	2.6%
	8th	Uruguay	1.9%	Germany	4.6%	UK	2.5%
	9th	Mexico	1.2%	Argentina	3.7%	Mexico	2.2%
	10th	Costa Rica	1.2%	Pakistan	3.2%	Nether.	2.0%
		Industry 6: Manufactured Goods		Industry 7: Machines, Transport Equip.		Industry 8: Misc. Manufacture Articles	
	1st	USA	28.9%	USA	35.3%	USA	48.3%
	2nd	Argentina	14.4%	Argentina	22.6%	Argentina	13.8%
	3rd	Japan	6.0%	Mexico	5.4%	UK	6.2%
	4th	Italy	4.7%	Germany	5.1%	Germany	4.7%
	5th	Germany	4.7%	Italy	4.6%	France	3.4%
	6th	Belgium	3.4%	France	2.3%	Uruguay	2.5%
	7th	Korea	3.2%	Canada	2.1%	Mexico	2.1%
	8th	UK	2.8%	Venezuela	1.9%	Canada	1.9%
	9th	Mexico	2.8%	Uruguay	1.9%	Nether.	1.9%
	10th	Nether.	2.5%	UK	1.7%	Paraguay	1.3%

Sources: *Trade Analysis System* of the United Nations. The re-export data is from the *World Trade Atlas* Database.

(2) Spillover effects: movements due to known linkages between countries and economies.
(3) Monsoon effects: movements due to common events that affect all markets.
(4) True contagion: the remaining movements in exchange rates unexplained by the three factors above. Similar to Calvo and Reinhart, Masson views true contagion as a residual process (unexpected turmoil).

Even though Masson's definitions are slightly different from that of Calvo and

Table 8.4 (c) Percentage of exports in 1999 to different destinations

Country	Rank	Industry 0: Food and Live Animals		Industry 1: Beverages and Tobacco		Industry 2: Crude Materials, inedible	
Chile	1st	USA	31.6%	USA	21.5%	Japan	32.6%
	2nd	Japan	20.6%	UK	21.5%	USA	12.4%
	3rd	Nether.	4.0%	Canada	6.6%	China	7.6%
	4th	Spain	3.7%	Germany	6.3%	Korea	7.0%
	5th	Mexico	3.7%	Japan	5.6%	Germany	6.2%
	6th	UK	3.3%	Denmark	4.6%	Mexico	5.4%
	7th	Germany	3.1%	Argentina	3.7%	Brazil	4.8%
	8th	Argentina	3.0%	Nether.	3.4%	Spain	3.0%
	9th	Canada	2.9%	Norway	3.2%	Italy	2.7%
	10th	Brazil	2.8%	Ireland	2.7%	Canada	2.2%
		Industry 3: Fuels and Lubricants, etc.		Industry 4: Animal,Veg.Oils,Fats, Wax		Industry 5: Chemical Reltd. Prod. Nes.	
	1st	USA	33.3%	Norway	40.7%	USA	22.9%
	2nd	Peru	16.0%	Mexico	11.1%	Brazil	11.6%
	3rd	Argentina	14.8%	Nether.	11.1%	Argentina	6.8%
	4th	Ecuador	12.3%	Japan	7.4%	Belgium	6.4%
	5th	Mexico	8.6%	Peru	7.4%	Peru	6.2%
	6th	Singapore	8.6%	Argentina	3.7%	Nether.	5.0%
	7th	Brazil	6.2%	Ecuador	3.7%	France	4.3%
	8th	-	-	Venezuela	3.7%	Spain	3.9%
	9th	-	-	Pakistan	3.7%	Mexico	3.7%
	10th	-	-	Germany	0.0%	Japan	3.4%
		Industry 6: Manufactured Goods		Industry 7: Machines, Transport Equip.		Industry 8: Misc. Manufacture Articles	
	1st	USA	17.7%	Argentina	21.4%	USA	27.8%
	2nd	Italy	12.1%	Mexico	19.1%	Argentina	21.4%
	3rd	Korea	10.4%	Brazil	10.3%	Brazil	16.9%
	4th	France	8.8%	Norway	6.3%	Peru	9.2%
	5th	Mexico	6.8%	Peru	6.0%	Mexico	7.8%
	6th	China	6.1%	USA	6.0%	Ecuador	2.0%
	7th	Brazil	5.6%	Venezuela	6.0%	Uruguay	2.0%
	8th	Argentina	5.1%	Russian	5.3%	Colombia	1.7%
	9th	UK	4.4%	Colombia	4.3%	Germany	1.4%
	10th	Japan	4.3%	Ecuador	1.8%	UK	1.4%

Sources: *Trade Analysis System* of the United Nations. The re-export data is from the *World Trade Atlas* Database.

Reinhart, Masson's definitions have become increasingly important because of their adoption by the IMF. In this chapter, we employ the definitions of Masson and we aim at examining the extent to which known linkages across countries, especially the trade and financial linkages, can account for the domino effects of the financial and currency crises during the 1995 Mexican Crisis and the 1997 Asian Crisis.

Table 8.4 (d) Percentage of exports in 1999 to different destinations

Country	Rank	Industry 0: Food and Live Animals		Industry 1: Beverages and Tobacco		Industry 2: Crude Materials, inedible	
China	1st	Japan	44.4%	HK (for re-export)	55.7% (15.61%)	Japan	29.8%
	2nd	HK (for re-export)	14.2% (3.79%)	Japan	9.5%	Korea	12.0%
	3rd	USA	8.3%	Singapore	7.7%	USA	11.9%
	4th	Korea	7.6%	Russian	3.8%	HK (for re-export)	7.2% (5.77%)
	5th	Malaysia	3.5%	Philip.	3.8%	Germany	6.9%
	6th	Germany	2.8%	Egypt	3.7%	Italy	6.7%
	7th	Singapore	2.1%	Macau	2.7%	Nether.	3.3%
	8th	France	1.7%	USA	2.7%	UK	2.8%
	9th	Spain	1.4%	UK	1.4%	Thaiiland	2.2%
	10th	Canada	1.3%	Australia	1.1%	Malaysia	1.7%
		Industry 3: Fuels and Lubricants, etc.		Industry 4: Animal,Veg.Oils,Fats, Wax		Industry 5: Chemical Reltd. Prod. Nes.	
	1st	Japan	30.3%	HK (for re-export)	46.0% (40.54%)	USA	18.6%
	2nd	HK (for re-export)	22.0% (0.28%)	Japan	8.0%	Japan	13.5%
	3rd	Korea	15.9%	USA	6.0%	HK (for re-export)	12.1% (4.91%)
	4th	USA	6.2%	Malaysia	6.0%	Korea	6.8%
	5th	Singapore	5.6%	Korea	5.0%	Germany	6.0%
	6th	France	2.2%	Germany	4.0%	France	3.7%
	7th	Russian	2.0%	UK	4.0%	Thailand	2.8%
	8th	Thailand	1.5%	Nether.	4.0%	Italy	2.8%
	9th	Macau	1.5%	Canada	3.0%	UK	2.3%
	10th	Germany	1.3%	Australia	3.0%	Belgium	2.2%
		Industry 6: Manufactured Goods		Industry 7: Machines, Transport Equip.		Industry 8: Misc. Manufacture Articles	
	1st	HK (for re-export)	26.6% (9.44%)	USA	29.7%	USA	32.8%
	2nd	USA	23.9%	HK (for re-export)	26.1% (14.05%)	HK (for re-export)	27.5% (15.03%)
	3rd	Japan	12.3%	Japan	9.9%	Japan	13.7%
	4th	Korea	5.7%	Germany	5.4%	Germany	4.5%
	5th	Germany	4.4%	Singapore	3.8%	France	2.8%
	6th	UK	2.1%	Korea	2.8%	Canada	2.3%
	7th	Italy	2.0%	France	2.8%	UK	1.8%
	8th	Canada	2.0%	UK	1.9%	Italy	1.8%
	9th	France	1.9%	Canada	1.8%	Australia	1.6%
	10th	Australia	1.8%	Nether.	1.6%	Spain	1.4%

Sources: *Trade Analysis System* of the United Nations. The re-export data is from the *World Trade Atlas* Database.

Table 8.4 (e) Percentage of exports in 1999 to different destinations

Country	Rank	Industry 0: Food and Live Animals		Industry 1: Beverages and Tobacco		Industry 2: Crude Materials, inedible	
Colombia	1st	USA	30.4%	USA	16.7%	USA	69.8%
	2nd	Germany	13.4%	Venezuela	16.7%	UK	7.3%
	3rd	Belgium	7.3%	Spain	13.3%	Canada	4.4%
	4th	Japan	6.6%	Algeria	10.0%	Spain	2.3%
	5th	Venezuela	4.4%	Germany	6.7%	Japan	2.2%
	6th	Italy	3.9%	Ecuador	6.7%	Nether.	2.2%
	7th	France	3.9%	Trinidad	6.7%	Germany	1.9%
	8th	Canada	3.8%	Mexico	6.7%	Singapore	1.1%
	9th	Spain	3.4%	France	3.3%	Korea	1.1%
	10th	Russian	1.8%	Belgium	3.3%	Venezuela	0.8%
		Industry 3: Fuels and Lubricants, etc.		Industry 4: Animal,Veg.Oils,Fats, Wax		Industry 5: Chemical Reltd. Prod. Nes.	
	1st	USA	74.0%	Nether.	28.6%	USA	34.9%
	2nd	UK	3.8%	Mexico	25.0%	Ecuador	13.7%
	3rd	Peru	3.3%	Venezuela	14.3%	Venezuela	12.7%
	4th	Trinidad	2.6%	UK	7.1%	Peru	11.7%
	5th	Brazil	2.4%	Germany	7.1%	Mexico	5.5%
	6th	Germany	1.9%	Belgium	7.1%	Costa Rica	3.8%
	7th	Nether.	1.9%	Honduras	3.6%	Brazil	3.7%
	8th	Israel	1.6%	Ecuador	3.6%	Guatemala	2.1%
	9th	Portugal	1.5%	USA	0.0%	Panama	1.9%
	10th	France	1.4%	Peru	0.0%	Honduras	1.2%
		Industry 6: Manufactured Goods		Industry 7: Machines, Transport Equip.		Industry 8: Misc. Manufacture Articles	
	1st	USA	30.5%	Venezuela	52.5%	USA	55.9%
	2nd	Venezuela	16.2%	Ecuador	9.9%	Venezuela	13.8%
	3rd	Ecuador	8.9%	Mexico	6.3%	Ecuador	6.3%
	4th	Peru	5.4%	Peru	4.6%	Mexico	5.1%
	5th	Mexico	4.1%	USA	4.3%	Peru	2.6%
	6th	Finland	3.4%	UK	3.6%	Argentina	2.1%
	7th	Italy	3.4%	Panama	2.6%	Panama	2.0%
	8th	Costa Rica	3.1%	Costa Rica	2.3%	Germany	1.8%
	9th	Japan	2.8%	Guatemala	2.0%	Costa Rica	1.5%
	10th	Belgium	2.8%	Italy	2.0%	Brazil	1.2%

Sources: *Trade Analysis System* of the United Nations. The re-export data is from the *World Trade Atlas* Database.

Channels of trade and financial linkages

Trade linkages

In the decade before the crises of June 1997 to December 1998, the East Asian countries had de facto pegged their exchange rates to the US dollar (Mckinnon, 2001). When a calamitous devaluation occurs in any one Asian economy (as in Thailand in June 1997), the rules of the currency–basket game require that

Table 8.4 (f) Percentage of exports in 1999 to different destinations

Country	Rank	Industry 0: Food and Live Animals		Industry 1: Beverages and Tobacco		Industry 2: Crude Materials, inedible	
India	1st	USA	20.0%	Russian	26.1%	Japan	23.5%
	2nd	Japan	16.3%	UK	18.0%	China	16.9%
	3rd	Russian	7.9%	USA	9.3%	USA	10.9%
	4th	UK	6.6%	Germany	6.8%	Italy	7.7%
	5th	Germany	3.9%	Poland	5.6%	Germany	4.9%
	6th	Malaysia	3.6%	Nether.	4.3%	HK	3.8%
	7th	Nether.	3.1%	Belgium	4.3%	Belgium	3.2%
	8th	Kuwait	2.8%	Singapore	3.7%	Korea	2.9%
	9th	Italy	2.7%	Egypt	3.1%	Nether.	2.7%
	10th	Korea	2.6%	Romania	1.9%	Russian	2.6%
		Industry 3: Fuels and Lubricants, etc.		Industry 4: Animal,Veg.Oils,Fats, Wax		Industry 5: Chemical Reltd. Prod. Nes.	
	1st	Japan	45.2%	USA	19.8%	USA	14.7%
	2nd	Singapore	13.5%	Japan	12.3%	Germany	6.4%
	3rd	Korea	9.6%	China	11.5%	Italy	5.0%
	4th	France	9.6%	Germany	11.5%	Russian	4.8%
	5th	Venezuela	7.7%	France	9.9%	Korea	4.6%
	6th	Thailand	4.8%	Thailand	5.8%	UK	4.2%
	7th	Australia	3.8%	Nether.	4.9%	Singapore	3.8%
	8th	Nether.	2.9%	Italy	3.7%	Mexico	3.2%
	9th	USA	1.0%	UK	3.7%	Brazil	3.1%
	10th	Banglad.	0.0%	Spain	2.9%	China	3.1%
		Industry 6: Manufactured Goods		Industry 7: Machines, Transport Equip.		Industry 8: Misc. Manufacture Articles	
	1st	USA	30.8%	USA	18.9%	USA	37.2%
	2nd	HK	13.2%	Germany	9.2%	UK	11.5%
	3rd	Belgium	7.4%	UK	8.3%	Germany	10.9%
	4th	Japan	5.2%	Singapore	5.0%	France	7.3%
	5th	UK	5.0%	Sri Lanka	4.6%	Italy	4.3%
	6th	Germany	4.3%	Malaysia	4.5%	Canada	3.4%
	7th	Italy	3.0%	Nigeria	3.5%	Nether.	3.2%
	8th	ISrael	2.6%	Italy	3.3%	Spain	2.0%
	9th	Korea	2.5%	France	2.8%	Belgium	1.9%
	10th	France	1.9%	Korea	2.8%	Japan	1.5%

Sources: *Trade Analysis System* of the United Nations. The re-export data is from the *World Trade Atlas* Database.

countries competing in common third markets in terms of trade, as the East Asian countries do, devalue as well. So the problem of contagious devaluation is built into the rules of the currency–basket regime. The probit estimation results of Eichengreen and Rose (1999), Glick and Rose (1999) and Forbes (2000) provide strong evidence of the role of trade in the propagation of recent crises.

Nevertheless, some other empirical papers argue that trade alone fails to explain the spread of the crisis from Thailand to other Asian countries in 1997. For instance, Masson (1998) calculates the loss in the trade competition of five

Table 8.4 (g) Percentage of exports in 1999 to different destinations

Country	Rank	Industry 0: Food and Live Animals		Industry 1: Beverages and Tobacco		Industry 2: Crude Materials, inedible	
Indonesia	1st	Japan	27.3%	USA	12.4%	Japan	27.7%
	2nd	USA	22.8%	Germany	12.4%	USA	12.5%
	3rd	HK	6.1%	Belgium	11.2%	China	12.2%
	4th	Germany	4.7%	Russian	10.0%	Korea	11.7%
	5th	Malaysia	4.5%	Nether.	9.4%	Spain	8.7%
	6th	Nether.	4.1%	Denmark	7.1%	Philip.	3.4%
	7th	Thailand	3.5%	Spain	5.9%	HK	2.8%
	8th	China	2.7%	HK	5.3%	Italy	2.5%
	9th	Korea	2.6%	Malaysia	4.7%	Malaysia	2.3%
	10th	UK	2.5%	UK	4.1%	Germany	1.9%
		Industry 3: Fuels and Lubricants, etc.		Industry 4: Animal,Veg.Oils,Fats, Wax		Industry 5: Chemical Reltd. Prod. Nes.	
	1st	Japan	52.8%	Germany	16.4%	China	16.6%
	2nd	Korea	23.0%	Nether.	15.7%	Japan	11.5%
	3rd	Australia	6.6%	China	14.9%	Thailand	9.3%
	4th	China	5.4%	Malaysia	10.0%	Malaysia	9.2%
	5th	USA	5.4%	USA	7.1%	HK	9.1%
	6th	Thailand	1.9%	Spain	6.1%	USA	7.6%
	7th	Spain	0.8%	UK	4.2%	Philip.	5.9%
	8th	Malaysia	0.8%	Turkey	3.3%	Korea	5.0%
	9th	HK	0.8%	Korea	3.0%	Australia	4.2%
	10th	Philip.	0.7%	Italy	2.7%	Nether.	2.4%
		Industry 6: Manufactured Goods		Industry 7: Machines, Transport Equip.		Industry 8: Misc. Manufacture Articles	
	1st	Japan	21.2%	USA	33.0%	USA	42.7%
	2nd	USA	14.4%	Japan	17.5%	Germany	9.3%
	3rd	China	9.9%	Malaysia	7.0%	Japan	8.5%
	4th	HK	6.3%	Germany	4.4%	UK	7.8%
	5th	Korea	5.4%	UK	4.2%	France	4.8%
	6th	Malaysia	4.2%	Thailand	3.3%	Nether.	4.0%
	7th	UK	3.9%	China	3.2%	Belgium	3.6%
	8th	Australia	3.9%	France	3.2%	Italy	2.6%
	9th	Germany	3.2%	HK	2.5%	spain	2.4%
	10th	Belgium	3.0%	Belgium	2.1%	Canada	1.9%

Sources: *Trade Analysis System* of the United Nations. The re-export data is from the *World Trade Atlas* Database.

Asian countries during the Asian Crisis, as measured by the changes in their real effective exchange rates. He finds that the competition effect is too small to explain for the spread of the Crisis from Thailand throughout Asia. Similarly, Baig and Goldfajn (1998) measure the direct and indirect trade linkages of the East Asian countries and do not find much evidence to support the trade linkage hypothesis. Their measures show that the third–country export profiles of the five infected East Asian countries are not similar enough to generate severe competitive pressure.

Table 8.4 (h) Percentage of exports in 1999 to different destinations

Country	Rank	Industry 0: Food and Live Animals		Industry 1: Beverages and Tobacco		Industry 2: Crude Materials, inedible	
S.Korea	1st	Japan	74.3%	Japan	52.5%	China	31.6%
	2nd	USA	6.5%	HK	15.0%	Japan	19.0%
	3rd	HK	3.5%	USA	11.9%	USA	11.2%
	4th	China	2.8%	Turkey	10.6%	HK	8.6%
	5th	Spain	1.8%	Greece	1.9%	Belgium	3.4%
	6th	Thailand	1.7%	Germany	1.3%	Malaysia	2.7%
	7th	Canada	1.1%	Oman	1.3%	Germany	2.3%
	8th	Philip.	1.0%	Russian	0.6%	Italy	2.3%
	9th	UK	1.0%	Singapore	0.6%	Singapore	2.2%
	10th	Italy	0.9%	China	0.6%	Thailand	1.5%
		Industry 3: Fuels and Lubricants, etc.		Industry 4: Animal,Veg.Oils,Fats, Wax		Industry 5: Chemical Reltd. Prod. Nes.	
	1st	Japan	41.0%	Japan	36.4%	China	40.3%
	2nd	China	29.3%	China	27.3%	HK	9.7%
	3rd	HK	11.0%	Russian	9.1%	Japan	9.3%
	4th	Singapore	7.4%	Thailand	9.1%	USA	8.8%
	5th	USA	6.8%	Philip.	9.1%	Thailand	3.2%
	6th	New Zeal.	0.9%	Israel	9.1%	Malaysia	2.6%
	7th	Thailand	0.7%	-	-	Philip.	2.3%
	8th	Australia	0.6%	-	-	Mexico	2.1%
	9th	Philip.	0.5%	-	-	Italy	1.5%
	10th	Russian	0.5%	-	-	UK	1.5%
		Industry 6: Manufactured Goods		Industry 7: Machines, Transport Equip.		Industry 8: Misc. Manufacture Articles	
	1st	China	26.9%	USA	32.1%	USA	38.0%
	2nd	USA	16.3%	Japan	8.5%	Japan	22.0%
	3rd	HK	12.6%	China	6.6%	China	6.0%
	4th	Japan	10.2%	UK	5.1%	Germany	4.7%
	5th	Thailand	2.4%	HK	5.0%	UK	3.6%
	6th	Mexico	2.3%	Germany	4.5%	HK	3.0%
	7th	Australia	2.0%	Singapore	4.2%	Canada	2.8%
	8th	UK	2.0%	Malaysia	3.7%	Mexico	2.3%
	9th	Singapore	1.9%	Mexico	2.3%	Singapore	2.1%
	10th	Malaysia	1.9%	Canada	2.2%	France	2.0%

Sources: *Trade Analysis System* of the United Nations. The re-export data is from the *World Trade Atlas* Database.

Financial linkages

Besides trade linkages, financial linkages are also important sources of contagion of financial and currency crises. The hypothesis that financial linkages are important channels for the contagion of currency crises was bolstered by the contagion of the 1995 Mexican Crisis to Argentina. Even though the bilateral and third–party trade linkages between Argentina and Mexico were weak, Argentina

Table 8.4 (i) Percentage of exports in 1999 to different destinations

Country	Rank	Industry 0: Food and Live Animals		Industry 1: Beverages and Tobacco		Industry 2: Crude Materials, inedible	
Malaysia	1st	Singapore	39.5%	Singapore	52.7%	Japan	22.5%
	2nd	Japan	9.7%	HK	21.3%	China	15.6%
	3rd	HK	7.3%	Thailand	10.7%	Singapore	10.1%
	4th	USA	7.3%	Japan	6.0%	Korea	6.1%
	5th	Nether.	5.4%	USA	2.7%	USA	5.4%
	6th	Australia	3.2%	Philip.	2.0%	HK	4.9%
	7th	UK	3.1%	China	1.3%	Thailand	4.6%
	8th	Germany	2.5%	Macau	0.7%	Nether.	4.1%
	9th	China	2.3%	France	0.7%	Germany	3.8%
	10th	Italy	2.1%	Kuwait	0.7%	Belgium	3.0%
	-	Industry 3: Fuels and Lubricants, etc.		Industry 4: Animal,Veg.Oils,Fats, Wax		Industry 5: Chemical Reltd. Prod. Nes.	
	1st	Japan	45.7%	Pakistan	14.4%	Singapore	17.0%
	2nd	Korea	20.7%	China	14.2%	Japan	14.0%
	3rd	Singapore	8.5%	Japan	8.1%	China	13.0%
	4th	USA	6.2%	Singapore	7.9%	HK	10.6%
	5th	Australia	5.9%	Nether.	6.7%	USA	10.2%
	6th	Thailand	4.7%	USA	6.5%	Thailand	6.6%
	7th	China	3.9%	Germany	4.7%	Korea	6.0%
	8th	Philip.	2.1%	Egypt	3.9%	Nether.	4.3%
	9th	New Zeal.	1.0%	Korea	3.3%	Philip.	3.5%
	10th	Sri Lanka	0.6%	S. Afr.	2.9%	Australia	3.3%
		Industry 6: Manufactured Goods		Industry 7: Machines, Transport Equip.		Industry 8: Misc. Manufacture Articles	
	1st	Singapore	19.8%	USA	32.1%	USA	32.4%
	2nd	Japan	15.8%	Singapore	21.9%	Singapore	24.1%
	3rd	Thailand	11.9%	Japan	9.6%	Japan	9.1%
	4th	USA	9.6%	HK	4.7%	UK	6.1%
	5th	China	9.3%	UK	4.3%	Germany	4.0%
	6th	HK	7.9%	Germany	3.5%	France	2.8%
	7th	Korea	3.7%	China	2.7%	Australia	2.7%
	8th	UK	3.2%	Nether.	2.6%	Belgium	2.0%
	9th	Australia	2.9%	Korea	2.6%	Canada	1.9%
	10th	Germany	1.8%	Australia	2.0%	HK	1.7%

Sources: *Trade Analysis System* of the United Nations. The re-export data is from the *World Trade Atlas* Database.

had close financial linkages to Mexico. The financial channels through which crises are transmitted across countries include mainly the following.

The role of international liquidity constraint Calvo (1998a) has stressed the role of liquidity in financial contagion. A leveraged investor facing margin calls needs to sell (to an uninformed counterpart) his/her asset holdings in order to raise liquidity. The strategy is not to sell assets the prices of which have already

Table 8.4 (j) Percentage of exports in 1999 to different destinations

Country	Rank	Industry 0: Food and Live Animals		Industry 1: Beverages and Tobacco		Industry 2: Crude Materials, inedible	
Mexico	1st	USA	77.3%	USA	82.9%	USA	59.8%
	2nd	Japan	6.4%	Canada	3.7%	Japan	13.5%
	3rd	Canada	3.4%	Germany	1.5%	Canada	3.5%
	4th	Algeria	1.2%	Spain	1.5%	Kkorea	2.8%
	5th	Spain	1.2%	Japan	1.1%	Belgium	2.4%
	6th	France	0.9%	France	1.1%	Germany	2.2%
	7th	Germany	0.8%	Denmark	0.8%	China	2.0%
	8th	Guatemala	0.7%	UK	0.7%	Russian	1.2%
	9th	Brazil	0.6%	Belgium	0.7%	Nether.	1.1%
	10th	Nether.	0.6%	Greece	0.5%	Italy	1.1%
		Industry 3: Fuels and Lubricants, etc.		Industry 4: Animal,Veg.Oils,Fats, Wax		Industry 5: Chemical Reltd. Prod. Nes.	
	1st	USA	83.5%	USA	78.8%	USA	43.1%
	2nd	Spain	6.9%	Japan	5.8%	Brazil	7.6%
	3rd	Japan	3.5%	Germany	3.8%	Argentina	4.6%
	4th	Canada	2.0%	UK	1.9%	Colombia	4.4%
	5th	Portugal	1.2%	Guatemala	1.9%	Venezuela	3.5%
	6th	UK	1.0%	France	1.9%	Guatemala	3.1%
	7th	Guatemala	0.5%	Venezuela	1.9%	Costa Rica	2.5%
	8th	El Salvador	0.4%	Panama	1.9%	Japan	2.3%
	9th	Brazil	0.2%	Spain	0.0%	Peru	2.2%
	10th	Panama	0.2%	Nether.	0.0%	Canada	2.1%
		Industry 6: Manufactured Goods		Industry 7: Machines, Transport Equip.		Industry 8: Misc. Manufacture Articles	
	1st	USA	82.1%	USA	86.3%	USA	91.2%
	2nd	Canada	3.9%	Canada	6.4%	Canada	3.6%
	3rd	Guatemala	1.3%	Germany	1.4%	Germany	0.7%
	4th	Venezuela	1.1%	Singapore	0.7%	Japan	0.6%
	5th	UK	1.1%	Japan	0.6%	France	0.5%
	6th	Coata Rica	1.0%	UK	0.4%	Guatemala	0.2%
	7th	Korea	0.8%	France	0.4%	Australia	0.2%
	8th	Japan	0.8%	Argentina	0.3%	UK	0.2%
	9th	Colombia	0.7%	Brazil	0.3%	Colombia	0.2%
	10th	Belgium	0.7%	Venezuela	0.2%	Costa Rica	0.2%

Sources: *Trade Analysis System* of the United Nations. The re-export data is from the *World Trade Atlas* Database.

collapsed, but rather to sell portfolio assets that have yet to lose their value. This causes the asset prices in other markets to crash. Goldfajn and Valdes (1997) also develops a model in which a crisis in a single country is contagious because it reduces the liquidity of international investors who participate in the markets of both the crisis country and elsewhere. Investors are forced to recompose their portfolios and to sell assets in countries that have yet to crash in order to satisfy margin calls.

Table 8.4 (k) Percentage of exports in 1999 to different destinations

Country	Rank	Industry 0: Food and Live Animals		Industry 1: Beverages and Tobacco		Industry 2: Crude Materials, inedible	
Philippines	1st	Japan	39.6%	HK	43.4%	Japan	50.6%
	2nd	USA	27.1%	Spain	14.1%	Germany	7.3%
	3rd	Korea	6.8%	USA	12.1%	USA	6.4%
	4th	HK	5.3%	Japan	5.1%	Korea	6.4%
	5th	Germany	3.0%	Germany	3.0%	China	5.1%
	6th	China	2.8%	Malaysia	3.0%	UK	4.9%
	7th	UK	2.1%	Thailand	3.0%	France	3.7%
	8th	Canada	1.9%	Egypt	2.0%	HK	2.9%
	9th	Nether.	1.5%	Singapore	2.0%	Malaysia	2.4%
	10th	Singapore	1.1%	UK	2.0%	Singapore	1.7%
		Industry 3: Fuels and Lubricants, etc.		Industry 4: Animal,Veg.Oils,Fats, Wax		Industry 5: Chemical Reltd. Prod. Nes.	
	1st	HK	22.9%	USA	43.7%	Japan	16.0%
	2nd	China	17.9%	Germany	17.9%	USA	15.6%
	3rd	Japan	17.9%	Nether.	15.0%	China	12.4%
	4th	Korea	16.9%	Japan	5.4%	HK	11.1%
	5th	Malaysia	8.5%	Belgium	3.1%	Korea	7.6%
	6th	Singapore	8.0%	France	2.9%	Thailand	7.1%
	7th	Thailand	2.5%	Italy	2.5%	Australia	6.2%
	8th	Macau	2.5%	Canda	1.8%	Malaysia	4.4%
	9th	Australia	1.5%	China	1.3%	Singapore	3.1%
	10th	Canada	1.0%	Mexico	1.1%	UK	3.1%
		Industry 6: Manufactured Goods		Industry 7: Machines, Transport Equip.		Industry 8: Misc. Manufacture Articles	
	1st	USA	25.4%	USA	34.4%	USA	65.1%
	2nd	Japan	17.8%	Japan	13.5%	Japan	9.7%
	3rd	China	10.9%	Singapore	11.1%	Germany	5.5%
	4th	Singapore	10.5%	Malaysia	6.3%	UK	3.2%
	5th	HK	5.6%	UK	5.5%	Canada	2.2%
	6th	Korea	5.0%	HK	4.9%	France	2.1%
	7th	Germany	3.1%	Germany	4.0%	HK	1.8%
	8th	Thailand	3.0%	Korea	3.5%	Nether.	1.6%
	9th	Malaysia	2.0%	Nether.	3.2%	Singapore	1.0%
	10th	UK	2.0%	Thailand	2.9%	Spain	1.0%

Sources: *Trade Analysis System* of the United Nations. The re-export data is from the *World Trade Atlas* Database.

The role of common creditors A common creditor is a country that lent heavily to the crisis countries and other major countries. There are several mechanisms of how common creditors, or banking centers, can cause cross–border spillovers. Losses in one country can lead banks to sell off assets in other countries in an attempt to restore their capital–adequacy ratios. Moreover, if banks are confronted with losses in their securities portfolio or a rise in non–performing loans in a given country, they are likely to try to reduce their overall value at risk. As indicated in Table 8.12(a)–Table 8.12(b), the US banks have an extensive exposure to

Table 8.4 (I) Percentage of exports in 1999 to different destinations

Country	Rank	Industry 0: Food and Live Animals		Industry 1: Beverages and Tobacco		Industry 2: Crude Materials, inedible	
Singapore	1st	Japan	25.8%	HK	72.1%	Japan	16.5%
	2nd	HK	12.8%	Malaysia	4.8%	USA	13.7%
	3rd	USA	11.0%	Philip.	4.8%	Malaysia	9.3%
	4th	Australia	8.2%	Thailand	4.1%	UK	8.7%
	5th	Philip.	6.6%	China	3.4%	HK	8.7%
	6th	Malaysia	4.7%	Sri Lanka	2.7%	Philip.	4.8%
	7th	Thailand	4.1%	UK	2.0%	China	4.4%
	8th	UK	3.9%	USA	1.4%	Thailand	4.0%
	9th	Nether.	1.9%	Japan	0.7%	Germany	3.4%
	10th	China	1.7%	France	0.7%	Korea	2.8%
		Industry 3: Fuels and Lubricants, etc.		Industry 4: Animal,Veg.Oils,Fats, Wax		Industry 5: Chemical Reltd. Prod. Nes.	
	1st	HK	32.6%	Kenya	18.3%	Malaysia	11.4%
	2nd	Malaysia	23.1%	Sri Lanka	8.8%	China	11.3%
	3rd	China	15.3%	China	6.7%	USA	11.1%
	4th	Japan	8.0%	Philip.	6.7%	UK	9.0%
	5th	Australia	4.8%	Japan	5.0%	HK	8.8%
	6th	USA	4.1%	Australia	4.6%	France	7.0%
	7th	Thailand	4.0%	Uganda	4.2%	Thailand	6.8%
	8th	Philip.	2.5%	Thailand	4.2%	Japan	6.3%
	9th	Korea	2.2%	Egypt	3.8%	Philip.	4.9%
	10th	Sri Lanka	1.2%	Sri Lanka	3.8%	Belgium	4.8%
		Industry 6: Manufactured Goods		Industry 7: Machines, Transport Equip.		Industry 8: Misc. Manufacture Articles	
	1st	Malaysia	21.9%	USA	29.0%	USA	24.7%
	2nd	HK	12.3%	Malaysia	11.3%	Japan	10.5%
	3rd	Thailand	12.1%	HK	8.8%	Malaysia	9.6%
	4th	China	6.9%	Japan	6.5%	HK	8.8%
	5th	USA	4.6%	Germany	5.0%	UK	7.8%
	6th	Japan	4.4%	UK	4.8%	Australia	4.9%
	7th	Korea	4.3%	China	4.1%	Hungary	4.6%
	8th	Philip.	4.3%	Nether.	4.0%	China	4.3%
	9th	UK	4.1%	Thailand	3.5%	Thailand	4.2%
	10th	Sri Lanka	3.6%	Ireland	3.4%	Germany	3.7%

Sources: *Trade Analysis System* of the United Nations. The re-export data is from the *World Trade Atlas* Database.

Latin America while the Japanese banks had an extensive exposure to Asia. When foreign banks recall loans and dry up credit lines, they exacerbate the original crises. The recalling of loans *elsewhere* by the foreign banks can also propagate crises. The fact that both US and Japanese credit are regionally concentrated helps us to understand why contagion is more regional than global. The probit regression results of Caramazza, Ricci and Salgado (2000) support this hypothesis. Their study shows that adding the common creditor variable greatly enhances the explanatory power of the regressions on the prediction of financial crises.

Table 8.4 (m) Percentage of exports in 1999 to different destinations

Country	Rank	Industry 0: Food and Live Animals		Industry 1: Beverages and Tobacco		Industry 2: Crude Materials, inedible	
Taiwan	1st	Japan	51.3%	HK	29.8%	China	29.4%
	2nd	USA	19.4%	USA	19.1%	Japan	20.4%
	3rd	HK	6.9%	Australia	14.9%	HK	12.9%
	4th	Thailand	4.7%	Japan	8.5%	USA	9.4%
	5th	Singapore	2.5%	Singapore	8.5%	Korea	5.7%
	6th	China	1.9%	UK	4.3%	Malaysia	4.3%
	7th	Philip.	1.8%	Germany	4.3%	Philip.	2.8%
	8th	Malaysia	1.8%	Czech	2.1%	Thailand	2.2%
	9th	Canada	1.5%	China	2.1%	UK	2.2%
	10th	Korea	1.3%	Cyprus	2.1%	Pakistan	1.6%
		Industry 3: Fuels and Lubricants, etc.		Industry 4: Animal,Veg.Oils,Fats, Wax		Industry 5: Chemical Reltd . Prod. Nes.	
	1st	China	22.8%	HK	21.1%	China	43.7%
	2nd	Singapore	21.6%	China	13.2%	HK	18.6%
	3rd	HK	21.3%	USA	10.5%	Japan	7.2%
	4th	Korea	5.6%	Japan	10.5%	USA	6.0%
	5th	USA	5.6%	El Salvador	10.5%	Thailand	3.4%
	6th	Japan	4.5%	Korea	7.9%	Malaysia	2.9%
	7th	New Zeal.	4.5%	Thailand	5.3%	Singapore	2.5%
	8th	Philip.	2.6%	Australia	5.3%	Korea	2.1%
	9th	Australia	1.9%	Philip.	5.3%	PHilip.	1.8%
	10th	Guatemala	1.9%	Egypt	5.3%	Australia	1.4%
		Industry 6: Manufactured Goods		Industry 7: Machines, Transport Equip.		Industry 8: Misc. Manufacture Articles	
	1st	China	26.7%	USA	30.1%	USA	41.6%
	2nd	USA	19.2%	China	9.9%	Japan	10.9%
	3rd	HK	15.5%	Japan	9.6%	HK	5.9%
	4th	Japan	5.1%	HK	8.2%	China	5.4%
	5th	Thailand	2.9%	Germany	5.3%	Germany	5.1%
	6th	Malaysia	2.8%	Singapore	4.2%	UK	4.4%
	7th	UK	2.3%	UK	3.8%	Singapore	2.6%
	8th	Germany	2.3%	Nether.	3.3%	Canada	2.5%
	9th	Philip.	2.1%	Malaysia	2.9%	France	2.2%
	10th	Canada	2.0%	Canada	2.7%	Australia	2.0%

Sources: *Trade Analysis System* of the United Nations. The re-export data is from the *World Trade Atlas* Database.

The role of cross country hedging and portfolio rebalancing Since cross–market hedging usually requires a high correlation of asset returns, the cross–country hedging and portfolio rebalancing hypothesis implies that countries whose asset returns exhibit a high degree of co–movement with the initial crisis countries (such as those of Argentina with Mexico and Malaysia with Thailand) will be more vulnerable to contagion via cross–market hedges. In addition, the value at risk model of Schinasi and Smith (1999) illustrates how shocks that seem purely local (for example, a financial crisis in one country) can have wider reverberations, in

Table 8.4 (n) Percentage of exports in 1999 to different destinations

Country	Rank	Industry 0: Food and Live Animals		Industry 1: Beverages and Tobacco		Industry 2: Crude Materials, inedible	
Thailand	1st	USA	24.8%	USA	33.7%	Japan	27.3%
	2nd	Japan	24.6%	Singapore	10.6%	China	13.2%
	3rd	HK	6.6%	Japan	7.7%	Malaysia	11.5%
	4th	Nether.	3.9%	Germany	5.8%	USA	11.3%
	5th	Malaysia	3.8%	France	5.8%	Korea	5.5%
	6th	Germany	3.4%	Malaysia	4.8%	HK	4.7%
	7th	Singapore	3.4%	UK	3.8%	France	3.4%
	8th	Canada	3.1%	Philip.	3.8%	Italy	3.3%
	9th	Australia	3.1%	Egypt	2.9%	Singapore	2.9%
	10th	UK	2.8%	HK	2.9%	Germany	2.6%
		Industry 3: Fuels and Lubricants, etc.		Industry 4: Animal,Veg.Oils,Fats, Wax		Industry 5: Chemical Reltd. Prod. Nes.	
	1st	Singapore	55.1%	Japan	21.2%	China	25.8%
	2nd	China	20.6%	Malaysia	18.2%	HK	19.8%
	3rd	Korea	7.3%	Korea	9.1%	Japan	13.8%
	4th	USA	4.1%	Spain	6.1%	Malaysia	7.0%
	5th	Japan	3.2%	Nether.	6.1%	Philip.	5.2%
	6th	Malaysia	2.7%	UK	6.1%	Singapore	4.8%
	7th	HK	2.7%	Germany	6.1%	USA	4.5%
	8th	Australia	2.7%	Belgium	6.1%	Pakistan	3.0%
	9th	Philip.	0.6%	Australia	3.0%	Australia	2.3%
	10th	France	0.3%	Singapore	3.0%	Korea	1.5%
		Industry 6: Manufactured Goods		Industry 7: Machines, Transport Equip.		Industry 8: Misc. Manufacture Articles	
	1st	USA	24.6%	USA	26.4%	USA	39.9%
	2nd	Japan	11.8%	Singapore	15.3%	Japan	14.6%
	3rd	HK	9.1%	Japan	13.0%	Germany	10.2%
	4th	China	6.5%	Malaysia	5.2%	France	8.7%
	5th	Singapore	5.1%	UK	4.4%	UK	6.3%
	6th	Belgium	4.4%	China	4.0%	HK	3.1%
	7th	Malaysia	4.3%	HK	3.8%	Canada	2.4%
	8th	UK	3.6%	Germany	3.8%	Belgium	2.4%
	9th	Germany	3.0%	Nether.	3.2%	Spain	1.6%
	10th	Australia	2.9%	Australia	2.8%	Nether.	1.5%

Sources: *Trade Analysis System* of the United Nations. The re-export data is from the *World Trade Atlas* Database.

cases in which basic principles of portfolio diversification give rise to "contagious selling" of financial assets. They show that if a shock occurs at period t which results in a reduction in equity capital available to a manager whose portfolio is leveraged, then the optimal strategy involves net sales of risky assets during period t. Because movements of the financial markets strongly impact the movements of exchange rates,[1] the Schinasi and Smith study of volatility spillovers in the financial markets is highly relevant to the understanding of spillovers in the foreign exchange market.

Table 8.4 (o) Percentage of exports in 1999 to different destinations

Country	Rank	Industry 0: Food and Live Animals		Industry 1: Beverages and Tobacco		Industry 2: Crude Materials, inedible	
Uruguay	1st	Brazil	44.3%	Paraguay	82.8%	China	20.2%
	2nd	USA	6.0%	Brazil	6.9%	italy	14.5%
	3rd	Israel	5.9%	UK	3.4%	Spain	14.5%
	4th	Argentina	5.7%	HK	3.4%	Germany	11.1%
	5th	UK	5.5%	Argentina	1.7%	Norway	5.7%
	6th	Germany	3.9%	USA	1.7%	USA	3.8%
	7th	Spain	3.3%	Philip.	0.0%	Argentina	3.8%
	8th	Venezuela	3.0%	Nether.	0.0%	UK	3.4%
	9th	Nether.	2.4%	Chile	0.0%	Brazil	3.4%
	10th	Canada	2.1%	Norway	0.0%	Turkey	3.1%
		Industry 3: Fuels and Lubricants, etc.		Industry 4: Animal,Veg.Oils,Fats, Wax		Industry 5: Chemical Reltd. Prod. Nes.	
	1st	Argentina	90.5%	Brazil	58.8%	Brazil	43.6%
	2nd	Brazil	4.8%	Argentina	5.9%	Argentina	21.0%
	3rd	USA	0.0%	Italy	5.9%	Paraguay	6.2%
	4th	Bolivia	0.0%	Spain	5.9%	Switz.	4.6%
	5th	Paraguay	0.0%	Colombia	5.9%	Japan	4.1%
	6th	-	-	Korea	5.9%	USA	4.1%
	7th	-	-	Belgium	5.9%	Ecuador	3.6%
	8th	-	-	Nether.	0.0%	Venezuela	3.1%
	9th	-	-	Israel	0.0%	Spain	1.0%
	10th	-	-	Banglad.	0.0%	Mexico	1.0%
		Industry 6: Manufactured Goods		Industry 7: Machines, Transport Equip.		Industry 8: Misc. Manufacture Articles	
	1st	Argentina	26.1%	Argentina	42.7%	Brazil	34.9%
	2nd	Brazil	25.8%	Brazil	26.7%	Argentina	33.3%
	3rd	USA	14.5%	France	21.3%	USA	13.3%
	4th	HK	6.3%	USA	2.2%	Germany	7.2%
	5th	Canada	5.8%	Paraguay	1.3%	Mexico	1.5%
	6th	Germany	2.9%	Venezuela	0.9%	Switz.	1.0%
	7th	Mexico	2.9%	Mexico	0.9%	Paraguay	1.0%
	8th	China	2.6%	Italy	0.4%	Canada	1.0%
	9th	Norway	1.8%	Israel	0.4%	UK	1.0%
	10th	Singapore	1.6%	Nether.	0.4%	Sweden	0.5%

Sources: *Trade Analysis System* of the United Nations. The re-export data is from the *World Trade Atlas* Database.

Measures of trade and financial linkages

Measures of direct trade linkages

Glick and Rose's measure of direct trade linkages Indexes of direct trade linkages focus on bilateral trade between two countries. Glick and Rose (1998) propose the following measure of direct trade between the initial crisis country

Table 8.4 (p) Percentage of exports in 1999 to different destinations

Country	Rank	Industry 0: Food and Live Animals		Industry 1: Beverages and Tobacco		Industry 2: Crude Materials, inedible	
Venezuela	1st	USA	44.8%	Colombia	61.2%	USA	29.7%
	2nd	Colombia	14.1%	Spain	10.2%	Italy	13.7%
	3rd	Belgium	6.1%	Nether.	7.1%	Japan	9.3%
	4th	Germany	5.5%	USA	6.1%	UK	6.4%
	5th	Spain	4.7%	Switz.	3.1%	Denmark	5.6%
	6th	France	4.5%	Peru	2.0%	Belgium	5.0%
	7th	Italy	3.3%	Italy	2.0%	Norway	4.7%
	8th	Brazil	3.3%	Germany	2.0%	Nether.	3.4%
	9th	Peru	2.2%	HK	2.0%	Canada	3.2%
	10th	Japan	1.8%	Brazil	1.0%	Colombia	2.9%
		Industry 3: Fuels and Lubricants, etc.		Industry 4: Animal,Veg.Oils,Fats, Wax		Industry 5: Chemical Reltd. Prod. Nes.	
	1st	USA	70.7%	Colombia	44.4%	USA	26.9%
	2nd	Brazil	6.5%	Ecuador	22.2%	Colombia	26.4%
	3rd	Canada	4.4%	Japan	11.1%	Peru	10.9%
	4th	Trinidad	2.0%	USA	11.1%	Brazil	4.9%
	5th	Germany	1.8%	Mexico	11.1%	Ecuador	4.3%
	6th	Costa Rica	1.3%	-	-	Spain	4.2%
	7th	Colombia	1.3%	-	-	Mexico	3.4%
	8th	PEru	1.2%	-	-	Nether.	2.4%
	9th	Guatemala	1.1%	-	-	Italy	1.9%
	10th	France	1.0%	-	-	France	1.3%
		Industry 6: Manufactured Goods		Industry 7: Machines, Transport Equip.		Industry 8: Misc. Manufacture Articles	
	1st	USA	38.5%	USA	59.1%	USA	44.1%
	2nd	Colombia	11.5%	Colombia	17.4%	Colombia	18.3%
	3rd	Japan	11.0%	Ecuador	3.7%	UK	9.7%
	4th	Mexico	10.0%	Brazil	2.4%	Ecuador	3.2%
	5th	Spain	3.8%	Mexico	2.4%	Mexico	3.2%
	6th	Peru	3.6%	UK	2.1%	Panama	3.2%
	7th	Italy	3.2%	Trinidad	1.6%	Peru	2.2%
	8th	Ecuador	2.1%	Panama	1.6%	Trinidad	2.2%
	9th	Brazil	1.9%	Italy	1.3%	Ireland	2.2%
	10th	Costa Rica	1.7%	Peru	1.3%	Nether.	1.1%

Sources: *Trade Analysis System* of the United Nations. The re-export data is from the *World Trade Atlas* Database.

(country 0) and any other country (country i):

$$DirectTradeIndx_i^{GlickRose} = 1 - | Exp_{i0} - Exp_{0i} | / (Exp_{i0} + Exp_{0i}).$$

This index measures the similarity of bilateral exports in terms of size between country i and the initial crisis country 0. The more similar the size of

Table 8.5 (a) Share of total credits in 1994 from various creditors

Borrowing Countries /Creditors	Argentina	Brazil	Chile	Colombia	Mexico	Uruguay	Venezuela
Austria	0.87%	0.54%	0.65%	0.28%	0.59%	0.00%	1.03%
Belgium	0.26%	0.43%	0.47%	0.48%	1.22%	0.03%	1.24%
Canada	1.99%	4.61%	3.95%	3.04%	4.30%	0.72%	4.90%
Finland	0.00%	0.02%	0.25%	0.02%	0.02%	0.03%	0.03%
France	7.55%	11.16%	5.09%	6.86%	8.93%	3.64%	11.04%
Germany	18.51%	13.18%	13.69%	11.62%	7.01%	6.13%	14.14%
Italy	9.72%	3.06%	2.86%	4.05%	2.51%	7.53%	5.18%
Japan	4.69%	8.86%	7.68%	11.52%	6.26%	0.89%	3.99%
Luxembourg	0.02%	0.02%	0.02%	0.00%	0.04%	0.00%	0.07%
Netherlands	4..31%	5.39%	5.35%	0.00%	3.13%	19.24%	5.66%
Spain	5.40%	2.89%	10.35%	7.45%	4.32%	10.88%	2.13%
UK	9.19%	9.77%	7.07%	9.99%	15.48%	8.68%	11.84%
US	**27.74%**	**22.59%**	**29.74%**	**26.14%**	**34.29%**	**31.76%**	**31.25%**
	China	India	Indonesia	S.Korea	Malaysia	Philip.	Taiwan
Austria	2.37%	0.82%	2.19%	0.67%	0.35%	1.05%	0.51%
Belgium	1.15%	2.05%	1.86%	3.14%	1.08%	0.98%	2.62%
Canada	0.97%	0.79%	0.11%	1.09%	0.81%	4.19%	3.05%
Finland	0.17%	0.10%	0.10%	0.19%	0.44%	0.16%	0.22%
France	15.35%	10.17%	7.30%	7.10%	10.35%	11.95%	16.48%
Germany	7.63%	13.77%	8.13%	7.74%	14.15%	8.62%	6.92%
Italy	2.33%	1.36%	0.25%	1.61%	0.70%	0.76%	1.97%
Japan	**34.22%**	**27.22%**	**52.48%**	**30.79%**	**43.22%**	13.94%	**25.66%**
Luxembourg	0.18%	0.09%	0.06%	0.32%	0.31%	0.01%	0.05%
Netherlands	2.77%	6.36%	3.94%	1.24%	3.47%	6.40%	2.86%
Spain	1.36%	0.13%	0.22%	0.25%	0.02%	1.00%	0.01%
UK	9.63%	18.53%	7.19%	11.47%	9.62%	10.44%	14.72%
US	2.32%	7.73%	7.02%	9.69%	10.18%	**37.41%**	12.12%
	Thailand	HK	Singapore				
Austria	1.08%	0.73%	0.79%	-	-	-	-
Belgium	1.72%	1.63%	2.75%	-	-	-	-
Canada	0.92%	0.83%	0.96%	-	-	-	-
Finland	0.34%	0.13%	0.50%	-	-	-	-
France	5.15%	5.04%	5.72%	-	-	-	-
Germany	6.54%	7.91%	10.27%	-	-	-	-
Italy	0.65%	2.19%	3.10%	-	-	-	-
Japan	**60.28%**	**62.24%**	**53.62%**	-	-	-	-
Luxembourg	0.15%	0.01%	0.37%	-	-	-	-
Netherlands	1.42%	1.22%	1.96%	-	-	-	-
Spain	0.06%	0.66%	0.80%	-	-	-	-
UK	7.07%	9.15%	10.20%	-	-	-	-
US	6.13%	3.05%	2.73%	-	-	-	-

bilateral exports from country i and country 0, the higher is the index. The results of this index are reported in Table 8.6. The table shows that among all the 17 countries in the sample, the five countries that have the highest direct trade linkages with Mexico during the 1994 Mexican Crisis were in the following order: Chile, Argentina, Venezuela, Uruguay and Colombia. The five countries that have the highest direct trade linkages with Thailand during the 1997 Thai Crisis were Singapore, Malaysia, China, Philippines and Taiwan.

This index indicates that both Malaysia and Philippines, the first two

Table 8.5 (b) Share of total credits in 1997 from various creditors

Borrowing Countries /Creditors	Argentina	Brazil	Chile	Colombia	Mexico	Uruguay	Venezuela
Austria	0.70%	0.87%	0.82%	0.64%	0.50%	0.70%	0.67%
Belgium	0.41%	0.93%	1.20%	0.64%	1.06%	0.28%	1.15%
Canada	3.05%	2.90%	4.74%	3.41%	5.31%	0.85%	4.81%
Finland	0.01%	0.10%	0.07%	0.01%	0.02%	0.00%	0.02%
France	9.04%	11.30%	6.21%	7.65%	9.33%	4.55%	5.95%
Germany	14.20%	14.03%	14.51%	11.83%	9.38%	14.52%	13.05%
Italy	6.93%	3.61%	2.35%	2.56%	2.94%	7.81%	5.31%
Japan	2.66%	6.52%	5.71%	8.09%	7.57%	0.28%	2.51%
Luxembourg	0.04%	0.16%	0.18%	0.01%	0.08%	0.08%	0.02%
Netherlands	5.06%	7.83%	9.74%	4.32%	5.06%	17.27%	6.47%
Spain	**20.57%**	5.46%	17.52%	**24.59%**	9.40%	14.44%	7.77%
UK	10.12%	5.97%	3.22%	6.95%	8.94%	4.79%	9.17%
US	17.43%	**20.69%**	**21.97%**	20.17%	**26.91%**	**21.86%**	**29.39%**
-	China	India	Indonesia	S.Korea	Malaysia	Philip.	Taiwan
Austria	2.37%	0.82%	2.19%	0.67%	0.35%	1.05%	0.51%
Belgium	1.15%	2.05%	1.86%	3.14%	1.08%	0.98%	2.62%
Canada	0.97%	0.79%	0.11%	1.09%	0.81%	4.19%	3.05%
Finland	0.17%	0.10%	0.10%	0.19%	0.44%	0.16%	0.22%
France	15.35%	10.17%	7.30%	7.10%	10.35%	11.95%	16.48%
Germany	7.63%	13.77%	8.13%	7.74%	14.15%	8.62%	6.92%
Italy	2.33%	1.36%	0.25%	1.61%	0.70%	0.76%	1.97%
Japan	**34.22%**	**27.22%**	**52.48%**	**30.79%**	**43.22%**	13.94%	**25.66%**
Luxembourg	0.18%	0.09%	0.06%	0.32%	0.31%	0.01%	0.05%
Netherlands	2.77%	6.36%	3.94%	1.24%	3.47%	6.40%	2.86%
Spain	1.36%	0.13%	0.22%	0.25%	0.02%	1.00%	0.01%
UK	9.63%	18.53%	7.19%	11.47%	9.62%	10.44%	14.72%
US	2.32%	7.73%	7.02%	9.69%	10.18%	**37.41%**	12.12%
	Thailand	HK	Singapore				
Austria	1.10%	0.73%	0.79%	-	-	-	-
Belgium	1.73%	1.63%	2.75%	-	-	-	-
Canada	1.30%	0.83%	0.96%	-	-	-	-
Finland	0.22%	0.13%	0.50%	-	-	-	-
France	8.02%	5.04%	5.72%	-	-	-	-
Germany	10.24%	7.91%	10.27%	-	-	-	-
Italy	0.57%	2.19%	3.10%	-	-	-	-
Japan	**56.38%**	**62.24%**	**53.62%**	-	-	-	-
Luxembourg	0.21%	0.01%	0.37%	-	-	-	-
Netherlands	2.85%	1.22%	1.96%	-	-	-	-
Spain	0.24%	0.66%	0.80%	-	-	-	-
UK	4.01%	9.15%	10.20%	-	-	-	-
US	4.30%	3.05%	2.73%	-	-	-	-

countries infected by the Thai Crisis, have a high index of direct trade with Thailand during 1997. However, it should be noted that this index focuses only on measuring the similarity of bilateral trade but not on the importance of bilateral trade between any two countries. For instance, this direct trade index takes the highest value 1 when bilateral exports between two countries are identical—a condition that obtains even when the bilateral exports between two countries are zero. The income effect index of Forbes (2001) (which is discussed below) complements the Glick and Rose direct trade index by providing accurate measures of the importance of bilateral exports between two countries. These

Table 8.5 (c) Share of total credits in 2001 from various creditors

Borrowing Countries /Creditors	Argentina	Brazil	Chile	Colombia	Mexico	Uruguay	Venezuela
Austria	0.09%	0.17%	0.13%	0.16%	0.19%	1.47%	0.10%
Belgium	0.54%	0.31%	0.56%	0.40%	0.37%	0.68%	1.27%
Canada	N/A	N/A	N/A	N/A	N/A	N/A	N/A
Finland	0.02%	0.05%	0.16%	0.15%	0.05%	0.00%	0.21%
France	4.83%	3.97%	4.33%	5.85%	2.11%	2.12%	6.26%
Germany	8.89%	8.55%	7.43%	10.39%	3.32%	11.25%	9.31%
Italy	8.34%	7.51%	2.16%	3.04%	0.87%	6.58%	3.69%
Japan	2.12%	2.94%	2.69%	6.33%	1.48%	0.34%	2.19%
Luxembourg	4.37%	9.74%	4.17%	6.77%	1.79%	10.94%	3.73%
Netherlands	0.05%	0.72%	0.05%	0.06%	0.01%	0.15%	0.20%
Spain	24.48%	17.98%	**47.47%**	**26.59%**	**40.61%**	17.79%	**41.61%**
UK	8.45%	12.27%	3.50%	7.62%	3.10%	6.87%	8.16%
US	**28.29%**	**25.10%**	17.02%	24.37%	36.16%	**29.64%**	15.36%
	China	India	Indonesia	S.Korea	Malaysia	Philip.	Taiwan
Austria	0.48%	0.77%	0.49%	0.62%	0.29%	0.62%	0.14%
Belgium	1.41%	0.66%	0.73%	0.70%	0.40%	2.46%	1.80%
Canada	0.40%	2.02%	1.66%	2.26%	0.00%	1.24%	2.53%
Finland	0.36%	0.07%	0.43%	0.05%	0.00%	0.29%	0.00%
France	9.34%	4.00%	6.82%	9.93%	3.75%	5.24%	5.64%
Germany	12.37%	15.80%	21.26%	9.66%	6.47%	16.13%	5.22%
Italy	1.34%	0.93%	0.29%	0.95%	0.25%	0.67%	0.42%
Japan	**19.74%**	8.11%	**24.12%**	15.53%	13.01%	15.41%	10.56%
Luxembourg	3.48%	6.99%	8.81%	4.18%	2.66%	4.59%	11.37%
Netherlands	0.03%	0.00%	0.00%	0.08%	0.02%	0.00%	0.00%
Spain	0.88%	0.04%	0.20%	0.20%	0.03%	0.63%	0.01%
UK	11.43%	**25.50%**	9.90%	9.31%	**26.22%**	11.95%	15.36%
US	8.59%	20.02%	9.31%	**22.88%**	14.69%	**22.34%**	**34.89%**
	Thailand	HK	Singapore				
Austria	0.29%	0.18%	0.13%	-	-	-	-
Belgium	0.34%	1.70%	1.52%	-	-	-	-
Canada	0.54%	0.96%	1.47%	-	-	-	-
Finland	0.95%	0.01%	0.14%	-	-	-	-
France	5.09%	4.21%	4.02%	-	-	-	-
Germany	10.38%	8.34%	9.52%	-	-	-	-
Italy	0.33%	0.82%	2.20%	-	-	-	-
Japan	**28.79%**	16.14%	17.22%	-	-	-	-
Luxembourg	10.90%	0.95%	4.29%	-	-	-	-
Netherlands	0.04%	0.00%	0.01%	-	-	-	-
Spain	0.00%	0.14%	0.07%	-	-	-	-
UK	11.03%	**48.92%**	**22.61%**	-	-	-	-
US	10.22%	7.37%	12.59%	-	-	-	-

indexes of Glick and Rose (1998) and Forbes (2001) taken together allow us to understand the two most important aspects of direct trade linkages: the similarity of bilateral trade and the importance of bilateral trade between any two countries.

Forbes' measure of direct trade linkages The income effect index of Forbes (2001) measures another important aspect of the direct trade linkages between two countries. The income effect index captures the impact of a crisis on a country's demand for exports from other countries. The index is measured as the total exports from country i to the initial crisis country 0 as a percentage of

Table 8.6 Glick and Rose's index of direct trade linkage

Glick and Rose's measure of direct trade linkage with Mexico								
	1994	1995	1996	1997	1998	1999	2000	2001
Argentina	**0.812**	0.580	0.646	0.577	0.800	0.939	0.923	0.923
Brazil	0.636	0.599	0.609	0.906	0.931	0.922	N/A	N/A
Chile	**0.930**	0.452	0.352	0.618	0.892	0.743	0.700	0.795
China	0.629	0.518	0.454	0.214	0.278	0.291	0.268	0.321
Colombia	**0.654**	0.336	0.334	0.362	0.445	0.707	0.664	0.611
HK	0.357	0.875	0.896	0.715	0.509	0.405	0.286	0.386
India	0.649	0.592	0.460	0.519	0.217	0.156	0.342	0.342
Indonesia	0.288	0.289	0.216	0.195	0.104	0.097	0.094	0.094
S.Korea	0.057	0.167	0.271	0.089	0.099	0.142	0.146	0.171
Malaysia	0.025	0.154	0.209	0.161	0.201	0.112	0.173	0.318
Mexico	1	1	1	1	1	1	1	1
Philippines	0.310	0.330	0.614	0.716	0.524	0.292	0.079	0.099
Singapore	0.489	0.953	0.763	0.888	0.916	0.805	0.383	0.680
Taiwan	N/A	N/A	N/A	N/A	N/A	N/A	N/A	N/A
Thailand	0.281	0.643	0.780	0.801	0.501	0.509	0.209	0.364
Uruguay	**0.768**	0.324	0.463	0.641	0.471	0.761	0.893	0.787
Venezuela	**0.809**	0.622	0.620	0.671	0.585	0.588	0.783	0.751
Glick and Rose's measure of direct trade linkage with thailand								
	1994	1995	1996	1997	1998	1999	2000	2001
Argentina	0.472	0	0.911	0.674	0.827	0.708	0.661	0.555
Brazil	0.403	0.591	0.621	0.762	0.801	0.786	0.882	0.660
Chile	0.437	0.486	0.525	0.508	0.837	0.891	0.648	0.981
China	0.844	0.835	0.799	**0.922**	0.799	0.783	0.875	0.884
Colombia	0.419	0.747	0.590	0.559	0.471	0.533	0.323	0.363
HK	0.700	0.711	0.716	0.708	0.692	0.673	0.692	0.736
India	0.658	0.771	0.724	0.798	0.879	0.874	0.889	0.783
Indonesia	0.879	0.858	0.896	0.764	0.826	0.794	0.876	0.882
S.Korea	0.475	0.497	0.548	0.619	0.604	0.763	0.771	0.789
Malaysia	0.667	0.703	0.768	**0.932**	0.869	0.906	0.894	0.855
Mexico	0.281	0.643	0.780	0.801	0.501	0.509	0.209	0.364
Philippines	0.833	0.681	0.862	**0.899**	0.909	0.891	0.918	0.931
Singapore	0.929	0.927	0.965	**0.946**	0.945	0.956	0.968	0.917
Taiwan	0.634	0.641	0.712	**0.817**	0.940	0.957	0.952	N/A
Thailand	1	1	1	1	1	1	1	1
Uruguay	0.583	0.361	0.152	0.307	0.287	0.325	0.769	0.717
Venezuela	0.625	0.335	0.608	0.018	0.317	0	0	0.735

country i's GDP. The income effect index is defined as follows:

$$IncomeEff_i^{Forbes} = Exp_{i0} / GDP_i,$$

where Exp_{i0} is the export from country i to the initial crisis country 0 and GDP_i is

Table 8.7 Forbes' measure of income effect

Forbes' measure of income effect of a devaluation in Mexican peso (in percentage)						
	1994	1995	1996	1997	1998	1999
Argentina	0.106	0.107	0.091	0.071	0.089	0.099
Brazil	0.238	0.072	0.084	0.071	0.128	0.200
Chile	**0.437**	0.216	0.222	0.103	0.714	0.941
China	0.041	0.030	0.028	0.523	0.073	0.080
Colombia	0.212	0.107	0.097	0.047	0.138	0.245
HK	0.428	0.281	0.228	0.117	0.392	0.442
India	0.024	0.014	0.019	0.284	0.053	0.053
Indonesia	0.086	0.046	0.059	0.024	0.252	0.130
S.Korea	0.318	0.192	0.233	0.085	0.421	0.493
Malaysia	**0.515**	0.377	0.197	0.336	0.400	0.349
Mexico	-	-	-	-	-	-
Philippines	0.061	0.049	0	0.050	0.101	0.157
Singapore	0.302	0.232	0.437	0.543	0.610	0.831
Taiwan	0.232	0.151	0.172	0.225	0.297	0.316
Thailand	0.078	0.032	0.038	0.096	0.228	0.232
Uruguay	0.314	0.088	0.148	0.164	0.121	0.210
Venezuela	**0.574**	0.290	0.347	0.440	0.254	0.194
Forbes' measure of income effect of a devaluation in Thai Baht (in percentage)						
	1994	1995	1996	1997	1998	1999
Argentina	0.011	0	0.053	0.035	0.036	0.059
Brazil	0.087	0.061	0.051	0.045	0.016	0.031
Chile	0.232	0.244	0.178	0.185	0.069	0.069
China	0.236	0.270	0.161	0.171	0.124	0.146
Colombia	0.004	0.010	0.006	0.007	0.006	0.011
HK	0.987	1.159	1.173	1.092	0.906	0.983
India	0.123	0.136	0.118	0.116	0.090	0.107
Indonesia	0.240	0.372	0.384	0.431	1.111	0.588
S.Korea	0.453	0.494	0.520	0.514	0.433	0.424
Malaysia	0.945	3.230	3.182	**3.006**	3.132	3.497
Mexico	0.004	0.007	0.015	0.033	0.022	0.020
Philippines	0	1.088	0.942	**1.099**	0.957	1.111
Singapore	7.943	8.464	7.997	**6.447**	5.025	6.037
Taiwan	1.016	1.178	1.022	0.908	0.733	0.735
Thailand	-	-	-	-	-	-
Uruguay	0.012	0.005	0.005	0.013	0.014	0.015
Venezuela	0.002	0.006	0.006	0.000	0.007	0

the gross GDP of country i.

The income effect index reported in Table 8.7 shows that the followings: (1) the income effects are highest for Venezuela, Malaysia and Chile during the 1994–1995 Mexican Crisis and highest for Singapore, Malaysia and Philippines during the 1997–1998 Thai Crisis. (2) The magnitude of the income effect for Singapore, Malaysia and Philippines during the 1997 Thai Crisis are much higher than that experienced by Venezuela, Malaysia and Chile during the 1994 Mexican Crisis. In fact, Malaysia and Philippines were the first two countries affected by the collapse of the Thai baht in 1997.

Measures of indirect trade linkages (degree of trade competition)

Glick and Rose's measure of trade competition Glick and Rose also compute an absolute trade competition index to measure the extent of trade competition between an initial crisis country and any other country. Glick and Rose's measure of trade competition is a weighted average of the importance of exports to destination m for the initial crisis country 0 and any other given country i. The index gives greatest weight to destination m when destination m is an export market of equal importance to both country 0 and i. This absolute trade competition index is written as follows:

$$AbsTradeComp_i^{GlickRose} = \sum_m \left\{ \frac{Exp_{0,m} + Exp_{i,m}}{Exp_0 + Exp_i} \right\} \left\{ 1 - \frac{| Exp_{0,m} - Exp_{i,m} |}{Exp_{0,m} + Exp_{i,m}} \right\},$$

where $Exp_{0,m}$ is the export from the initial crisis country 0 to the destination country m. Exp_0 is the total export of country 0.

The absolute trade competition index is reported in Table 8.8(a). It shows that Malaysia, the first country affected by the Thai Crisis, had the highest degree of trade competition with Thailand before the Thai Crisis. Nevertheless, the index shows that Argentina, the country most affected by the 1995 Mexican Crisis, did not have high degree of trade competition with Mexico prior to the Mexican Crisis. This indicates that the contagion of the Mexican Crisis to Argentina was through a channel other than trade. Using a GARCH Model (which is discussed in a latter section), this chapter finds that the financial linkage is an important channel through which the Mexican Crisis was spillover to Argentina.

A variant of the absolute trade competition index is the relative trade competition index. This index uses trade shares instead of the absolute value of trade in the measure of trade competition. It is measured as follows:

$$RelTradeComp_i^{GlickRose} = \sum_m \left\{ \frac{Exp_{0,m} + Exp_{i,m}}{Exp_0 + Exp_i} \right\} \left\{ 1 - \frac{\left| \frac{Exp_{0,m}}{Exp_0} - \frac{Exp_{i,m}}{Exp_i} \right|}{\frac{Exp_{0,m}}{Exp_0} + \frac{Exp_{i,m}}{Exp_i}} \right\}.$$

The result of this index is reported in Table 8.8(b). Similar to the *absolute* trade competition index, this *relative* trade competition index indicates that Malaysia, the country first infected by the Thai Crisis, was most vulnerable to the trade competition effect of the devaluation in Thai baht. Also, this index indicates that

Table 8.8 (a) Glick and Rose's absolute trade competition index

Glick and Rose's measure of absolute trade competition with Mexico								
	1994	1995	1996	1997	1998	1999	2000	2001
Argentina	**0.388**	0.386	0.397	0.357	0.319	0.275	0.266	0.324
Brazil	0.278	0.252	0.250	0.215	0.207	0.206	0.200	0.246
Chile	0.167	0.168	0.168	0.152	0.131	0.115	0.104	0.157
China	0.303	0.295	0.297	0.298	0.321	0.326	0.317	0.370
Colombia	0.179	0.162	0.152	0.150	0.132	0.129	0.120	0.131
HK	**0.396**	0.373	0.352	0.348	0.348	0.342	0.326	0.325
India	0.200	0.194	0.196	0.183	0.191	0.193	0.174	0.212
Indonesia	0.200	0.187	0.184	0.171	0.165	0.148	0.141	0.194
S.Korea	0.340	0.320	0.274	0.256	0.270	0.293	0.300	0.336
Malaysia	0.282	0.275	0.239	0.225	0.236	0.234	0.209	0.231
Mexico	1	1	1	1	1	1	1	1
Philippines	0.217	0.212	0.201	0.203	0.204	0.188	0.170	0.212
Singapore	0.291	0.279	0.270	0.252	0.252	0.235	0.207	0.228
Taiwan	**0.437**	0.401	0.371	0.367	0.370	0.356	0.328	N/A
Thailand	0.262	0.233	0.215	0.209	0.215	0.207	0.196	0.219
Uruguay	0.045	0.046	0.043	0.037	0.032	0.023	0.021	0.026
Venezuela	0.266	0.241	0.239	0.224	0.161	0.160	0.202	0.228
Glick and Rose's measure of absolute trade competition with Thailand								
	1994	1995	1996	1997	1998	1999	2000	2001
Argentina	0.226	0.214	0.234	0.218	0.230	0.231	0.233	0.231
Brazil	0.527	0.508	0.515	0.478	0.482	0.497	0.515	0.517
Chile	0.283	0.313	0.308	0.322	0.298	0.294	0.307	0.360
China	0.439	0.420	0.427	0.388	0.375	0.402	0.367	0.338
Colombia	0.246	0.204	0.219	0.228	0.225	0.230	0.238	0.240
HK	0.368	0.385	0.379	0.372	0.387	0.422	0.416	0.440
India	0.519	0.503	0.536	0.525	0.547	0.548	0.578	0.590
Indonesia	0.659	0.633	0.670	**0.666**	0.664	0.659	0.692	0.699
S.Korea	0.503	0.487	0.488	0.479	0.476	0.498	0.481	0.478
Malaysia	0.701	0.689	0.674	**0.674**	0.679	0.672	0.677	0.677
Mexico	0.263	0.235	0.218	0.213	0.219	0.211	0.197	0.222
Philippines	0.410	0.413	0.478	**0.543**	0.618	0.608	0.626	0.684
Singapore	0.457	0.446	0.448	0.453	0.493	0.510	0.505	0.510
Taiwan	0.233	0.240	0.243	0.232	0.227	0.234	0.230	N/A
Thailand	1	1	1	1	1	1	1	1
Uruguay	0.039	0.038	0.042	0.044	0.041	0.034	0.036	0.039
Venezuela	0.340	0.311	0.294	0316	0.280	0.292	0.340	0.322

Argentina was not a strong trade competitor of Mexico.

Forbes' measure of trade competition Forbes (2001) constructs a trade competition index that takes into account the composition of trade. Indeed, two countries should be considered strong trade competitors with each other only if they are exporting in the same industries. In addition, compared to the Glick and

Table 8.8 (b) Glick and Rose's relative trade competition index

Glick and Rose's measure of relative trade competition with Mexico								
	1994	1995	1996	1997	1998	1999	2000	2001
Argentina	0.204	0.154	0.172	0.159	0.160	0.212	0.213	0.239
Brazil	0.322	0.312	0.325	0.296	0.306	0.347	0.359	0.396
Chile	0.330	0.295	0.335	0.310	0.326	0.353	0.318	0.434
China	0.232	0.227	0.245	0.241	0.266	0.279	0.260	0.293
Colombia	0.550	0.546	**0.608**	0.577	0.571	**0.675**	**0.685**	**0.675**
HK	0.281	0.272	0.267	0.277	0.294	0.307	0.295	0.300
India	0.320	0.299	0.325	0.327	0.338	0.362	0.362	0.357
Indonesia	0.243	0.235	0.239	0.232	0.246	0.249	0.234	0.271
S.Korea	0.286	0.268	0.241	0.236	0.257	0.287	0.295	0.327
Malaysia	0.291	0.286	0.263	0.267	0.305	0.308	0.286	0.292
Mexico	1	1	1	1	1	1	1	1
Philippines	0.539	0.509	0.470	0.493	0.477	0.431	0.430	0.436
Singapore	0.240	0.233	0.238	0.236	0.261	0.258	0.230	0.241
Taiwan	0.376	0.356	0.367	0.366	0.370	0.369	0.344	N/A
Thailand	0.304	0.272	0.279	0.293	0.328	0.325	0.340	0.329
Uruguay	0.179	0.176	0.194	0.170	0.157	0.177	0.203	0.272
Venezuela	**0.635**	**0.637**	0.595	**0.620**	**0.575**	0.647	0.644	0.646
Glick and Rose's measure of relative trade competition with Thailand								
	1994	1995	1996	1997	1998	1999	2000	2001
Argentina	0.276	0.239	0.238	0.231	0.252	0.281	0.263	0.272
Brazil	0.502	0.490	0.493	0.454	0.470	0.497	0.499	0.480
Chile	0.550	0.523	0.565	0.551	0.543	0.566	0.562	0.582
China	0.640	0.636	0.669	0.652	0.667	**0.691**	0.706	0.710
Colombia	0.145	0.152	0.135	0.144	0.144	0.134	0.127	0.149
HK	0.538	0.525	0.541	0.539	0.563	0.564	0.576	0.573
India	0.623	0.594	0.622	0.620	0.606	0.610	0.638	0.633
Indonesia	0.667	0.649	**0.678**	0.668	0.666	0.676	0.695	0.701
S.Korea	0.646	0.641	0.625	0.615	0.616	0.682	0.691	0.663
Malaysia	**0.701**	**0.689**	0.674	**0.674**	**0.679**	0.672	0.677	0.677
Mexico	0.305	0.274	0.280	0.296	0.330	0.327	0.340	0.330
Philippines	0.650	0.621	0.656	0.646	0.662	0.671	**0.718**	**0.724**
Singapore	0.568	0.558	0.588	0.598	0.616	0.617	0.598	0.600
Taiwan	0.233	0.240	0.243	0.232	0.227	0.234	0.230	N/A
Thailand	1	1	1	1	1	1	1	1
Uruguay	0.289	0.311	0.343	0.316	0.317	0.331	0.360	0.346
Venezuela	0.293	0.260	0.237	0.241	0.290	0.256	0.263	0.257

Rose index, Forbes' index has the advantage that it does not assume symmetry in the trade competition between two countries. It weighs different countries differently according to the relative importance of various industries in their total exports. Forbes' trade competition index is defined as follows:

$$TradeComp_i^{Forbes} = \frac{100}{\max_j\{TradeComp_j^{Forbes}\}} \sum_k \left\{ \frac{Exp_{0,W,k}}{Exp_{W,W,k}} \times \frac{Exp_{i,W,k}}{GDP_i} \right\},$$

where $Exp_{0,W,k}$ is the export from the initial crisis country 0 in industry k to the world (W). $Exp_{W,W,k}$ is the export from every country in the world in industry k to every other country in the world. GDP_i is the gross domestic product of country i.

The first term inside the summation sign of the index measures the exports from the initial crisis country 0 in a given industry k as a share of the world's exports in that industry. The second term inside the summation sign of the index captures the importance of exports from country i in the same industry relative to its GDP. The products of these two terms for each industry are then summed over all industries. The resulting value is then normalized by the maximum calculated value and multiplied by 100. As before, the initial crisis countries examined in this chapter include Mexico in 1994 and Thailand in 1997.

Forbes' trade competition index is reported in Table 8.9. The index indicates that Singapore and Malaysia had the highest degree of trade competition with Mexico and Thailand during both the Mexican and Thai Crises.[2] However, one drawback of this index is that it does not take into account the destinations of export. The export destinations are important in determining the degree of trade competition across countries as two countries are competing with each other only if they are exporting similar items to the same destinations. For this reason, we develop a new trade competition index that takes into account both the composition and destination of export. The index is discussed in the next section.

Lau and Yan's measure of trade competition that takes into account the composition and destination of trade The new trade competition index proposed in this chapter has the advantage of matching the export industries with the export destinations. The index is defined as follows:

$$TradeComp_{it}^{LauYan} = \frac{Exp_i}{GDP_i} \sum_k \left\{ \frac{Exp_{i,k}}{Exp_i} \times \frac{1}{\sum_m (w_{i,m,k} - w_{0,m,k})^2} \right\},$$

where $Exp_{i,k}$ is the export of country i in industry k. Exp_i is the total export of country i. GDP_i is the gross domestic product of country i. $w_{i,m,k} = Exp_{i,m,k}/Exp_{i,k}$ measures the share of country i's exports to destination m in industry k.

The term $\Sigma_m(w_{i,m,k} - w_{0,m,k})^2$ captures the similarity of both the composition and the destinations of exports between country i and the initial crisis country 0. $Exp_{i,k}/Exp_i$ captures the importance of exports in industry k relative to the total exports of country i. The products of these two terms are then summed over all industries. The output is multiplied by Exp_i/GDP_i to capture the importance of

Table 8.9 Forbes' trade competition index that takes into account the composition of trade

Forbes' measure of trade competition with Mexico					
	1995	1996	1997	1998	1999
Argentina	5.66	5.83	6.26	5.51	4.16
Brazil	4.58	4.14	4.45	4.40	5.49
Chile	14.80	13.97	12.56	11.15	11.12
China	27.67	26.37	27.87	26.44	27.14
Colombia	10.19	9.07	9.71	8.84	10.05
HK	32.18	29.53	27.70	28.47	28.88
India	5.92	6.19	6.08	5.69	4.79
Indonesia	17.88	17.07	20.39	40.53	25.01
S.Korea	19.00	19.17	23.51	29.25	26.54
Malaysia	80.53	78.68	87.77	**100**	**100**
Mexico	-	-	-	-	-
Philippines	22.49	26.42	36.98	46.75	45.39
Singapore	**100**	**100**	**100**	91.63	86.69
Taiwan	40.28	41.65	42.61	42.57	40.95
Thailand	26.08	25.96	34.41	39.85	39.76
Uruguay	10.05	9.19	9.63	9.45	6.89
Venezuela	28.05	33.96	27.46	13.93	14.56
Forbes' measure of trade competition with Thailand					
	1995	1996	1997	1998	1999
Argentina	12.56	13.64	13.00	11.24	9.09
Brazil	9.64	9.10	8.94	7.85	10.22
Chile	40.43	39.48	33.05	27.55	28.73
China	46.19	41.21	39.04	32.53	33.64
Colombia	19.26	15.71	16.48	15.19	14.02
HK	47.98	41.63	35.90	32.35	33.18
India	11.60	12.83	11.13	9.77	8.35
Indonesia	24.35	23.53	26.07	52.89	31.47
S.Korea	23.45	23.04	27.15	30.40	27.81
Malaysia	96.46	92.75	99.37	**100**	**100**
Mexico	22.98	29.40	33.39	30.37	26.22
Philippines	34.98	36.70	46.27	50.25	48.20
Singapore	**100**	**100**	**100**	82.90	80.25
Taiwan	53.61	53.63	50.88	45.00	43.93
Thailand	-	-	-	-	-
Uruguay	27.86	27.95	26.45	23.10	16.98
Venezuela	9.92	14.13	12.23	7.51	7.28

the export relative to the GDP of country i. Comparatively large value indicates that a given country is a strong trade competitor of a given initial crisis country. The results of this index for various Southeast Asian and Latin American countries are reported in Table 8.10.

The index indicates that there is a gradual increase in the trade competition among the countries in the last decade, which is a direct result of the trade liberalization process in the emerging countries. It is also worth noting that this index performs well in indicating the countries that are vulnerable to the contagion of crises. The countries most affected by the Thai Crisis—namely, Taiwan, Singapore, Malaysia, Indonesia, Philippines and S.Korea—have the highest value of the trade competition index with Thailand.

Measures of financial linkages

Financial linkages are important in understanding why some countries that do not have close trade ties with the crisis countries are still vulnerable to the contagion effect. The literature on contagion emphasizes two major types of transmission mechanisms or linkages associated with the financial markets: the common creditors linkages and volatility spillover mechanism. The common creditor effect arises when a crisis in a given country causes foreign creditors to withdraw funds not only from the crisis country but also from other borrowing countries. Factors that give rise to the volatility spillover of financial markets include international liquidity constraints, portfolio rebalancing, the asymmetric information and herding behaviors on the part of investors.

Measures of the common creditor effect Three sets of indexes have been developed in the literature to measure the common creditor effect, the Caramazza, Ricci and Salgado indexes (2000), the Kaminsky and Reinhart indexes (1998) as well as the Rijckeghem and Weder indexes (1999). The Caramazza, Ricci and Salgado indexes consist of three variables. The first variable (CRS1) measures the importance of common creditors for the borrowing countries, calculated as the share of total credit borrowed from the major banking centers—the US and Japanese banks. The second variable (CRS2) measures the importance of borrowers to common lenders (CRS2), expressed as a borrowing country's credit as a share of a given creditor's total cross–border lending. The third variable (CRS) measures the mutual importance of lenders and borrowers, calculated as the product of CRS1 and CRS2. The three variables associated with the credits from the US banks are written as follows (the three variables associated with the credits from the Japanese banks are defined likewise):

$$CRS1_i^{US} = \frac{B_i^{US}}{B_i},$$

$$CRS2_i^{US} = \frac{B_i^{US}}{B^{US}}$$

and

$$CRS_i^{US} = CRS1_i^{US} \times CRS2_i^{US},$$

where B_i^{US}/B_i denotes the international borrowing of country i from US banks

Table 8.10 Lau and Yan's trade competition index that takes into account both the composition and destination of trade

Lau and Yan's measure of trade competition with Mexico					
	1995	1996	1997	1998	1999
Argentina	0.177	0.198	0.183	0.182	0.155
Brazil	0.266	0.238	0.222	0.322	0.298
Chile	0.786	0.899	0.813	0.954	0.961
China	1.062	0.925	0.947	2.342	0.561
Colombia	1.836	1.481	1.476	1.973	4.838
HK	0.929	0.795	0.706	2.075	0.356
India	0.365	0.388	0.380	0.607	0.267
Indonesia	0.700	0.674	0.753	3.293	0.736
S.Korea	0.703	0.664	0.793	1.506	0.888
Malaysia	2.833	2.543	2.621	4.694	3.019
Mexico	-	-	-	-	-
Philippines	1.495	1.291	1.743	6.030	1.293
Singapore	3.311	3.282	3.170	3.381	2.648
Taiwan	1.670	1.584	1.576	2.738	1.260
Thailand	0.847	0.821	1.100	2.560	1.104
Uruguay	0.256	0.288	0.283	0.308	0.206
Venezuela	**10.360**	18.898	13.983	8.847	6.165
Lau and Yan's measure of trade competition with Thailand					
	1995	1996	1997	1998	1999
Argentina	1.03	1.21	1.23	1.31	1.22
Brazil	1.37	1.32	1.41	1.74	2.27
Chile	11.58	9.03	10.81	10.32	12.44
China	4.40	4.11	4.57	4.32	4.70
Colombia	1.17	1.19	1.30	1.60	1.53
HK	7.11	6.01	5.67	6.00	5.49
India	5.72	5.01	4.35	4.01	4.05
Indonesia	12.32	9.79	**13.17**	45.58	30.04
S.Korea	6.23	6.05	8.76	16.40	13.59
Malaysia	11.53	11.76	**14.98**	20.02	19.19
Mexico	0.499	0.61	0.73	0.82	0.70
Philippines	5.82	5.92	**10.82**	25.21	39.46
Singapore	12.74	12.77	**16.39**	23.44	22.36
Taiwan	14.62	16.62	**26.94**	32.66	34.36
Thailand	-	-	-	-	-
Uruguay	1.79	2.15	2.08	2.12	1.52
Venezuela	1.46	1.47	1.43	1.23	0.95

B_i denotes the total borrowing of country i from all international banks B^{US} denotes the total international claims of US banks.

The results for the variables CRS1, CRS2 and CRS are reported in Table 8.11, Table 8.12 and Table 8.13 respectively. Table 8.11 shows that there is a strong regional pattern in international lending. The Latin American countries

Table 8.11 (a) Percentage of various countries' international borrowings from the US banks ($CRS1_{US}$)

	1994	1995	1996	1997	1998	1999	2000	2001
All countries (excluding the lending country)	12.2%	11.9%	13.1%	11.3%	10.5%	9.3%	8.5%	14.5%
Latin American Countries								
Argentina	27.7%	29.2%	29.5%	17.4%	18.3%	16.4%	16.2%	28.2%
Bolivia	25.0%	38.8%	38.6%	39.9%	16.3%	16.8%	18.1%	25.1%
Brazil	22.5%	25.1%	27.1%	20.6%	17.3%	23.3%	21.2%	25.1%
Chile	29.7%	30.1%	27.9%	21.9%	18.7%	18.8%	16.5%	17.0%
Colombia	26.1%	27.8%	24.5%	20.1%	22.6%	22.2%	20.5%	24.3%
Mexico	34.2%	31.0%	28.9%	26.9%	27.9%	28.0%	23.8%	36.1%
Uruguay	31.7%	27.8%	30.2%	21.8%	20.6%	17.7%	16.5%	29.6%
Venezuela	31.2%	24.1%	25.5%	29.3%	25.7%	22.6%	21.1%	15.3%
Southeast Asian Countries								
China	2.3%	3.5%	4.8%	4.0%	3.2%	3.1%	2.2%	8.5%
HK	3.0%	3.0%	4.1%	4.0%	3.6%	4.3%	5.6%	7.3%
India	7.7%	9.9%	8.8%	8.6%	8.0%	8.1%	9.5%	20.0%
Indonesia	7.0%	6.2%	9.5%	8.3%	7.8%	8.4%	7.8%	9.3%
S.Korea	9.6%	9.7%	9.3%	10.1%	9.6%	11.5%	10.5%	22.8%
Malaysia	10.1%	9.0%	10.5%	6.4%	4.1%	7.8%	5.1%	14.6%
Philippines	37.4%	35.3%	29.3%	16.3%	16.4%	17.9%	10.8%	22.3%
Singapore	2.7%	3.1%	3.0%	1.8%	1.8%	2.0%	2.9%	12.5%
Taiwan	12.1%	12.4%	14.2%	8.3%	5.8%	6.4%	11.7%	34.8%
Thailand	6.1%	6.5%	7.2%	4.3%	3.3%	2.9%	3.5%	10.2%

borrow heavily from the US banks while Asian countries borrow heavily from the Japanese banks. For instance, in the 1994 Mexican Crisis, 34.2 percent of Mexico's international credits were from the US banks. Argentina, the country most affected by the Mexican Crisis, borrowed as much as 27.7 percent of its international credits from the US banks. Prior to the 1997 Asian Crisis, 56.3 percent of Thailand's international credits were from the Japanese banks. Table 8.12 indicates that, among all the sample countries in 1994, Mexico's share of US claims on the emerging markets was the highest. It amounted to 23.3 percent of US's total claim. Likewise, Thailand's share of Japanese claims on emerging markets in 1997 was the highest. It amounted to 20.3 percent of Japan's total claim.

Kaminsky and Reinhart (1998) constructed another set of indexes to measure the common creditor effect. Their indexes are dummy variables that take the value of 1 if a country obtains the majority of its funds from US banks, or from Japanese banks. Table 8.14 reports the result of the dummy variables. Just as there exists a regional pattern for trade, there also exist regional blocs that depend heavily on common creditor countries. Prior to the Mexican Crisis of 1994, all Latin American countries in the sample relied on US banks as their

Table 8.11 (b) Percentage of various countries' international borrowings from the Japanese banks ($CRS1_{Jap}$)

	1994	1995	1996	1997	1998	1999	2000	2001
All countries (excluding the lending country)	19.3%	18.9%	17.1%	14.5%	11.7%	15.6%	15.9%	11.7%
Latin American Countries								
Argentina	4.6%	4.4%	3.9%	2.6%	3.2%	2.5%	2.6%	2.1%
Bolivia	0.5%	0.2%	0.0%	0.0%	0.1%	0.0%	0.0%	0.0%
Brazil	8.8%	8.3%	7.6%	6.5%	5.7%	5.5%	4.2%	2.9%
Chile	7.6%	7.2%	5.2%	5.7%	5.4%	5.7%	5.2%	2.6%
Colombia	11.5%	11.4%	7.8%	8.0%	8.9%	10.0%	9.6%	6.3%
Mexico	6.2%	7.8%	8.9%	7.5%	7.1%	4.5%	4.0%	1.4%
Uruguay	0.8%	0.5%	0.8%	0.2%	0.3%	0.3%	0.2%	0.3%
Venezuela	3.9%	4.9%	4.2%	2.5%	3.4%	4.0%	4.0%	2.1%
Southeast Asian Countries								
China	34.2%	36.4%	32.3%	30.9%	25.9%	25.2%	17.7%	19.7%
HK	62.2%	55.3%	42.2%	36.0%	29.4%	32.3%	32.0%	16.1%
India	27.2%	23.7%	20.9%	20.1%	15.4%	11.2%	9.6%	8.1%
Indonesia	52.4%	47.1%	39.6%	37.7%	36.5%	30.6%	25.3%	24.1%
S.Korea	30.7%	27.6%	24.3%	21.5%	25.9%	20.7%	17.5%	15.5%
Malaysia	43.2%	43.6%	36.9%	31.0%	31.8%	33.2%	26.8%	13.0%
Philippines	13.9%	11.8%	11.7%	13.3%	14.3%	17.4%	18.3%	15.4%
Singapore	53.6%	39.9%	31.0%	30.0%	23.5%	21.3%	26.6%	17.2%
Taiwan	25.6%	14.3%	12.0%	13.4%	10.2%	13.1%	16.5%	10.5%
Thailand	60.2%	58.6%	53.4%	56.3%	55.0%	46.0%	36.8%	28.7%

most important source of credits. Similarly, with the exception of the Philippines, all Asian countries relied on Japanese banks as their principal source of funds.

However, one limitation of the Caramazza, Ricci and Salgado indexes (2000) and the Kaminsky and Reinhart indexes (1998) discussed above is that they only consider the relationship between a country and one single creditor (US or Japan). Their indexes do not consider simultaneously the relationships between a country and multiple lenders. The indexes constructed by Rijckeghem and Weder (1999) rectify this deficiency by including the information of multiple creditors. As a result, these indexes are more comprehensive. The set of indexes proposed by Rijckeghem and Weder include the absolute fund competition index and the relative fund competition index. The indexes are weighted averages of the importance of a common lender for both country i and the initial crisis country 0. As stated in the formula below, the first component of the index measures the overall importance of the common lender for countries i and 0. The second component captures the extent to which i and 0 compete for funding from common creditors.

Table 8.12 (a) Percentage of US's international lending to various countries ($CRS2_{US}$)

	1994	1995	1996	1997	1998	1999	2000	2001
Latin American Countries								
Argentina	**10.4%**	**10.7%**	**10.1%**	**8.3%**	**9.9%**	**6.9%**	**8.2%**	**6.9%**
Bolivia	0.0%	0.1%	0.1%	0.2%	0.2%	0.2%	0.1%	0.1%
Brazil	**12.0%**	**13.9%**	**14.1%**	**12.4%**	**11.1%**	**9.1%**	**10.6%**	**10.3%**
Chile	3.8%	3.9%	3.2%	3.6%	3.6%	2.4%	2.7%	2.1%
Colombia	2.7%	2.9%	3.1%	2.9%	3.4%	1.9%	1.7%	1.2%
Mexico	**23.3%**	**17.1%**	**13.4%**	**13.1%**	**15.9%**	**10.8%**	**11.2%**	**22.4%**
Uruguay	1.1%	1.0%	0.9%	0.8%	1.0%	0.6%	0.6%	0.5%
Venezuela	4.5%	2.7%	2.1%	2.8%	2.8%	1.9%	2.0%	0.9%
Southeast Asian Countries								
China	1.0%	1.6%	2.0%	2.0%	1.6%	0.9%	0.9%	1.5%
HK	7.7%	6.9%	6.6%	6.8%	4.1%	3.0%	4.5%	6.0%
India	1.2%	1.4%	1.1%	1.3%	1.3%	1.1%	1.5%	2.1%
Indonesia	2.5%	2.6%	4.0%	3.8%	3.1%	2.1%	2.3%	1.1%
S.Korea	5.7%	7.3%	7.1%	7.5%	5.5%	4.4%	4.5%	5.0%
Malaysia	1.4%	1.4%	1.8%	1.4%	0.7%	0.9%	0.8%	2.1%
Philippines	2.6%	2.8%	3.0%	2.5%	2.3%	1.9%	1.3%	1.4%
Singapore	5.0%	5.9%	4.4%	2.9%	2.0%	1.3%	2.1%	5.0%
Taiwan	2.6%	2.7%	2.4%	1.7%	1.0%	0.8%	1.5%	3.3%
Thailand	2.8%	3.9%	3.8%	2.0%	1.1%	0.5%	0.7%	1.2%

Table 8.12 (b) Percentage of Japan's international lending to various countries ($CRS2_{Jap}$)

	1994	1995	1996	1997	1998	1999	2000	2001
Latin American Countries								
Argentina	1.1%	1.0%	1.0%	0.9%	1.5%	0.6%	0.7%	0.6%
Bolivia	0.0%	0.0%	0.0%	0.0%	0.0%	0.0%	0.0%	0.0%
Brazil	2.9%	2.9%	3.0%	3.0%	3.2%	1.2%	1.1%	1.4%
Chile	0.6%	0.5%	0.4%	0.7%	0.9%	0.4%	0.4%	0.4%
Colombia	0.7%	0.7%	0.7%	0.9%	1.1%	0.5%	0.4%	0.3%
Mexico	2.7%	2.7%	3.1%	2.8%	3.6%	1.0%	1.0%	1.1%
Uruguay	0.0%	0.0%	0.0%	0.0%	0.0%	0.0%	0.0%	0.0%
Venezuela	0.3%	0.3%	0.2%	0.1%	0.3%	0.2%	0.2%	0.1%
Southeast Asian Countries								
China	9.4%	10.6%	10.4%	11.9%	11.8%	4.4%	4.0%	4.3%
HK	N/A	N/A	N/A	N/A	N/A	N/A	N/A	N/A
India	2.7%	2.2%	2.0%	2.4%	2.3%	0.9%	0.8%	1.0%
Indonesia	**12.2%**	**12.6%**	**12.9%**	**13.4%**	**12.8%**	**4.7%**	**4.0%**	**3.5%**
S.Korea	**11.6%**	**12.9%**	**14.3%**	**12.4%**	**13.2%**	**4.7%**	**4.0%**	**4.2%**
Malaysia	3.9%	4.4%	4.8%	5.2%	5.1%	2.2%	2.2%	2.3%
Philippines	0.6%	0.5%	0.9%	1.6%	1.8%	1.1%	1.1%	1.1%
Singapore	N/A	N/A	N/A	N/A	N/A	N/A	N/A	N/A
Taiwan	3.6%	1.9%	1.5%	2.1%	1.6%	1.0%	1.1%	1.2%
Thailand	**17.7%**	**22.2%**	**22.1%**	**20.3%**	**17.5%**	**4.9%**	**3.8%**	**4.3%**

Table 8.13 (a) ($CRS_{US} = CRS1_{US} \times CRS2_{US}$)

-	1994	1995	1996	1997	1998	1999	2000	2001
Latin American Countries								
Argentina	2.8%	3.1%	3.0%	1.4%	1.8%	1.1%	1.3%	1.9%
Bolivia	0.0%	0.0%	0.0%	0.0%	0.0%	0.0%	0.0%	0.0%
Brazil	2.7%	3.5%	3.8%	2.5%	1.9%	2.1%	2.2%	2.6%
Chile	1.1%	1.1%	0.9%	0.8%	0.6%	0.4%	0.4%	0.3%
Colombia	07%	0.8%	0.7%	0.5%	0.7%	0.4%	0.3%	0.2%
Mexico	**8.0%**	**5.3%**	**3.8%**	**3.5%**	**4.0%**	**3.0%**	**2.6%**	**8.1%**
Uruguay	0.3%	0.2%	0.2%	0.1%	0.2%	0.1%	0.1%	0.1%
Venezuela	1.4%	0.6%	0.5%	0.8%	0.7%	0.4%	0.4%	0.1%
Southeast Asian Countries								
China	0.0%	0.0%	0.1%	0.0%	0.0%	0.0%	0.0%	0.1%
HK	0.2%	0.2%	0.2%	0.2%	0.1%	0.1%	0.2%	0.4%
India	0.1%	0.1%	0.1%	0.1%	0.1%	0.0%	0.1%	0.4%
Indonesia	0.1%	0.1%	0.3%	0.3%	0.2%	0.1%	0.1%	0.1%
S.Korea	0.7%	0.7%	0.6%	0.7%	0.5%	0.5%	0.4%	1.1%
Malaysia	0.1%	0.1%	0.1%	0.0%	.0%	0.0%	0.0%	0.3%
Philippines	1.0%	1.0%	0.8%	0.4%	0.3%	0.3%	0.1%	0.3%
Singapore	0.1%	0.1%	0.1%	0.0%	0.0%	0.0%	0.0%	0.6%
Taiwan	0.3%	0.3%	0.3%	0.1%	0.0%	0.0%	0.1%	1.1%
Thailand	0.2%	0.2%	0.2%	0.0%	0.0%	0.0%	0.0%	0.1%

Table 8.13 (b) ($CRS_{Jap} = CRS1_{Jap} \times CRS2_{Jap}$)

-	1994	1995	1996	1997	1998	1999	2000	2001
Latin American Countries								
Argentina	0.05%	0.05%	0.04%	0.03%	0.05%	0.02%	0.02%	0.01%
Bolivia	0.00%	0.00%	0.00%	0.00%	0.00%	0.00%	0.00%	0.00%
Brazil	0.26%	0.24%	0.23%	0.20%	0.19%	0.07%	0.05%	0.04%
Chile	0.05%	0.04%	0.02%	0.04%	0.05%	0.03%	0.02%	0.01%
Colombia	0.09%	0.09%	0.06%	0.07%	0.11%	0.05%	0.04%	0.02%
Mexico	0.17%	0.21%	0.28%	0.22%	0.26%	0.05%	0.04%	0.02%
Uruguay	0.0%	0.0%	0.00%	0.00%	0.00%	0.00%	0.00%	0.00%
Venezuela	0.01%	0.02%	0.01%	0.00%	0.01%	0.01%	0.01%	0.00%
Southeast Asian Countries								
China	3.24%	3.88%	3.39%	3.71%	3.08%	1.13%	0.72%	0.85%
HK	N/A	N/A	N/A	N/A	N/A	N/A	N/A	N/A
India	0.74%	0.53%	0.44%	0.48%	0.36%	0.11%	0.08%	0.09%
Indonesia	6.44%	5.96%	5.15%	5.08%	4.71%	1.445%	1.02%	0.85%
S.Korea	3.59%	3.58%	3.49%	2.67%	3.44%	0.99%	0.71%	0.65%
Malaysia	1.69%	1.93%	1.79%	1.62%	1.65%	0.76%	0.59%	0.30%
Philippines	0.09%	0.07%	0.11%	0.21%	0.26%	0.19%	0.22%	0.18%
Singapore	N/A	N/A	N/A	N/A	N/A	N/A	N/A	N/A
Taiwan	0.93%	0.28%	0.19%	0.29%	0.17%	0.13%	0.20%	0.13%
Thailand	10.67%	13.05%	11.83%	11.45%	9.69%	2.28%	1.43%	1.25%

Table 8.14 (a) A dummy that = 1 if a country obtains the majority of its funds from the US

	1994	1995	1996	1997	1998	1999	2000	2001
Latin American Countries								
Argentina	1	1	1	0	0	0	0	1
Bolivia	1	1	1	1	0	0	0	0
Brazil	1	1	1	1	1	1	1	1
Chile	1	1	1	1	1	0	0	0
Colombia	1	1	1	0	1	1	1	0
Mexico	1	1	1	1	1	1	1	0
Uruguay	1	1	1	1	1	0	0	1
Venezuela	1	1	1	1	1	1	1	0
Southeast Asian Countries								
China	0	0	0	0	0	0	0	0
HK	0	0	0	0	0	0	0	0
India	0	0	0	0	0	0	0	0
Indonesia	0	0	0	0	0	0	0	0
S.Korea	0	0	0	0	0	0	0	1
Malaysia	0	0	0	0	0	0	0	0
Philippines	1	1	1	1	1	1	0	1
Singapore	0	0	0	0	0	0	0	0
Taiwan	0	0	0	0	0	0	0	1
Thailand	0	0	0	0	0	0	0	0

Table 8.14 (b) A dummy that = 1 if a country obtains the majority of its funds from Japan

	1994	1995	1996	1997	1998	1999	2000	2001
Latin American Countries								
Argentina	0	0	0	0	0	0	0	0
Bolivia	0	0	0	0	0	0	0	0
Brazil	0	0	0	0	0	0	0	0
Chile	0	0	0	0	0	0	0	0
Colombia	0	0	0	0	0	0	0	0
Mexico	0	0	0	0	0	0	0	0
Uruguay	0	0	0	0	0	0	0	0
Venezuela	0	0	0	0	0	0	0	0
Southeast Asian Countries								
China	1	1	1	1	1	1	1	1
HK	1	1	1	1	1	1	1	0
India	1	1	1	1	0	0	0	0
Indonesia	1	1	1	1	1	1	1	1
S.Korea	1	1	1	1	1	1	1	0
Malaysia	1	1	1	1	1	1	0	0
Philippines	0	0	0	0	0	0	0	0
Singapore	1	1	1	1	0	1	1	0
Taiwan	1	0	0	0	0	0	1	0
Thailand	1	1	1	1	1	1	1	1

Table 8.15 (a) Rij et al.'s (absolute) measure of competition with Mexico for international funds

-	1994	1995	1996	1997	1998	1999	2000	2001
Latin American Countries								
Argentina	**0.56**	**0.62**	**0.68**	**0.69**	**0.69**	**0.69**	**0.75**	**0.48**
Bolivia	0.01	0.01	0.01	0.01	0.05	0.07	0.04	0.01
Brazil	**0.67**	**0.74**	**0.76**	**0.71**	**0.70**	**0.75**	**0.75**	0.01
Chile	0.28	0.33	0.35	0.45	0.46	0.46	0.49	**0.31**
Colombia	0.22	0.29	0.39	0.42	0.38	0.34	0.29	0.14
Mexico	1.00	1.00	1.00	1.00	1.00	1.00	1.00	1.00
Uruguay	0.09	0.11	0.12	0.13	0.14	0.14	0.13	0.05
Venezuela	0.32	0.31	0.27	0.29	0.29	0.31	0.31	0.17
Southeast Asian Countries								
China	0.41	0.46	0.52	0.51	0.51	0.53	0.42	0.23
HK	0.26	0.25	0.31	0.31	0.39	0.40	0.42	0.20
India	0.33	0.33	0.34	0.37	0.32	0.37	0.40	0.23
Indonesia	0.34	0.41	0.50	0.50	0.48	0.50	0.49	0.21
S.Korea	0.46	0.45	0.46	0.48	0.54	0.57	0.49	0.32
Malaysia	0.28	0.33	0.41	0.43	0.39	0.31	0.31	0.19
Philippines	0.19	0.23	0.33	0.41	0.36	0.37	0.37	0.15
Singapore	0.31	0.29	0.30	0.29	0.38	0.42	0.38	0.27
Taiwan	0.40	0.49	0.47	0.52	0.43	0.41	0.35	0.24
Thailand	0.32	0.39	0.43	0.40	0.37	0.33	0.31	0.18

Table 8.15 (b) Rij et al.'s (absolute) measure of competition with Thailand for international funds

-	1994	1995	1996	1997	1998	1999	2000	2001
Latin American Countries								
Argentina	0.36	0.37	0.40	0.35	0.33	0.29	0.27	0.35
Bolivia	0.01	0.01	0.01	0.02	0.03	0.06	0.05	0.03
Brazil	0.37	0.39	0.42	0.37	0.34	0.35	0.30	0.28
Chile	0.30	0.28	0.27	0.31	0.41	0.45	0.43	0.34
Colombia	0.27	0.25	0.26	0.29	0.37	0.39	0.42	0.38
Mexico	0.32	0.39	0.43	0.40	0.37	0.33	0.31	0.18
Uruguay	0.12	0.09	0.09	0.12	0.18	0.21	0.20	0.18
Venezuela	0.35	0.27	0.23	0.24	0.32	0.37	0.42	0.34
Southeast Asian Countries								
China	0.60	**0.61**	**0.62**	**0.65**	**0.62**	**0.64**	0.49	**0.61**
HK	0.28	0.37	0.45	0.40	0.44	0.36	0.31	0.19
India	0.44	0.30	0.30	0.39	0.44	0.50	0.50	0.55
Indonesia	**0.77**	**0.69**	**0.71**	**0.72**	**0.73**	**0.71**	**0.63**	**0.71**
S.Korea	**0.62**	0.59	0.58	0.53	0.61	0.55	0.49	0.54
Malaysia	0.45	0.38	0.43	0.54	0.59	0.63	**0.61**	0.50
Philippines	0.26	0.22	0.29	0.39	0.44	0.55	0.55	0.54
Singapore	0.37	0.44	0.48	0.42	0.46	0.40	0.34	0.38
Taiwan	0.52	0.43	0.42	0.46	0.47	0.47	0.49	0.56
Thailand	1.00	1.00	1.00	1.00	1.00	1.00	1.00	1.00

Table 8.16 (a) Rij et al.'s (relative) measure of competition with Mexico for international funds

-	1994	1995	1996	1997	1998	1999	2000	2001
Latin American Countries								
Argentina	**0.70**	**0.72**	**0.72**	**0.69**	**0.69**	**0.69**	**0.76**	**0.68**
Bolivia	0.58	0.45	0.48	0.47	0.34	0.43	0.52	**0.71**
Brazil	**0.69**	**0.74**	**0.78**	**0.70**	**0.69**	**0.74**	**0.75**	0.58
Chile	**0.71**	**0.77**	**0.71**	**0.70**	**0.71**	**0.74**	**0.78**	**0.71**
Colombia	0.68	**0.76**	**0.72**	**0.73**	**0.76**	**0.78**	**0.78**	**0.68**
Mexico	1.00	1.00	1.00	1.00	1.00	1.00	1.00	1.00
Uruguay	0.63	0.61	0.60	0.58	0.61	0.56	0.65	0.65
Venezuela	**0.76**	0.71	**0.72**	**0.75**	**0.78**	**0.75**	**0.73**	**0.70**
Southeast Asian Countries								
China	0.43	0.45	0.51	0.51	0.49	0.49	0.41	0.23
HK	0.36	0.42	0.47	0.48	0.48	0.46	0.43	0.21
India	0.50	0.51	0.52	0.52	0.51	0.50	0.51	0.33
Indonesia	0.41	0.45	0.50	0.50	0.51	0.51	0.51	0.21
S.Korea	0.48	0.46	0.48	0.50	0.54	0.57	0.50	0.36
Malaysia	0.49	0.46	0.49	0.46	0.46	0.51	0.47	0.29
Philippines	**0.74**	**0.72**	**0.73**	0.60	0.61	0.61	0.54	0.35
Singapore	0.40	0.46	0.49	0.47	0.47	0.48	0.38	0.26
Taiwan	0.59	0.57	0.61	0.56	0.53	0.51	0.51	0.44
Thailand	0.37	0.38	0.43	0.40	0.42	0.42	0.40	0.23

Table 8.16 (b) Rij et al.'s (relative) measure of competition with Thailand for international funds

-	1994	1995	1996	1997	1998	1999	2000	2001
Latin American Countries								
Argentina	0.33	0.32	0.37	0.35	0.37	0.38	0.37	0.41
Bolivia	0.15	0.12	0.17	0.14	0.12	0.23	0.25	0.22
Brazil	0.38	0.38	0.42	0.41	0.43	0.44	0.45	0.50
Chile	0.36	0.35	0.36	0.36	0.42	0.47	0.45	0.34
Colombia	0.39	0.39	0.41	0.41	0.44	0.52	0.50	0.50
Mexico	0.37	0.38	0.43	0.40	0.42	0.42	0.40	0.23
Uruguay	0.23	0.22	0.24	0.24	0.29	0.32	0.33	0.41
Venezuela	0.30	0.30	0.34	0.31	0.37	0.44	0.43	0.42
Southeast Asian Countries								
China	**0.61**	**0.65**	**0.66**	**0.65**	**0.63**	**0.67**	**0.47**	**0.61**
HK	**0.88**	**0.83**	**0.73**	**0.68**	**0.64**	**0.66**	**0.61**	0.51
India	0.58	0.56	0.57	0.55	0.52	0.50	0.49	0.53
Indonesia	**0.82**	**0.77**	**0.75**	**0.72**	**0.73**	**0.71**	**0.67**	**0.71**
S.Korea	0.61	0.58	0.59	0.54	**0.61**	0.55	0.50	0.57
Malaysia	**0.73**	**0.73**	**0.70**	**0.65**	**0.68**	**0.73**	**0.64**	**0.49**
Philippines	0.43	0.40	0.44	0.47	0.51	**0.60**	**0.58**	**0.60**
Singapore	**0.81**	**0.67**	**0.62**	**0.59**	0.56	0.59	0.50	**0.59**
Taiwan	0.57	0.44	0.45	0.47	0.47	0.49	0.49	0.55
Thailand	1.00	1.00	1.00	1.00	1.00	1.00	1.00	1.00

The absolute fund competition index ($FundCompAbs_i^{RijWed}$) is calculated using the absolute value of credit obtained from the common lender while the relative fund competition index ($FundCompSh_i^{RijWed}$) is calculated using the share of credit obtained from the common lender. The two indexes are defined as follows:

$$FundCompAbs_i^{RijWed} = \sum_c \frac{B_{0c} + B_{ic}}{B_0 + B_i}\left(1 - \frac{B_{0c} - B_{ic}}{B_{0c} + B_{ic}}\right)$$

and

$$FundCompSh_i^{RijWed} = \sum_c \frac{B_{0c} + B_{ic}}{B_0 + B_i}\left(1 - \frac{B_{0c} / B_0 - B_{ic} / B_i}{B_{0c} / B_0 + B_{ic} / B_i}\right),$$

where B_{0c} is the foreign borrowing of the initial crisis country (country 0) from creditor c and B_0 is the total foreign borrowing of country 0.

The absolute fund competition index and the relative fund competition index are reported in Table 8.15 and Table 8.16 respectively. The absolute fund competition index indicates that Brazil and Argentina have been Mexico's two strongest competitors for international funds while Indonesia, South Korea and China have been Thailand's strongest competitors. A similar regional pattern is also observed in the relative fund competition index.

Measuring volatility spillovers across financial markets

Volatility contagion and spillovers across financial markets provide a key transmission channel of crisis. The propagation of volatility emerges from a number of sources, including international liquidity constraints (Calvo,1998), cross–country hedging and portfolio rebalancing (Schinasi and Smith,1999) as well as the herding behavior of investors (Calvo,1999). Edwards (1998) formulates an augmented GARCH Model to measure volatility spillovers across countries. He modifies the traditional GARCH Model by including Mexico–specific volatility variables in the estimation of the conditional variance equation. The estimated coefficients of the volatility indicators in the GARCH Model allow him to test whether or not there had been volatility spillovers during the 1994 Mexican Crisis. Edwards' results suggest that Argentina was highly vulnerable to volatility spillover during the Mexican Crisis, but other countries like Chile were not.

This chapter extends the Edwards model to examine the extent of volatility spillovers across stock markets during the 1994 Mexican Crisis and the 1997 Thai Crisis. To control for possible common exogenous shocks from the US and Japanese stock markets, the Edwards model is augmented with volatility indicators of the US and the Japanese stock markets. The augmented GARCH model is given as follows:

$$\Delta n = \phi_0 + \phi_1 \Delta n_{-1} + \varepsilon_t$$
$$\varepsilon_t \sim N(o, \sigma_t^2)$$
$$\sigma_t^2 = \alpha_0 + \alpha_1 \varepsilon_{t-1}^2 + \beta_1 \sigma_{t-1}^2$$
$$+ \theta_{Mex} VOLIND_{t-1}^{Mex} + \theta_{Thai} VOLIND_{t-1}^{Thai} + \theta_{Jap} VOLIND_{t-1}^{Jap} + \theta_{US} VOLIND_{t-1}^{US}$$
$$\theta_{Mex}, \theta_{Thai}, \theta_{Jap}, \theta_{US} \geq 0,$$

where r_t is the stock return at time t, σ_t^2 is the conditional volatility at period t and $VOLIND^{Mex}$, $VOLIND^{Tha}i$, $VOLIND^{Jap}$, and $VOLIND^{US}$ are the volatility indicators of Mexico, Thailand, Japan and US respectively.

The stock returns used in the estimation are weekly returns from January 1986 to January 2002, computed using the stock market index of Datastream. The volatility indicators of Mexico and Thailand (the two initial crisis countries during the 1994 Mexican Crisis and the 1997 Asian crisis) as well as Japan and US (the two largest financial centers in the world) are the estimated conditional variances from a standard first order GARCH model. In the augmented GARCH model stated above, a significant θ is evidence of strong spillover effect in the stock markets. The estimated coefficients of the volatility indicators in the augmented GARCH Model are reported in Table 8.17. The estimation suggests that there are significant volatility spillovers from the Mexican stock market to the stock markets of Argentina, Brazil and Chile, even after controlling for common exogenous shocks from the US and the Japanese stock markets. Likewise, there are significant volatility spillovers from the Thai stock market to the stock markets of Hong Kong, Indonesia, South Korea, Malaysia, Philippines, Singapore and Taiwan. The estimated conditional variances of the countries in the sample are shown in Figure 8.1 and 8.2.

Conclusions

This chapter examines the role of trade and financial linkages in the contagion of currency crises and presents empirical evidence on the importance of different transmission channels in the contagion of the 1994 Mexican Crisis and 1997 Asian Crisis. This chapter first employs Glick and Rose as well as Forbes' direct trade–linkage indexes to measure the extent of direct trade linkages across countries. Forbes' direct trade index indicates strong direct trade linkages among the South–east Asian countries that were affected by the 1997 Asian Crisis. The direct trade linkages were much weaker among the Latin American countries during the Mexican Crisis. For the indirect trade linkages (trade competition), Glick and Rose's index indicates that Malaysia had the highest degree of trade competition with Thailand before the Thai Crisis. Malaysia was indeed the first country being affected by the Thai Crisis. Nevertheless, the index shows that Argentina, the country most affected by the Mexican crisis, did not have high trade competition with Mexico prior to the Mexican crisis. It is shown in this chapter that financial linkages are actually the culprits that result in the contagion of the crisis from

Table 8.17 Estimates of the contagion coefficients based on the augmented GARCH Model

	θ_{Mexico}	θ_{Thai}	θ_{Japan}	θ_{US}
Latin American Countries				
Argentina	0.537 (0.231)**	0.106 (0.131)	0.049 (0.076)	0.247 (0.271)
Brazil	0.323 (0.171)	0.223 (0.182)	0.016 (0.016)	1.475 (0.849)*
Chile	0.357 (0.195)*	0.123 (0.214)	0.001 (0.011)	0 -
Colombia	0 -	0 -	0 -	0.018 (0.031)
Mexico	N/A -	0.335 (0.242)	0 -	0 -
Venezuela	0.077 (0.064)	0.088 (0.047)*	0.014 (0.015)	0 -
Southeast Asian Countries				
China	0.045 (0.063)	0.026 (0.043)	0.022 (0.044)	0 -
HK	0.421 (0.378)	0.220 (0.129)*	0 -	0.297 (0.108)**
India	0 -	0.050 (0.256)	0 -	0.041 (0.043)
Indonesia	0.067 (0.120)	0.490 (0.247)*	0 -	0 -
S.Korea	0.178 (0.155)	0.133 (0.077)*	0 -	0 -
Malaysia	0 -	0.318 (0.016)*	0 -	0 -
Philippines	0.084 (0.071)	0.024 (0.011)	0 -	0.215 (0.126)
Singapore	0 -	0.120 (0.075)*	0 -	0.050 (0.029)*
Taiwan	0.135 (0.194)	0.010 (0.006)*	0.002 (0.014)	0.180 (0.086)**
Thailand	0.016 (0.184)	N/A -	0 -	0.477 (0.305)*

[a] The numbers in parentheses are the std. errors.
[b] '*' means the coefficient is significant at a 10% level.
[c] '**' means the coefficient is significant at a 5% level.

Mexico to Argentina. This chapter also makes use of a new trade competition index that takes into account the composition and destinations of trade to measure the extent of trade competition among the countries. This new index treats two

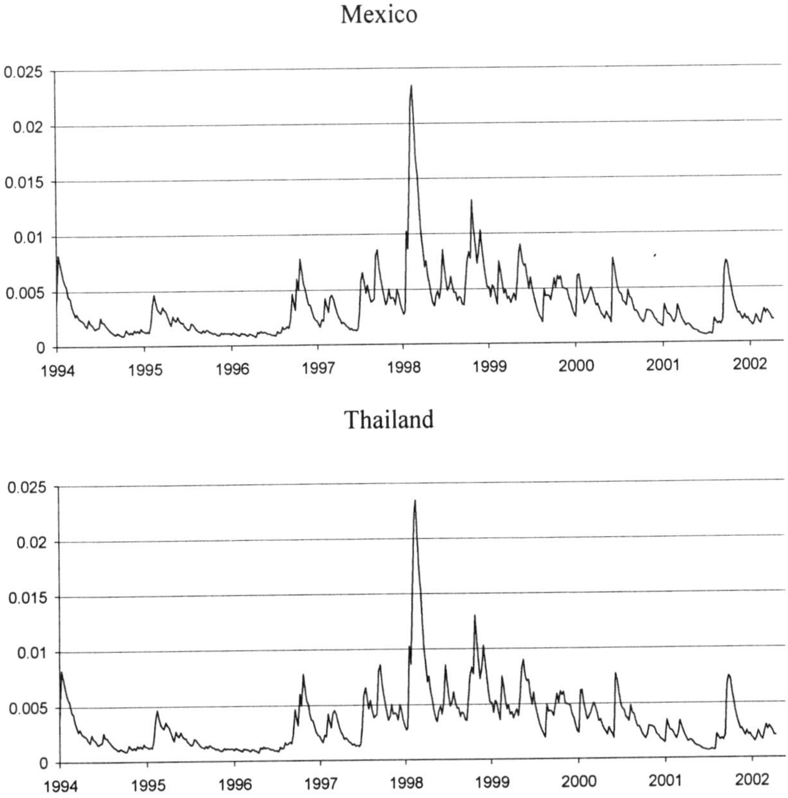

Figure 8.1 Conditional volatilities of stock return for the initial crisis countries

countries as strong trade competitors only when they are exporting products in the same industries to the same destinations. The index indicates that there is a gradual increase in the trade competition among the countries in the last decade, which is adirect result of the trade liberalization process in the emerging countries. It is also worth noting that this index performs well in indicating the countries that are vulnerable to the contagion of crises. The countries most affected by the Thai Crisis—namely, Taiwan, Singapore, Malaysia, Indonesia, Philippines and S. Korea—have the highest value of the trade competition index with Thailand.

Two types of financial linkages are also examined in this chapter. They are the 'common creditor effect' and 'volatility spillover'. The common creditor linkage is studied using the common creditor indexes of Caramazza, Ricci and Salgado (2000), Kaminsky and Reinhart (1998) as well as the fund competition indexes of Rijckeghem and Weder (1999). All three indexes show that there is a strong regional pattern in international lending. The indexes of Caramazza, Ricci and Salgado as well as Kaminsky and Reinhart indicate that the Latin American

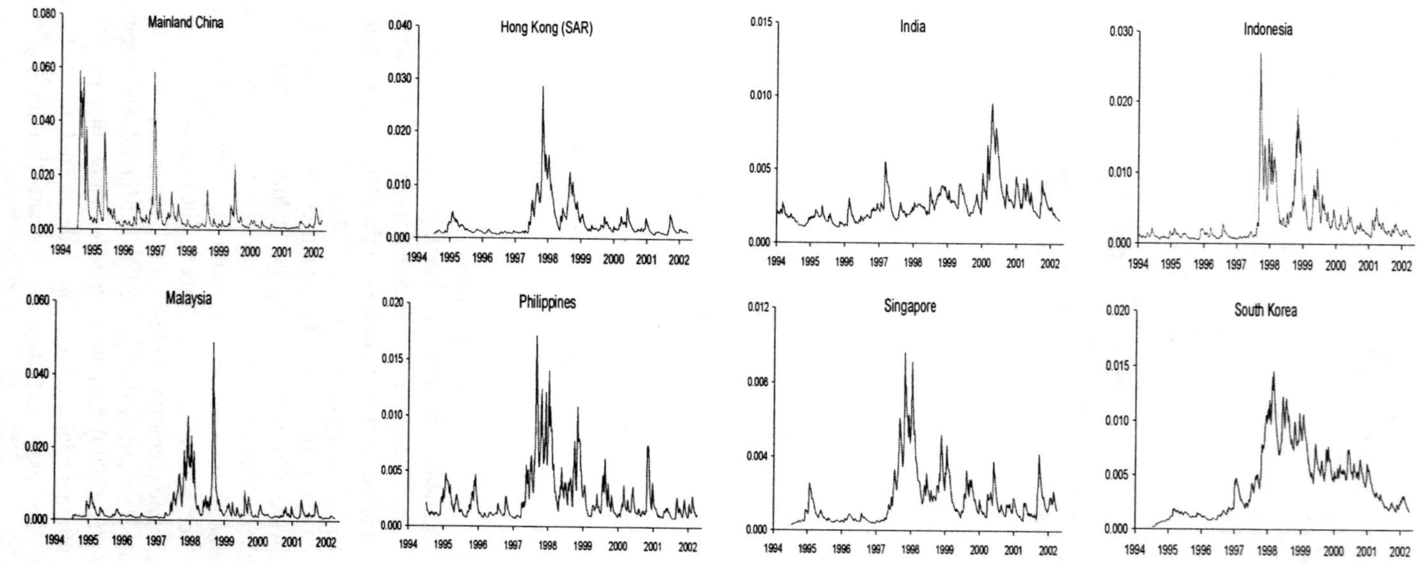

Figure 8.2 Conditional volatilities of stock return for various Southeast Asian and Latin American countries

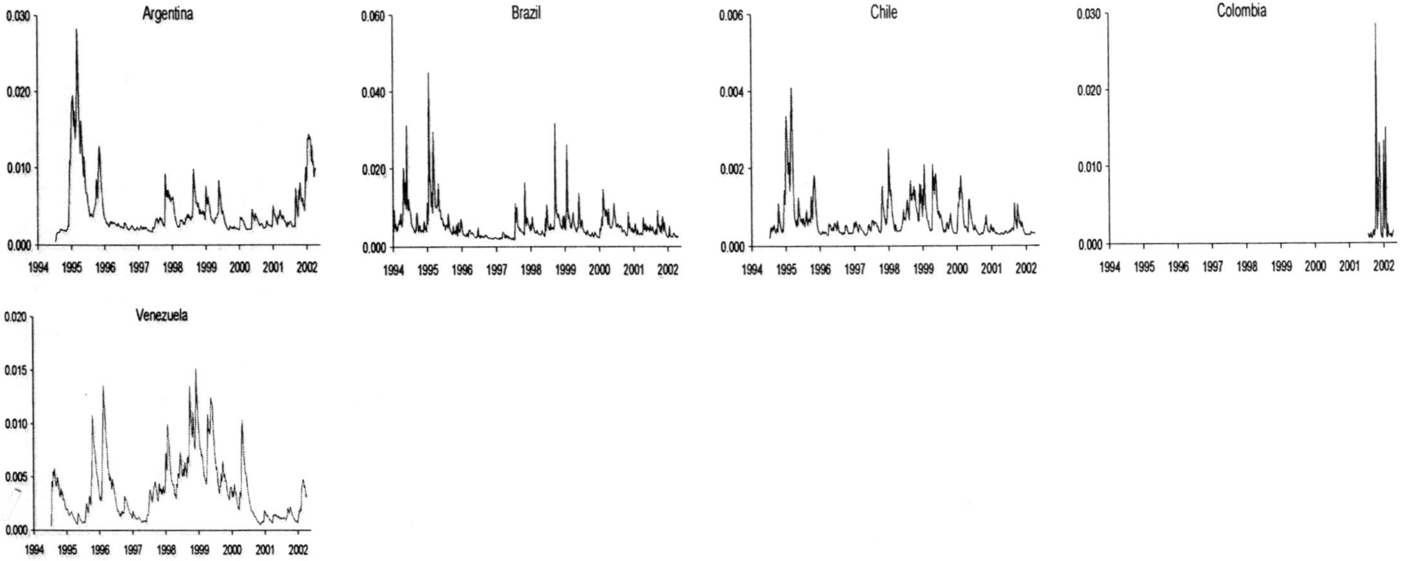

Figure 8.2 Continued

countries borrow the majority of their bank credits from US banks while Asian countries borrow mainly from Japanese banks. The absolute and relative fund competition index of Rijckeghem and Weder indicates that Brazil and Argentina have been Mexico's two most important competitors while Indonesia, South Korea and China have been Thailand's major competitors for international funds. Using a GARCH model, this chapter further shows that the spillover from the Mexican financial market to the Argentine financial market was an important channel that resulted in the contagion of the Mexican crisis to Argentina. In conclusion, this chapter provides evidence that both trade and financial linkages are important in the contagion of currency crises.

Appendix: data description

The countries included in the sample are Argentina, Brazil, Chile, Colombia, Mexico, Uruguay and Venezuela from Latin America as well as Mainland China, Hong Kong (SAR), India, Indonesia, South Korea, Malaysia, Philippines, Singapore, Taiwan and Thailand from the Southeast Asia. The sample period is 1986Q1 to 2000Q4, subject to the availability of data. The table below summaries the data sources regarding the measurements of the trade and financial linkages. The data regarding the economic fundamentals are quarterly data extracted mainly from IMF's International Financial Statistics. Details are documented in Lau and Yan (2003). The stock returns data used in the GARCH model is weekly data from Datastream. Weekly data is used to avoid the problem of non–synchronous trading and the day–of–the–week effects (Ng, 2000). The stock indexes include the Merval Index of Argentina, the Bovespa Index of Brazil, the General (IGPA) Index of Chile, the Shanghai Composite Index of China, the CSE Index of Colombia, the Hang Seng Index of Hong Kong, the BSE National Index of India, the Jakarta Stock Exchange Composite Index of Indonesia, the Korea Stock Exchange Composite Index of South Korea, the Kuala Lumpur Stock Exchange Composite Index of Malaysia, the IPC (BOLSA) Index of Mexico, the Philippines Stock exchange Index of the Philippines, the Stock Exchange All Share Index of Singapore, the Stock Exchange Weighted Price Index of Taiwan, the Bangkok Stock Exchange Price Index of Thailand, the Stock Exchange General Price Index of Venezuela, the Tokyo Stock Price Index of Japan and Standard and Poor 500 Index of the United States.

Variables	**Data Sources**
Bilateral Exports	*Direction of Trade* Database (from the IMF).
Exports by industries and destinations	*Trade Analysis System for PC* Database (from the International Trade Center of UN's Statistics Division). 1–digit SITC classification is used in the calculation.

International lending of selected banking centers to various countries	Bank for International Settlements.
Stock Market Index	Datastream.

Notes

1 For instance, Nagayasu (2000) uses Granger causality tests and cointegration tests to identify the statistical significance of stock indices in explaining exchange rate movements. He finds that some stock indexes—in particular those that concentrate on the banking and financial sectors—are often the driving forces of currency devaluations.

2 Singapore had such high value of Forbes's trade competition index because of its large trade sector. Singapore's total export amounted to 142% of its GDP in 1995 and 132% of its GDP in 1997. Even after the re–export was excluded, Singapore's domestic export amounted to 83% and 76% of its GDP in 1995 and 1997 respectively. This gives rise to high value of the component $Exp_{i,W,k}/GDP_i$ in Forbes' trade competition index.

References

Baig, T. and Goldfajn, L. (1998), 'Financial Market Contagion in the Asian Crisis', International Monetary Fund Working Paper No.WP/98/155.

Bordo, M.D., Bruce, M. and Schwartz, A.J. (1995), 'Real versus Pseudo International Systematic Risk: Some Lessons from History', NBER Working Paper No.5371.

Calvo, G.A. (1998a), 'Understanding the Russian Virus: with special reference to Latin America', manuscript, see http://www.bsos.umd.edu/econ/ciecalvo.htm/.

Calvo, G.A. (1998b), 'Capital Flows and Capital–Market Crises: The Simple Economics of Sudden Stop', *Journal of Applied Economics* **1**(1), pp. 35–54.

Calvo, G.A. (1999), 'Contagion in Emerging Market: When Wall Street is The Carrier', manuscript, see http://www.bsos.umd.edu/econ/ciecalvo.htm/.

Calvo, S. and Reinhart, C.M. (1996), 'Capital Flows to Latin America: Is There Evidence of Contagion Effects', in G. Calvo, M. Goldstein, and E. Hochreiter (eds), *Private Capital Flows to Emerging Markets*, Washington D.C.: Institute for International Economics.

Caramazza, F.. Ricci, L. and Salgado, R. (2000), 'Trade and Financial Contagion in Currency Crises', IMF Working Paper WP/00/55.

Eichengreen, B. and Rose, A. (1999), 'Contagious Currency Crises: Channels of Convergence', in T. Ito and A. Kruger (eds), *Changes in Exchange Rates in Rapidly Developing Countries: Theory, Practice, and Policy Issues*, University of Chicago Press.

Eichengreen, B., Rose, A. and Wyplosz, C. (1997), 'Contagious Currency Crises', CEPR Discussion Papers 1453.

Forbes, K. (2001), 'Are Trade Linkages Important Determinants of Country Vulnerability to Crises', NBER Working Paper w8194.

Forbes, K. and Rigobon, R. (1999), 'Measuring Contagion: Conceptual and Empirical Issues', Paper prepared for the 1999 UNU–WIDER conference on Financial Contagion in Finland.

Forbes, K. and Rigobon, R. (2000), 'No Contagion, Only Interdependence: Measuring Stock

Market Co–movements', M.I.T Working Paper.

Frankel, J.A. and Schmukler, S.L. (1998), 'Crisis, Contagion, and Country Funds: Effects on East Asia and Latin America', in R. Glick (eds), *Managing Capital Flows and Exchange Rates*, Cambridge University Press.

Glick, R. and Rose, A. (1998), 'Contagion and Trade: Why are Currency Crises Regional', NBER Working Paper w6806.

Goldfajn, L. and Valdés, R. (1997), 'Capital Flows and the Twin Crises: The Role of Liquidity', IMF Working Paper no. 97–87.

Kaminsky, G.L. and Reinhart, C.M. (1998), 'Financial Crises in Asia and Latin America: Then and Now', *American Economic Review* **88**(2).

Lau, L.J. and Yan, I.K. (2003), 'Predicting Currency Crises with a Nested Logit Model', manuscript, Stanford University.

Masson, P.R., (1998), 'Contagion: Monsoonal Effects, Spillovers, and Jumps Between Multiple Equilibria', IMF Working Paper WP/98/142.

Masson, P.R., (1999), 'Multiple Equilibria, Contagion, and the Emerging Market Crises', IMF Working Paper WP/99/164.

Mckinnon, R.I. (2001), 'After the Crisis, the East Asian Standard Resurrected', in J. Stiglitz and S. Yusuf (eds), *Rethinking the East Asian Miracle*, World Bank and Oxford University Press.

Nazmi, N. (2001), *Americas Perspectives*, Banc One Capital Markets, Inc.

Ng, A. (2000), 'Volatility Spillover Effects from Japan and the US to the Pacific–Basin', *Journal of International Money and Finance* **19**, pp. 207–233.

Rijckeghem, C. and Weder, B. (1999) 'Sources of Contagion: Finance or Trade', IMF Working Paper WP/99/146, International Monetary Fund.

Schinasi, G.J. and Smith, R.T. (1999), 'Portfolio Diversification, Leverage, and Financial Contagion', IMF Working Papers 99/136, International Monetary Fund.

Sebastian, E. (1998a), 'Interest Rate Volatility, Capital Controls and Contagion', NBER Working Paper 6756.

Sebastian, E. (1998b), 'Interest Rate Volatility, Contagion and Convergence: An Empirical Investigation of the Cases of Argentina, Chile and Mexico', *Journal of Applied Economics* **1**(1), pp. 55–86.

Chapter 9

Exchange Rate Dynamics: Where is the Saddle Path?

Yin–Wong Cheung, Javier Gardeazabal and Jesús Vázquez

Introduction

Undeniably, exchange rate behavior is one of the most intensely studied topics in the international finance literature. The overshooting model *à la* Dornbusch provides a prominent explanation for high variability of (real) exchange rates. Since its publication in the 1970s (Dornbusch, 1976), the over–shooting model occupies a key position in modeling exchange rate dynamics (Frankel and Rose, 1995). A notable feature of the model is the saddle–path dynamics, which follows from the assumption that the price of goods and the exchange rate have different adjustment speeds. Under the sticky price assumption, the exchange rate overshoots its new equilibrium level in response to shocks so that the system reaches a new saddle–path trajectory and converges to the new equilibrium position. Strictly speaking, 'overshooting dynamics' is the consequence of the presence of 'saddle–path dynamics'.[1] In the literature, nonetheless, 'overshooting' is commonly used to describe this class of exchange rate models. Thus, for convenience, in the following sections the terms 'overshooting dynamics' and 'saddle–path dynamics' are used interchangeably.

Several approaches have been adopted to test the overshooting model. For instance, some empirical studies are based on the reduced form exchange rate equation derived from the model. Despite the initial success of the model to describe observed data, the subsequent evidence is far from supportive (Frankel, 1979; Driskill, 1981; Driskill and Sheffrin, 1981). Other studies examine the relationship between real interest rate differentials and real exchange rates. Again, the empirical evidence is usually not in favor of the model (Meese and Rogoff, 1988; Edison and Pauls, 1993).

Engel and Morley (2001) consider a modified overshooting model that does not require exchange rates and prices to have the same adjustment speed. Using an unobserved component specification, the authors find prices adjust faster toward their equilibrium values—a result that lends support to the modified overshooting model. Cheung, Lai and Bergman (2004), on the other hand, compare the individual contributions of exchange rate and price movements to real exchange rate dynamics. It is found that real exchange rate dynamics are mainly driven by exchange rate adjustments while the reversion to real exchange rate equilibrium is attributable to price adjustments. Also, exchange rate movements tend to amplify and prolong deviations from the equilibrium real exchange rate. The finding is at odds with the adjustment mechanism predicted by the standard overshooting model.

Several studies directly evaluate the effect of monetary shocks on exchange rates and, hence, infer the validity of the overshooting hypothesis. Eichenbaum and Evans (1995), for instance, find that exchange rate overshooting exists but the maximal impact of a monetary shock on exchange rates occurs with a lag of two to three years. The finding is not entirely consistent with the overshooting model *à la* Dornbusch, which predicts exchange rate overshooting is instantaneously triggered by the shock. The non–instantaneous overshooting phenomenon appears to be a common empirical regularity (Cheung and Lai, 2000; Clarida and Gali, 1994). Faust and Rogers (1999), however, argue that the observed non–instantaneous overshooting effect derived from a vector autoregression (VAR) system can be spurious. These authors point out that the timing of the maximum monetary shock effect depends on the assumptions used to identify the VAR system. They show that the identification scheme proposed by Faust (1998) can be used to obtain the almost immediate overshooting effect.

This study offers an alternative perspective to evaluate the validity of the overshooting hypothesis. Essentially, we exploit the implication of the saddle–path mechanism, which is the driving force of the overshooting result, for data dynamics. The intertemporal dynamics of a given system are governed by the roots of its characteristic polynomial. In the exchange rate literature, the saddle–path property that yields the overshooting phenomenon is defined by the presence of both explosive and stationary roots. Typically, some transversality conditions are imposed to limit the effects of explosive roots so that the system can settle on the saddle path that leads to the steady state.

To a certain extent, the characterization of saddle–path dynamics is comparable to, but different from, that of cointegration. Both saddle–path and cointegration dynamics depend upon the roots of the system's characteristic polynomial. Such a similarity suggests that a test for cointegration may be adopted to test for the presence of saddle–path dynamics.

This chapter explores whether the Johansen procedure, a standard approach to test for cointegration, is a useful tool to detect saddle–path dynamics. Instead of testing for non–stationary behavior directly, the Johansen test exploits the implications of cointegration for the rank of the coefficient matrix defined by the characteristic polynomial and uses the rank condition to infer system dynamics. By using rank conditions, the Johansen test sidesteps some technical issues of hypothesis testing in the presence of non–stationarity. Indeed, it can be shown that the saddle–path and cointegration dynamics have different implications for the rank of the coefficient matrix defined by the characteristic polynomial. Specifically, the presence of cointegration is not consistent with saddle–path dynamics. Thus, the Johansen procedure can be used to discriminate between the two types of system dynamics.

When we apply the Johansen procedure to study the interaction between exchange rates and relative prices, we find that exchange rates and relative prices are cointegrated. The empirical results are suggestive of the absence of the Dornbusch–type overshooting behavior in the data.

A canonical Dornbusch–type overshooting is presented in the next section. After this, we describe the design of the Monte Carlo experiment and reports the empirical power of the Johansen procedure for detecting saddle–path dynamics. The results of testing for cointegration in monthly data from five industrial countries are presented in the following section. Finally, we offer some concluding remarks.

An overshooting model

For illustrative purposes, we present a standard overshooting model *à la* Dornbusch. The sticky–price assumption is a key element of the standard Dornbusch model. Although the purchasing power parity is assumed to hold in the long run, prices are assumed to be inflexible in the short run and do not react instantaneously to a shock. The overshooting phenomenon occurs because, in respond to a monetary shock, the exchange rate has to adjust to clear not just the foreign exchange market but also the goods market to attain a short–run equilibrium. The gradual price adjustment is the mechanism bringing the system to the long–run equilibrium.

A stochastic version of Dornbusch's overshooting model can be formulated as follows (Azariadis, 1993, chapter 5):

(9.1) $$i_t - i_t^* = E_t e_{t+1} - e_t$$

(9.2) $$m_t - p_t = \phi y_t - \eta i_t + u_t$$

(9.3) $$y_t = \delta(e_t + p_t^* - p_t) - \sigma(i_t - E_t(p_{t+1} - p_t)) + \varepsilon_t$$

(9.4) $$E_t p_{t+1} - p_t = \alpha(y_t - \bar{y})$$

where all variables (except the interest rates) are in logarithms and all parameters are non–negative. Equation (9.1) captures the uncovered interest rate parity condition: with e_t being the nominal exchange rate defined as the domestic price of foreign currency and $i_t\,(i_t^*)$ being the domestic (foreign) interest rate. The domestic nominal interest rate can exceed the foreign rate when the market anticipates a depreciation of the domestic currency. Equation (9.2) describes a money–market equilibrium relationship, where m_t is the nominal money supply, p_t is the price level and y_t is the real national income. The shock to the monetary equilibrium is given by u_t. Equation (9.3) states that the income level is demand determined. A real depreciation raises demand and so does a fall in the real interest rate. ε_t is a real demand shock. Equation (9.4) governs the price adjustment scheme. Although prices are predetermined and do not respond instantly to current realizations of other variables, they adjust gradually over time in response to the excess of aggregate demand over the natural/full employment output level ($\bar{y}$).

Conceptually, the model generates overshooting behavior in the following manner. With short–run price stickiness, an unanticipated monetary expansion induces a fall in domestic interest rates and leads to a capital outflow that will lead to the overshooting of the domestic currency to the point where the expected rate of appreciation exactly offsets the interest differential. Moreover, aggregate demand is boosted by the currency depreciation and lower interest rates. In response to higher aggregate demand, prices begin to rise slowly, thereby reducing the real money supply and pushing domestic interest rates back up. The domestic currency then appreciates gradually over time, along with rising prices. The gradual price adjustment will drive both the exchange rate and the real exchange rate to converge asymptotically to their corresponding equilibrium levels.

The implications of the equations (9.1) to (9.4) for exchange rate dynamics can be seen from the solution of the model. Following the standard procedure, we assume the foreign interest rate, the foreign price, and the domestic money supply are constant; that is, $i_t^* = i^*$, $p_t^* = p^*$, $m_t = m$. The resulting solutions of the exchange rate and price paths are given by a system of first–order simultaneous difference equations:

$$(9.5)\quad e_{t+1} - e_t = (1/\eta)(p_t - \bar{p}) + v_{1t+1}$$

$$(9.6)\quad p_{t+1} - p_t = (\alpha\delta/(1-\alpha\sigma))(e_t - \bar{e}) - (\alpha(\delta + (\sigma/\eta))/(1-\alpha\sigma))(p_t - \bar{p}) + v_{2t+1}$$

where $\bar{e}$ and $\bar{p}$ are the respective steady–state values of the exchange rate and the price level. The zero mean disturbance terms v_{1t+1} and v_{2t+1} are combinations of monetary shocks, real shocks and prediction errors. The system can be compactly written as

$$(9.7)\quad \Delta X_{t+1} = \mu + AX_t + V_{t+1}$$

where $X_{t+1} = (e_{t+1}, p_{t+1})'$, $\Delta = (1-L)$, L is the lag operator, the constant μ is a function of the parameters and the steady–state values of the exchange rate and price, and

$$(9.8)\quad A = \begin{pmatrix} 0 & \dfrac{1}{\eta} \\ \dfrac{\alpha\delta}{1-\alpha\sigma} & -\dfrac{\alpha(\delta+(\sigma/\eta))}{1-\alpha\sigma} \end{pmatrix}.$$

Let $\theta_1 < \theta_2$ be the two roots of the characteristic equation $|A - \theta I| = 0$.[2] Depending on parameter configuration, the model can generate different types of dynamics. For instance, under the assumption that $\alpha\sigma < 1$, then the determinant of A, $|A| = \theta_1\theta_2$

$= -(\alpha\delta/(1 - \alpha\sigma)\eta) < 0$, the two roots have different algebraic signs, implying that $\theta_1 < 0 < \theta_2$. Therefore, θ_2 is the explosive root and θ_1 is the stationary root. In this case, the system exhibits saddle–path dynamics and the associated overshooting behavior.

The popular cointegration dynamics are also encompassed under (9.7). Note that equation (9.7) is already in an error correction format. For cointegration to take place, the rank of matrix A should be equal to one and $|A| = 0$. For instance, the rank condition is satisfied when $\delta = 0$; that is, aggregate demand does not respond to the real exchange rate. When $\delta = 0$, the roots are $\theta_1 = -(\alpha\sigma/(1 - \alpha\sigma)\eta) < 0$ and $\theta_2 = 0$. Therefore, cointegration dynamics can be viewed as a limiting case of saddle–path behavior, in particular, when δ tends to zero.

Figures 9.1 and 9.2 illustrate the saddle–path and cointegration dynamics respectively. Technically speaking, the saddle–path dynamics are described by the unique manifold that leads the system towards its steady state. Appropriate initial conditions place the economy on the saddle–path manifold. Figure 9.1 gives a canonical phase diagram for a saddle–path system. The arrows indicate the system dynamics. The unique trajectory that brings the system to its steady state is the saddle–path line, denoted by the SP line in Figure 9.1.

For a cointegrated system, only one common $I(1)$ process drives the evolution of the system components. The system converges to its steady state disregarding the initial conditions. Under cointegration, there are an infinite number of trajectories that bring the system to its equilibrium. Notice that the slope of the phase line $\Delta p_t = 0$ is equal to $\alpha\delta/(\alpha(\delta + (\sigma/\eta)))$. Therefore as δ tends to zero, the phase line $\Delta p_t = 0$ rotates clock–wise until it overlaps with the $\Delta e_t = 0$ phase line. Figure 9.2 depicts the phase diagram of a cointegrated system, where the two lines overlap. When δ tends to zero, the explosive region in Figure 9.1 disappears and there is an infinite number of paths leading to the line where the two phase lines overlap. The manifold where the two phase lines overlap is known as the 'attractor' of the system.

There is another case that deserves attention. When $\alpha = 0$, the price level follows a random walk (a martingale difference process, to be precise), the rank of matrix A is null, and there is no cointegration between prices and exchange rates. Apparently, this case is not relevant to empirical data on exchange rates and prices examined in Section 4 because these data are typically non–stationary and prices do not follow a martingale.

Detecting saddle–path behavior

The discussion in the previous section suggests that the rank of A can be used to infer the dynamics of the system. Instead of deriving a new testing method, we observe that the Johansen's procedure, which is a standard test for cointegration, uses the rank of A to infer the system dynamics. Thus, we explore the possibility of using the Johansen's procedure to discriminate the saddle–path and stationary systems from a cointegrated system.

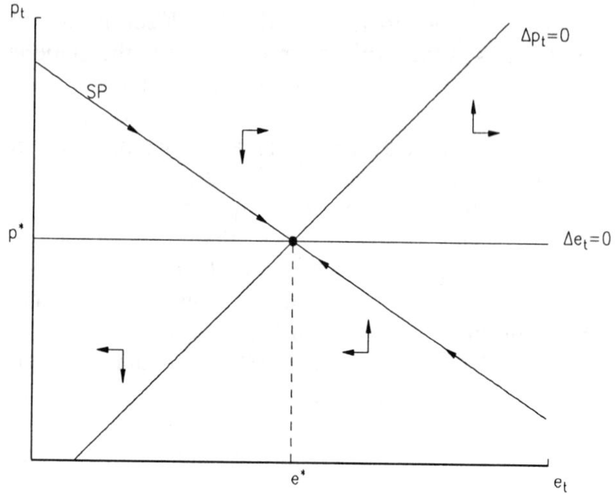

Figure 9.1 Saddle path dynamics

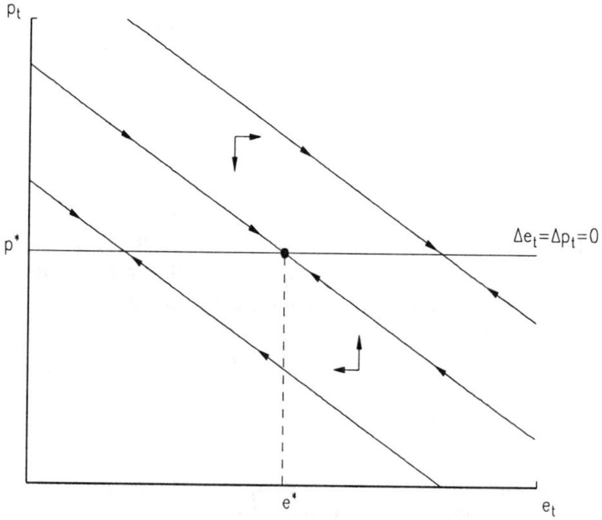

Figure 9.2 Cointegration dynamics

Table 9.1 The empirical power of the Johansen Maximum Eigenvalue Statistic against saddle-path alternatives

	Roots		T = 100		T = 300	
	θ_2	θ_1	H_0 *vs* H_1	H_0 *vs* H_1	H_0 *vs* H_1	H_0 *vs* H_1
	0.20	-0.20	1.0	0.7845	1.0	1.0
	0.20	-0.10	1.0	0.5119	1.0	0.9944
	0.20	-0.01	1.0	0.1027	1.0	0.2023
	0.10	-0.20	1.0	0.5186	1.0	0.9936
$\sigma_0 = 0.0$	0.10	-0.10	1.0	0.3703	1.0	0.9508
	0.10	-0.01	1.0	0.1087	1.0	0.1977
	0.01	-0.20	1.0	0.1120	1.0	0.2004
	0.01	-0.10	1.0	0.1244	1.0	0.1938
	0.01	-0.01	1.0	0.1686	1.0	0.1566
	0.20	-0.20	0.9995	0.8355	1.0	1.0
	0.20	-0.10	0.9715	0.5779	1.0	0.9980
	0.20	-0.01	0.9283	0.1114	1.0	0.1956
	0.10	-0.20	0.9981	0.5565	1.0	0.9974
$\sigma_0 = 0.1$	0.10	-0.10	0.8976	0.4221	1.0	0.9640
	0.10	-0.01	0.7304	0.1391	1.0	0.1867
	0.01	-0.20	0.9943	0.1148	1.0	0.2052
	0.01	-0.10	0.7893	0.1313	1.0	0.2028
	0.01	-0.01	0.4326	0.1301	0.7625	0.1688
	0.20	-0.20	0.8881	0.9573	1.0	1.0
	0.20	-0.10	0.5943	0.8082	1.0	0.9995
	0.20	-0.01	0.5732	0.0343	1.0	0.0521
	0.10	-0.20	0.8253	0.7037	1.0	0.9997
$\sigma_0 = 1.0$	0.10	-0.10	0.3279	0.5974	1.0	0.9939
	0.10	-0.01	0.2619	0.0672	0.9487	0.0544
	0.01	-0.20	0.8304	0.1163	1.0	0.2014
	0.01	-0.10	0.2393	0.2173	1.0	0.1997
	0.01	-0.01	0.2429	0.0543	0.2119	0.1369

For a bivariate difference–stationary system, the Johansen procedure is usually implemented as follows. First, the maximum eigenvalue statistic of the Johansen procedure tests the null hypothesis H_0: $rank(A) = 0$ against the alternative H_1: $rank(A) = 1$. Under H_0, the unit root components of two individual series are driven

Table 9.1 Continued

	Roots		T = 100		T = 300	
	θ_2	θ_1	H_0 *vs* H_1	H_0 *vs* H_1	H_0 *vs* H_1	H_0 *vs* H_1
	0.20	-0.20	0.7946	0.9911	1.0	1.0
	0.20	-0.10	0.4929	0.9503	1.0	1.0
	0.20	-0.01	0.4770	0.0027	1.0	0.0057
	0.10	-0.20	0.7024	0.7809	1.0	1.0
σ_0 = 10.0	0.10	-0.10	0.2123	0.7612	1.0	0.9999
	0.10	-0.01	0.1951	0.0046	0.9017	0.0065
	0.01	-0.20	0.7479	0.1223	1.0	0.2087
	0.01	-0.10	0.1465	0.2874	1.0	0.2077
	0.01	-0.01	0.2180	0.0234	0.1244	0.0748

Note: The empirical rejection frequencies of applying the Johansen maximum eigenvalue test to artificial data generated according to saddle–path dynamics are reported. The rejection frequencies are based on 10,000 replications and a 5% critical value. Two sample sizes; T = 100 and T = 300, are considered. The hypotheses are defined by H_0: *rank*(A) = 0, H_1: *rank*(A) = 1, and H_2: *rank*(A) = 2. Two rejection frequencies are recorded. The first one reported under the column 'H_0 *vs* H_1' is the frequency of H_0 being rejected. The second one reported under 'H_0 *vs* H_1' is the frequency of H_1 being rejected conditioning on the rejection of H_0. The characteristic roots of the system are given by θ_1 and θ_2. The standard deviation of the initial condition is given by σ_0. See the text for a more detailed description of the simulation.

by two different $I(1)$ processes and there is no cointegration. Under H_1, the variables are cointegrated and the two variables are driven by one common $I(1)$ process and one stationary process. If H_0 is rejected, the procedure then considers the hypothesis H_1: *rank*(A) = 1 against the alternative H_2: *rank*(A) = 2. While the cointegration dynamics is consistent with the non–rejection of H_1, either a stationary system or a saddle–path system implies A has full rank. It is interesting to recall that, in the previous section, it is shown that a cointegration system can be interpreted as a limiting case of either a saddle–path system or a stationary system.

In the literature, there are several studies examining the empirical performance of the Johansen procedure (Cheung and Lai, 1993b; Gonzalo 1994). Typically these studies consider the cointegration rather than the saddle–path alternative. The Johansen procedure is constructed to test for the rank of A and, at least theoretically, can be used to detect saddle–path behavior. The natural question to ask is: 'What is the empirical power of the Johansen's tests against the saddle–path alternative?' A Monte Carlo experiment is designed to shed some insights on the power issue. Again, a bivariate system that has the form of (9.7) is used to illustrate the point.

The Monte Carlo experiment is conducted as follows. First, T observations of X_t are generated according to saddle–path dynamics. The Appendix contains information on the procedure used to generate the data. Second, the maximum eigenvalue statistic is used to test the hypothesis H_0: $rank(A) = 0$ against the alternative H_1: $rank(A) = 1$. If H_0 is rejected in favor of H_1, then H_1 is tested against the alternative H_2: $rank(A) = 2$. Third, the procedure is repeated N times. Two rejection frequencies are recorded. The first one is the frequency of H_0 being rejected. The second one is the frequency of H_1 being rejected, conditioning on the rejection of H_0. The following parameter values are considered: $T = (100, 300)$, $N = 10{,}000$, $\theta_1 = (-0.20, -0.1, -0.01)$, $\theta_2 = (0.20, 0.1, 0.01)$, and $\sigma_i^2 = \text{var}(v_{it}) = 0.01$. An additional parameter is the variance of the distribution (σ_0^2) from which the initial observation is drawn. The values of σ_0 used in the experiment are 0, 0.1, 1, and 10.

Because the Johansen's methodology is a standard test procedure, we refer the reader to, for example, Johansen and Juselius (1990), for a detailed discussion of the procedure and of the construction of the maximum eigenvalue statistic.

The simulations results are reported in Table 9.1. The rejection frequencies are derived using the 5% critical value. One relatively easy to interpret result is that the power increases with the sample size. Conditional on the other parameter values, the rejection frequency increases with the sample size—that is, the test is consistent. The implications of the roots θ_1 and θ_2 for the rejection frequencies are quite intuitive. In general, the further away the roots are from zero, the higher is the rejection frequency. Exceptions occur when $T = 100$, $\theta_1 = -0.01$ and $\theta_2 = 0.01$. In some of these cases, the rejection frequency for H_1 against H_2 is higher than in some other parameter combinations in which the roots are further away from zero. However, the apparent odd result disappears when the rejection frequency for H_1 against H_2 is computed without conditioning on the rejection of H_0.

It is interesting to observe that, for the two tests H_0 against H_1 and H_1 against H_2, both θ_1 and θ_2 have comparable effects on the rejection frequencies. The observation is consistent with the fact that the Johansen procedure is a test for the rank of the relevant coefficient matrix. When either θ_1 or θ_2 is approaching zero, the rank of the relevant matrix is approaching one, the system dynamics are shifting towards H_1, and it is getting more and more difficult to reject H_1. As a general rule, when both θ_1 and θ_2 are close to zero, the rank is close to zero and the test has low power to reject H_0. It is not too surprising to observe the limited power of the test, especially when $\theta_1 = -0.01$ and $\theta_2 = 0.01$. Statistical tests always have low power for alternatives that are very close to the null hypothesis.

The effect of σ_0 appears intricate. When $\sigma_0 = 0$, all simulated time series are initially at the steady state. The system moves away from the steady state in the presence of random shocks and, then, follows the saddle–path to the new steady state. When $\sigma_0 > 0$, the initial position of the system is not necessarily at the steady state. The greater σ_0, the more likely the system is initially far away from the

Table 9.2 The empirical power of the Johansen Maximum Eigenvalue Statistic against stationary alternatives

Roots		$T = 100$		$T = 300$	
θ_2	θ_1	H_0 *vs* H_1	H_1 *vs* H_2	H_0 *vs* H_1	H_1 *vs* H_2
-0.20	-0.20	1.0	0.8349	1.0	1.0
-0.20	-0.10	1.0	0.5641	1.0	0.9974
-0.20	-0.01	1.0	0.1042	1.0	0.1972
-0.10	-0.20	1.0	0.5485	1.0	0.9975
-0.10	-0.10	1.0	0.3980	1.0	0.9613
-0.10	-0.01	1.0	0.1135	1.0	0.1862
-0.01	-0.20	1.0	0.1064	1.0	0.2028
-0.01	-0.10	1.0	0.1128	1.0	0.1939
-0.01	-0.01	1.0	0.1326	1.0	0.1551

Note: The empirical rejection frequencies of applying the Johansen maximum eigenvalue test to artificial data generated according to stationary dynamics are reported. The rejection frequencies are based on 10,000 replications and a 5% critical value. Two sample sizes; $T = 100$ and $T = 300$, are considered. The hypotheses are defined by H_0: $rank(A) = 0$, H_1: $rank(A) = 1$, and H_2: $rank(A) = 2$. Two rejection frequencies are recorded. The first one reported under the column 'H_0 *vs* H_1' is the frequency of H_0 being rejected. The second one reported under 'H_1 *vs* H_2' is the frequency of H_1 being rejected conditioning on the rejection of H_0. The characteristic roots of the system are given by θ_1 and θ_2. See the text for a more detailed description of the simulation.

steady state. In fact, the σ_0 parameter can have two opposite effects on the empirical power. On the one hand, when σ_0 is large, the initial shock moves the system far away from the steady state and, hence, the system stays for a long time on the converging saddle path. Intuitively, it would be easier for the test to reveal the saddle–path dynamics. On the other hand, a large σ_0 introduces a high level of noise and, subsequently, makes it more difficult to reject the nonstationarity (null) hypothesis and less easy to uncover saddle–path dynamics.

The results in Table 9.1 indicate that the effect of σ_0 depends on the roots θ_1 and θ_2. It is instructive to compare the two extremes cases ($\theta_1 = -0.20$ and $\theta_2 = 0.20$) and ($\theta_1 = -0.01$ and $\theta_2 = 0.01$). In the former case, the roots are quite different from zero and the system is far away from H_0 and H_1. An increase in the value of σ_0 from 0 to 1 is accompanied with an increase in the number of cases in which favorable evidence is gardened for H_2. The result holds when either the conditional rejection frequency (the one reported in the table) or the total rejection frequency is considered. Thus, for this parameter configuration, an increase in the value of σ_0 from 0 to 1 improves the ability to detect saddle–path dynamics. The rejection frequency falls, however, when σ_0 is increased from 1 to 10. Thus, when the noise level associated with σ_0 is high (relative to the distance from H_0 and H_1), σ_0 negatively affects the power of the test to detect saddle–path dynamics. For the case $\theta_1 = -0.01$ and $\theta_2 = 0.01$, the system is very close to having two zero roots. Under this situation, an increase in the value of σ_0 makes it more difficult to discern the saddle–path dynamics and, thus, lowers the ability of the test to reject H_0 and H_1. The positive (negative) effect of σ_0 on ability to reveal saddle–path dynamics dominates when the system dynamics is far away from (close to) those implied by H_0 and H_1.

In conducting the simulation experiment, the Johansen trace statistics were also computed. However, the empirical power estimates based on the trace statistic are very similar to those based on the maximum eigenvalue statistic. Different values of σ_1^2 and σ_2^2 were also included in the experiment. It turns out that the simulation results are quite insensitive to a) the value of σ_1^2 and σ_2^2, and b) the relative size of of σ_1^2 and σ_2^2. Thus, the simulation results related to the trace statistic and different combinations of σ_1^2 and σ_2^2 are not reported for brevity. These results are available from the authors upon request.

While the results indicate that the Johansen procedure has a reasonable power to uncover saddle–path behavior, it is noted that a stationary bivariate system can lead to similar rejection results. It is instructive to assess the power of the test in the presence of stationary data. To this end, we apply the Johansen procedure to data generated under stationary alternatives. The stationary roots considered are θ_1, $\theta_2 = (-0.2, -0.10, -0.01)$. The other parameters are the same as those considered in Table 9.1. Table 9.2 reports the power of the Johansen procedure against the stationary alternatives when we set $\sigma_0 = 0$.

Similar to the saddle–path experiment, the empirical power in Table 9.2 is increasing with the sample size and the distance of the roots from zero. Compared with results in Table 9.1, results in Table 9.2 indicate that the Johansen maximum eigenvalue statistic has reasonable power in detecting the full rank condition—no matter it is generated by saddle–path or stationary dynamics.

Exchange rate dynamics

In this section, we use the Johansen procedure to infer whether the saddle–path and the related overshooting dynamics are an appropriate description of exchange rate dynamics. Four dollar–based exchange rates namely British pound, French franc, German mark, and Italian lira are included in the sample. Monthly data of nominal exchange rates and consumer price indexes from April 1973 to December 1998 were retrieved from the International Financial Statistics data CD–ROM. These data are expressed in logarithms. As commonly conceived, the individual exchange rate and price series display $I(1)$ non–stationarity. Following the literature, the bivariate system comprising of the nominal exchange rate and the relative price is

Table 9.3 Johansen cointegration test results

	Max. Eigenvalue Stat.		Trace Stat.	
	rank(*A*) = 0	*rank*(*A*) = 1	*rank*(*A*) = 0	*rank*(*A*) = 1
British Pound				
Lag = 2	21.3878*	5.3478	26.7356*	5.3478
French Franc				
Lag = 4	34.7165*	4.3357	39.0522*	4.3357
German Mark				
Lag = 1	15.9658**	3.9937	19.9595*	3.9937
Italian Lira				
Lag = 1	26.6205*	4.9276	31.5481*	4.9276

Note: The Johansen tests for cointegration between nominal exchange rates and relative prices are presented. Both the maximum eigenvalue statistic 'Max. Eigenvalue Stat.' and the trace statistics 'Trace Stat.' are reported. The null hypotheses are given underneath the statistic labels. The alternatives for the maximum eigenvalue statistic are *rank*(*A*) = 1 and *rank*(*A*) = 2 and the those for the trace statistic are *rank*(*A*) > 0 and *rank*(*A*) > 1. The lag parameter 'Lag =' is selected using the Akaike information criterion. Significance at the 5% and 1% levels are indicated by '**' and '*' according to the finite sample critical values in Cheung and Lai (1993b). The hypothesis of *rank*(*A*) = 0 is rejected by both statistics but the hypothesis of *rank*(*A*) = 1 is not rejected.

employed to study the cointegration relationship between exchange rates and relative prices.

For notational purposes, a bivariate system as (9.7) is re–writen in its general form:

$$(9.9)\quad \Delta X_t = \mu + AX_{t+1} + \sum_{i=1}^{k-1} A_i X_{t-i} + V_t$$

where no parameter restriction is imposed on matrices A and A_i. The lagged X_t's are included to ensure that V_t follows a white noise process and that the Johansen result is not distorted by serial correlation in the error term. In implementing the test, the lag parameter k is selected using the Akaike information criterion. Both the Johansen maximum eigenvalue and trace statistics are calculated. Again we refer readers to Johansen and Juselius (1990) for the construction of these test statistics.

The results of the Johansen tests are reported in Table 9.3. Both the maximum eigenvalue and trace statistics reject the null hypothesis H_0: *rank*(*A*) = 0 but not the null hypothesis H_1: $rank(A) = 1$. Thus, the exchange rate and the relative price are cointegrated and the two series in each bivariate system are driven by a common $I(1)$ process. Individually, each series evolves as a non–stationary $I(1)$ process. However, a unique combination of the two series governed by the cointegrating vector is stationary. Typically, the cointegration result is interpreted as the evidence of the presence of an empirical long–run relationship between exchange rates and prices, which constitutes a necessary condition for long–run purchasing power parity (Cheung and Lai, 1993a; Kugler and Lenz, 1993).

The results in the previous sections allow us to use the rank of A to infer the system dynamics from a different perspective. In addition to the long–run relationship interpretation, our results also indicate that neither the notion of saddle–path nor stationary dynamics are consistent with the inference that the rank of A is equal to one. Because exchange rates and relative prices are $I(1)$ processes, the bivariate system consisting of these two variables is not stationary. Thus, the strength of the result is its implications for the irrelevance of using saddle–path and the related overshooting dynamics to describe exchange rate behavior.

There are a few caveats in generalizing the cointegration results. First, the empirical illustration includes only a few countries even though these are the key industrial countries. It is fair to say that a more definite inference on the relevancy of saddle–path dynamics still awaits additional results from a larger set of dollar–based exchange rates and cross–rates. Second, as indicated in the simulation experiment, the ability to detect saddle–path dynamics is severely handicapped when the explosive root is very close to one. Further analyses are required to rule out this possibility. Nonetheless, the cointegration results in Table 9.3 cast doubt on the general validity of saddle–path/overshooting exchange rate dynamics.

Concluding remarks

The overshooting model *à la* Dornbusch is a prominent explanation for the volatile exchange rate behavior in the current floating period. Assuming prices are sticky, the model displays a saddle–path pattern and yields overshooting dynamics that induces high short–term exchange rate volatility. Using a bivariate system, this study illustrates the implications of saddle–path, cointegration, and stationary dynamics for the characteristic roots that determines the system's intertemporal behavior. It is shown that a cointegration system can be interpreted as a limiting case of a system that displays either saddle–path or stationarity dynamics. A Monte Carlo experiment is designed to illustrate the usefulness of the Johansen tests to uncover saddle–path dynamics. The simulation results indicate that the Johansen tests have a) reasonable power to detect saddle–path dynamics, and b) similar power to reject the cointegration hypothesis in favor of saddle–path or stationarity alternatives.

Our empirical example shows that exchange rates and prices are cointegrated. Because the variables in a saddle–path system are not supposed to display a cointegrating relationship, the empirical evidence is indicative of the absence of saddle–path dynamics in the data under investigation. Exchange rate models that do not rely on saddle–path properties and over–shooting dynamics may deserve some more serious attention.

It is conceivable that the implications of the current study go beyond the exchange rate saddle–path behavior. There are models in different areas in economics exhibiting saddle–path properties. For instance, the neo–classical growth model (Cass, 1965) is an early example in which saddle–path dynamics are used to elaborate balanced–growth. Other models that utilize saddle–path dynamics to elucidate relationships between economic variables include those of Bruno and Fischer (1991) for interest rates and inflation, Evans and Yarrow (1981) for real money balances and inflation. The saddle–path property in these models, however, is not commonly subject to direct empirical test.

Nonetheless, it is noted that some studies report cointegrating relationship between a) output, investment, and consumption (King *et al.*, 1991)[3] and between interest rates and inflation (Bonham, 1991). These cointegration results imply the saddle–path models may not be appropriate for these variables.

While the Johansen procedure, as illustrated in previous sections, can be used to test for saddle–path dynamics, further studies on other testing procedures for saddle–path dynamics are warranted; especially given the widespread use of saddle–path models in economics.

Appendix: Generating data that exhibit saddle–path dynamics

The simulation experiment dealing with saddle–path dynamics is conducted as follows. First, we find a solution to equation (9.7) under the saddle–path hypothesis. Second, using the saddle–path solution, we simulate X_t of length T. T = 100 and T = 300 are considered in the exercise. Third, the Johansen test statistic is calculated from the simulated data. The above steps are repeated N times and N is set to 10,000. The N sample Johansen statistics are then compared with the 5% critical value to tally the rejection frequency.

We follow the standard procedure to obtain the saddle–path solution to equation (9.7). Let B be a (2x2) matrix whose columns contain the eigenvectors of $(A + I)$. Pre–multiplying system (9.7) by B^{-1}, we obtain $Z_t = \Lambda Z_t + U_t$ where $Z_t = B^{-1}X_t$, $\Lambda = B^{-1}(A + I)$ is a diagonal matrix with the eigenvalues of $(A + I)$ along the diagonal and $U_t = B^{-1}V_t$. Then, we solve each of the first–order difference equations $z_{it} = (1 + \theta_i)z_{it-1} + u_{it}$; i = 1,2 where $Z_t = (z_{1t}, z_{2t})'$ and $U_t = (u_{1t}, u_{2t})'$. Under the saddle–path hypothesis, $\theta_1 < 0$ and $\theta_2 > 0$. We solve the first equation backward and the second equation forward. The solutions can be expressed as the sum of two terms:

$$z_{it} = z_{it}^{*} + (1+\theta_i)^t c_{i0}$$

where

$$z_{1t}^{*} = \sum_{i=0}^{\infty} (1+\theta_1)^i u_{1t-i},$$

$$z_{2t}^{*} = \sum_{i=0}^{\infty} \left(\frac{1}{1+\theta_2} \right)^{i+1} u_{2t+i+1}$$

and $c_{i0} = z_{i0} - z_{i0}^{*}$. In economics, these two terms are usually labeled the 'steady state' and the 'bubble'. The saddle–path solution is obtained by setting the terminal condition $c_{20} = 0$ so that the resulting sequence is not explosive. The original variables of the system are then recovered using $X_t = BZ_t$.

The steady state $Z_t^{*} = (z_{1t}^{*}, z_{2t}^{*})'$ is approximated by the sum of a finite number of elements. We first generate the series U_t of length $3T$ using a normal random number generator. The first T simulated numbers are used to generate z_{11}^{*}, the first $T + 1$ simulated numbers are used to generate z_{12}^{*}, ..., and so on. The last T simulated numbers are used to generate z_{2T}^{*}, the last $T + 1$ simulated numbers are used to generate z_{2T-1}^{*}, ..., and so on. In addition, the initial condition c_{10} is required to calculate the solution. In the experiment, the initial condition c_{10} is drawn from a normal distribution with zero mean and variante σ_0^2. The idea of the random choice is to capture the existence of a continuum of equilibria (each indexed by a different initial condition) lying on the unique stable manifold converging to the steady state.

Notes

1 Strictly speaking, overshooting implies saddle–path but the opposite is not true.

2 Notice that if equation (9.7) is written as $X_{t+1} = \mu + \Pi X_t + V_{t+1}$, where $\Pi = A + I$, then the roots of Π, say λ_1 and λ_2, are related to the roots of A according to $\lambda_i = 1 + \theta_i$, $i = 1, 2$. Therefore, a unit root of Π is equivalent to a zero root of A.

3 King *et al.* (1991) show in a neoclassical growth framework that (the logs of) output, consumption and investment are cointegrated when thechnology shocks follow an $I(1)$ process, whereas certain ratios characterizing the balanced–growth path (for instance, the consumption–output and the investment–output *great ratios*) exhibit saddle–path dynamics.

References

Azariadis, C. (1993), *Intertemporal Macroeconomics*, Blackwell Publishers, Oxford.

Bonham, C. (1991), 'Correct Cointegration Tests of the Long–Run Relationship between Nominal Interest and Inflation', *Applied Economics* **23**, pp. 1487–1492.

Bruno, M. and Fischer, S. (1991), 'Seigniorage, Operating Rules, and the High Inflation Trap', *Quarterly Journal of Economics* **105**, pp. 353–374.

Cass, D. (1965), 'Optimum Growth in an Aggregative Model of Capital Accumulation', *Review of Economic Studies* **32**, pp. 233–240.

Cheung, Y.W. and Lai, K.S. (1993a), 'Long–Run Purchasing Power Parity During the Recent Float', *Journal of International Economics* **34**, pp. 181–192.

Cheung, Y.W. and Lai, K.S. (1993b), 'Finite–Sample Sizes of Johansen's Likelihood Ratio Tests for Cointegration', *Oxford Bulletin of Economics and Statistics* **55**, pp. 313–328.

Cheung, Y.W. and Lai, K.S. (2000), 'On the Purchasing Power Parity Puzzle', *Journal of International Economics* **52**, pp. 321–330.

Cheung, Y.W., Lai, K.S. and Bergman, M. (2004), 'Dissecting the PPP Puzzle: The Unconventional Roles of Nominal Exchange Rate and Price Adjustments', *Journal of International Economics* (forthcoming).

Clarida, R. and Gali, J. (1994), 'Sources of Real Exchange Fluctuations: How Important are Nominal Shocks?', *Carnegie–Rochester Conference Series on Public Policy* **41**, pp. 1–56.

Dornbusch, R. (1976), 'Expectations and Exchange Rate Dynamics', *Journal of Political Economy* **84**, pp. 1161–1176.

Driskill, R.A. (1981), 'Exchange Rate Dynamics, An Empirical Analysis', *Journal of Political Economy* **89**, pp. 357–371.

Driskill, R.A. and Sheffrin, S.M. (1981), 'On the Mark: Comment', *American Economic Review* **71**, pp. 1068–1074.

Edison, H.J. and Pauls, B.D. (1993), 'A Re–Assessment of the Relationship between Real Exchange Rates and Real Interest Rates: 1974–1990', *Journal of Monetary Economics* **31**, pp. 165–187.

Eichenbaum, M. and Evans, C.L. (1995), 'Some Empirical Evidence on the Effects of Shocks to Monetary Policy on Exchange Rates', *Quarterly Journal of Economics* **110**, pp. 975–1009.

Engel, C. and Morley, J.C. (2001), 'The Adjustment of Prices and the Adjustment of the Exchange Rate', manuscript, University of Wisconsin.

Evans, J. and Yarrow, G. (1981), 'Some Implications of Alternative Expectations Hypotheses in the Monetary Analysis of Hyperinflations', *Oxford Economic Papers* **33**, pp. 61–80.

Faust, J. (1998), 'The Robustness of Identified VAR Conclusions About Money', *Carnegie–Rochester Conference Series on Public Policy* **41**, pp. 1–56.

Faust, J. and Rogers, J.H. (1999), 'Monetary Policy's Role in Exchange Rate Behavior', *International Finance Discussion Paper* #652, Board of Governors of the Federal Reserve System.

Frankel, J. (1979), 'On the Mark: A Theory of Floating Exchange Rates Based on Real Interest Differentials', *American Economic Review* **69**, pp. 610–622.

Frankel, J. and Rose, A. (1995), 'Empirical Research on Nominal Exchange Rates', Chapter 33 in G. Grossman and K. Rogoff, (eds), *Handbook of Internationl Economics* Vol. 3, pp. 1689–1729, Elsevier, Amsterdam.

Gonzalo, J. (1994), 'Five Alternative Methods of Estimating Long–Run Equilibrium Relationships', *Journal of Econometrics* **60**, pp. 203–233.

Johansen, S. and Juselius, K. (1990), 'Maximum Likelihood Estimation and Inference on Cointegration – With Applications to the Demand for Money', *Oxford Bulletin of Economics and Statistics* **2**, pp. 169–210.

King, R., Plosser, C., Stock, J. and Watson, M. (1991), 'Stochastic Trends and Economic Fluctuations', *American Economic Review* **81**, pp. 819–840.

Kugler, P. and Lenz, C. (1993), 'Multivariate Cointegration Analysis and the Long–Run Validity of PPP', *Review of Economics and Statistics* **75**, pp. 180–184.

Meese, R. and Rogoff, K. (1988), 'Was it Real? The Exchange Rate–Interest Rate Differential Relation over the Modern Floating–Rate Period', *The Journal of Finance* **43**, pp. 933–948.

Chapter 10

How Well Has the Currency Board Performed? Evidence from Hong Kong

Yum K. Kwan and Francis T. Lui

Introduction

The recent global financial turmoil has changed the currency board from a relatively obscure and unstudied monetary regime to an exchange rate system that has attracted widespread attention. It has been recommended as the definitive solution to stabilize the currency and the economy in Mexico, Indonesia, Russia and Brazil. Part of the enthusiasm may be due to its property of having a stable exchange rate. Its smooth adoption in a number of countries, notably Argentina (1991), Estonia (1992), Lithuania (1994) and Bulgaria (1997) must have also created greater confidence in the system.[1] If the renewed interest could be sustained and more countries were to adopt currency boards eventually, then as Schwartz (1993) had commented, 'a watershed would have been reached in the annals of political economy'.

Currency board, first introduced in the British colony of Mauritius in 1849, is a rule–based monetary institution different from a central bank. Although there are variations, a typical currency board has two essential characteristics. First, the board has the obligation to exchange on demand local currency for some major international currency, which is often called the reserve currency, and vice versa, at a fixed exchange rate stipulated in the legislation. Second, local currency is issued based on at least 100 percent reserve of securities denominated mainly in the reserve currency.

Since the nineteenth century, dozens of currency boards had been established in British colonies and other places, often in response to monetary or exchange rate disturbances.[2] However, when these colonies became independent nations after World War II, most of them decided to replace the currency board with a central bank. Only very few currency boards still survive today. This may be the reason why some people believe that this form of monetary institution has already lost its practical importance. This judgment is premature. Recent events have shown that currency stability is of central importance in policy making in many countries. Currency board is among the few viable options to achieve this end.

Do the benefits of currency board outweigh their costs? This is an important policy question for countries considering adopting it. Some of the theoretical advantages and disadvantages of currency boards are well known, many of which are the same as those of a commodity–standard monetary system.[3] For example, convertibility of currency is guaranteed and there is little or no uncertainty about the exchange rate. On the other hand, in times of domestic liquidity crisis, a currency board arrangement cannot act as a lender of last resort. In theory, its reserve currency can only be used to buy local currency or foreign securities. It would be a violation of its basic principle if the reserve were to be used to purchase the assets of a domestic bank suffering from a run.[4] Moreover, since currency board is a rule–based arrangement, discretionary monetary policies are precluded. Whether this macroeconomic self–discipline is regarded as an advantage, however, is more controversial.

To assess the viability of adopting currency boards as the monetary institution, we should not confine ourselves to theoretical discussions alone. Since they have been in existence for almost one and a half centuries, a more fruitful approach is to analyze rigorously the empirical data generated from actual experience. This literature is generally lacking. In this chapter, we shall analyze the macroeconomic implications of a currency board regime using Hong Kong data by the structural vector autoregressive method developed by Blanchard and Quah (1989) and Bayoumi and Eichengreen (1993, 1994). The viability of the regime is also discussed.

In the next section, we shall briefly discuss the institutional background of Hong Kong's currency board and argue why its experience provides us with a unique natural experiment to evaluate some aspects of the system. This is followed by an outline of the structural vector autoregressive model implemented in this chapter and the empirical results. We conclude the chapter by summarizing some general properties and implications about currency boards that we have learned from the Hong Kong experience.

Institutional background of Hong Kong's currency board

The currency system of Hong Kong, following that of China, was based on the silver standard in the nineteenth and early part of the twentieth centuries.[5] In 1934, the United States decided to buy silver at a very high fixed rate and that led to large outflow of silver from Hong Kong and China.[6] As a result, both governments abandoned the silver standard. In December 1935, Hong Kong enacted the Currency Ordinance, which was later renamed as the Exchange Fund Ordinance, and purchased all privately held silver coins. At the same time, the note–issuing banks, which were private enterprises, had to deposit their silver reserves with the newly created Exchange Fund and received Certificates of Indebtedness (CIs) in return. The Exchange Fund sold the silver in the London market for sterling. From then on, if an authorized bank wanted to issue more notes, it was obligated to purchase more CIs from the Exchange Fund with sterling at a fixed rate of sixteen

HK dollars to one pound. The Exchange Fund would also buy the CIs from the banks if the latter decided to decrease the money supply. Thus, the monetary system had all the features of a currency board, with the exception that legal tenders were issued by authorized private banks rather than directly by the board.

The peg to the sterling lasted for more than three decades, despite four years of interruption during World War II. In 1967, because of devaluation of the sterling, the sixteen HK dollar peg could no longer be sustained. In July 1972 further pressure from the devaluation of the sterling forced the eventual abolition of the link between the sterling and HK dollar. The latter was pegged to the US dollar at a rate within an intervention band. This also did not last long. Again devaluation of the US dollar and an inflow of capital to Hong Kong led to the decision of free–floating the HK dollar against the US dollar. The currency board system was no longer operating.

Under the free–floating system from 1974 to 1983, authorized banks still had to purchase CIs, which at this time were denominated in HK dollar, from the Exchange Fund if they wanted to issue more notes. The Fund maintained an account with these banks. The payment for the CIs was simply a transfer of credit from the banks to the account of the Exchange Fund. Starting from May 1979, the note–issuing banks were required to maintain 100–percent liquid–asset cover against the Fund's short–term deposits. This cover did not imply that the Exchange Fund could effectively limit the creation of money because the banks could borrow foreign currency to obtain the liquid assets. Money growth in this period was higher and more volatile than before. In 1978, the government also decided to transfer the accumulated HK dollar fiscal surplus to the Exchange Fund, which has since then become the government's *de facto* savings account.

During the initial phase of the free–floating period, the HK dollar was very strong. However, from 1977 onwards, it was subject to considerable downward pressure. Trade deficit was growing. Money supply, M2, increased at the rate of almost 25 percent a year, mainly because of even faster growth in bank credit. The start of the Sino–British negotiations over the future of Hong Kong in 1982 led to a series of financial crises: stock market crash, real estate price collapse, runs of small banks, and rapid depreciation of the HK dollar. On 17 October 1983, the government decided to abolish interest–withholding tax on HK dollar deposits and more importantly, to go back to the currency board system again. The exchange rate was fixed at US$1 = HK$ 7.8. Banks issuing notes had to purchase CIs with US dollar at this rate from the Exchange Fund. The reserves accumulated were invested mainly in interest–bearing US government securities. Table 10.1 summarizes the historical evolution of Hong Kong's monetary institutions.

Several institutional changes to the currency board system of Hong Kong, now popularly known as the 'linked exchange rate system', had been introduced since 1983. In 1988, the Exchange Fund established the new 'Accounting Arrangements' which in effect empowered it to conduct open market operations. Legislative changes also allowed the government to have more flexibility in manipulating the interest rates. Since March 1990, the Fund was permitted to issue several kinds of 'Exchange Fund Bills', instruments that were similar to short–term Treasury

Table 10.1 The exchange rate regimes for the Hong Kong dollar

Date	*Exchange rate regime*	*Reference rate*
Until 4 Nov 1935	Silver standard	-
6 Dec 1935	Pegged to Sterling	£1 = HK$16
23 Nov 1967		£1 = HK$14.55
6 July 1972	Fixed to US dollar with ±2.25%	US$1 = HK$5.65
14 Feb 1973	Intervention bands around a central rate	US$1 = HK$5.085
25 Nov 1974	Free float	-
17 Oct 1983	Pegged to US dollar	US$1 = HK$7.80

Source: Nugee (1995).

bills. In 1992, a sort of discount window was opened to provide liquidity to banks. The Hong Kong Monetary Authority (HKMA) was established in December 1992 to take over the power of the Exchange Fund Office and the Commissioner of Banking. The HKMA has since then been active in adjusting interbank liquidity in response to changes in demand conditions. Table 10.2 presents the Exchange Fund's balance sheet in recent years.

The main instrument used by the HKMA to adjust interbank liquidity is the interest rate. For a long time, it has relied on interest rate arbitrage to stabilize the exchange rate, in the sense that a capital outflow will push up interest rate and consequently lend support to the Hong Kong dollar. On 9 December 1996, the HKMA introduced a new inter–bank payment system known as the 'real time gross settlement' (RTGS). Each bank is required to open an account with positive balance at the HKMA for interbank settlement purpose. Because the RTGS has been very efficient, the aggregate balance of the banking system, i.e., the sum of the balances in the individual accounts, tends to be very small, say, at the level of HK$ 2 billion. However, as discussed in details in Lui, Cheng and Kwan (2003), the small size of the aggregate balance has caused great interest rate volatility. An outflow of capital exceeding the amount in the aggregate balance may, given the particular institutional arrangements, completely drain the latter and force the interest rate to rise to some exceedingly high level.[7] According to the econometric evidence reported in Kwan, Lui and Cheng (2000), contrary to the belief of the HKMA, the higher interest rate during the financial crisis of 1997–98 was not only harmful to the economy, but also detrimental to the credibility of the exchange rate. Rather than being a stabilizing factor in attracting inflow of foreign funds, the high interest rate simply signaled the increased risks in holding the Hong Kong dollar.

Several remarks should be made here. First, the monetary institution in Hong Kong has not been a static system. In less than half a century, it has evolved from the silver standard to a currency board with sterling being the reserve currency, and then to a free–floating regime, and finally returned to the currency board with a

Table 10.2 Exchange fund balance sheet

HK$mn	1989	1990	1991	1992	1993	1994	1995	1996	1997
ASSETS									
Foreign currency assets	149,152	192,323	225,333	274,948	335,499	381,233	428,547	493,802	588,475
Hong Kong dollar assets	9,625	3,874	10,788	12,546	12,987	24,617	32,187	40,715	48,215
	158,777	196,197	236,121	287,494	348,486	405,850	460,734	534,517	636,690
LIABILITIES									
Certificate of Indebtedness	37,191	40,791	46,410	58,130	68,801	74,301	77,600	82,480	87,015
Fiscal Reserve Account	52,546	63,226	69,802	96,145	115,683	131,240	125,916	145,898	237,629
Coins in circulation	2,012	2,003	2,299	2,559	2,604	3,372	3,597	4,164	5,399
Exchange Fund Bills and Notes	0	6,671	13,624	19,324	25,157	46,140	53,125	83,509	89,338
Balance of banking system	978	480	500	1,480	1,385	2,208	1,762	474	296
Other liabilities	1,603	391	4,834	3,220	7,314	22,815	38,600	45,130	26,802
	94,330	113,562	137,469	180,858	220,944	280,076	300,600	361,655	446,479
ACCUMULATED EARNINGS	64,447	82,635	98,652	106,636	127,542	125,774	160,134	172,862	190,211

Source: Hong Kong Monetary Authority Annual Report, various issues.

US dollar link. More recently, as Schwartz (1993) has observed, there has been some 'dilution' of the features that distinguish a currency board. Given historical hindsight, one can hardly believe that the present system will last forever, despite the persistent assurance by the Hong Kong Government that the linked exchange rate is there to stay permanently. This view is supported by the observation that historically all fixed exchange rate regimes could not be sustained for very long periods.[8] This motivates us to conduct simulation experiments to investigate the conditions under which the Hong Kong currency board might collapse.

Second, from 1974 to now, Hong Kong has experienced two polar cases of monetary systems, namely, free–floating (1974–83) and currency board (1983–now). There have been no other economic institutional changes of comparable order of magnitude. The government still adopts the 'positive non–interventionism' policy formulated more than two decades ago. It has been persistently keeping the size of the government small and leaving small budgetary surpluses in most fiscal years. It has also refrained from using fiscal policy as a fine–tuning tool. The legal system has remained intact and Hong Kong's economic freedom has always been rated at the highest level by international agencies. These similarities in the two periods provide us with a relatively homogeneous setting to compare the implications of the two systems as if under a natural controlled experiment.

Third, while structural homogeneity is needed for the controlled experiment on the one hand, sufficiently rich variations in data are necessary for statistical purpose on the other. If the economic conditions of the two periods had remained perfectly stable, then the data would hardly contain enough information for inferring the macroeconomic performance of the two systems. We need to observe how the two regimes respond to external shocks. Indeed Hong Kong as a small open economy is extremely sensitive to external shocks that may overshadow the 'treatment effect' of a currency board system. Fortunately, by adopting the approach in Blanchard and Quah (1989), it is possible to isolate the transitory and permanent shocks during the two periods. Counter–factual simulations can be performed to identify the effects of the change in monetary regime.

Fourth, Hong Kong has gone through a number of major economic shocks from 1974 to now. This period covers the time span of several business cycles. There have also been big swings in real estate and stock markets. The quarterly data available are reasonably rich in variations which allow us to make meaningful inferences.

Fifth, the economic health and significant financial strength of Hong Kong provide an almost ideal situation to test the vulnerability of a currency board system when it is confronted with a crisis. At the end of 1997, foreign currency assets in the Exchange Fund amounted to US$ 75.5 billion, which was the world's third largest. The ratio of foreign currency assets in the Exchange Fund to currency in circulation was bigger than five. The value of the government's accumulated fiscal reserve was also substantial. In fact, it was contributing to one–third of the Exchange Fund (see the Fund's balance sheet in Table 10.2). If simulations show that Hong Kong's currency board has to face a crisis when it is subject to shocks of specified magnitude, then it is hard to imagine that the currency board in a country with poorer economic health can survive under the same scenario.

Lastly, we do not see the performance of the macroeconomy during the financial crisis of 1997–98 truly representative of the consequence of the currency board. The Hong Kong government at the time had adopted a mechanism that was conducive to excessive interest rate volatility. The problem was remedied in September 1998 when eight technical measures aimed at interest rate stability were introduced by the HKMA. In this chapter we have therefore confined our empirical analyses to the period up to the last quarter of 1997, when the effects of the high interest rate policy were not as apparent as in 1998. The readers are referred to Kwan et al. (2000) and Lui et al. (2003) for detailed discussions of the currency crisis.

Empirical model

In this Section, we discuss a framework that will be used to compare the macroeconomic performance of the flexible and linked exchange rate regimes when they are subject to exogenous shocks. To properly take into account the heterogeneity induced by these shocks, we adopt Blanchard and Quah's (1989) approach to identify them explicitly.

Our empirical framework is the structural vector autoregressive (VAR) model initiated by Blanchard and Watson (1986), Sims (1986), and Bernanke (1986). Following Blanchard and Quah (1989) and Bayoumi and Eichengreen (1993, 1994), we formulate a bivariate model in output growth and inflation rate to identify two series of structural shocks: (1) those whose effects on output level are only transitory, and (2) those that have permanent effects on the output level. Shocks of the first type can be interpreted as demand shocks originated from innovations in the components of aggregate demand, while the second type are supply shocks originated from innovations in productivity and other factors that affect aggregate supply. We now briefly describe the model and refer the reader to the above references and the surveys in Giannini (1992) and Watson (1994) for details.

Let $X_t = (\Delta y_t , \Delta p_t)'$, where y_t and p_t denote the logarithm of output and price level, respectively, and Δ is the first–difference operator. X_t is assumed to be covariance stationary and have a moving average representation of the form

$$(10.1) \quad X_t - \mu = B_0 e_t + B_1 e_{t-1} + B_2 e_{t-2} + \ldots \equiv B(L)e_t$$

where $e_t = (e_{dt} , e_{st})'$ is a bivariate series of serially uncorrelated shocks with zero mean and covariance matrix Ω, $B(L) = B_0 + B_1L + B_2L^2 + \ldots$ is a short–hand notation for the matrix polynomial in backshift operator L, and μ is the mean of X_t. (10.1) is taken to be structural in that e_{dt} and e_{st} have a behavioral interpretation of being the demand shock and supply shock, respectively. The coefficient matrices in

$B(L)$ capture the propagation mechanism of the dynamic system. In particular, the (i, j) element of B_k is the kth step impulse response of the ith endogenous variables with respect to a one unit increase in the jth shock.

Equation (10.1) is not directly estimated. We proceed in the following steps. First, we estimate a VAR in X_t:

$$(10.2) \quad A(L)(X_t - \mu) = u_t$$

where $\{u_t\}$ is a bivariate series of serially uncorrelated errors with zero mean and covariance matrix Σ, and $A(L)$ is a matrix polynomial in L. Second, we invert the estimated autoregressive polynomial in (10.2) to obtain the Wold moving average representation, which is the reduced form to (10.1).

$$(10.3) \quad X_t - \mu = u_t + C_1 u_{t-1} + C_2 u_{t-2} + \ldots \equiv C(L)u_t$$

Again, $C(L) = I + C_1L + C_2L^2 + \ldots$ is short–hand for the matrix polynomial as stated. In our implementation the reduced form VAR is estimated with six lags and the Wold representation in (10.3) is expanded up to 200 lags which is more than adequate. Given estimates of the reduced form parameters, $C(L)$ and Σ, and the reduced form residuals u_t, is it possible to recover the structural parameters, $B(L)$ and Ω, and the structural residuals e_t? This is a classical identification problem in simultaneous equation models and the answer is yes provided that enough *a priori* restrictions have been placed on the structural parameters. Comparing (10.1) and (10.3) it can be checked that the structural and reduced form are related by the following relationships:

$$(10.4) \quad B_0 e_t = u_t \quad \forall t.$$

$$(10.5) \quad B_j = C_j B_0, \quad j = 0,1,2,\ldots$$

$$(10.6) \quad B_0 \Omega B_0' = \Sigma.$$

Equations (10.4) and (10.5) imply that the structural form in (10.1) can be recovered from the reduced form in (10.3) once B_0 is determined. Thus, the identification problem boils down to imposing sufficiently many restrictions so that B_0 can be solved from (10.6).

In our bivariate system, there are seven structural parameters in B_0 and Ω, but only three reduced form parameters in Σ; we thus need four restrictions to just–identify the structural model. The first three restrictions come from assuming Ω to be the identity matrix. The zero covariance restriction dictates that the two structural shocks are uncorrelated, implying that any cross–equation interaction of the two shocks on the dependent variables are captured by the lag structure in $B(L)$. The two unit–variance restrictions imply that B_0 is identified up to multiple of the two standard deviations. Thus B_j has the interpretation of being the jth step impulse response with respect to a one–standard–deviation innovation in the structural shocks. The last restriction comes from Blanchard and Quah's (1989) idea of restricting long–run multiplier. Since demand shocks are assumed to have no permanent effects on output level, this translates into the restriction that the long–run multiplier (i.e., the sum of impulse responses) of demand shocks on output growth must be zero, i.e.,

$$(10.7)\quad B_{11}(1) \equiv B_{11,0} + B_{11,1} + B_{11,2} + \ldots = 0$$

where $B_{11}(1)$ and $B_{11,j}$ are the upper left–hand corner of $B(1)$ and B_j respectively.

To see how (10.7) can be translated into a restriction on B_0, let J be the lower triangular Cholesky factor of Σ and notice that (10.6) can be written as (after assuming $\Omega = \mathrm{I}$)

$$(10.8)\quad B_0 B_0' = \Sigma = JJ'$$

Thus B_0 can be determined from J up to an orthogonal transformation S, i.e.,

$$(10.9)\quad B_0 = JS, \quad SS' = I.$$

Orthogonality implies that S (up to one column sign change) must be of the form

$$(10.10)\quad S = \begin{bmatrix} a & \sqrt{1-a^2} \\ \sqrt{1-a^2} & -a \end{bmatrix}$$

(10.5) and (10.9) imply

$$(10.11)\quad B(1) = C(1)B_0 = HS, \quad H = C(1)J$$

(10.7) then implies a restriction

$$(10.12)\quad H_{11}a + H_{12}\sqrt{1-a^2} = 0$$

which determines a and hence S. Once S is found, B_0 can be determined by (10.9). Given B_0, the structural parameters and the structural shocks can then be recovered from the reduced form via (10.4) and (10.5).

The output and price data are quarterly Hong Kong real per capita GDP (in 1990 price) and the corresponding GDP deflator from 1973:1 to 1997:4, taken from various issues of *Estimates of Gross Domestic Product* published by Hong Kong Government.[9] Both output and price series exhibit strong seasonality and they are deseasonalized before use by a spectral method by Sims (1974) and implemented in Doan (1992, section 11.7). To check our model specification, we perform standard unit root test and cointegration test to the output and price level series. Testing the null hypothesis of $I(1)$ with non–zero drift against the alternative of trend stationarity, the Dickey–Fuller t–statistic register values of –2.14 and –1.47 for the output and price series, respectively, which are way above the 5% critical value of –3.45 (Hamilton, 1994, Table B6, Case 4). Thus, the covariance stationarity assumption for the first–differenced series is warranted. Equation (10.2) as a first–difference VAR would be invalid if the two series were cointegrated. Testing the null hypothesis of no cointegration, we run cointegrating regressions for the two series and apply augmented Dickey–Fuller (ADF) unit root test to the residuals. With output being the dependent variable in the cointegrating regression, the ADF statistic registers a value of –2.86, which is above the 5% critical value of –3.42 (Hamilton, 1994, Table B9, Case 3) and hence not significant. When the price level is instead the dependent variable in the cointegrating regression, the calculated ADF statistic is –2.70, again not statistically significant at the 5% level. Thus, we conclude that the output and price level series are not cointegrated and the VAR system in (10.2) is valid.

Results and interpretations

In this Section, we present the empirical results and interpret them. In particular, we use these results to compare the macroeconomic performance of the free–floating and currency board regimes from several perspectives.

Institutional effect or environment effect?

Figure 10.1 displays the data for the full sample period, covering both the free–floating (1975:1–1983:3) and currency board (1983:4–1997:4) regimes. It can be seen that both inflation and output growth are somewhat more stable during the currency board years than the free–floating years. More precisely, the standard deviation of output growth rates during the free–floating and currency board years are 2.84 and 2.01, respectively, and that of the inflation rates are 1.56 and 1.18, respectively. What is behind the observed reduction in volatility in both output growth rates and inflation rates? Some believe that this is simply because of a more congenial international environment during the 1980s than the 1970s. On the other hand, advocates of fixed exchange rate and currency board, including the Hong Kong government, sometimes argue that this is due to the inherent superiority of the linked exchange rate regime over the free–floating system (e.g., Sheng, 1995). Granted that both arguments are reasonable and neither can be rejected *a priori*, it is then necessary to disentangle the 'institutional effect' from the 'environment effect'. In our structural VAR model, the structural parameters, B_j's, play the role of institution and the structural shocks, u_t, represent the external environment. By estimating two separate structural models for the two exchange rate regimes, we obtain two sets of structural parameters representing the two monetary institutions and two sets of supply and demand shocks representing two different external

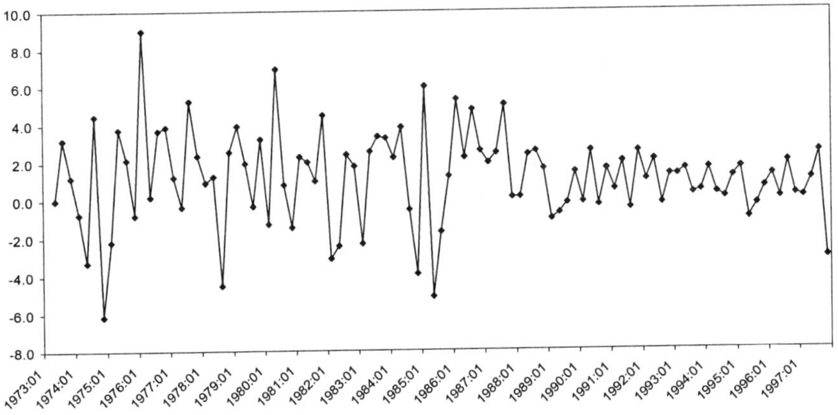

(A) Per capita real GDP growth rate (percent)

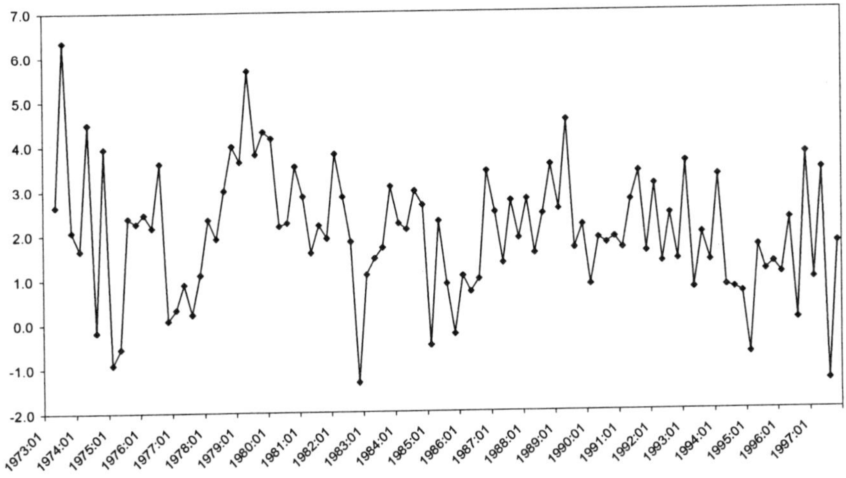

(B) Inflation rate (percent)

environments. As will be shown later, both the parameters and the shocks have significantly changed across the two regimes.

The estimated reduced form, (10.2) and (10.3), are not of direct interest and hence not reported. Since the structural model is just identified, there is a one–to–one relationship between the reduced form and the structural parameters. This implies that a stability test for the structural equation (10.1) can be done equivalently by means of the reduced form equation (10.2). Using this approach, we find that the parameters for the structural equation (10.1) are indeed statistically

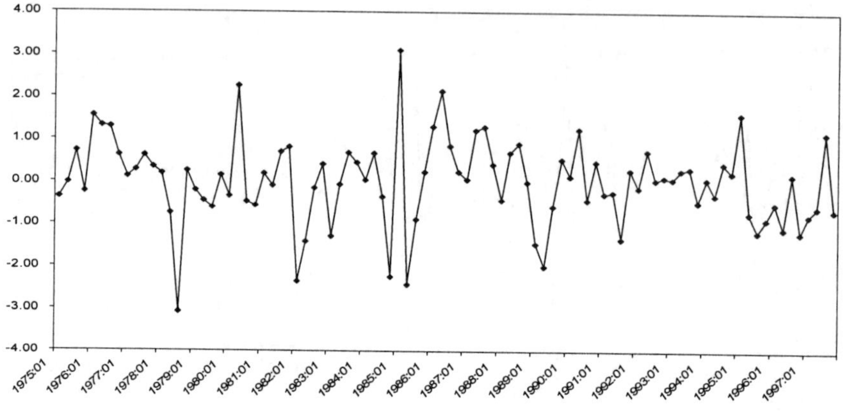

(A) Demand shocks

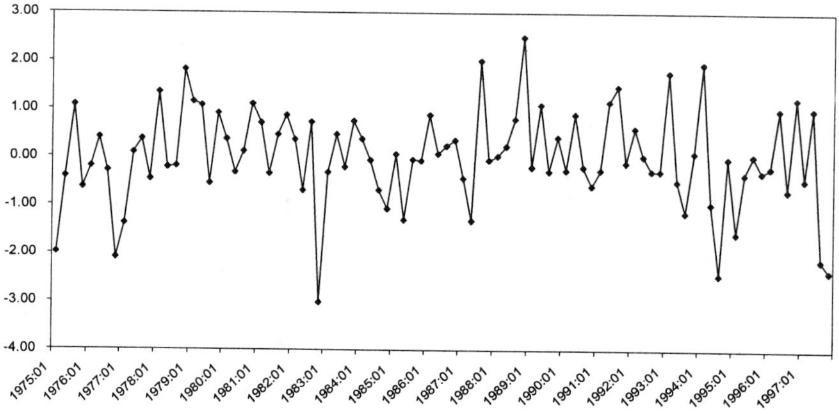

(B) Supply shocks

Figure 10.2 Demand shocks (A) and supply shocks (B)

different across the two regimes. This is evident from a likelihood–ratio version of the Chow test, which rejects the null hypothesis of no structural change at the 5 percent level.[10] The result supports the Lucas Critique. We need to use a different set of structural parameters to capture the institutional effect due to a change in the monetary regime. It is assumed, however, that these parameters are invariant to the exogenous shocks.

Figure 10.2 presents the quarterly demand and supply shocks (1975–97) that are identified by our econometric model. Many of the shocks can be identified

Table 10.3 Characteristics of structural disturbances

	Demand shocks				Supply shocks			
	Free–floating		Currency Board		Free–floating		Currency Board	
Skewness	-0.91	[0.01]	-0.04	[0.89]	-0.76	[0.04]	0.15	[0.63]
Kurtosis	4.11	[0.11]	3.45	[0.37]	4.74	[0.02]	3.95	[0.09]
Maximum	1.81		2.49		2.24		3.09	
Minimum	-3.01		-2.44		-3.07		-2.42	

Note: Numbers in squared brackets are p–values for testing either the population skewness = 0 (symmetry) or kurtosis = 3 (normal shape).

with well–known historical episodes. For example, the Sino–British negotiations over the future of Hong Kong (1982:4), the government's intervention to suppress housing price (1994:2), and the Asian financial crisis (1997:3) have created significant negative demand shocks. On the other hand, large supply shocks are apparent during the second oil crisis (1978:3) and the 1989 political events at Tiananmen Square (1989:2).

Table 10.3 reports sample statistics of the shocks. By the skewness and kurtosis tests, one can observe that both types of shocks during the free–floating period exhibit substantial non–normality, which can be attributed to a few large negative shocks. Shocks during the currency board period, on the contrary, show no strong evidence against normality, as is clear from the skewness and kurtosis tests. This indicates that the two exchange rate regimes are subject to exogenous shocks of different characteristics. Simply comparing the macroeconomic performance in the two periods without properly controlling for the environment effect can be misleading.

Variance decomposition and impulse response

In addition to having different characteristics, the demand and supply shocks also differ in their relative importance in explaining the data. This is demonstrated by the results on variance decomposition of the shocks. Table 10.4 shows the percentages of variance in output growth rate and inflation that can be explained by the demand shocks in n quarters, where n is the corresponding number in the first column. The percentages explained by the supply shocks are given by 100 minus the table entries. As can be readily seen, during the free–floating regime, demand shocks explain a relatively small fraction of output variations but a substantial fraction of inflation variations. In other words, output variations during the free–floating regime are mainly attributed to supply shocks. In contrast, during the currency board regime, demand shocks play a dominant role and can explain much of the variations in output and price movements.

Table 10.4 Percentage of forecast error variance explained by demand shocks

Quarter	Output growth rate Free-floating	Output growth rate Currency Board	Inflation rate Free-floating	Inflation rate Currency Board
1	1.35	15.56	92.02	62.28
4	7.06	16.36	90.12	64.60
8	7.87	18.81	84.14	62.19
12	8.54	19.26	84.73	61.03
16	8.64	19.39	84.40	59.87
20	8.65	19.33	84.45	59.38
24	8.66	19.33	84.41	59.12
28	8.67	19.33	84.40	58.97
32	8.67	19.32	84.40	58.89

Note: The corresponding percentages explained by supply shocks are given by 100 minus the table entries.

Table 10.5 Counter-factual simulation

	Output growth rate %		Inflation rate %	
	Mean	Standard dev.	Mean	Standard dev.
Case 1 (1975-83)				
Actual (FF)[a]	1.54	2.84	2.13	1.56
Simulated (CB)[b]	0.98	2.26	1.65	1.30
Case2 (1983-97)				
Actual (CB)	1.04	2.01	1.80	1.18
Simulated (FF)	1.59	2.62	2.22	1.33

a FF = Free-floating.
b CB = Currency board.

Figure 10.3 depicts the impulse responses of output level with respect to demand and supply shocks during the two monetary regimes. The figure reveals an interesting asymmetric response pattern. Under the currency board regime, demand shocks appear to have a bigger impact on output than supply shocks. The opposite is true for the free–floating regime during which supply shocks appear to have a bigger impact. In other words, the currency board regime seems to be relatively more supply shocks resistant than the free–floating regime, but relatively more vulnerable to demand shocks.

We can draw the following conclusions from the results above. The output in Hong Kong under a currency board seems to be less susceptible to supply shocks, which are usually not induced by government short–term policies. However, demand shocks do cause greater short–term volatility in output under the currency board system. If a government with a currency board is able to discipline itself to pursue a stable and predictable fiscal policy, the volatility of the economy may be lower than that under free–floating. An explanation of why Hong Kong's economy has been less volatile after the adoption of the linked exchange rate is that stable fiscal policy has, at least until recently, been the philosophy of the financial branch of its government.

Counter–factual simulations

As discussed above the two periods under consideration are subject to shocks with different properties. In other words, the environment effect would have to be properly controlled for if we were to do a meaningful comparison of the macroeconomic performance for the two periods. One way to proceed is to consider the following two counter–factual cases:

Case 1 What would have happened to the economy if the currency board system were adopted from 1975 to 1983?

Case 2 What would have happened to the economy if the free–floating system were adopted from 1983 to 1997?

To answer the question in Case 1, we apply the demand and supply shocks of 1975 to 1983 to equation (10.1) which has been estimated for the currency board regime, and compare the simulated results with the actual time path. To answer the second question, we do the simulations in a similar way, but this time we apply the shocks of 1983 to 1997 to equation (10.1) for the free–floating regime. The approach is based on the assumption that the supply and demand shocks identified by the estimation procedure are invariant to the changes in exchange rate regime. This exogeneity assumption makes a lot of sense for Hong Kong. In this small open economy whose external sector is much larger than its GDP, most of the supply and demand shocks are external, and there is no reason why these external shocks would depend on institutional changes in Hong Kong. Moreover, the government has been following the same stable fiscal policy throughout the two periods under consideration, and there is no central bank in Hong Kong to determine the money supply which is largely rule–based in both regimes and automatically adjusts to external shocks. Thus, there is no *a priori* reason to believe that the supply and demand shocks are regime dependent.

The counter–factual exercise amounts to replacing the structural residual e_t in equation (10.1) by a hypothetical residual e_t* and then simulating a new data path X_t*, given structural parameters μ and $B(L)$. For example, in Case 1, e_t, μ, and $B(L)$ are the residual and structural parameters for the free–floating regime, while e_t* is taken to be the residual for the currency board regime. In practice, however, the moving average representation in equation (10.1) is difficult to work with. We instead perform the simulation by equation (10.2) with a reduced form residual u_t*

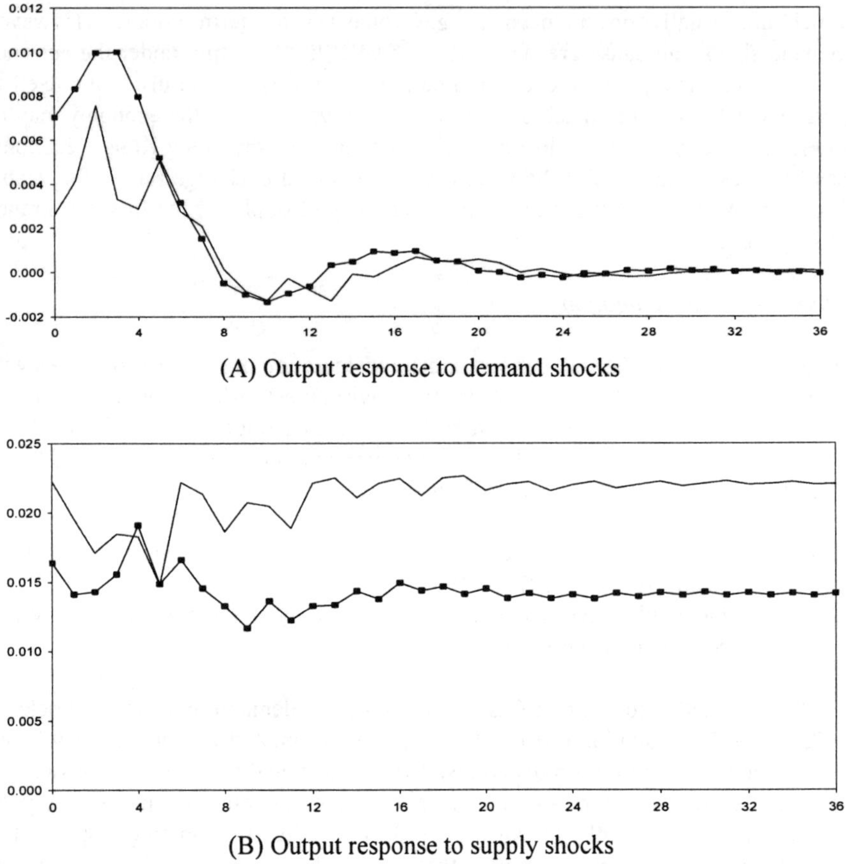

Note: Boxed line = currency board; plain line = free–floating.

Figure 10.3 Impulse responses of output level with respect to demand shocks (A) and supply shocks (B)

constructed from e_t* via equation (10.4). It is straightforward to check that our two–step procedure is equivalent to a direct simulation of equation (10.1).

Summaries of these counter–factual simulations are presented in Table 10.5. The results show that if the currency board system were adopted in the first period, then the average growth rate would have declined, but inflation would have gone down also. Since the standard deviations are also lower, we can say that both output growth and inflation would have been more stable. The simulation patterns for the

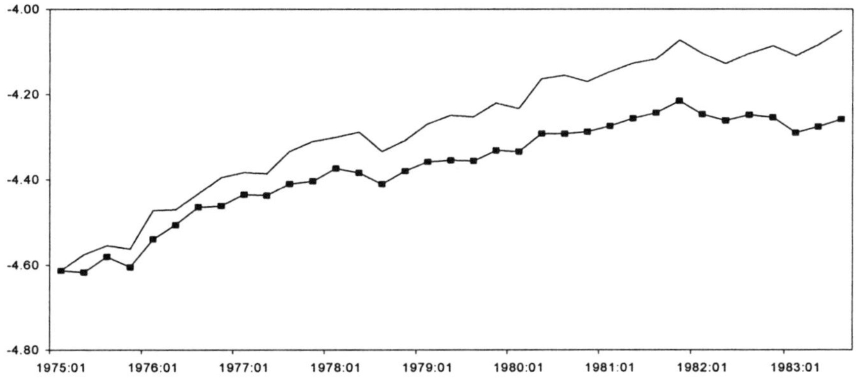

Output level (in log)

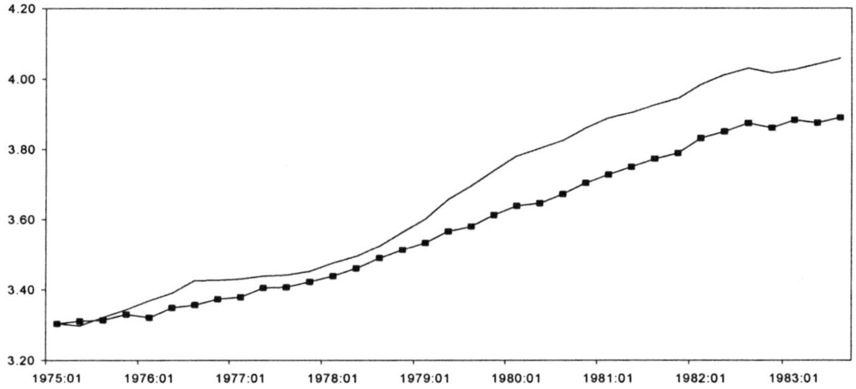

Price level (in log)

Note: Boxed line = currency board (simulated); Plain line = free–floating (actual).

Figure 10.4 Counter–factual simulation case 1

second period are similar. The cost of a currency board system is lower output growth. However, there are also benefits. Inflation rate decreases and the economy is less volatile. The tradeoff is transparent when the comparison is in terms of levels (rather than growth rates) as depicted in Figures 10.4 and 10.5.

The counter–factual simulations disentangle the effects of regime shift and changes in the external environment. As an example, consider the reduction in

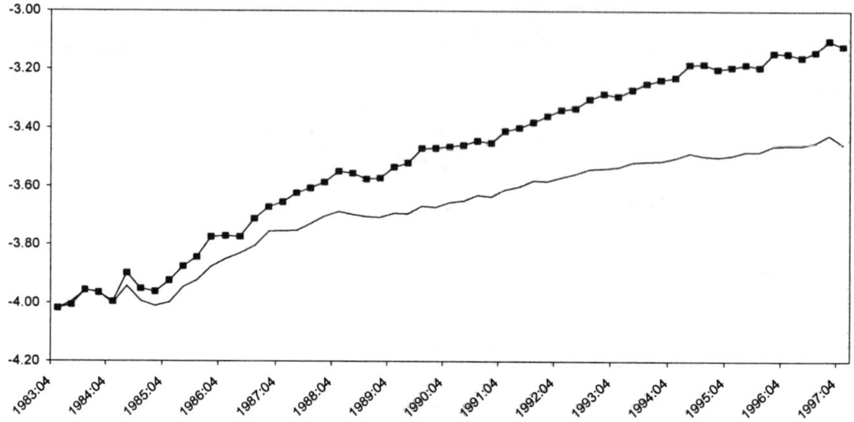

Output level (in log)

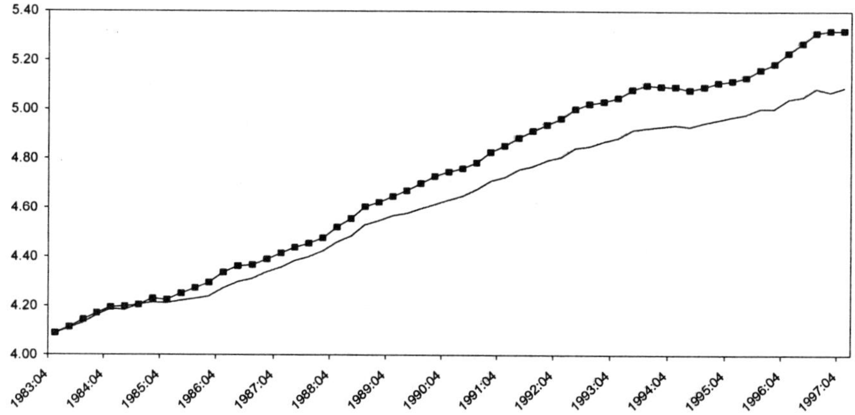

Price level (in log)

Note: Boxed line = free–floating (simulated); Plain line = currency board (actual).

Figure 10.5 Counter–factual simulation case 2

output growth volatility when the monetary system changes from free–floating to currency board. The standard deviation of output growth rates goes down from 2.84 to 2.01, a roughly 29 percent reduction in volatility. From simulation case 1, we see that if the currency board system were adopted to the environment of the 1970s, output volatility would have declined to 2.26, a 20 percent reduction from 2.84.

This implies that about 69 percent of the reduction in output volatility that we actually observe from the data is due to the adoption of the currency board, while the remaining 31 percent is due to a more tranquil external environment in the 1980s. Similarly, the marginal effect of the currency board on inflation volatility is to reduce it from 1.56 to 1.30, or about 17 percent reduction. The observed reduction, however, is from 1.56 to 1.18, or a decline of 24 percent. One can then have the following decomposition. The difference in external environment during the 1970s and 1980s accounts for 29 percent of the reduction in inflation volatility, while the change in the monetary regime explains the remaining 70 percent of the reduction.

Currency and banking crises

The Hong Kong government has been vehemently claiming that the Exchange Fund is financially strong and the linked exchange rate will be defended. As can be seen from the balance sheet of the Fund in Table 10.2, Hong Kong indeed owns one of the largest foreign reserves in the world. Does it mean that the HK$ 7.8 link is immune of the possibility of crisis? In theory, a crisis does not occur even when people exchange all the currency for foreign assets because of the 100 percent back–up. However, we should note that foreign reserves are enough only to provide partial support to M3. Take the end of 1997, when speculative attacks occurred, as an illustrative example. Total M3 was HK$ 2827 billion, 41 percent of which was in bank deposits denominated in foreign money. Suppose people decided to change the portfolio of M3 by exchanging HK dollar deposits for foreign money. If the change were big enough, the banking sector would have to sell its domestic assets for foreign money to avoid bank runs. It is not clear whether the Fund would be willing to buy these domestic assets. However, the Exchange Fund Ordinance would allow the Financial Secretary the flexibility to do so even though Hong Kong's monetary institution had been a currency board.[11] Suppose the Exchange Fund would indeed provide the foreign liquidity to avoid bank runs. If people decided to increase their foreign exchange holdings from 41 percent to 48 percent of M3, the accumulated earnings in the balance sheet of the Fund would disappear. If the foreign deposits ratio went up further to 56 percent, all the fiscal reserve would be used up.

These rather simplistic calculations tell us that a run on the Hong Kong dollar could occur even though the change in people's portfolio holdings is not exceptionally large. We do not have an estimate of the portfolio holdings as a function of other variables. However, one can reasonably speculate that the confidence in the HK dollar will suffer significantly and the link will face a crisis if the fiscal reserve is completely depleted.

The amount of fiscal reserve is affected by shocks to the economy. Since the Hong Kong government, until recently, has been following a reasonably stable fiscal policy, we focus our attention on supply shocks here. How big are the supply shocks if the fiscal reserve is to be eliminated? This can be answered by making use of the empirical estimates in this chapter.

Table 10.6 Expenditure and revenue (as percent of GDP)

Year	*Expenditure*	*Revenue*
1982	19.2	16.7
1983	18.6	14.7
1984	16.0	15.5
1985	16.6	16.7
1986	15.9	16.1
1987	14.5	16.5
1988	14.9	16.7
1989	16.4	16.5
1990	16.3	15.3
1991	16.2	17.1
1992	15.8	17.3
1993	17.3	18.6
1994	16.3	17.2
1995	17.8	16.7
1996	17.7	17.5
1997	18.4	20.7
Mean	16.7	16.9

The long–run impulse response of the logarithm of $y(t)$ with respect to a supply shock of one standard deviation is 0.0141. This means that a one–standard–deviation supply shock will reduce output permanently by 1.41 percent, other things being equal. Thus, we can calculate the post–shock output level $y(t)^*$ by the formula $y(t)^* = (1 - 0.0141x)y(t)$ for a supply shock of size x standard deviations. Similarly for K periods of negative supply shocks, each of size x, the post–shock output level should be $y(t)^* = (1 - 0.0141x)^K y(t)$. Table 10.6 reports the expenditure and revenue (as percentages of GDP) of the Hong Kong government from 1982 to 1997. It can be seen that the government has managed to achieve small budget surplus in most years and the average expenditure and revenue rates are 16.7% and 16.9%, respectively. Suppose the Hong Kong government is to maintain her traditional fiscal restraint, we may assume that the expenditure and revenue rates are to be fixed at the mentioned long–term average values. Then the post–shock revenue would be $0.169y(t)^* = [0.169(1 - 0.0141x)^K]\, y(t)$. Thus, the effect of the supply shock on revenue is equivalent to a 'tax–cut' with the new, effective tax rate being $0.169(1 - 0.0141x)^K$. These rates are shown in Table 10.7. Making use of Table 10.7, one can come up with results in different scenarios. For example, it only takes a 2–standard–deviation shock lasting for one quarter to throw the budget into deficit. If there are negative 3–standard–deviation supply shocks lasting for two years, then the deficit every year will be approximately HK$ 51.6 billion. It only takes about three years for the fiscal reserve to be completely depleted if political pressures prohibit the government from reducing its expenditures accordingly.

Table 10.7 Post–shock effective revenue–output ratio percent

	Size of negative supply shocks (in standard deviation)			
Duration (quarters)	1	2	3	4
1	16.7	16.4	16.2	15.9
2	16.4	16.0	15.5	15.0
3	16.2	15.5	14.8	14.2
4	16.0	15.1	14.2	13.4
5	15.7	14.6	13.6	12.6
6	15.5	14.2	13.0	11.9
7	15.3	13.8	12.5	11.3
8	15.1	13.4	12.0	10.6

Currency crises can lead to bank runs. But bank runs can occur because of other reasons too. Since the typical currency board does not provide a lender of last resort, bank runs are often regarded as the Achilles Heel of the system. Indeed banking crises did occur in Hong Kong a number of times, all during the currency board years. The government and the banking system resorted to several ways to deal with them.

In 1994 there were 180 licensed banks in Hong Kong, 16 of which were owned mostly by local shareholders (Hong Kong Monetary Authority, 1994, pp. 90–91). Government policies towards runs on local and foreign banks seemed to be different. It did not attempt to support the Citibank in 1991 when rumors caused a short–lived run, nor did it try to rescue the Bank of Credit and Commerce International's Hong Kong branch before its collapse in the same year. However, it moved to take over two small local banks in the mid 1960s and three more in the period of 1982–86. It also provided some emergency funds to support five banks in the same period, four of which were later acquired by others. The note–issuing banks also played an important role in cushioning the shocks from the runs. They supported one bank in 1961, three in 1965–66, and took over three more in the same period. Thus, in the 1960s, the government was relying mainly on the financially strong note–issuing banks to either lend to or take over the troubled local banks. In more recent years, the government seemed to have resorted to the Exchange Fund for playing the role of lender of last resort.[12] This is another reason to say that some of the features of a currency board have been diluted in Hong Kong.

What can we learn from Hong Kong's experience?

The general performance of the currency board in Hong Kong has been good in the sense that it has contributed to greater stability. Counter–factual exercises indicate that when both free–floating and currency board regimes are subject to the same exogenous shocks, output and prices are less volatile under the latter.

The stability result is not general. Simulations on impulse response show that output is less sensitive to supply shocks under currency board than under free–floating. On the other hand, demand shocks can cause stronger short–term volatility in output in a currency board system. The relative stability in output in Hong Kong to a large extent must have come from the government's self–discipline in fiscal policy, which is based on two rules: balanced budget or small surplus, and keeping government size small. Other countries without a stable rule–based fiscal policy may not do well to reduce output volatility even if they have currency boards.

The fiscal restraint not only affects output stability, but also the credibility of the exchange rate system. A weakness of the currency board system is that people may doubt the determination and capability of the government to maintain perfect convertibility at the specified rate. The conservative fiscal policy has been instrumental in creating surpluses for almost every budgetary year. Without the significant fiscal reserve, confidence in the Hong Kong dollar may suffer. In recent years, since the Exchange Fund has been acting as if it could be the lender of last resort, its financial strength, which is partly supported by a large fiscal reserve, is all the more important. Perhaps a reason why fiscal policy in Hong Kong is coordinated with its monetary system is that the Financial Secretary has the authority to control both.

Despite the financial strength of the Exchange Fund, the Hong Kong dollar has for several times been subject to considerable speculative pressure, especially during the Asian financial turmoil. In each occasion, the forward rate of the Hong Kong dollar has depreciated, although the spot rate remains relatively robust. Do people have enough confidence in the Hong Kong dollar? Typically more than 40 percent of M3 is in deposits denominated in foreign currency. This large portion is an indication that people only have limited confidence in the future of the Hong Kong dollar, in spite of all the assurance that the government has provided.

Should other countries adopt the currency board system? The above analysis indicates that the decent performance in Hong Kong has been due to a combination of favorable factors, and yet, the possibility of monetary collapse cannot be ruled out. It is doubtful that many countries have equal or better conditions.

Notes

1 See Hanke et al. (1993) and Balino et al. (1997), among others.

2 For more detailed discussion of the history of currency boards, see Walters and Hanke (1992), Schwartz (1993), and Hanke and Schuler (1994).

3 Williamson (1995) provides a useful summary of the advantages and disadvantages of currency boards.

4 The currency board of Hong Kong is an exception to this rule. There is no formal legislation prohibiting the board from using its foreign reserve to purchase domestic assets, although the board has so far refrained from doing so in a significant way. See the balance sheet in Table 10.2. One interpretation is that the legislature

provides an 'escape clause' with which the board can act as a lender of last resort during financial crises. As long as the escape clause is only invoked in truly exceptional and justifiable situations, it will not undermine the credibility of the currency board rule. Bordo and Kydland (1995, 1996) interpret the classical gold standard as such kind of contingent monetary rule with an escape clause (i.e., suspension of convertibility). It should be noted that when the Hong Kong government spent US$ 15 billion to buy domestic stocks in August 1998, it was using money from fiscal reserves, but not from the currency board.

5 For more details on the historical development of the monetary regime in Hong Kong, see Jao (1990), Schwartz (1993), Greenwood (1995), and Nugee (1995).

6 See Friedman and Schwartz (1963, pp. 483–491) and Friedman (1992) for the silver–purchase program in 1934 and its deflationary effect on China.

7 On 23 October 1997, the overnight interbank rate reached 280 percent. It has often been pointed out that the HKMA might have deliberately pushed up interest rate further by delaying the injection of liquidity back into the economy.

8 Eichengreen (1994) casts doubt on the future of any pegged exchange rate regime in the 21st century. He predicts that only the two extremes of flexible exchange rate and monetary union will survive.

9 Quarterly population figures are obtained by log–linearly interpolating the annual data.

10 The likelihood ratio statistic $LR = -2(\mathit{ln}L_0 - \mathit{ln}L_1 - \mathit{ln}L_2) = -2(771.16 - 291.47 - 500.49) = 41.6$ rejects the null hypothesis of no structural change at the 5 percent level according to a chi–squared distribution with 26 degrees of freedom. $\mathit{ln}L_0$, $\mathit{ln}L_1$, and $\mathit{ln}L_2$ are the log likelihood values of the VAR in (2) estimated by using the full sample (75:1–97:4), the free float period (75:1–83:3), and the currency board period (83:4 – 97:4), respectively.

11 The Exchange Fund Ordinance, Section 3 (2), states that 'The Fund, or any part of it, may be held in Hong Kong currency or in foreign exchange or in gold or in silver or may be invested by the Financial Secretary in such securities or other assets as he, after having consulted the Exchange Fund Advisory Committee, considers appropriate.' (Hong Kong Monetary Authority, 1994, p. 51).

12 See Jao (1993, Chap. 13) and Ho et al. (1991, Chap.1) for more details about banking crises in Hong Kong.

References

Balino, T., Enoch, C., Ize, A., Santiprabhob, V. and Stella, P. (1997), 'Currency Board Arrangements: Issues and Experiences', *IMF Occasional Paper* **151**.

Bayoumi, T. and Eichengreen, B. (1993), 'Shocking Aspects of European Monetary Integration', in F. Torres and F. Giavazzi (eds), *Adjustment and Growth in the European Monetary Union*, Cambridge University Press.

Bayoumi, T. and Eichengreen, B. (1994), 'Macroeconomic Adjustment Under Bretton Woods and the Post–Bretton–Woods Float: An Impulse Response Analysis', *Economic Journal* **104**, pp. 813–827.

Bernanke, B. (1986), 'Alternative Explanations of the Money–income Correlation', *Carnegie–Rochester Conference Series on Public Policy* **25**, pp. 49–99.

Blanchard, O.J. and Watson, M. (1986), 'Are Business Cycles All Alike?' in R. Gordon (ed.), *The American Business Cycle: Continuity and Change*, University of Chicago Press.

Blanchard, O.J. and Quah, D. (1989), 'The Dynamic Effects of Aggregate Demand and Supply Disturbances', *American Economic Review* **79**, pp. 655–673.

Bordo, M. and Kydland, F. (1995), 'The Gold Standard As a Rule: An Essay in Exploration', *Explorations in Economic History* **32**, pp. 423–464.

Bordo, M. and Kydland, F. (1996), 'The Gold Standard As a Commitment Mechanism', in T. Bayoumi, B. Eichengreen and M. Taylor (eds), *Modern Perspectives on the Gold Standard*, Cambridge University Press.

Doan, T. (1992), *RATS User's Manual Version 4*, Estima.

Eichengreen, B. (1994), *International Monetary Arrangements for the 21st Century*, The Brookings Institution.

Friedman, M. and A.J. Schwartz, A.J. (1963), *A Monetary History of the United States: 1867–1960*, Princeton University Press.

Friedman, M. (1992), 'Franklin D. Roosevelt, Silver, and China', *Journal of Political Economy* **100**, pp. 62–83.

Giannini, C. (1992), *Topics in Structural VAR Econometrics*, Springer–Verlag.

Greenwood, J. (1995), 'The Debate on the Optimum Monetary System', *Asian Monetary Monitor* **19**, pp. 1–5.

Hamilton, J. (1994), *Time Series Analysis*, Princeton University Press.

Hanke, S.H., Jonung, L. and Schuler, K. (1993), *Russian Currency and Finance: A Currency Board Approach to Reform*, Routledge.

Hanke, S.H. and Schuler, K. (1994), *Currency Boards for Developing Countries*, Institute for Contemporary Studies Press.

Ho, R.Y.K., Scott, R. and Wong, K.A. (1991), *The Hong Kong Financial System*, Oxford University Press.

Hong Kong Census and Statistics Department (1995), *Estimates of Gross Domestic Product 1961 to 1995*, Hong Kong Government Printer.

Hong Kong Monetary Authority (1994, 1995), *Annual Report*, Hong Kong Monetary Authority.

Hong Kong Monetary Authority (1998), *Monthly Statistical Bulletin,* September issue.

Jao, Y.C. (1990), 'From Sterling Exchange Standard to Dollar Exchange Standard: The Evolution of Hong Kong's Contemporary Monetary System 1967–89', in Y.C. Jao and F. King (eds), *Money in Hong Kong: Historical Perspective and Contemporary Analysis*, University of Hong Kong Press.

Jao, Y.C. (1993), *Hong Kong's Financial System Towards the Future*, Joint Publishing Company.

Johnson, N.L. and Kotz, S. (1970), *Distributions in Statistics—Continuous Univariate Distribution 1*, Wiley.

Kwan, Y.K., Lui, F.T. and Cheng, L.K. (2000), 'Credibility of Hong Kong's Currency Board: The Role of Institutional Arrangements', in T. Ito and A.O. Krueger (eds), *Regional and Global Capital Flows: Macroeconomic Causes and Consequences*, NBER–East Asia Seminar on Economics, Vol. 9, University of Chicago Press.

Lui, F.T., Cheng, L.K. and Y.K. Kwan (2003), 'Currency Board, Asian Financial Crisis, and the Case for Put Options', in L.S. Ho and C.W. Yuen (eds), *Exchange Rate Regimes and Macroeconomic Stability*, Kluwer.

Nugee, J. (1995), 'A Brief History of the Exchange Fund', in *Money and Banking in Hong Kong*, Hong Kong Monetary Authority.

Schwartz, A.J. (1993), 'Currency Boards: Their Past, Present and Possible Future Role', *Carnegie–Rochester Conference Series on Public Policy* **39**, pp. 147–187.

Sheng, A. (1995), 'The Linked Exchange Rate System: Review and Prospects', *Hong Kong Monetary Authority Quarterly Bulletin*, pp. 54–61.

Sims, C.A. (1974), 'Seasonality in Regression', *Journal of the American Statistical Association* **69**, pp. 618–626.

Sims, C.A. (1986), 'Are Forecasting Models Usable for Policy Analysis?', *Federal Reserve Bank of Minneapolis Quarterly Review* **10**, pp. 2–16.

Walters, A.A. and Hanke, S. (1992), 'Currency Boards', in P. Newman, M. Milgate and J. Eatwell (eds), *The New Palgrave Dictionary of Money and Finance*, Macmillan.

Watson, M. (1994), 'Vector Autoregression and Cointegration', in R. Engle and D. McFadden (eds), *Handbook of Econometrics* Vol. 4, Elsevier.

Williamson, J. (1995), *What Role for Currency Boards?* Institute for International Economics.

PART IV
SOCIOECONOMIC ISSUES

Chapter 11

A Modified Harris–Todaro Model of Rural–Urban Migration for China

Derek Laing, Chuhwan Park and Ping Wang

Introduction

With the advent of the *open–door* economic reforms two decades ago, China has experienced a prolonged period of rapid growth. While this has resulted in its per capita income increasing by more than 12 times, an unpleasant by–product is the socioeconomic consequences of *mangliu* ('peasant flood'), or illegal internal migration, which has arisen from regionally unbalanced development and the shift in the surplus of labor from agricultural to industrial sectors.[1] In attempt to stem this tide the Chinese government has adopted a *hukou* system (i.e., a household registration system), which limits legal migration by *legislating* an individual's location choices.[2] Despite this, the presence of significant economic incentives for locating urban employment, has led to a flood of illegal migrants who have moved into major industrial cities, such as Shanghai and Shenzhen. For instance, based on the retrospective questions in China's 1990 census (conducted by the State Statistical Bureau) it has been estimated that over 20 million legal migrants, during the 5–year period from 1985 to 1990, located themselves in Guangdong, Beijing and Shanghai.[3] Among all non–hukou migrants over this period, more than 75 percent have been from rural areas, almost two–thirds between age 20 and 39, almost 60 percent relocating for job–related reasons, only less than 12 percent with senior high school education, and approximately two–thirds working in retail, hotel/restaurant service, and manufacturing industries.

Figure 11.1 below presents the natural population growth rates in Chinese rural and urban areas.[4] While both series exhibited a downward trend (from about 1.65 and 1.1 percent down to 10.5 and 9 percent, respectively, for rural and urban (areas), it is clearly seen that the gap between the two was narrowed over the past decade. At the same time, the urbanization ratio continued to rise, from approximately 24 to 30 percent, as suggested by Figure 11.2.

It is expected that the urbanization ratio will reach 70 percent by 2050 as a result of an estimated net migration from rural to urban area of 50 million persons. Currently, China has about 660 cities and 19,000 towns. By 2050, 80 percent of towns will grow into small or medium–sized cities and by then, China will have 50 large metropolis, each with more than 2 million people, 150 big cities, 500 medium–sized cities and 1,500 small cities.

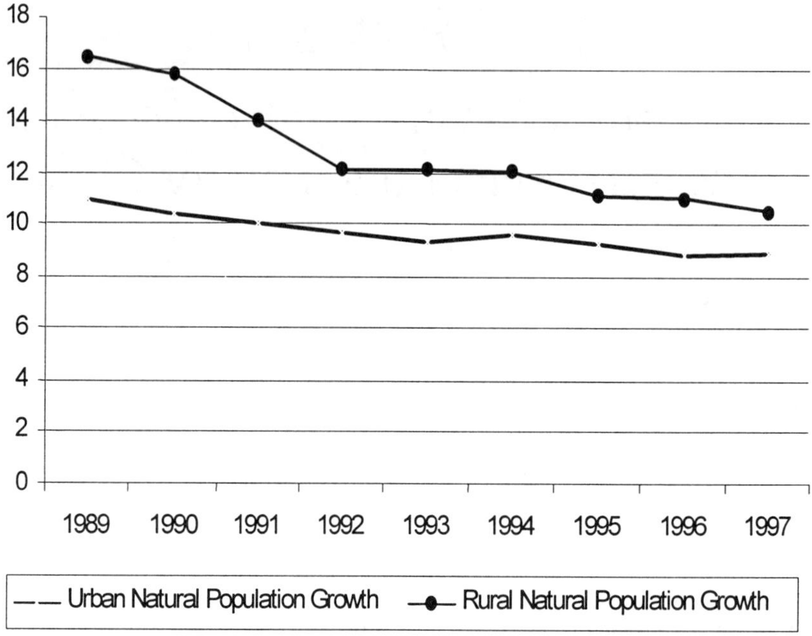

Figure 11.1 Natural population growth rates in China: rural vs urban (%)

Note: Data prior to 1990 are based on interpolation of China's 1982 and 1990 national population censuses; afterwards, data are estimated based on the annual National Sample Survey on Population Change (NSSPC). All data exclude the population of Hong Kong and Macao, but include military personnel.

A key factor of such rural–urban migration is the on–going increase in the per capita income differential between the two areas. From Figure 11.3, we can see that the urban–rural per capital annual disposable income differential was only about 341 yuan in 1980, but rose sharply to 3,060 yuan in 1997.

Todaro (1969) and Harris and Todaro (1970) set up a seminal framework of migration between rural and urban areas. They hypothesize that individuals migrate to urban sectors with the aim of obtaining employment in the formal sector and that informal sector employment is a transitional phase during which migrants are searching for formal sector job. In their decision to migrate, potential migrants balance the probability of unemployment against the real income differentials between the urban formal sector and the rural area. That is, there may be higher

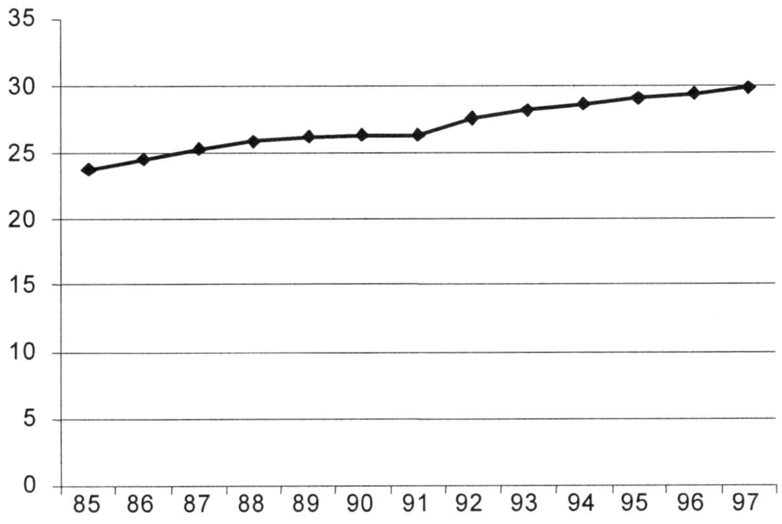

Figure 11.2 Urbanization ratio (%)

Note: Data prior to 1990 are based on interpolation of China's 1982 and 1990 national population censuses; afterwards, data are estimated based on the annual National Sample Survey on Population Change (NSSPC). All data exclude the population of Hong Kong and Macao, but include military personnel.

unemployment in the urban sector due to the existing uncertainty of finding work in the formal sector even though the expected income in the urban sector is higher than that of the rural sector. Recently, Bencivenga and Smith (1997) analyzed the interaction between migration and unemployment, in which economic development is accompanied by migration from rural to urban employment and is associated with significant urban unemployment. According to their results, adverse selection in the urban sector keeps the unemployment pools away from the formal urban market so that employers hire only a very small proportion of unemployed workers from the unemployment pools. This adverse selection becomes particularly acute when the economic profits decline in the urban labor markets. In Brueckner and Zenou (1999), the urban land market is explicitly incorporated into the Harris–Todaro framework. As a result, the interactions between rural–urban migration and urban land rent are examined. They find that the increased urban land rent reduces the incentive for a rural resident to migrate to the city, which provides a partial explanation of the reversed pattern of rural–urban migration (suburbanization) in the U.S. since 1960.

In this chapter, we construct a model particularly suitable for the study of

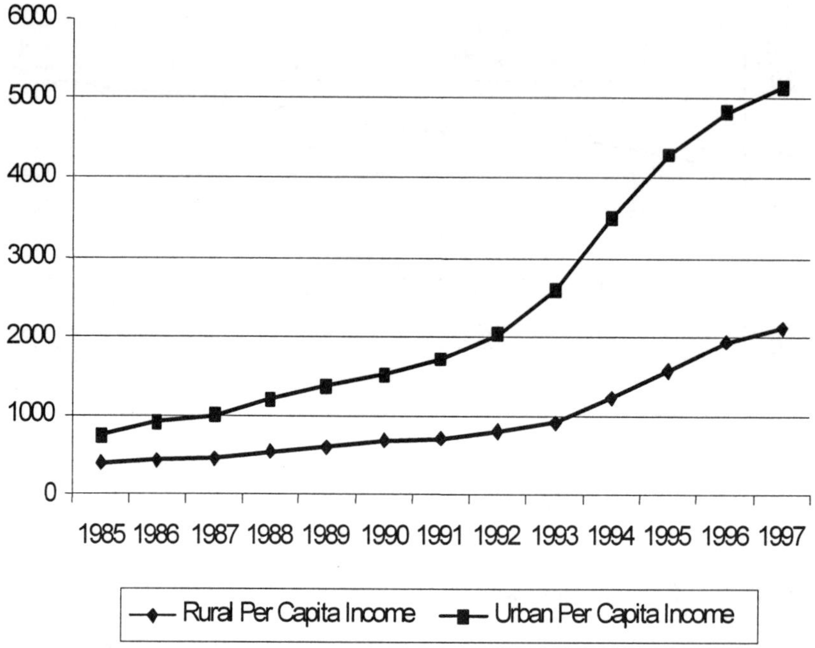

Figure 11.3 Per capita income in China: rural versus urban (in Yuan)

Note: Data prior to 1990 are based on interpolation of China's 1982 and 1990 national population censuses; afterwards, data are estimated based on the annual National Sample Survey on Population Change (NSSPC). All data exclude the population of Hong Kong and Macao, but include military personnel.

rural–urban migration in China. Following Coulson, Laing and Wang (2001) and Park (1999), we adopt a search theoretic approach where both the migration flows and migration probabilities are endogenously determined.[5] Due to the household registration policy, illegal immigrants may be penalized in two forms: (i) if they fail to submit a legal document to their employers, they receive lower *equilibrium* wages than those enjoyed by legal residents and (ii) as a result of government auditing, they are more likely to lose their jobs than are legal residents. Both legal and illegal workers in the urban labor market conduct job search that is mediated via a random matching technology. The technology is such that each vacancy can be filled by at most one worker and each worker can hold at most one job at any given point in time. By endogenizing individuals' migration and job–search decision, we determine endogenously the wage schedules for both legal and illegal workers, under a symmetric Nash bargain where workers and firms equally divide the joint surplus accrued from their successful matching.

In a steady–state equilibrium, (i) rural legal residence must have no incentive to migrate to the urban area (or what we call a 'no–arbitrage' migration relationship), (ii) population net flows from and to each employed and unemployed pool must be zero and the number of filled jobs must equal to the number of employed workers (or what we call a 'steady–state matching' relationship), and (iii) firms continue to enter until their expected market value equals to the fixed entry cost (or what we call an 'equilibrium entry' relationship). We show that under a rather weak condition, the steady–state equilibrium exists and is unique. By performing comparative–static analysis, we find that the enforcement of the household registration rule can discourage illegal migration, which in turn leads to a higher job finding rate and reduces the urban unemployment rate.

The remainder of this chapter is organized as follows. In the next section, we present the basic structure of the model. While the following section determines the wage schedules for legal and illegal workers by a symmetric Nash bargain, the subsequent section proves the existence and uniqueness of the steady–state equilibrium in which there is no net migration flow. We then characterize the steady–state equilibrium in the penultimate section and finally provide some concluding remarks, including possible avenues for future research.

The basic environment

We consider a continuous time closed economy that consists of two sectors corresponding to the rural and city sectors. The total population is normalized to one. The household registration system is such that, the mass of residents who are *legally* obliged to live in the *rural* sector is N. The mass $1–N$ of workers are permitted to move to the city.[6] All agents discount the future at the rate, $r > 0$. All workers are identical except for their legal residency status. Each worker is endowed with a unit of labor which can be supplied to firms inelastically.

The one–time interregional migration cost of moving from the rural sector to the city (or *vice versa*) is captured by $Z > 0$. We assume that legally registered rural residents can search for jobs in the city without incurring any explicit search costs (although search is time consuming). All agents must present their household registration must be presented when they apply for a job. However, even unregistered households can search for work. If they successfully match with an employer, they become illegal (working) migrants. We assume that they suffer faster job break ups than formal workers and, later prove, that they will earn lower wages as well. The decision regarding whether a rural resident will choose to move to the city depends upon the expected discounted value of income in each of the two regions. We label those who decide to remain in the rural sector by a superscript 'R' and those who *illegally* move to the city by 'M'. Legal residents in the city are, indexed by 'C'. These individuals always search for jobs in the city (under a condition that ensures the payoff of a city job is sufficiently high).

There is free entry of firms into the urban labor market, in the sense that any firms can enter the market upon incurring a fixed cost $K > 0$, which captures both firms' start–up and capital costs. Firms can exit the labor market without cost.

The rural labor market is assumed to be perfectly competitive. However, in the urban labor market the interactions between workers and firms are governed by random matching processes. This reflects the specialization of labor that occurs in urban labor, and captures the time consuming and difficult task of matching the 'right worker' with the 'right task'. Each firm consists of a single vacancy that can be filled by a single worker. The mass of unfilled vacancies in the economy is denoted V. All vacancies are completely durable and identical in every respect.

Upon a successful match, the worker–firm pair negotiates a wage and production takes place immediately. In steady–state equilibrium, there is no migration flow between two regions, as all of those who wish to move to the city do so at the beginning of the period. It follows that our analysis is one that applies to the distribution of a given group of workers between the urban and rural labor markets.[7] One of the key economic relationships in our model is a *no arbitrage* condition. This condition basically ensures that in steady state equilibrium there are no incentives to move from one location to another. (If this condition were to be violated, then a *mass* of workers would 'jump' from one sector to another, which would discretely reduce the value of searching in that sector.)

Given the matching process, urban workers are either currently employed (E) or else unemployed (U) and searching for work. Likewise, employers are in one of two states. They either have a filled vacancy and are producing output, or alternatively they have an open vacancy and are searching for labor. These two states are denoted by (F) and (V) respectively. Thus, the total workforce in each region is described by

$$(11.1)\quad N = R + \Lambda = R + E^M + U^M;\quad 1 - N = E^C + U^C.$$

In view of the fact that each vacancy is filled by at most one worker, the total number of city jobs equals the total number of city employees $E^M + E^C$. In view of this, the fraction of workers who illegally migrate to the city is: $\lambda \equiv \Lambda/N = (E^M + U^M)/N$.

The flow output per worker in the rural sector is given by

$$(11.2)\quad y^R = A,$$

where $A > 0$. To capture the observed phenomenon, output per worker in the city is specified as

$$(11.3)\quad y = A + \Delta,$$

where $\Delta > 0$ denotes the rural–urban productivity differentials, which is the primary economic incentive that induces rural–urban migration.

Let $\alpha \equiv U^M/(U^M + U^C)$ denote the fraction of searching workers with legal residence in the rural region. (It follows that α is the fraction of searching workers who are legally allowed to reside in the city). Denote the flow probability that a worker locates a vacancy as μ and that a vacancy locates a worker as η. It follows that searching vacancies meet illegal immigrants into the city and legal residents at different rates according to the fraction α. More specifically, the effective flow probability with which a vacancy locates an illegal migrant is $\eta\alpha$, while it meets a legal resident is $\eta(1-\alpha)$.

We assume that worker–firm matches break up for exogenous reasons. Accordingly let δ denote the flow break–up probability between jobs and legal workers. Jobs and illegal migrants into the city break up at the rate, $(\delta+\beta)$. Here $\beta > 0$ is an additional job break up component, reflecting the city's enforcement of the residency laws. For simplicity, the government's enforcement behavior and financing are not explicitly modeled in the present paper.

Denote the (endogenous) market wage rate of legal workers by w. The wage of illegal immigrants is defined as: $v \equiv (1-\theta)w$, where $\theta \in (0, 1)$ captures the (endogenous) wage reduction of illegal workers. Further, let J_E^M and J_U^M denote the respective present–discounted value of a employed and unemployed illegal migrants (more specifically, workers who are officially domiciled in the rural sector, but work or search for work in the urban labor market. The corresponding asset values for legal residents are J_E^C and J_U^C. Finally, Π_F^i and Π_V, respectively, denote the present–discounted value of a filled vacancy with a worker of type–i ($i = M, C$) and the expected present–discounted value of an unfilled vacancy (which obviously, is independent of the worker's type).

The associated Bellman equations determining agents' steady state asset values equal

$$(11.4)\quad rJ^R = A,$$

$$(11.5)\quad rJ_E^M = v + (\delta+\beta)(J_U^M - J_E^M),$$

$$(11.6)\quad rJ_U^M = \mu(J_E^M - J_U^M),$$

$$(11.7)\quad rJ_E^C = w + \delta(J_U^C - J_E^C),$$

$$(11.8)\quad rJ_U^C = \mu(J_E^C - J_U^C),$$

$$(11.9)\quad r\Pi_F^M = y - v + (\delta+\beta)(\Pi_V - \Pi_F^M),$$

$$(11.10)\quad r\Pi_F^C = y - w + \delta(\Pi_V - \Pi_F^C)$$

and

$$(11.11)\quad r\Pi_V = \eta[\alpha\Pi_F^M + (1-\alpha)\Pi_F^C - \Pi_V].$$

These asset value equations have intuitive interpretations. To begin with, the competitive labor market assumption implies that workers' flow incomes in this sector are trivially equal to A. As indicated by (11.4), J^R is equal to the lifetime wealth of a rural worker (A/r) given the discount rate r. Equation (11.5) says that the flow value of an illegal—but employed worker—equals the net flow value of wage income, v, plus the expected value of the change in state that arises because of job break–ups (i.e., becoming an unemployed and searching for another job in the urban labor market) which occurs with flow probability $\delta + \beta$. Equation (11.6) indicates that, because of the absence of either flow income while unemployed, or flow costs while searching, the flow value of an unemployed illegal migrant is simply the flow value of the expected capital gain of finding urban employment. Precisely analogous interpretations hold for the asset values (11.7) and (11.8).

Finally, (11.9) and (11.10) describe the asset values of employers. Equation (11.9) equals the flow value of a filled vacancy with a worker of type–i. It equals the sum of its flow profits (flow output net of wages) in conjunction with the the expected flow value of suffering a capital loss due to a job break–up. In equation (11.11), the expected flow value of holding open an unfilled vacancy is simply the expected flow capital gain from successfully hiring either a legal resident or illegal migrant.

The aggregate mass of unemployed workers in the economy is: $U \equiv U^M + U^C$. Since a vacancy can be filled by exactly one worker and each worker work in at most one job, it is clear that steady–state matching in the urban labor market must satisfy:

(11.12) $\mu U = \eta V = \Gamma(U,V)$,

where the first equality says that the instantaneous flow of successful matches of searching workers must equal the flow rate at which unfilled vacancies find workers. The second equality states that these flow matching rates are governed by a random - matching technology Γ *a lá* Diamond (1982). We make standard assumptions about Γ. More specifically, $\Gamma(\cdot)$ is strictly increasing and strictly concave in the masses of the two searching parties, U and V. It exhibits constant returns to scale in U and V. Finally, it satisfies the Inada conditions ($lim_{j\to 0}\Gamma_j = \infty$ and $lim_{j\to\infty}\Gamma_j = 0$, for $j \in \{U, V\}$) and the boundary conditions ($\Gamma(0, V) = \Gamma(U, 0) = 0$). A Cobb–Douglas function, for example, satisfies all of these conditions. These ensure a well–behaved, Beveridge curve in which the absence of either side of the matching parties would result in no matches. By utilizing the constant–returns property, straightforward manipulation of (11.12) yields $\eta = \Gamma(U/V, 1) = \Gamma(\eta\backslash\mu, 1)$, or,

(11.13) $\eta = \eta(\mu)$,

where $\eta_\mu = -(\eta/\mu^2)/(1 - U\Gamma_U/\Gamma) < 0$. This will be referred to as the *steady–state matching* (SS) locus, which gives a negative relationship between the two flow probabilities in the steady state. It is immediate from (11.12) and (11.13) that the mass of vacancy is given by

$$(11.14) \qquad V = \frac{\mu}{\eta(\mu)} U,$$

which is increasing in worker's flow matching probability μ.

Wage bargaining in the urban labor market

We now turn to the determination of the wage in the urban labor market. Although the flow probabilities η and μ are endogenously determined in equilibrium, workers and firms treat them as parametrically given in making their decisions. Furthermore, as vacancies are atomistic, the expected value of an unfilled vacancy is also taken as parametric throughout the analysis (see Pissarides, 1987 and Laing, Palivos and Wang, 1995 for detailed discussions).

For simplicity, we further assume that the two parties bargain cooperatively to maximize their equally weighted joint surplus: $(J_E^i - J_U^i)^{1/2}(\Pi_F^i - \Pi_V)^{1/2}$, for $i = M$, C. This optimization problem is characterized by a symmetric Nash bargaining solution. Thus, the wage offers made to illegal migrants, v, and legal residents, w, must satisfy

$$(11.15) \quad J_E^i - J_U^i = \Pi_F^i - \Pi_V > 0.$$

First, manipulating (11.5) and (11.6) implies

$$(11.16) \quad J_E^M - J_U^M = \frac{r}{r+\mu} J_E^M = \frac{v}{r+\delta+\beta+\mu}.$$

Similarly, (11.7) and (11.8) together give

$$(11.17) \quad J_E^C - J_U^C = \frac{r}{r+\mu} J_E^C = \frac{w}{r+\delta+\mu},$$

whereas (11.9) and (11.10) can be rewritten as

$$(11.18) \quad \Pi_F^M - \Pi_V = \frac{1}{r+\delta+\beta}[y - v - r\Pi_V]$$

and

$$(11.19) \quad \Pi_F^C - \Pi_V = \frac{1}{r+\delta}[y - w - r\Pi_V].$$

Next, substituting (11.16)–(11.19) into (11.15), we can obtain the wage offer functions and characterize their properties as follows:

Proposition 1 (*wage offers*)

The unique wage offer functions determined by the symmetric Nash bargain between a vacancy and a type i $\in \{M, C\}$ *are given by*

$$(11.20)\ v = \frac{r+\delta+\beta+\mu}{2(r+\delta+\beta)+\mu}(y - r\Pi_V)$$

and

$$(11.21)\ w = \frac{r+\delta+\mu}{2(r+\delta)+\mu}(y - r\Pi_V).$$

They possess the following properties:

$$\frac{\partial v}{\partial \mu} > 0; \quad \frac{\partial v}{\partial \Pi_V} < 0; \quad \frac{\partial v}{\partial \beta} < 0; \quad \frac{\partial w}{\partial \mu} > 0; \quad \frac{\partial w}{\partial \Pi_V} < 0; \quad \frac{\partial w}{\partial \beta} = 0.$$

Intuitively, an increase in the flow probability with which a worker locates a job (μ) enhances his bargaining power, and leads to a higher wage offer. In contrast an increase in the value of an unfilled vacancy, Π_V, reduces the wage offer since it increases the option value to the firm of keeping the vacancy open. An increase in the government's enforcement efforts to capture illegal migrants is captured by an increase in β. The effect of this is to lower the present discounted value of the surplus that accrues to an illegal worker–firm pair, which in turn reduces the *relative* wage offer made to illegal migrants.

Recall that θ is defined by the condition $v \equiv (1 - \theta)w$, where $\theta \in (0, 1)$. Using (11.20) and (11.21), we can compute the wage 'mark–down,' $\theta \equiv (w - v)/w$, facing illegal workers. It is given by:

Proposition 2 (*the wage discount factor* θ)

The wage discount rate facing an illegal worker in the urban labor market is given by

$$(11.22)\ \theta(\mu;\beta) = \frac{\beta\mu}{(r+\delta+\mu)[2(r+\delta+\beta)+\mu]}.$$

It possesses the following properties:

$$\frac{\partial\theta}{\partial\mu} > 0 \ \textit{if} \ \beta < \beta_0 \ \textit{and} \ \frac{\partial\theta}{\partial\mu} < 0 \ \textit{if} \ \beta > \beta_0; \quad \frac{\partial\theta}{\partial\beta} > 0.$$

The second result is straightforward: an increase in the city government's attempts to detecting illegal migration (higher β) enlarges the wage gap between legal and illegal workers, thus raising the wage mark–down (higher θ). The first result says that *provided* the city government's attempts to detecting illegal migration are sufficiently weak (low β) an increase in market thickness that makes it easier for workers to locate jobs (high μ) increases the gap between the wage offers made to legal and illegal migrants. Alternatively, if detection efforts are vigorous, then an increase in the matching rate μ lowers the wage mark–down. This effect can be explained as follows. As μ rises it is easier for all workers to find jobs. However, as β rises as well, the value of matches between firms and illegals declines, but at slower rate at the margin. As a result, there exists a critical enforcement rate β after which further increases in the matching rate, μ, start to reduce the wage mark–down.

Steady–state equilibrium

In steady–state equilibrium, the free entry of vacancies implies the market value of an unfilled vacancy must be equal its fixed entry cost:

(11.23) $\Pi_V = K.$

By substituting (11.3) and (11.23) into (11.20) and (11.21), the equilibrium wage schedules can be written as

(11.24) $$v(\mu;\beta,K) = \frac{r+\delta+\beta+\mu}{2(r+\delta+\beta)+\mu}(A+\Delta-rK)$$

and

(11.25) $$w(\mu;\beta,K) = \frac{r+\delta+\mu}{2(r+\delta)+\mu}(A+\Delta-rK),$$

where $\Delta = y - y^R$. Manipulating (11.9)–(11.11) and (11.13) to express Π_V as a function of (μ , v, w), we can rewrite (11.23) as:

(11.26) $$\frac{\eta(\mu)}{r+\eta(\mu)}\left[\alpha\frac{y-v(\mu)+(\delta+\beta)K}{r+\delta+\beta}+(1-\alpha)\frac{y-w(\mu)+\delta K}{r+\delta}\right] = K.$$

Substituting (11.3), (11.24) and (11.25) into (11.26) and manipulating, we obtain

$$(11.27)\quad \Psi(\mu,\alpha;\beta,K,\Delta) \equiv \frac{\eta(\mu)(A+\Delta-rK)}{2(r+\delta+\beta)+\mu}\left[1+\frac{2\beta(1-\alpha)}{2(r+\delta)+\mu}\right]-rK=0.$$

Straightforward differentiation of this expression yields

$$(11.28)\quad \frac{\partial\Psi}{\partial\mu}<0,\quad \frac{\partial\Psi}{\partial\alpha}<0,\quad \frac{\partial\Psi}{\partial\beta}<0,\quad \frac{\partial\Psi}{\partial K}<0,\ and\ \frac{\partial\Psi}{\partial\Delta}<0.$$

This condition can be used to derive an *equilibrium entry* (EE) relationship:

Lemma 1 (equilibrium entry)

The equilibrium entry condition is given by,

$$(11.29)\quad \alpha=\alpha(\mu;\beta,K,\Delta)\equiv 1-\frac{2(r+\delta)+\mu}{2\beta}\left\{\frac{rK[2(r+\delta+\beta)+\mu]}{\eta(\mu)(A+\Delta-rK)}-1\right\},$$

satisfying the following properties:

(i) $\frac{\partial\alpha}{\partial\mu}<0,\ \frac{\partial\alpha}{\partial\beta}<0,\ \frac{\partial\alpha}{\partial K}<0,\ and\ \frac{\partial\alpha}{\partial\Delta}<0;$

(ii) $\alpha\to\infty\ as\ \mu\to 0\ and\ \alpha\to\alpha_{\min}>0\ as\ \mu\to\infty.$

The *EE* locus gives the set of matching rates μ and η such that the net *ex ante* value to a firm from creating a new vacancy is precisely zero. Crucially, the *EE* locus takes into account the fact that firms recognize that their subsequent wage agreements are determined according to the Nash bargaining solution described in propositions 1 and 2.

The *EE* locus establishes a *negative* relationship between the flow probability with which workers locate jobs, μ, and the fraction of illegal migrants, α, in the population of urban job seekers.

In steady–state equilibrium, there are no net migration flows. This means that at t = 0 rural residents make a decision regarding whether they will remain where they are or, alternatively, search for work in the urban labor market. In order to ensure that there is no migration in steady state it is necessary that the present–discounted value of remaining a rural worker must equal the expected present–discounted value of *illegal* job seekers in the urban sector, *net* of the migration cost Z.[8] This gives rise to a *no–arbitrage* (NA) condition, which takes the form:

(11.30) $J_U^M - Z = \frac{A}{r} = J^R > 0$

or, using (11.3), (11.6), (11.16) and (11.20),

(11.31) $\frac{A}{r} + Z = J_U^M = \frac{\mu}{2(r+\delta+\beta)+\mu}\left(\frac{A+\Delta}{r} - K\right).$

Straightforward manipulation and differentiation establish

Lemma 2 (no–arbitrage)

The no–arbitrage condition is given by

(11.32) $\mu = \Phi(\beta, K, Z, \Delta) \equiv \frac{2(r+\delta+\beta)(A+rZ)}{\Delta - r(K+Z)},$

satisfying

$$\frac{\partial\Phi}{\partial\beta} > 0; \quad \frac{\partial\Phi}{\partial K} > 0; \quad \frac{\partial\Phi}{\partial Z} > 0; \quad \frac{\partial\Phi}{\partial\Delta} < 0.$$

One of the appealing features of this condition is that it uniquely determines the flow probability μ and does so independently of the fraction of illegals, α in the population. This means the *NA* locus is vertical in (μ, α) space at a given value of μ. Figure 11.4 depicts the (unique) steady–state equilibrium at point *E*. It occurs at the point where the negatively sloped *EE* locus intersects the vertical *NA* locus.

Moreover, the urban labor market must exhibit no net flows for either type of workers and hence,

(11.33) $(\delta+\beta)E^M = \mu U^M$

and

(11.34) $\delta E^C = \mu U^C.$

which can be combined with (11.1) to yield the masses of employed and unemployed workers:

(11.35) $E^M = \frac{\mu N \lambda}{\delta+\beta+\mu},$

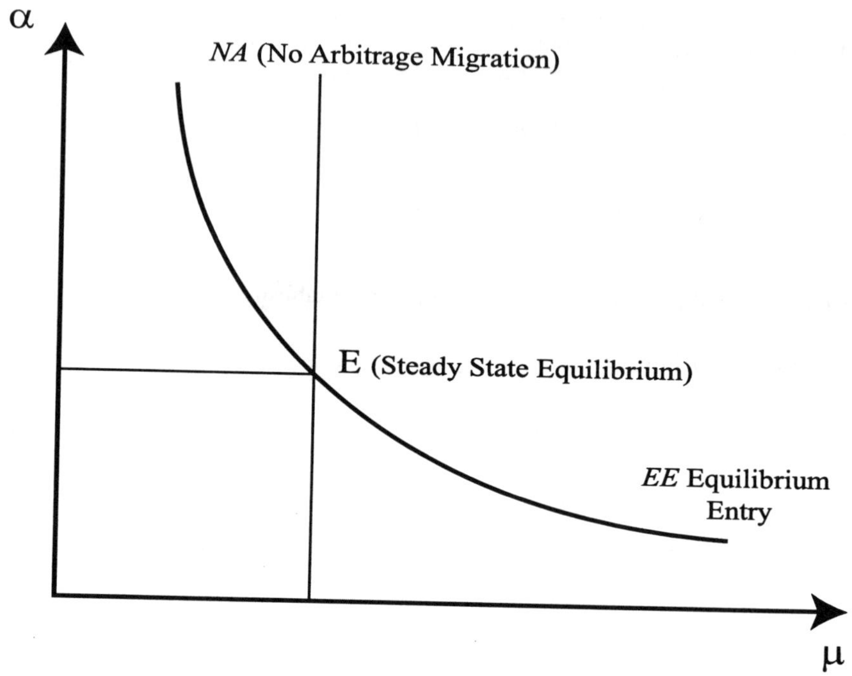

Figure 11.4 Steady–state equilibrium

$$(11.36)\quad E^C = \frac{\mu(1-N)}{\delta+\beta},$$

$$(11.37)\quad U^M = \frac{(\delta+\beta)N\lambda}{\delta+\beta+\mu}$$

and

$$(11.38)\quad U^C = \frac{\delta(1-N)}{\delta+\beta}.$$

A thicker urban labor market—measured by a higher flow probability μ—raises employment and reduces unemployment. For a given thickness measure, a greater enforcement on illegal workers by the city government results in a higher unemployment rate for illegal workers, a lower unemployment rate for legal workers, and a reduced mass of employment for either type of workers.

The definition of α and equation (11.38) together give

Lemma 3 (*aggregate unemployment*)

The aggregate unemployment rate in the society is given by

$$(11.39)\ U(\mu,\alpha) \equiv U^M + U^C = \frac{\delta(1-N)}{\delta+\beta}\frac{1}{\alpha},$$

satisfying

$$\frac{\partial U}{\partial \mu} < 0; \quad \frac{\partial U}{\partial \alpha} > 0.$$

That is, a thicker urban labor market decreases aggregate unemployment, whereas more illegal workers tends to increase it. Plugging (11.39) into (11.14), we have

$$(11.40)\ V(\mu,\alpha;\beta) = \frac{\delta(1-N)}{\delta+\beta}\frac{\mu}{\alpha\eta(\mu)},$$

which is increasing in μ and decreasing in α and β. Finally, substitution of (11.37) and (11.38) into the definition of α leads to

Lemma 4 (*migration rate*)

The rural migration rate into the city is given by

$$(11.41)\ \lambda(\mu,\alpha;\beta) = \frac{1-N}{N}\frac{\delta}{\delta+\beta}\frac{\alpha}{1-\alpha}\left(1+\frac{\beta}{\delta+\mu}\right),$$

satisfying

$$\frac{\partial \lambda}{\partial \mu} < 0; \quad \frac{\partial \lambda}{\partial \alpha} > 0; \quad \frac{\partial \lambda}{\partial \beta} < 0.$$

Intuitively, a thicker urban labor market increases the disadvantages of illegal migrants relative to legal workers, as it is easier for legal residents to find work. In turn, this discourages rural migration into the city. This property contrasts the partial–equilibrium probabilistic model of migration due to Todaro (1969) and Harris and Todaro (1970). While a higher rural migration rate is consistent with a larger fraction of unemployed illegal workers in the city, a strengthened city government's enforcement on illegal workers reduces the rural migration rate into the city.

Definition (*steady–state equilibrium*)

A steady–state equilibrium is a pair of wage functions, $v(\mu\,;\beta, K)$ and $w(\mu\,;\beta, K)$, together with a tuple of quantities (μ, η, α, λ, E^M, E^C, U^M, U^C, V), satisfying the following conditions:

(*i*) (*Symmetric Nash Wage Bargain*): (*11.24*) *and* (*11.25*);
(*ii*) (*Steady–State Matching*): *the SS locus* (*11.13*);
(*iii*) (*Equilibrium Entry*): *the EE locus* (*11.29*);
(*iv*) (*No–Arbitrage*): *the NA locus* (*11.32*);
(*v*) (*Migration Rate*): (*11.41*);
(*vi*) (*Steady–State Population*): (*11.35*)–(*11.38*) *and* (*11.40*).

Condition E

$\Delta > r(K + Z)$, *i.e., the productivity gap is sufficiently high relative to the entry and migration costs.*

As it can be seen from (11.32), condition E is necessary and sufficient to ensure a positive value of μ in steady–state equilibrium. Moreover, it is also sufficient to guarantee positive wages and non–trivial migration from rural to urban. Utilizing lemmas 1–4, we can establish:

Proposition 3 (*existence and uniqueness of the steady–state equilibrium*)

Under Condition E, the steady–state equilibrium exists and is unique.

Comparative statics

To characterize the steady–state equilibrium, it is useful to understand the recursive nature of the model. First, the *EE* locus (11.29) and the *NA* locus (11.32) together determine the steady–state equilibrium values of μ and α. These are then substituted into (i) (11.24), (11.25) and (11.22) to pin down the two wage schedules (v and w) and the wage mark–down θ facing illegal migrants. Once the contact rates α and μ are determined, equations (11.13) and (11.41) pin down firm's flow matching probability (η) and the migration rate (λ). Once all of the Poisson arrival rates have been determined, equations (11.35)–(11.38) and (11.40) can be used to derive the steady–state equilibrium masses of the employed, the unemployed and the vacancies (E^M, E^C, U^M, U^C, V)). Finally, equation (11.39) can be used to determine the steady–state equilibrium rate of aggregate unemployment (U). Applying lemmas 1–4 as well as equation (11.41) yields

Proposition 4 (*characterization of the steady–state equilibrium*)

Under condition E, the unique steady–state equilibrium possesses the following properties:

(i) (*thickness of the urban labor market*):

$$\frac{\partial \mu}{\partial \beta} > 0; \quad \frac{\partial \mu}{\partial K} > 0; \quad \frac{\partial \mu}{\partial Z} > 0; \quad \frac{\partial \mu}{\partial \Delta} < 0;$$

(ii) (*fraction of illegal workers in the city*):

$$\frac{\partial \alpha}{\partial \beta} < 0; \quad \frac{\partial \alpha}{\partial K} < 0; \quad \frac{\partial \alpha}{\partial Z} < 0; \quad \frac{\partial \alpha}{\partial \Delta} > 0;$$

(iii) (*wage mark–down facing illegal workers*):

$$\frac{\partial \theta}{\partial \beta} > 0; \quad \frac{\partial \theta}{\partial K} > 0; \quad \frac{\partial \theta}{\partial Z} > 0; \quad \frac{\partial \theta}{\partial \Delta} < 0 \textit{ for sufficiently small } \beta;$$

(iv) (*migrate rate from rural to urban*):

$$\frac{\partial \lambda}{\partial \beta} < 0; \quad \frac{\partial \lambda}{\partial K} < 0; \quad \frac{\partial \lambda}{\partial Z} < 0; \quad \frac{\partial \lambda}{\partial \Delta} > 0;$$

(v) (*aggregate unemployment rate*):

$$\frac{\partial U}{\partial \beta} < 0; \quad \frac{\partial U}{\partial K} < 0; \quad \frac{\partial U}{\partial Z} < 0; \quad \frac{\partial U}{\partial \Delta} > 0.$$

Many of these results carry over the intuition embodied in the partial–equilibrium relationships described in the earlier lemmas and propositions to a general–equilibrium environment in which all of the matching rates, populations, and wage offers are endogenously determined. Accordingly we discuss only the most noteworthy findings.

Key among them is that an increase in the enforcement rate β *increases* the rate at which *all* workers (both legal and illegal migrants) locate jobs: $\partial\mu/\partial\beta > 0$. The intuition is that an increase in β increases the job break up rate which means that in steady state, there are a greater number of unfilled vacancies searching for a given number of unemployed job seekers.

An increase in the migration cost Z also raises the rate at which workers find jobs. The explanation is that an increase in Z reduces illegal migration. As a result, the fraction α of illegals in the urban population falls ($\partial\alpha/\partial Z < 0$). In turn, this raises the *ex ante* value to firms of entering the city as they are *less likely* to see their matches terminate as a result of government enforcement of residency requirements, since a greater fraction of their employees are legally domiciled. In turn, the greater number of firms makes it easier for workers to find jobs, so that μ rises. Evidently, an increase in enforcement efforts (i.e., an increase in β) also reduces the fraction of illegal migrants in the city, α, as well as the extent of illegal migration λ. In this regard a notable result is that greater enforcement increases the wage gap: $\partial\theta/\partial\beta > 0$. Essentially this is a resurfacing of the partial–equilibrium result reported in proposition 2 to a general–equilibrium setting.

From a policy perspective, one of the most significant findings is that an increase in the city government's enforcement activities (raising β) reduces the level of unemployment: $\partial U/\partial\beta < 0$—and does so, even though the penalty in the event of detection is the termination of the match. This is a general equilibrium result. It arises because the increase in β deters so many illegal rural migrants from entering the city in the first place.

The results pertaining to the entry cost K are of some interest, since the government may enjoy some ability in implementing policies that make it more or less costly for firms to enter the market. (For example, the government could devise low tax enterprise zones to encourage entry). As the results make clear this is a double edged sword. While it certainly makes it easier for workers to find jobs (μ rises) it also encourages illegal immigration into the city.

Conclusions

China, it would seem, never does 'anything by halves'. Its per capital growth rate over the past twenty years or so has been utterly staggering, leading to a twelve fold increase in per capita incomes over the period. However, growth has been uneven. The resultant difference in per capita incomes enjoyed by urban and rural dwellers is now precipitous. This has generated enormous amounts of internal migration, as workers abandon the land in search of urban employment. The labor flows are staggering. Over the five year period 1985–1990, the migration to *three* of China's major cities equaled about half the population of France.

To deal with the problems generated by the mass exodus from the land and the even greater social and economic problems that arise from their movement to the city, China has attempted to control internal migration through a *Hukou*—household registration—system. The snag, of course, is that the economic incentives to migrate are so great that many individuals simply flout the law and illegally migrate from the rural to the urban sector in search of work. This chapter is unique in that it extends the basic Harris Todaro model to a search equilibrium setting that includes both legal and illegal migrants. One of the main findings is that stricter enforcement of registration laws may reduce unemployment levels in the city. However, in its attempt to promote economic growth policies that reduce the cost of capital, and that encourage the entry of vacancies into the city, may only make internal migration policies even more acute.

We believe that this chapter can be extended in a variety of ways. Following Laing, Palivos, and Wang (1995) it would be of interest to admit a non trivial educational decision. In this case, illegal migrants—by making it more difficult and time consuming for legal residents to find work—reduce the value of education. As a result, a vigorously enforced household registration system may be welfare enhancing by fostering investment in human capital. Our model shares with the canonical Harris (1969) and Harris and Todaro (1970) models of migration the unappealing feature that all migration takes place *ex ante* at the very beginning of the period. An interesting extension would be to admit an endogenous migration flow from the rural to the urban sector that arises because of (initially) increasing returns to urban employment. In this case, it would be of great interest to investigate just how the hukou registration system impacts the *distribution of income* during the process of economic development.

Notes

1 For an elaboration on peasant flood in China, the reader is referred to Chan (1988) and Wan (1995). For a discussion of the shift of labor force, see Lewis (1954) and Kuznets (1982). With regard to the socio–economic consequences, the Shenzhen City Police Report suggests that crimes committed by non–hukou migrants accounted for approximately 90 percent of the total.

2 See Yang (1993) for a detailed description of the hukou system.

3 Based on transportation flows prior to the New Year holiday, the total non–hukou migration is estimated at least 35 million. Based on the 1990 Census questionaire, non–hukou migration is believed almost as large as hukou migration (cf. Chan, Liu and Yang 1999).

4 Though China's population control policy has brought the total fertility rate down from 5 to 1.8 percent over the period of 1970–95, China did not achieve its goal of stabilizing population at 1.2 billion in 2000. Instead, the total population grew over 1.3 billion and its projection is towards 1.5 billion by 2025. For issues concerning China's population policy, the reader is referred to Scotese and Wang (1995).

5 Conventional urban matching models do not consider the stochastic nature of the search process. For example, see Helsley and Strange (1990) and Abdel–Rahman and Wang (1995).

6 For simplicity, we (harmlessly) ignore those who currently reside in the city, since our focus is on the process of rural to urban migration.

7 Laing, Park, and Wang (2002) consider the *dynamics* of migration between the city and rural areas.

8 Recall that all, $1 - N$, legally registered workers move to the city. This means that at the margin, it is the decisions of the N non registered migrants that are crucial.

References

Abdel–Rahman, H. and Wang, P. (1995), 'Toward a General Equilibrium Theory of a Core–Periphery System of Cities', *Regional Science and Urban Economics* **25**, pp. 529–546.

Bencivenga, V.R. and Smith, B.D. (1997), 'Unemployment, Migration, and Growth', *Journal of Political Economy* **105**, pp. 582–608.

Brueckner, J.K. and Zenou, Y. (1999), 'Harris–Todaro Models with A Land Market', *Regional Science and Urban Economics* **29**, pp. 317–339.

Chan, K.W. (1988), 'Rural–urban Migration in China, 1950–1982: Estimates and Analysis', *Urban Geography* **9**, pp. 53–84.

Chan, K.W., Liu, T. and Yang, Y. (1999), 'Hukou and Non–hukou Migrations in China: Comparisons and Contrasts', *International Journal of Population Geography* **5**, pp. 425–448.

Coulson, N.E., Laing, D. and Wang, P. (2001), 'Spatial Mismatching in Search Equilibrium', *Journal of Labor Economics* **19**, pp. 949–972.

Diamond, P.A. (1982), 'Wage Determination and Efficiency in Search Equilibrium', *Review of Economic Studies* **49**, pp. 217–227.

Harris, J.R., and Todaro, M.P. (1970), 'Migration, Unemployment, and Development: A Two–Sector Analysis', *American Economic Review* **61**, pp. 126–141.

Helsley, R.W. and Strange, W. (1990), 'Matching and Agglomeration Economies in a System of Cities', *Regional Science and Urban Economics* **20**, pp. 189–222.

Kuznets, S. (1982), 'The Pattern of Shift of Labor Force from Agriculture, 1950–1970', in M. Gersoritz et al. (ed.), *The Theory and Experience of Economic Development*, George Allen & Unwin, London, UK, pp. 43–59.

Laing, D., Palivos, T. and Wang, P. (1995), 'Learning, Matching and Growth', *Review of Economic Studies* **62**, pp. 115–129.

Lewis, W.A. (1954), 'Economic Development with Unlimited Supplies of Labour', *Manchester School of Economic and Social Studies* **22**, pp. 131–191.

Park, C. (1999), 'Three Essays on Migration, Labor Market Performance and Economic Growth', Ph.D. Dissertation, The Pennsylvania State University, University Park, PA.

Pissarides, C.A. (1987), 'Search, Wage Bargains and Cycles', *Review of Economic Studies* **54**, pp. 473–483.

Scotese, C. and Wang, P. (1995), 'Can Government Enforcement Permanently Alter Fertility? The Case of China', *Economic Inquiry* **33**, pp. 552–570.

Todaro, M.P. (1969), 'A Model of Labor Migration and Urban Unemployment in Less Developed Countries', *American Economic Review* **60**, pp. 138–148.

Todaro, M.P. (1986), 'Internal Migration and Urban Employment: Comment/Reply', *American Economic Review* **77**, pp. 566–572.

Wan, G. (1995), 'Peasant Flood in China: Internal Migration and Its Policy Determinants', *Third World Quarterly* **16**, pp. 173–219.

Yang, X. (1993), 'Household Registration, Economic Reform and Migration', *International Migration Review* **27**, pp. 796–818.

Chapter 12

The 'Banker Effect' on Chinese Stock Pricing

Yuan Shu and Guoqiang Bin

Introduction

It is a hotspot of debate about the development of Chinese Stock Market among economists in China. The debating became more furious since the *Caijing* (Finance and Economy) magazine disclosed in October 2000 some inside stories of mutual funds, which told us how the mutual funds manipulated stock prices and cheated investors. Some famous Chinese economists, such as Wu Jinglian, Li Yining, Xiao Zhuoji, Dong Fureng, Xu Xiaonian, Justine Yifu Lin[1] and Zhang Weiying, held a serious debate[2] about the role of stock market, speculation, bubbles, high P/E ratio, 'banker' behaviors and the regulation of Chinese stock market. Despite they held different opinions, no one denied the fact that stock price manipulations of 'bankers' had extensive and important impact on stock pricing.

As a young emerging market, it is inevitable that Chinese stock market has many defects in institution, ownership structure, corporate governance, regulatory and pricing mechanism etc. Any of these defects may contribute to inefficient resource allocation. Stock price manipulation is now a public secret in China, though it is illegal by the law. Up till now the China Securities Regulatory Commission (CSRC) has no effective measures to prevent these behaviors.

Though it is well known that there are serious stock price manipulations in Chinese stock market, there are few theoretical and empirical researches on this topic. One explanation might be that it is difficult to measure the behavior of 'bankers' or test the 'banker effect' on stock price manipulates. Using the stock holder distribution data from Shenzhen Stock Exchange, Wu Qihua, Liu Jing and Rao Gang (2001) did some tentative work. They prove that share concentration, stock–holding proportion of the accounts with more than 100,000 shares of a listed company, is significantly related to the fluctuation of the stock price in a single factor regression model. But they did not give any theoretical explanation to this relationship.

In this chapter, the authors will use a theoretical model to discuss the pricing mechanism of the Chinese stock market. Based on descriptions of stock price manipulation behavior, we try to use share concentration as an indicator of 'banker behavior', develop a multiple factor pricing model to examine the 'banker effect'

Table 12.1 Large transaction distribution at Shenzhen Stock Exchange

Turnovers of large transactions/total turnovers[a]	*Number of companies*	*% of total listed companies*
<10%	315	63.0%
10%~20%	83	16.6%
20%~30%	56	11.2%
>30%	46	9.2%
Total	500	100.0%

[a] Transactions that exceed 100,000 Yuan.

Source: http://www.cninfo.com.cn.

on stock price and make further empirical investigation on the dynamic relationship of 'banker' behavior, share concentration, stock price and corporate performance.

The remainder of the chapter is as follows. The next part is a simple theoretical model. After this come empirical studies and the last part contains our conclusions.

A simple theoretical model

Stock 'bankers' in the Chinese stock market

The past 10 years has witnessed the miracle of the rapid growth of stock market in China. According to the March 2002 statistics of China Securities Regulatory Commission (CSRC), there are now 1171 listed companies and the total market capitalization is RMB 4305.05 billion among which RMB 1426.43 billion are tradable shares. The total number of investor accounts exceeds 67.31 million. The total stock exchange turnover during April 2001 to March 2002 was RMB 3613.75 billion. The average turnover of each investor was RMB 55,300 in one year, which shows that majority of the investors in Chinese stock market are small individual private investors. However, institutional investors grew rapidly and their transaction behaviors have important impacts on the stock pricing.

The stock 'banker' phenomenon is well known in China. The so–called stock 'bankers' are mainly some institutional investors with huge funds, who control large part of the tradable public A shares[3] of certain listed companies and manipulate the stock prices. These investors include some mutual funds, securities companies, listed companies, big state owned companies, private–raised funds, and some rich private investors. In most of the price manipulation cases, the banker is in collusion with the listed company. Though stock price manipulation is illegal in

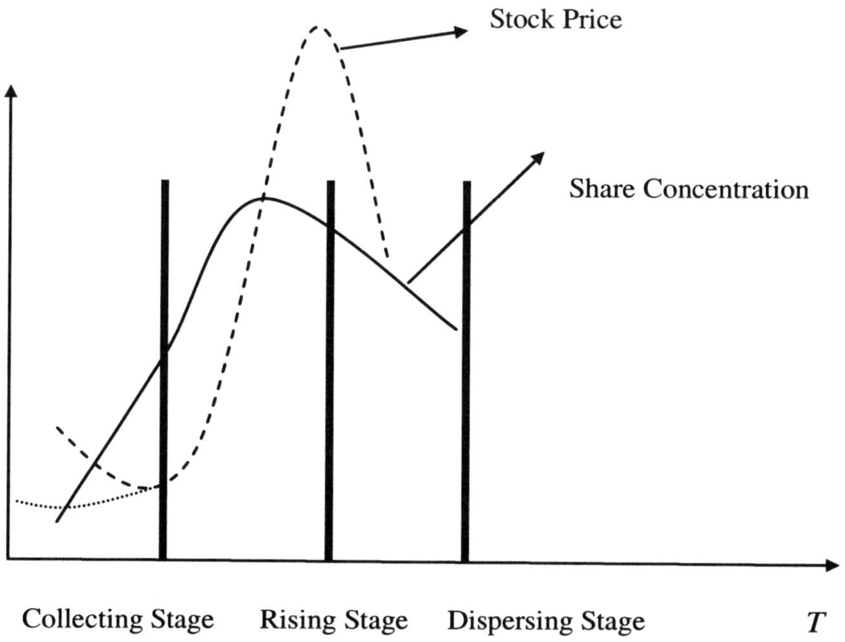

Figure 12.1 A typical stock price manipulation

China, the 'banker' phenomena are publicly discussed in all kinds of public media, or even in the chartered securities information disclosing media. Books discussing about how to find and follow the 'banker' are sold widely in China.

According to the statistics of Shenzhen Stock Exchange in August 2000, turnovers of many companies are brought about by large transaction orders exceeding 100,000 Yuan (see Table 12.1). The result shows that 'bankers' shape the stock prices of many companies.

How the 'Banker' manipulates the stock price?

A typical stock price manipulation process of the stock 'bankers' can be divided into three stages, i.e. collecting stage, rising stage and dispersing stage. (See Figure 12.1.)

Collecting stage In the first stage, the banker will stealthily buy a large proportion of the tradable A shares of a certain listed company it will manipulate, usually reaching 30%–70% of the total tradable shares. According to the Chinese securities law, a stock-holding company is obliged to disclose to public when its holding excesses 5% of the total share of a listed company. The banker will not buy all the stocks in a single share account but in a series of secret accounts to evade this regulation. In order to reduce the cost, stock price will not rise too much or even fall to a lower level at this stage by some low price sale and/or bad news about the company. The share concentration will rise gradually as the banker collects more shares.

Rising stage While the share concentration rises and the banker collects enough shares for price manipulation, it comes into the second stage—rising stage. In this stage, stock price rises sharply to a high level in a short period of time. As a large part of the tradable shares are under the control of the banker, it is not very difficult for him to raise the stock price. The more stocks under control, the easier for he/she to manipulate the price. Share concentration degree gets higher in this stage. The listed companies will disclose some 'good' news to allure other investors to buy the shares with a very high price.

Dispersing stage The banker has huge profit at the rising stage, though the profit is not realized. In order to realize the profit, he has to sell the shares to other investors. While the price is high, the banker will gradually sell out his shares. When most of the stock shares go to a large number of scattered investors, share concentration and stock price will both fall.

A simple theoretical model

Based on the consumption–based asset model, we develop a simple theoretical model to explain the pricing mechanism in Chinese stock market. In a two period model, the investor is to maximize his utility under his income constraint.

$$\max u(c_t, c_{t+1}) \; or \; \max_{\{\xi\}} u(c_t) + \beta E_t[u(c_{t+1})]$$

$$s.t.$$

$$c_t = e_t - p_t \xi$$

$$c_{t+1} = e_{t+1} - x_{t+1} \xi$$

where β is the discount factor; e is investor's income; ξ is the amount that investor invests on asset; p is the asset price; x is the total revenue including asset price and the dividend ($x_{t+1} = p_{t+1} + d_{t+1}$). Solving this optimal problem, we get the following result

$$p_t = E_t[\beta \frac{u'(c_{t+1})}{u'(c_t)} x_{t+1}] = E_t[\beta \frac{u'(c_{t+1})}{u'(c_t)} (p_{t+1} + d_{t+1})].$$

Obviously, stock price is determined by the expectation of stock price at the next stage and the cash dividend. In an infinite model, we get a similar result

$$p_t = E_t \sum_{j=0}^{\infty} [\beta^j \frac{u'(c_{t+j})}{u'(c_t)} d_{t+j}].$$

Stock price is determined by the cash dividends expectation only. The result is useful in a mature market. When it goes to the case of Chinese stock market, the situation is very different.

Due to the special ownership structure and inefficiency of corporate governance, the life cycle of listed company is rather short and cash dividends are seldom adopted. According to the statistics,[4] the total transaction costs, stamp duties and transaction commissions of security exchanges in China were more than RMB 90 billion in 2000, while the total profits of all the listed companies were about RMB 80 billion and cash dividends were less than RMB 10 billion. The cash dividends are not enough to compensate the transaction costs. It means that it was a negative sum game in Chinese stock exchanges.

It is impossible for an investor to make profit by holding the stock for a long period of time. People buy stocks and just expect to sell them at a higher price at a later stage. Suppose the stocks are to sell at time $t + s$, we revise the pricing equation as following

$$p_t = E_t \sum_{j=0}^{s} [\beta^j \frac{u'(c_{t+j})}{u'(c_t)} d_{t+j}] + E_t [\beta^s \frac{u'(c_{t+s})}{u'(c_t)} p_{t+s}].$$

As the dividends are less important in Chinese stock market, stock price is mainly determined by the expectation of stock price at time $t + s$. In the weakly regulated market, manipulation is the most effective way to change the expectation of stock price.

Following the above analysis on banker behavior, share concentration and stock pricing, we introduce a share concentration Ω in the theoretical model

$$p_t(\Omega_t) = E_t \sum_{j=0}^{s} [\beta^j \frac{u'(c_{t+j})}{u'(c_t)} d_{t+j}] + E_t [\beta^s \frac{u'(c_{t+s})}{u'(c_t)} p_{t+s}(\Omega_{t+s})].$$

where $\partial p / \partial \Omega > 0$.

We uses share concentration Ω as an indicator of 'banker behavior' to test stock price manipulation in Chinese stock market. To examine the robustness of our theoretical model, we develop a multiple regression model to estimate the 'banker effect' of share concentration on stock pricing by using cross section data. The econometric model is

$$p_i = \beta H_i + \alpha E_i + \lambda NV_i + \varphi LQ_i + \varepsilon,$$

H_t: share concentration,

Table 12.2 The share concentration of listed companies at Shenzhen

	H_1	H_2	H_3	H_4
Mean	47.29	3.16	49.28	18.83
Median	26.11	2.03	45.75	12.50
Max	1221.89	48.58	98.59	92.74
Min	8.02	0.83	12.70	0.58
Standard Deviation	87.80	3.68	20.01	17.06
Observations	501	501	501	501

Source: The website of SZ Stock Exchange http://www.cninfo.com.cn.

E_t : earning per share,
NV_t : net asset per share,
LQ_t : logarithm of total tradable A shares of the listed company.

The latter three variables are control variables. E_t and NV_t reflect the company fundamentals of profitability and net asset value. LQ_t indicates the size of the listed company and the feasibility of price manipulation.

Empirical studies

The sample data of our empirical studies are from the website of SZ Stock Exchange. They are data of the total 501 listed companies of different industries and regions at Shenzhen Stock Exchange, which is one of the two stock exchanges in China. Our sample is a well proxy of the whole stock market in China. We build 4 indicators to measure the share concentration of tradable A share of listed companies at Shenzhen Stock Exchange. (Look at Table 12.2.)

H_1: Average market value of tradable A shares of a stock holder/1,000.
H_2: Average number of tradable A shares of a stock holder/1,000.
H_3: Cumulative holding proportion of stock holders who have more than 10,000 shares.
H_4: Cumulative holding proportion of stock holders who have more than 100,000 shares.

From Table 12.2, we see that share concentration of the listed companies at Shenzhen Exchange differs widely. Take H_2 as an example, the most concentrated list company has average 48,580 shares in each investor account while the most

Table12.3 The most concentrated 15 listed companies at Shenzhen

Code	*Company*	*Shareholders*	*H2*	*H4*	*H3*
0549	Xiang Huo Ju A	3,421	48.58	71.669	98.587
0633	He Jin Tou Zi	2,325	37.38	57.551	97.588
0012	Shen Nan Bo A	5,941	17.97	92.737	96.104
0510	Jin Lu Ji Tuan	12,502	15.45	62.883	94.932
0602	ST Jin Ma	2,302	18.93	14.609	94.377
0702	Zheng Hong Si Liao	4,205	15.45	20.045	93.952
0425	Xu Gong Ke Ji	9,564	12.68	41.427	93.833
0627	Bai Ke Yao Ye	4,829	15.11	20.057	93.158
0885	Chun Du A	3,270	18.35	78.290	92.542
0540	Shi Ji Zhong Tian	4,821	13.74	25.825	92.077
0557	Yin Guang Xia A	17,520	16.03	68.103	91.948
0881	Da Lian Guo Ji	5,709	12.87	40.315	91.937
0028	Shen Yi Li A	4,930	11.11	76.266	91.473
0048	Zhong Ke Chuang Ye	14,783	7.72	61.099	91.295
0801	Si Chuan Hu Shan	3,838	7.88	57.769	91.045

dispersed one has only 830 shares. As for H_4, for a dispersed company large shareholders only possess 0.58% of the total tradable shares, while 92.74% of the total tradable shares are under the control of several large shareholders in the most concentrated case. For the 67 million stock investors in China, majority of them are small individual private investors and it is impossible for them to hold 100,000 shares of one company or do such a big transaction.

Table 12.3 shows us 15 the most concentrated listed companies at Shenzhen Stock Exchange. Most of them were 'famous' stars in the market. Most of their tradable shares were under the control of several large shareholders and their prices rose a lot during the past several years, some were even 10 times more than their original price level, such as Xiang Huo JU A and He Jin Tou Zi which were controlled by the most powerful banker in China—the Delong Group. Zhong Ke Chuang Ye and Yin Guang Xia were the two famous security–cheating scandals. Many investors suffered great loss from the collapse of these companies.

Static stock pricing model

The static model will not tell you whether a stock price is over–valued or under–valued. The purpose of the static stock pricing model is to test whether share concentration has significant impact on stock price. The empirical results in Table 12.4 show that our theoretical analysis is correct.

Table 12.4 Static stock pricing model[5]

Dependent Variables	*P*	*P*	*P*	*P*
Constant	94.44	97.89	92.96	99.55
	(21.62)	(21.38)	(19.43)	(21.64)
E	3.65	3.85	3.74	3.58
	(4.51)	(4.51)	(4.31)	(4.16)
NV	0.87	0.89	0.87	0.82
	(7.97)	(7.69)	(7.44)	(7.09)
LQ	–4.65	–4.85	–4.57	–4.54
	(–19.46)	(–19.36)	(–18.67)	(–19.60)
H_1	0.0020	-	-	-
	(10.88)	-	-	-
H_2	-	0.356	-	-
	-	(7.67)	-	-
H_3	-	-	0.056	-
	-	-	(6.42)	-
H_4	-	-	-	0.072
	-	-	-	(7.19)
R^2	0.57	0.52	0.51	0.52
Adjusted R^2	0.56	0.52	0.50	0.51
F	159.00	131.17	122.92	127.85
D. W.	1.73	1.78	1.87	1.89
Obs.	482	482	482	482

Note: The stock prices were the closing prices at 29 Jun, 2001. All the variables pass the 1% significant test.

(1) Share concentration has significant positive impact on stock pricing.
(2) The impact of company fundamentals such earning and net asset is also significant in the static model. Though speculation factors are very important, the Chinese market is not completely irrational.
(3) The size of tradable A share of the listed company is significant but negative. The smaller the companies are, the easier they can be manipulated.

As many factors can influence stock price, we are satisfied with the R–squared at 0.5 level. The explaining power of the endogenous variables is robust and appropriate.

Dynamic relationship of share concentration, stock price and corporate performance

The static model can be used to test the static 'banker effect' on stock price. It

Table12.5 Relationship between changes of share concentration and price

Dependent Variables	*DP(%)*	
	Coefficient	t–test value
DN	–0.67	–10.31
C	50.68	12.72
DN^2	0.00	7.48
DN^3	–9.82E–06	–6.26
DN^4	5.83E–09	5.55
R^2	0.37	-
Adjusted R^2	0.36	-
D. W.	1.62	–
Obs.	211	-

Note: DN is the percentage change of the number of shareholders during 2000 and DP is the percentage change of stock price at the same period.

cannot reveal the dynamic process of stock price manipulation. We build another model to test the dynamic 'banker effect' on stock price.

From Table 12.5, we found that as the number of stockholder reduces, the share concentration increases and the stock price rises sharply. The more changes of the number of shareholders (DN), the more changes of the stock price (DP). The result is accord with our theoretical analysis in the second part.

Someone may argue that changes of share concentration may not necessarily reflect price manipulation. Institutional investors may buy stocks according to private information of company fundamentals. In order to test these assumptions, we run another regression to test the relationship between changes of share concentration and company performance. We found that there is no significant relation between these two variables. (Table 12.6.)

Due to the limitation of data, it is impossible to examine all aspects of stock price manipulations. And the robustness of our conclusions is limited and it will be examined in further studies.

Conclusion

In this chapter, we used share concentration as an indicator of 'banker behavior' to test stock price manipulation in Chinese stock market. We found that banker behavior has significant effects on stock pricing in the static model; the changes

Table 12.6 Relationship between changes of share concentration and company performance

Dependent Variables	*DE(%)*	
	Coefficients	t–test values
DN	0.13	0.45
C	–33.37	–0.69
R^2	0.0015	-
D. W.	5.53	-
Obs.	135	-

Note: DE is the percentage change of earning per share in 2000. DN is the same indicator as the above.

of share concentration result in changes of stock price; the relationship between share concentration and the performance of listed company is not significant. Our results show that price manipulations do exist in Chinese stock market and that price manipulation is not based on the fundamentals of listed companies. As the pricing mechanism in China is distorted by vicious manipulations, the resource allocation efficiency of stock market is greatly reduced. What Mr. Wu Jinglian worried about is justified. The government should improve the regulatory mechanism to fight for securities cheating and manipulation.

Unless the market behaviors change drastically, our results also make sense in investment decision–making. Generally speaking, stock price will not rise too much without institutional investors playing a major role in the trading. Share concentration gives us a good hint to judge the transaction timing. If the share concentration is low, it will be too early to buy the stock. If it is too high, the banker is ready to sell his stocks at any time and investors should be careful of the danger of buying this kind of stocks. The optimal strategy is to buy stocks that have passed collecting stage and is going to the rising stage.

The share concentration is also a good indicator for the regulatory authority to regulate the manipulations behaviors. By taking a close look at the most concentrated stocks and their relative accounts, the authority can find illegal trading behaviors and take timely action.

Notes

1 From http://www.ccer.edu.cn the discussing series of 'the prospects and worries of Chinese Securities Market'.

2 The debate is described in Wu (2001) *Shi Nian Fen Yun Hua Gu Shi* (Papers on

diverse and confused Stock Market in the Past Ten Years).

3 Stocks listed at Shanghai and Shenzhen Stock Exchange can be classified into A shares and B share. A shares are for domestic Chinese investors. B shares are for foreign investors, investors invested in USD in Shanghai Exchange and HKD in Shenzhen Exchange. A shares can be divided into three categories, state–owned shares, legal person shares and tradable A shares. Only the tradable A shares can be exchanged at the stock exchanges.

4 Data from CSRC.

5 All the empirical studies are calculated with Eviews 3.1.

References

Chen, D., Zhou, C., Xiao, L., and Peng, C. (1996), 'Research on Stock Pricing in Capital Market', *China Management Science* **4**, pp. 9–17.

James, F. and Walter, R. (2000), *Portfolio Management: Theory and Application (Chinese Version)*, Machine Industry Publishing Company.

Liu, B. (1997), *Empirical Research on China Securities Market*, Xuelin Publishing Company.

Lu, Y. (2000), *Teltham–Ohlson Valuation Model & the Value–relevance of P/B and P/E*, Shanghai Sanlian Publishing Company.

Ma, S.I., Song, L. and Wang, W. (2000), 'An Empirical Research on the Factors that Affect Stock Price in Shanghai Stock Market', *Statistics Research* **8**, pp. 24–28.

Mackay, C. and Vega, J. (2000), *Extraordinary Popular Delusions and the Madness of Crowds (Chinese Version)*, Hainan Publishing Company.

Wu, J. (2001), *Shi Nian Fen Yun Hua Gu Shi*, Shanghai Far East Publishing Company.

Wu, Q., Jing, L. and Gang, R. (2001), 'An Empirical Research on the Relationship between Share Concentration Degree and Stock Price Fluctuation', *Securities Market Herald* **6**, pp. 4–9.

Chapter 13

China's Food Economy and Its Implications for the Rest of the World

Ninghui Li

Introduction

It is well known that China's rapid economic development in the past two decades is unparalleled in recent world history. From 1978 to 1999, China's real average annual GDP growth rate was 9.14 percent, making it one of the fastest–growing economies in the world. Real agricultural GDP growth rate was 5.92 percent. Its foreign trade expanded more rapidly than its overall economic growth. With the rapid growth of external sector, foreign trade has been playing a big role in the national economy since reforms started in the late 1970s. The real annual growth rate of the total value of China's foreign trade was 14.59 percent in 1978–99, and the ratio of trade to GDP increased from 9.8 percent in 1978 to 32.8 percent in 1999. China is already the world's fifth–largest trading country in terms of trade volume, and the second largest recipient of foreign investment for several years. China's population, which stood at 1.259 billion in 1999, is expected to reach nearly 1.43 billion people by 2020. Recent economic reform brought about accelerating income growth. As a result, demand for food, particularly meat, grew – and continues to grow. The increase in demand for meat has, in turn, accelerated the demand for feed grain.

National strategy, therefore, aims to increase national grain production as well meat production. In line with the strategy, a policy environment geared toward increasing production has implications on sustainable agricultural development in accordance with comparative advantage as determined by the market forces. However, the ratio of world prices to domestic prices of agricultural commodities affects comparative advantage, food security and overall economy performance. Also, the impact of market forces that induce production (in accordance with comparative advantage) and efficient allocation of resources depends not only on the level of liberalization in the international trade but also on the level of liberalization in the domestic market. The policy issues and options facing China are, therefore, complex.

The sheer size of its economy, its rapid growth, and its increasing integration into the global economy will make China a crucial player in the future development of world markets for inputs and outputs of agricultural activities. Small adjustments in China's agricultural supply and demand may have significant implications on world agricultural trade and its trading partners. This will make China's long–term agricultural supply, demand, and trade activities an issue of both national and international significance.

More attention should therefore be focused on the supply, demand and trade of agricultural commodities, on the analysis of how and to what extent China's agricultural policy can affect its national food balance and developments in the world market, and how China's food market responds to changes in the world market.

In order to realize these objectives, China's Agricultural Policy Simulation Model (CAPSiM) is used which can comprehensively and simultaneously account for the major driving forces and policies determining China's domestic food demand and supply.[1] The influence of the linkages of China's economy with the rest of the world is examined by linking Global Trade Analysis Project (GTAP) and CAPSiM in two scenarios, i.e., the baseline scenario and the WTO scenario, to be described in detail below.

CAPSiM and GTAP

CAPSiM (China's Agricultural Policy Simulation Model)

China's Agricultural Policy Simulation Model (CAPSiM) is an equilibrium model within the agricultural sector. CAPSiM is a formal framework that has been regularly used for agricultural commodity projection and policy simulation, including agricultural sector wide and commodity specific policies, and macroeconomic and trade policies.

Most of the elasticities and parameters used in CAPSiM are estimated econometrically with imposition of theoretical constraints. In the projection or policy simulation, prices can be determined endogenously or exogenously. The model explicitly accounts for urbanization and market development (demand side), technology, agricultural investment, environmental trends and competition for labor and land use (supply side), as well as the price responses of both demand and supply. The model can be used for both main short–run and long–run policy simulation and projection for key agricultural variables in response to the changes in exogenous shocks to the economy. It is also designed for analyzing the likely impact of specific policies on key variables such as crop's sown area, yield, production, prices, consumption, commodity demand and its components (food, feed and other use), stock, and export and import for about 20 agricultural commodities or commodity groups.

GTAP[2]

The Global Trade Analysis Project (GTAP) was established with the objective of supporting the analysis of international trade, environment, and resource issues in an economy–wide context. GTAP consists of several components:

- A global database,
- A standard modeling framework,
- Software for manipulating the data and implementing the standard model,
- A global network of researchers with a common interest in multi–region trade analysis, and
- A consortium of 18 national and international agencies providing support and relationship.

GTAP model and its database are based on input–output tables provided by each country. The latest released version of GTAP is version 5 that contains 57 sectors and 66 regions. This version of GTAP contains a CGE module for China. The main contribution of this model in GTAP has been identified to add the international trade dimension between China and its trading partners and to provide the overall global background for scenario analysis.

The linkage between CAPSiM and GTAP

The partial equilibrium price of agriculture products with trade Figure 13.1 shows the interactive response between China's food market and world food market in partial equilibrium model when the markets are linked. This theoretical mechanism is not only embodied in trade sub–model of CAPSiM, but is also realized in the linkage of CAPSiM and GTAP for simulation and projection.

Suppose that, in the absence of trade, China produces and consumes at point A at P1 in Panel A, while Rest of the World produces and consumes at point A' at P3 in panel C. Panel B represents trade market in the world. With the opening of trade, the price of agriculture products in the world market will be somewhere between P1 and P3 since China is a large country.

Assume that the production of agriculture products in China increases and that in the rest of the world, production is still at the same level as before. Then, the supply curve in panel A will shift from SC to SC', and in turn, the supply curve in panel B will shift from SW to SW' because China will export more and the equilibrium price in the world market goes down from the price at E* to the price at E*'.

The decrease in world market will induce less export from China, more import into China, increase in Chinese consumption and decrease in Chinese food production, so that, in panel A, the supply curve will shift inward and demand curve shift outward. These shifts will induce changes in world market again. These two markets will interact continually until a new equilibrium point is reached. A similar analysis can be done whenever there is some change in the demand in China, as well as some changes in the supply and/or demand in the rest of the world.

Therefore, given the fact that China is not a price–taker in the world market, the price of agriculture products in the world market will be subject to change endogenously in order to reach the equilibrium point of the market whenever there is some change in the supply of or demand for agriculture products in the world market.

Table 13.1 Linkage between two models

	CAPSiM	*GTAP*
Output	Import and export by commodity (to GTAP) Production and various consumption (household demand, feed, seed, industry use and waste) by commodity Population (total, urban and rual) Income (urban and rural) Agriculture research expenditure Agriculture research stock Investment in irrigation Rural wage	QXW and QIW (by CAPSiM commodity and to CAPSiM for China) GDP EV (welfare) Value change by commodity Price change by commodity Quantity change by commodity
Input	Growth rates of world prices by commodities which will be imposed on by percentage changes in world price index for total good i supplies (PW) (from GTAP) Exchange rate assumption Consumer's and producer's subsidy equivalence assumption NTB assumption Growth rate of population (total, urban and rural) Growth rate of real income (urban and rural) Growth rate of agriculture research expenditure Growth rate of investment in irrigation Growth rate of market development Inflation rate (national, urban and rural) Various elasticities and other parameters Erosion and salinity assumption Price policy assumption Grain stock policy assumption	Percentage changes in aggregate imports of product i into China (QIW), CIF weights, and aggregate exports of product i from China (QXW), FOB weights Growth rates of real GDP (all regions) Growth rates of skilled and unskilled labor (all regions) Growth rate of population (all regions) Growth rates of TFP (Total Factor Productivity) (all regions) Growth rates of capital (all regions)
Comparison	The trend of change in production, trade, consumption and welfare, etc.	

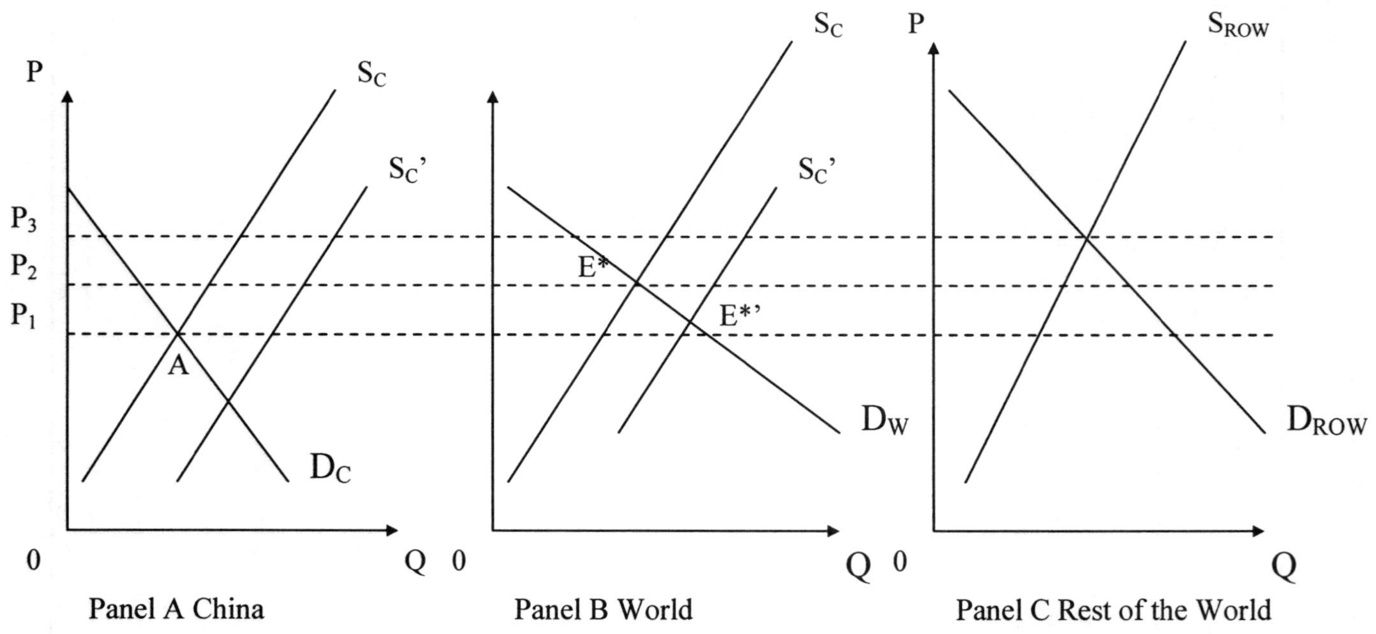

Figure 13.1 The partial equilibrium price of agriculture products with trade

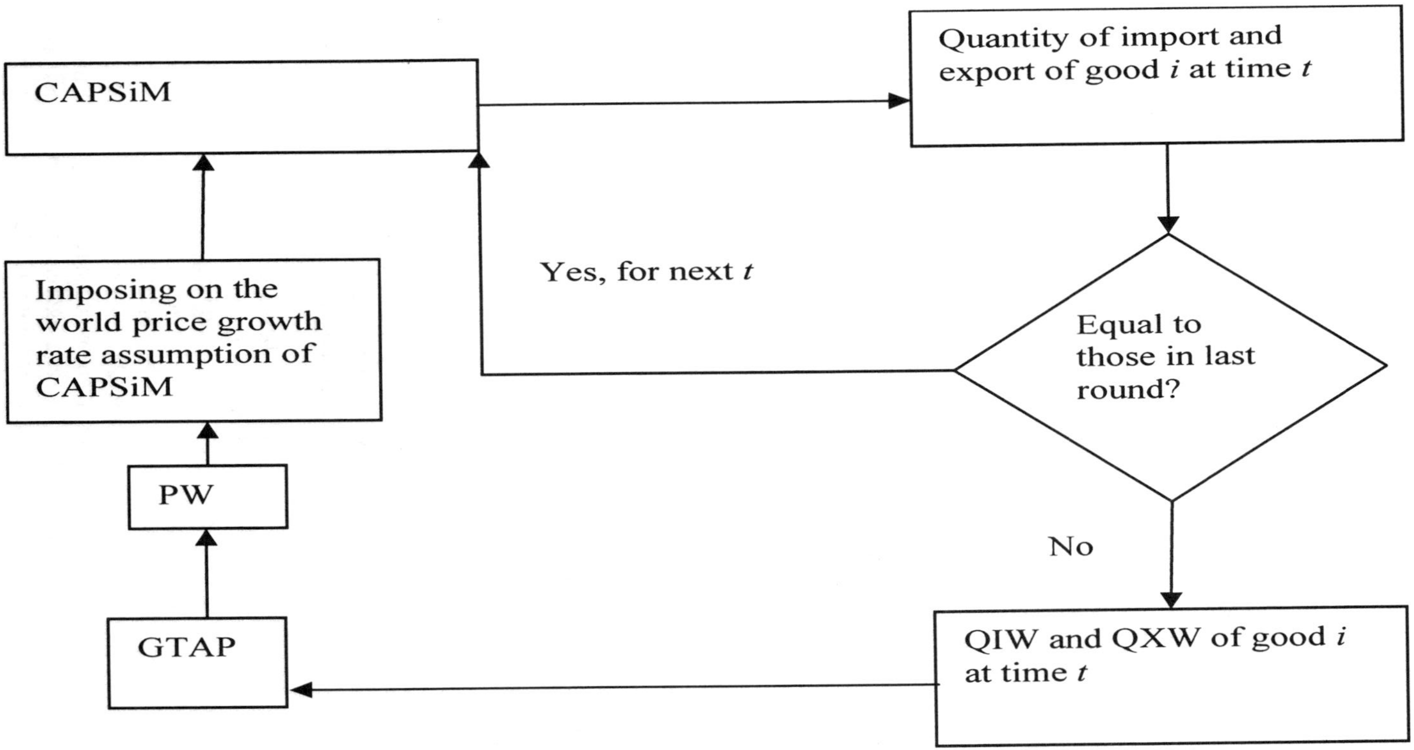

Figure 13.2 **Iterative linkage between the two models (t=2005, 2010, 2015, 2020)**

Table 13.2 Assumption of population growth rate in baseline scenario

	Nation	*Urban*	*Rural*
2000	0.81	2.4017	0.1228
2001	0.77	2.3896	0.0548
2002	0.7434	2.3776	0.005
2003	0.7309	2.3656	–0.0253
2004	0.7184	2.3535	–0.0561
2005	0.7059	2.3415	–0.0875
2006	0.6871	2.3355	–0.1319
2007	0.6778	2.3204	–0.1585
2008	0.6684	2.3054	–0.1858
2009	0.659	2.2903	–0.2134
2010	0.6496	2.2752	–0.2416
2011	0.6697	2.3059	–0.2499
2012	0.6456	2.2679	–0.2896
2013	0.6214	2.23	–0.3297
2014	0.5973	2.1921	–0.3698
2015	0.5732	2.1542	–0.4102
2016	0.5643	2.1373	–0.4393
2017	0.5325	2.0889	–0.4862
2018	0.5008	2.0404	–0.533
2019	0.4691	1.992	–0.58
2020	0.4373	1.9435	–0.6271

GTAP aggregation There are 66 regions, 57 sectors and 5 factors in the GTAP database version 5, which are mapped into 12 new regions, 17 new sectors and 5 factors in this study, respectively. The 12 new regions aggregated are: China, Hong Kong, Taiwan, Japan and Korea, South East Asia, Other Asia countries, Australia and New Zealand, NAFTA, South and Central American, EU, Central and Eastern Europe, and the rest of the World. The 17 new sectors aggregated are: rice (including paddy and processed), wheat, coarse grains, oil seeds and vegetable oils, sugar raw and processed, plant based fibers, other crops, cattle and red meat, pig and poultry, raw milk and dairy products, fish, other food products, natural resources and extracts, textile and leather, labor intensive manufacturing, capital intensive manufacturing, and services and other activities. The 5 factors are: land, unskilled labor, skilled labor, capital, and natural resources.

Linkage Both CAPSiM and GTAP will be run based on two scenarios: baseline and WTO framework. Assumptions used in each scenario for China are the same across the models. Growth rates of real GDP, labor and capital endowments will be used in the two models as exogenous variables. Figure 13.1 gives the theoretical framework of linking China's food market and world food market. To put this framework into practice in this article, firstly, CAPSiM estimates the quantities of import and export of good i and delivers percentage changes in aggregate imports of product i into China (QIW), CIF weights, and aggregate exports of product i from China (QXW), FOB weights. These feed into GTAP. The most crucial component is that GTAP delivers percentage changes in world price index for total product i supplies (PW), this feeds into CAPSiM as an exogenous variable and is imposed on the world price index in CAPSiM. Subsequently, a CAPSiM run results in import and export volumes again. These feed into GTAP, etc., until convergence is achieved. The flow chart given in Figure 13.2 describes this procedure.

Baseline projection serves as the reference point for the scenarios. As such, it is a very important element. It establishes a view of the future, starting from the present situation and taking current policies into account. Since the subsequent scenarios consist mainly of imposed policy changes during the projections period, the quality and features of the baseline are very important. Table 13.1 summarizes the procedure.

Simulation and projection

Baseline scenario

CAPSiM Income growth and population growth will remain important determinants of food balance in the future. Population growth of China peaked in the late 1960s and early 1970s. Since then, fertility rate and the nature rate of population growth have begun to fall. The growth rates of population from 2000 to 2020 in urban and rural areas, and the nation as a whole, are inferred by using moving average method based on World Bank's estimation and listed in Table 13.2. According to this projection, the growth rate of population in the urban areas is much higher than that in the rural areas due to the urbanization trend in China resulting from its economic development. The share of urban population will rise from 31.4 percent in 2000, to 34.0 percent in 2005, 36.9 percent in 2010, and 43.1 percent in 2020.

Baseline per capita income growth rate is forecasted at an average rate of about 4 percent in rural areas and 4.5 percent in urban areas. Growth rate in the late 1980s and the early 1990s was substantially above this level in the urban economy (around 6–7 percent), and significantly below this in rural areas (less than 1 percent per year between 1985 and 1992). However, in recent years the overheated urban grow has slowed, and rural economy has begun to pull out of its recession, growing at 4 percent per year since 1991.

China is a country with a vast agricultural base, as well as a vast population. Agricultural security—food security in particular—is a pressing issue. China bases its agricultural policies on domestic agricultural supply, especially on balances supply and demand of grains. Meanwhile, China actively sought international resources as a necessary supplement. In terms of these policies, China made extensive use of price controls in the agricultural sector for a long time. During the continued reform of China's price system, however, the share of government prices has dropped substantially and that of market–regulated prices has increased. At present, for agricultural products, the share of government prices is 9.1 percent, government guidance prices, 7.1 percent, and market–regulated prices, 83.3

percent. Products used in CAPSiM that are subject to government guidance pricing include wheat, maize, rice, soybean, soybean oil, and cotton.

Due to the price policies, the prices of agricultural products are less responsive to changes in the world markets. In the baseline scenario, the prices will be endogenously determined, assuming the current trade policy (tariff levels and non–tariff–restrictions) remains.

Supply will primarily respond to prices, new technology and irrigation investment. The fertilizer price is assumed to be constant in the projection period, but the opportunity costs of land for crop production and labor for the whole agricultural sector are assumed to grow at 1 percent and 2 percent, respectively.

Technological change significantly contributed to China's agricultural growth in the past (Huang and Rozelle 1996; Fan and Pardey 1997). However, annual expenditures on research declined from 1985 to 1990, and irrigation expenditure dropped from 1975 to 1985. Because of the lagging effects, these early investment decreases will keep baseline projections of investment growth below histories' rate in the early projection period. The recent recovery in research and irrigation investment, together with the experience of other Asian countries and China's commitment to a strong domestic grain economy, lead to the expectation that China will sustain its recent upturn in investment funding over the long run. The annual growth rates of research and irrigation expenditure are assumed to be 4 percent and 3.5 percent, respectively. Erosion and salinization are expected to increase continually at a steady but slow pace, that is, both the ratio of erosion area to total land area and the ration of salinity area to cultivate area are assumed to reach 0.2 percent.

GTAP Table 13.3 lists the main assumptions used in GTAP.

WTO scenario

Based on the agreements signed, the changes in Table 13.4 and Table 13.5 will be included in the Consumer and Producer Subsidy Equivalence assumption, taking account of variables compatibility between the two models.

In this scenario, commodity price in the domestic market and commodity border price will be compared, and the former will be exogenously forced to change annually to be equal to the latter in 2005 in terms of the WTO framework. Border prices imply two kinds of prices: CIF world prices for importable and FOB world prices for exportable.

Results of simulation and projection

Baseline scenario

This is done based on the assumptions and procedure given above for 2005, 2010, 2015, and 2020.

Table 13.3 Assumption of growth rates in baseline scenario (percentage change)

Region	Period	China	H.K.	Taiwan	Jap/Korea	SEA	Oth Asia	Aus/Nzl	Nafta	SAM	EU	CEEC	ROW
Real GDP	00–05	7.8	4.525	3.6	1.192	4.55	5.05	3.233	2.605	2.925	2.475	4.25	2.65
	06–10	7.66	4.42	4.82	2.288	5.0	5.3	2.846	2.823	3.9	2.5	3.4	2.9
	11–15	7.51	4.1	4.8	2.6	5.277	5.1	2.76	2.581	3.5	2.7	3.5	2.93
	16–20	7.3	4.0	4.4	2.2	5.27	4.97	2.74	2.399	2.938	2.6	3.3	2.4
Unskilled labor	00–05	0.514	0	0.332	–0.698	1.903	2.011	–0.36	0.122	1.628	–1.03	–0.561	1.021
	06–10	0.423	0.037	0.302	–0.764	1.834	1.96	–0.268	0.284	1.573	–0.873	–0.498	1.068
	11–15	0.195	0.053	0.204	–0.792	1.574	1.908	–0.269	0.234	1.493	–0.726	–0.406	1.046
	16–20	–0.047	0.21	0.123	–0.441	1.041	1.811	–0.3	0.259	1.372	–0.524	–0.271	1.131
Skilled labor	00–05	3.6	3.9	3.7	3.47	2.97	3.53	3.41	2.94	3.87	3.17	2.82	3.4
	06–10	3.86	3.05	3.2	2.95	3.03	3.62	2.89	2.5	3.82	2.42	2.19	2.82
	11–15	3.9	2.1	2.69	1.83	3.08	3.71	2.36	2.06	3.77	1.67	1.56	2.61
	16–20	3.95	1.2	2.19	1.3	3.24	3.9	1.94	1.55	3.73	1.01	0.92	2.02
Population	00–05	0.731	0.7	0.71	0.062	1.235	1.4	0.767	0.904	1.3	–0.1	0.41	1.36
	06–10	0.668	0.567	0.577	0.032	1.035	1.37	0.667	0.744	1.27	–0.13	0.38	1.33
	11–15	0.621	0.433	0.443	0.012	0.835	1.34	0.567	0.584	1.24	–0.16	0.35	1.31
	16–20	0.501	0.3	0.31	–0.018	0.635	1.31	0.467	0.424	1.21	–0.19	0.32	1.29
TFP	00–20	1.8	0.25	0.7	0.3	0.16	1.38	0.81	1.19	0.68	1.05	0.9	0.53
Capital	00–05	12.4	3.3	3.3	–1.129	4.219	6.2	2.145	3.798	4.8	2.433	6.09	2.7
	06–10	10.8	3.9	3.9	–0.201	5.126	5.8	4.1	4.387	3.4	2.1	6.5	4.0
	11–15	10.0	4.0	4.0	0.598	4.656	5.3	3.406	3.449	1.9	1.7	6.4	3.3
	16–20	9.9	3.8	3.8	0.5	4.2	5	3.3	3.4	1.8	1.6	6.3	3.2

Note: Unskilled labor growth rates are inferred from skilled labor growth rates by referencing total labor growth rate. Let SUnSkilled be the share of unskilled labors in total labors, SSkilled the share of skilled labors in total labors, RUnSkilled, RSkilled and RLabor the growth rates of unskilled labors, skilled labors and total labors, respectively. Then, we have SUnSkilled * (1+ RUnSkilled) + SSkilled * (1+ RSkilled) = (1+ RLabor).

Table 13.4 Tariff reduction for agricultural products used

Commodity	*Present*	*Protocol in*	*Commodity*	*Present*	*Protocol in*
Rice	1%	1%	Sugar	30%	15%
Wheat	1%	1%	Vegetable	13%	13%
Maize	1%	1%	Pork	20%	12%
Sweet Potato	13%	13%	Beef	45%	12%
Potato	13%	13%	Mutton	23%	12%
Other Coarse	3%	3%	Poultry	20%	10%
Soybeans	3%	3%	Eggs	25%	10%
Cotton	3%	3%	Milk	45%	10%
Edible oil	13%	9%	Fish	15%	10%

The linkage between the world market and China's food market In terms of the linkage given above, we can calculate the percentage change in the quantity of commodity import into and export from China, and the percentage change in the world price index, given the baseline scenario assumptions. We can also incorporate the two percentage changes to calculate percentage changes in commodity import into and export from China with respect to a unit of percentage changes in world price, listed in the following two tables, in order to analyze more closely the linkage between world food market and China's food market.

The ratios in Table 13.6 show how much percentage change in the quantity of commodity i imported into China occurs in order to reach new equilibrium whenever there is a 1 percent change in the world price induced by the change in the quantity of the commodity import into China. Similarly, the ratios in Table 13.7 show how much percentage change in the quantity of commodity i exported from China occurs in order to reach new equilibrium whenever there is a 1 percent change in the world price induced by the change in the quantity of the commodity export from China. These ratios give the direction and amount of adjustments in order to settle the markets in China and in the world at new equilibrium for all the agricultural products.

These ratios show the high sensitivity of China's agricultural products trade to the world market. However, such a high sensitivity does not make that much sense to China's food market because of the low ratios of trade to productions and trade to consumptions of these agricultural products. It also does not make that much sense to the world market price index, similarly because of the low quantity of agricultural products traded in the world market in the baseline scenario, which is based on the real economy at present. Nevertheless, we see that the absolute values of the ratios given in Tables 13.6 and 13.7 will decrease as the quantities traded in the world market increase. This trend represents the diminishing marginal utility trade.

Is China's food production enough to meet its demand in the future? The projections of production and consumption given by CAPSiM with baseline

Table 13.5 Tariff rate quota for major bulk agricultural commodities

Commodities	*TRQ in 2000 (MMT)*	*TRQ in 2005 (MMT)*	*TRQ tariff rate (%)*	*Preferential tariff rate (%)*
Rice	2.6	5.3	1.00	65.00
Wheat	7.3	9.3	1.00	114.00
Maize	4.5	7.2	1.00	114.00
Cotton	0.743	0.894	3.00	67.00
Edible oil	3.4	3.3	13.00	121.60

assumptions show that:[3]

(1) There are 9 products in which production is greater than consumption: rice, wheat, sweet potato, soybean, pork, mutton, eggs, milk, and fish.
(2) There are 2 products in which production is less than consumption: other coarse grains, cotton.
(3) There are 6 products in which production is nearly equal to consumption: maize, potato, edible oil, sugar, vegetable, and beef.
(4) There is 1 product, i.e., poultry, in which production surpasses consumption before year 2009, and after that, consumption surpasses production.

Other coarse grains are mainly used in the food processing industry and as feed in the livestock sectors. They are not Chinese staple. Therefore, their shortage does not make much difference to Chinese daily life. The shortage of domestic supply of edible oils also mainly results from the increasing demand from the food processing industry. China imports cotton as an intermediate good into the textile industry. The imported cheaper cotton lowers the prices of textile and leather, making China's textile industry more competitive in the world.

On all accounts, we can say that China's food production can adequately meet its food demand and that the country will be able to maintain its highly self-sufficient food economy in the future in the baseline scenario.

Hicksian equivalent variation Regional real income gains are usually summarized by the Hicksian equivalent variation (EV). EV represents the income that consumers would be willing to forgo to achieve new well-being (up) at new equilibrium compared with the initial well-being (ui) at initial prices (pi) of initial equilibrium.

$$EV = E(pi, up) - E(pi, ui),$$

where E represents the expenditure function to achieve utility level u given a vector of prices p.

Table 13.8 shows that China's total welfare will improve, but per capita welfare

Table 13.6 Baseline scenario, percentage change in commodity import into China with respect to a unit of percentage change in world price

Import	*2005*	*2010*	*2015*	*2020*
Rice	–13.3324	–10.5569	–10.0791	–9.7360
Wheat	–12.9971	–10.4820	–10.7396	–10.4144
Coarse grains	–22.1115	–22.7909	–7.1089	–6.9972
Oilseeds	–2.0799	–1.8316	–1.9527	–2.0193
Sugar	–12.2757	–8.4251	–8.4985	–8.4966
Fibers	–11.7605	–8.0166	–6.6691	–7.0529
Other Crops	–22.9886	–14.9337	–9.8974	–8.2318
Red meat	–14.0390	–11.4793	–10.4860	–10.3034
Pig & poultry	–11.2178	–9.5917	–9.5246	–9.4066
Milk	–13.0922	–11.0029	–10.7063	–10.8149
Fish	–12.6321	–10.1470	–15.9341	–8.7108

gain decrease as time goes on, given the baseline scenario assumption.

We can trace the sources of China's EV by decomposing the various contributions to total EV. Herein, we consider three kinds of contributions, i.e., contribution to EV of allocation effects, contribution to EV of primary factor augmenting technology change, and contribution to EV of changes in the supplies of endowment commodity, i.e., land, unskilled labor, skilled labor, and natural resources. The first one represents how much welfare China can gain through the optimal reallocation of production behavior and consumption behavior at new equilibrium. The second one represents how much welfare China can gain through primary factor technology progress, i.e., TFP in this model, at new equilibrium.

Table 13.9 shows that the more advantage one sector has or the higher value added one sector owns, the more gains China will reap from that sector, given the baseline scenario assumptions. The highest value–added sector, the capital–intensive manufacturing sector, contributes the most. Service sector, which is heavily labor–intensive, contributes the second due to China's advantage in labor. These two sectors' notable contribution can also be attributed to the fact that, in China, (1) the developments in the two sectors are still at low levels, (2) these two sectors are undergoing rapid expansion, and (3) the market allocation of these two sectors is subject to be more efficient. Therefore, the marginal returns of optimal allocation in these two sectors are high.

The contribution from the textile sector ranks third. China has a big advantage in the textile sector for a long time and will likely be able to maintain this for at least two decades. At present, there are several restrictions for China to export textile products to developed countries, especially the U.S. Such restrictions mainly are implemented by those regions in terms of the Multifibre Arrangement (MFA). China is expected to gain more from the textile sector after its accession to WTO because all of the restrictions will be eliminated by 2005 according to agreements for China's accession to WTO.

Table 13.7 Baseline scenario, percentage change in commodity export from China with respect to a unit of percentage change in world price

Export	*2005*	*2010*	*2015*	*2020*
Rice	14.624	8.95942	9.03376	9.07179
Wheat	11.371	9.36187	9.27290	9.20941
Coarse	19.218	27.69724	8.88951	8.60825
Oilseeds	4.919	2.08597	1.52999	0.34848
Sugar	9.161	8.09546	8.11996	8.57879
Fibers	8.912	14.06201	10.13387	10.16533
Other Crops	12.832	11.81590	10.45721	10.54993
Red meat	11.462	11.73257	8.22435	10.51374
Pig &	11.102	10.36355	9.92971	10.24072
Milk	12.115	10.10592	10.25628	10.21413
Fish	11.716	10.40533	7.63307	11.07923

Table 13.8 Baseline scenario, China's EV, US$ million

EV	*2005*	*2010*	*2015*	*2020*
Total	53014	53562	53039	51460
Per capita (US$)	40.77	39.84	38.23	36.15

Among agricultural products, there are relatively more contributions to EV of allocation effects from rice, oilseeds, other crops, and pig and poultry sectors. There are relatively less contributions to EV of allocation effects from wheat, coarse grains, sugar, fibers, red meat, milk, and fish sectors. Herein, a positive number in one sector means that China will gain in the sector and the sector will expand, and a negative number in one sector means China will lose in the sector and the sector will shrink after the optimal allocation. There are 4 sectors with negative contribution to EV of allocation effects in 2005: wheat, coarse grains, sugar, and fibers. However, as a whole, China stands to gain from the allocation effects.

The welfare gain listed in Table 13.10, to some extent, represents the contributions to EV of TFP. The table shows that all sectors gain from the primary factor augmenting technology change, because this change results in higher productivity, more efficiency in production, and lower cost of inputs. Comparing Table 13.10 with Table 13.9, we see that all sectors, except capital–intensive manufacturing sector, gain more through primary factor augmenting technology change than through allocation effect. This means that the technology development and technology application in almost all sectors in China are still at low levels and the marginal return of primary factor augmenting technology change is high.

Table 13.9 Baseline scenario, total contribution to EV of allocation effects, US$ million

China	*2005*	*2010*	*2015*	*2020*
Rice	69.02	61.54	62.23	60.27
Wheat	−15.21	7.6	5.25	6.02
Coarse grains	−9.45	12.75	16	22.31
Oilseeds	329.92	393.53	423.46	430.53
Sugar	−9.61	3.89	4.18	5.73
Fibers	−9.18	8.69	11.23	12.18
Other crops	81.17	85.83	88.56	85.77
Red meat	10.33	12.04	11.53	11.59
Pig & poultry	96.24	97.81	99.47	96.98
Milk	3.44	5.21	6.45	5.97
Fish	14.74	16.19	16.13	15.9
Other food	660.33	659.3	644.27	623.96
Natural extracts	297.66	271.49	253.59	247.8
Textile	1094.08	1083.7	1077.56	1024.75
Labor inten. manuf.	719.02	648.71	625.59	617.64
Capital inten. manuf.	3883.4	3553.34	3361.98	3297.04
Services	2832.74	2720.37	2602.14	2556.38

China can benefit more from TFP, which expands the production frontier, than from reallocation of resources, which usually makes production behavior and consumption behavior move along frontier curves.

From table 13.11, the change in capital contributes so much to EV that it dominates the changes in two other endowments. Unskilled labor contributes the least and even provides a negative contribution to EV in 2020. While the contributions to EV of the changes in capital decrease, those of the changes in skilled labors increase as time goes on. This means that there are opposite trends of marginal gain from skilled labor and capital, and that skilled labor plays an increasingly important role in China's agricultural economy development, as well as in China's whole economy development.

WTO scenario

In addition to all the assumptions used in the baseline scenario, several protocols of China's accession to WTO given in the Report of the Working Party on the Accession of China are integrated into this scenario. The simulation and projection in the WTO scenario proceeds in the following ways:

(1) Forcing the prices of agricultural products in domestic free market used in CAPSiM to be equal to border prices by 2005.
(2) Adjusting the changes in producer and consumer subsidy equivalence used

in CAPSiM according to the agreements of China's accession to WTO.

(3) Adjusting the tariff rate used in GTAP according to the agreements of China's accession to WTO.

(4) Adjusting non–tariff barriers used in CAPSiM according to the agreements of China's accession to WTO.

(5) Adjusting exchange rate assumption. China's forex reserve quickly grew during the last ten years from 21.2 billion US$ in the end of 1993 to 203 billion US$ in the end of October 2001, and the trend will remain. Together with the fast growth rate of the GDP, this high forex reserve will usually induce an appreciation of Chinese yuan. At present, the current account open, but capital account is still controlled. Government control exchange rate by buying forex in the open market to keep the yuan from appreciating. In this case, it is subject to induce inflation as the government keeps buying forex and selling yuan while forex supply keeps going up. China is going to loose the control of capital account, and more buyers can enter the open market. This will release part press of appreciation resulting from more buyers. However, if the supply is still greater than demand, the yuan has to be appreciated. It is estimated that China's forex supply will surpass demand for the next two decades, and more and more operations will be played by the market force after accession to WTO. Taken this into account, it is necessary to adjust exchange rate downward.

Exchange rate assumption in WTO scenario

2000	2001	2002	2003	2004	2005	2006	2007	2008
8.2796	8.2768	8.2755	8.2742	8.273	8.2718	8.2705	8.2693	8.268

2009	2010	2011	2012	2013	2014	2015	2016	2017
8.2667	8.2654	8.2641	8.2628	8.2615	8.2602	8.259	8.2578	8.2565

2018	2019	2020
8.2552	8.254	8.2517

(6) Others are the same as those in the baseline scenario.

The linkage between world market and China's food market and comparison of the results between baseline scenario and WTO scenario Here, we just analyze the difference of the percentage changes in commodity import into China and export from China with respect to a unit of percentage change in world price between the baseline scenario and the WTO scenario. This difference represents the change in sensitivity of China's food market to the world market when the circumstance of China's food economy shifts from the baseline scenario to the WTO scenario.

Table 13.10 Baseline scenario, contribution to EV of primary factor augmenting technology change, US$ million

China	*2005*	*2010*	*2015*	*2020*
Rice	468.13	468.88	468.78	468.36
Wheat	96.63	96.04	95.91	95.77
Coarse grains	152.71	151.41	151.09	150.73
Oilseeds	119.13	118.29	117.65	117.38
Sugar	13.9	13.5	13.46	13.36
Fibers	46	44.36	44.45	44.5
Other crops	974.53	972.73	971.14	969.73
Red meat	67.22	67	66.88	66.72
Pig & poultry	659.55	659.52	658.44	657.61
Milk	23.99	23.9	23.8	23.78
Fish	252.46	250.9	249.67	248.87
Other food	214.04	215.09	215.51	215.35
Natural extracts	740.84	735.88	732.24	731.07
Textile	812.19	815.6	816.22	814.73
Labor inten. manuf.	710.43	710.25	710.27	709.77
Capital inten.	2873.64	2874.59	2874.56	2872.34
Services	4835.44	4845.41	4846	4843.23

Given the percentage changes in the world price index in the baseline scenario and in the WTO scenario, a positive number in Table 13.12 means that China will import more in the WTO scenario than in the baseline scenario, a negative number means that China will import less in the WTO scenario than in the baseline scenario. Conversely, in Table 13.13, a positive number means that China will export more in the WTO scenario than in the baseline scenario, and a negative number means that China will export less in the WTO scenario than in the baseline scenario.

Therefore, we see that:

(1) As a whole, China's accession to WTO will bring more imports of agricultural products into China, and will reduce the export of most agricultural products.

(2) Since the magnitude of the number in each sector represents the degree of impact of China's accession to WTO on that sector, most agricultural sectors in China will face the largest shocks in the next five years. As we know, the next five years cover the period of protection for China to adjust its production structures and economic policies to join WTO, most changes required by WTO protocols will occur during the period.

(3) If both the number in Table 13.12 and the number in Table 13.13 for one sector in the same year are positive, there is a trade expansion in the sector in that year (as a result of China's accession to WTO). Oppositely, if both

the number in Table 13.12 and the number in Table 13.13 for one sector in the same year are negative, there is trade shrinkage in the sector in that year (again, resulting from China's accession to WTO). Therefore, rice trade will expand in 2005 and will then shrink. Sugar trade will shrink after 2015. Fish trade will expand in 2005, 2015 and 2020, and will shrink in 2010. Pig and poultry trade will expand in 2005 and 2015.

(4) The net import of wheat will increase before 2020 and then subsequently decrease. The net import of coarse grains will decrease in 2005 and 2010, and then increase. The net import of oilseeds will increase in all years, so will the net import of cattle and red meat.

China's food security in the WTO scenario The projections of production and consumption given by CAPSiM with WTO assumptions show that:[4]

(1) There are 9 products in which production is greater than consumption (they are the same as those in baseline scenario): rice, wheat, sweet potato, soybean, pork, mutton, eggs, milk, and fish.

(2) There are 3 products in which production is less than consumption (edible oil is added into this category in WTO scenario): other coarse grains, cotton, and edible oil.

(3) There are 3 products in which production is nearly equal to consumption (edible oil, sugar, and beef are excluded which were in this category in the baseline scenario): maize, potato, and vegetable.

(4) There are 3 products in which production surpasses consumption at first, and after some years, consumption surpasses production (sugar and beef are added into this category in WTO scenario): sugar in 2019, beef in 2011, and poultry in 2006.

Although there are some changes in the pattern of production, trade and consumption of several agricultural products mentioned above from the baseline scenario to the WTO scenario, there is no change in the pattern of production, trade and consumption of Chinese staple food. Therefore, on all accounts, we can still say that China's food production can adequately meet its food demand and that China will be able to maintain its highly self–sufficient food economy in the future in the WTO scenario.

Hicksian equivalent variation As we did in the baseline scenario, we present the Hicksian equivalent variation in the WTO scenario in Table 13.14.

Similar to Table 13.8, we see that China's total welfare will improve, but per capita welfare gain will decrease as time goes on, given the WTO scenario assumption. The difference between this table and Table 13.8 is very limited and can therefore be ignored. It means that there will be no significant changes in regional welfare resulting from the changes in China's agricultural sectors after China's accession to WTO. Nevertheless, we can trace in which contribution there is biggest difference between the baseline scenario and the WTO scenario by decomposing the total contributions to EV into three contributions.

Table 13.11 Baseline scenario, contribution to EV of changes in endowment commodity, US$ million

China	*2005*	*2010*	*2015*	*2020*
Unskilled labor	1662.39	1370.33	632.44	–152.49
Skilled labor	2669.53	866.25	2897.16	2932.17
Capital	32095.21	28181.4	26186.83	25917.6

Table 13.12 Differences of percentage change in commodity import into China with respect to a unit of percentage change in world price between the WTO scenario and the baseline scenario

Import	*2005*	*2010*	*2015*	*2020*
Rice	0.58542	–0.05949	–0.05913	–0.05971
Wheat	0.24202	0.22666	0.17913	–0.12982
Coarse grains	–6.04971	–1.82235	0.25077	0.24607
Oilseeds	0.52851	0.31062	0.28299	0.25611
Sugar	0.35274	0.09790	–0.04899	–0.10135
Fibers	2.11022	–0.27937	–0.72734	–0.02105
Other crops	7.65122	14.93376	3.31049	–0.05682
Red meat	2.41873	2.03581	0.72119	0.40564
Pig & poultry	0.85193	0.10022	0.32620	0.29198
Milk	0.74785	0.04827	–0.00229	0.13006
Fish	0.56466	–0.39246	15.93415	0.58829

Given the assumptions in the WTO scenario, we see that the textile and leather sector will contribute the most in the next five years through the allocation effects after China's accession to WTO. The next largest contribution comes from the wheat sector, followed by oilseeds and pig and poultry. In fact, all the agricultural sectors except rice make a positive contribution in the next five years after China's accession to WTO. Therefore, at least in the next five years, China will benefit by optimizing the allocation of production, consumption, and trade based on the world market after its accession to WTO.

Comparing the table with Table 13.15, the numbers in Table 13.16 are small and can therefore be ignored. This means that there will be almost no changes in China's welfare coming from primary factor augmenting technology changes after China's accession to WTO. Similarly, the welfare changes reported in Table 13.17 are also small and can be ignored. Therefore, we can say that the changes in China's welfare resulting from China's accession to WTO will mainly come from the optimal allocation of production, consumption, and trade based on the whole world market.

Table 13.13 Differences of percentage change in commodity export from China with respect to a unit of percentage change in world price between the WTO scenario and the baseline scenario

Export	*2005*	*2010*	*2015*	*2020*
Rice	0.17018	–0.04187	–0.04911	–0.05789
Wheat	–0.13459	0.10959	–0.08693	0.00245
Coarse	6.18090	2.28449	–0.27396	–0.18957
Oilseeds	–1.46811	–0.64666	–1.00579	–0.92918
Sugar	–0.21214	–0.17892	–0.19475	–0.22351
Fibers	–0.45397	–4.24775	5.07931	–2.15687
Other	0.10228	0.06036	–0.03328	–0.03207
Red meat	–0.10050	–0.17743	1.26732	–2.87332
Pig &	0.51230	–0.56134	0.49400	–0.14352
Milk	–0.04582	–0.05509	–0.07338	–0.09494
Fish	0.10558	–0.03447	0.05149	1.73742

Table 13.14 WTO scenario, China's EV, US$ million

EV	*2005*	*2010*	*2015*	*2020*
Total	52981	53564	53042	51461
Per capita (US$)	40.75	39.84	38.23	36.15

Conclusions

Before any conclusion can be made, it should be noted that:

(1) What have been done above focuses on the change from an initial steady state to a new steady state under various assumptions given in the two scenarios. The methodology that has been adopted is a combination of dynamic analysis and static analysis. Simulation and projection are implemented by a partial equilibrium model (agricultural sector specific), CAPSiM, for China, and a CGE model, GTAP, for all the regions.

(2) The linkage between CAPSiM and GTAP is done by the communication of changes in China's agricultural products trade, without consideration of the changes in other sector's trade, given by CAPSiM, with the changes in world market price, given by GTAP. Therefore, the effects of changes in agricultural sectors on other sectors can be simulated by GTAP, but the effects of changes in other sectors on agricultural sectors cannot be simulated directly by CAPSiM, and cannot be wholly simulated by GTAP as well because CAPSiM cannot transfer this information to GTAP.

Nevertheless, we can safely say this shortcoming, if any, is limited and will not incompatibly change what we have generated because a) the agriculture sector is independent of other sectors in China, and b) the omitted effects are indirect ones which are small.

(3) All assumptions and parameters given in two scenarios are inferred by some other econometric models, e.g. AIDS, or experts' experience inference based on the available information. Nevertheless, some unforeseen changes will occur in the future. It is possible that these unanticipated changes will, to some extent, alter the patterns or behaviors of production or consumption. These kinds of change will mostly result from new high technologies. In that case, some commodities which are important in people's daily life at present will become less important, or will even be replaced by some newly developed commodities in the future, and vice versa. Historically, occurrences of such changes are not unusual. However, people have no other choice but to keep doing such inference as what we have done in this study, to guide their behaviors in the future, making some adjustments as time goes by. We can also worry less about what we have done (focus on agriculture sector) because food economy is more stable than other sectors in the whole economy, yet the period of projection in this study is long enough to be manageable.

Based on historical data and projection, we see that China's food economy has moderate impact on the rest of the world. The smooth and moderate interaction between China's food economy and global food economy does not mean that China's food economy is not important, but shows that China's food economy is stable and healthy, as well as comparatively independent.

Undeniably, China's agricultural products trade share in the world will increase after China enters WTO. According to the simulation, however, the changes will also be moderate and will not bring about abnormal shocks in the world market. Most shocks may occur in the next five years when China's economy is expected to experience the interim to accommodate the new circumstances.

China's accession to WTO will bring many changes to China's economy. China will gain in some sector and lose in some other sectors after accession to WTO. But as a whole, gain is more than loss.

China's food security

According to the projection done by CAPSiM, there are 9 products (both in baseline scenario and WTO scenario) whose productions are greater than their consumptions, i.e., rice, wheat, sweet potato, soybean, pork, mutton, eggs, milk and fish. There are 6 products in the baseline scenario and 3 products in the WTO scenario whose productions are nearly equal to their consumptions. These products largely account for the Chinese' daily food demand. There are 3 products whose productions are less than their consumptions in the WTO scenario, i.e., other coarse grains, cotton and edible oil. Among these products, other coarse grain is mostly demanded as feed use and industry use; cotton is mainly used in textile

Table 13.15 Change in contribution to EV of allocation effects from the baseline scenario to the WTO scenario, US$ million

China	*2005*	*2010*	*2015*	*2020*
Rice	–0.03	–0.03	–0.02	–0.01
Wheat	10.4	–0.06	–0.02	0.07
Coarse grains	2.93	1.34	1.63	2.14
Oilseeds	9.74	2.41	1.29	0.7
Sugar	3.21	–0.01	0	–0.04
Fibers	7.2	1.11	0.63	0.18
Other crops	0.15	0.02	–0.37	0.05
Red meat	2.31	–0.02	0.03	0.01
Pig & poultry	6.46	0.09	–0.32	–0.2
Milk	1.88	0.01	0	–0.01
Fish	0.28	–0.01	–0.01	0.01
Other food	0.12	0.1	0.02	0.08
Natural extracts	–0.25	0.1	0.09	0.06
Textile	19.15	–2.92	–3.15	–2.64
Labor inten. manuf.	0.13	0.11	0.08	0.06
Capital inten.	–0.71	0.97	0.81	0.6
Services	0.31	0.02	–0.01	–0.01

industry (mostly for textile products export); only edible oil has a direct effect on people's daily life, yet part of it is used in the food processing industry. The shortage of these products can be made up in the world market without affecting China's food security.

On all accounts, we can say that China's food production can adequately meet its food demand and will be able to maintain its highly self–sufficient food economy in the future, even after accession to WTO.

Trade and linkage

China's agricultural products trade, especially Chinese staple food products trade, with the rest of the world has been a supplement to balance supply of and demand for agricultural products, and will still be in the future. This is determined by China's status: China is a big country with one–fifth of the total world population, China's food security can be ensured only by China. As a result, the mutual impact of China's market and world market is lessened. Even if there are such special shocks as China's accession to WTO or uncertainty shocks to China's food market (both on the supply side and demand side), there will not be any significant variations in the two markets and the interaction of the two markets is acceptable.

As China's economy develops, there will be a stronger linkage between its food market and that of the world. On the positive side, this linkage will benefit China's optimizing resources allocation and its optimizing supply and demand in the world

Table 13.16 Change in contribution to EV of primary factor augmenting technology change from the baseline scenario to the WTO scenario, US$ million

China	*2005*	*2010*	*2015*	*2020*
Rice	0	0	0	0
Wheat	–0.17	0	0	0
Coarse grains	–0.09	–0.02	–0.02	–0.03
Oilseeds	–0.02	–0.01	0.01	0.03
Sugar	–0.06	0	0	0
Fibers	–0.14	0.05	0.05	0.04
Other crops	–0.07	0.01	0.02	0
Red meat	–0.1	0	–0.01	0.01
Pig & poultry	–0.19	–0.01	0.01	0.01
Milk	–0.06	0	0	0
Fish	0.01	–0.01	0	0.01
Other food	0.03	0	0	0
Natural extracts	0.02	0.02	0.01	0.01
Textile	0.59	–0.1	–0.1	–0.08
Labor inten. manuf.	0.04	0	0	0
Capital inten. manuf.	0.17	0.02	0	0
Services	0	0	0	0

market. Based on the law of comparative advantage and in view of the fact that the costs in most of China's agricultural production are higher than world average, this growing linkage will induce China to import more and export less in most agriculture products.

On the negative side, this linkage may also bring about more risks in the implementation of China's food security policy and in maintaining the stability of the world market. Fortunately, the probability of this case is low, based on the results of the simulation. Trading the risk off the high cost to maintain high self–sufficiency, it will be beneficial to ensure China's food security with a more efficient linkage with the rest of the world by reducing the level of food self–sufficiency and more actively entering the world market to balance food supply and demand.

Welfare

In this article, we use the Hicksian equivalent variation to measure welfare. According to the simulation, Chinese welfare will improve, but the welfare gain will decrease as time goes on. Herein, diminishing marginal return works in the gain from stronger linkage with the rest of the world.

When analyzing the components of total EV by sectors, we see how the law of comparative advantage works. The sectors having more competitive advantages

Table 13.17 Contribution to EV of changes in endowment commodity from baseline scenario to WTO scenario, US$ million

China	*2005*	*2010*	*2015*	*2020*
Unskilled labor	0.09	–0.01	–0.01	0
Skilled labor	0.29	–0.03	–0.04	–0.03
Capital	3.36	–0.27	–0.34	–0.26

stand to gain more, and the sectors having less competitive advantages subsequently gain less. Meanwhile, the more important one sector in the whole economy is, the more is gained from the sector, and vice versa.

There are many factors contributing to people's real income. We decomposed China's EV by sector into three contributions, i.e., contribution to EV of allocation effects, contribution to EV of primary factor augmenting technology change, and contribution to EV of changes in the supplies of endowment commodity, i.e., land, unskilled labor, skilled labor, and natural resources.

By comparing the welfare gained under different scenarios, we see that the changes caused by China's accession to WTO are less significant, and the most relevant change, in this case, will occur over the next five years, and China will benefit more from allocation effects after entering WTO. This also represents that more effects of agricultural sectors on China's welfare will come from domestic market rather than the world market.

China will experience more adjustment in agricultural production structure in the next five years. This adjustment will definitely bring about welfare redistribution and will not necessarily be advantageous to all people in all sectors. Some people or some sectors will gain less or even lose. Those losses are the costs of the structure adjustment, though as a whole China's welfare will increase.

Comparing the contribution to EV of allocation effects versus the contribution to EV of primary factor augmenting technology change, we see that the latter contributes more. This means that China will benefit more from improvement of technology than from adjustment in structure.

Skilled labor contributes more to the welfare than unskilled labor. It is also shown that contribution to China's EV of changes in endowment commodity is dominated by the contribution to EV of changes in capital. This means that capital formation and capital stock is the most important factor to improve welfare.

China is rich in labor. This is China's advantage in labor–intensive industry, and this advantage will last at least 20 years because there is still a huge labor stock in rural areas, although population growth rate is not high and is actually going down. However, the ratio of skilled labor to total labor is low compared with that in advanced regions, and this status will remain for a long time though it is gradually improving. Therefore, any development in the labor–intensive industry will more directly improve Chinese welfare, while an increase in capital formation will improve the capacity of the whole Chinese economy.

China's food economy will affect global food economy in two ways: direct effect which works within agricultural industry; and indirect effect which works through the changes in other industries induced by the change in the agricultural industry. Obviously, the first effect dominates the second, and both of them work through international trade. In this study, these two effects are implied in the simulation of GTAP and in the projection of CAPSiM through the linkage of the two models. In IV, we see that the mutual impact of two economies is not much and is smooth. This does not mean that China's food economy is less important; instead, it shows that China's food economy is stable and healthy, as well as comparatively independent.

Without a doubt, China's stable and healthy food economy plays an important role in the stability and healthy development of the global food economy. Although China's food economy does not play a dominant role in the world, it at least ensures that the global food economy will not be disturbed adversely by China. This relationship exists and will be strengthened after China's accession to WTO.

Therefore, both China and the rest of the world need a stable and healthy Chinese food economy. In view of this importance, Chinese government has endeavored to ensure China's food security. However, there is a tradeoff between food security and efficiency. In the past, Chinese government paid much more attention to food security than food economy efficiency. In fact, to some extent, the achievement in food security was made at the expense of losing efficiency, typically represented by a higher procurement price in rural areas than selling price in urban areas in order to protect producers in rural areas and consumers in urban areas. This protection cannot be sustained, especially in a market–driven economy, not only because of the heavy financial burden but also because of the distortion in the food market. Fortunately, this distortion has been corrected without jeopardizing the food market after the onset of food marketing system reforms. Obviously, this success is based on the achievement of food security and economy development in rural areas. What is more, this success soundly supports China's food economy development under new market conditions, especially under the WTO framework.

To encapsulate, China's food economy is stable and healthy, and a stable and healthy Chinese food economy benefits not only China, but also the whole world.

Notes

1 So far, there are several models in the world which have been developed aimed primarily at predicting China's future food situations as well as determining its potential impacts on the world market, among which the most popular are: Brown's model, IMPACT, CAPSiM, CAAP, OECF, Mitchell model, Nyberg model. See Fan and Agcaoili–Sombilla (1997).

2 Hertel (1997).

3 Li (2002).

4 Li (2002).

References

Bigman, D. (1985), *Food Policies and Food Security under Instability – Modeling and Analysis*, Lexington Books.

Chung, J.W. (1994), *Utility and Production Functions*, Blackwell, Oxford UK and Cambridge USA.

Commodities Team Development Prospect Group (2000), *A Comprehensive Review and Price Forecast*, The World Bank.

Deaton, A. and Muellbauer, J. (1980), *Economics and Consumer Behavior*, Cambridge University Press.

Elbehri, A. and Pearson, K.R. (2000), 'Implementing Bilateral Tariff Rate Quotas in GTAP using GEMPACK', GTAP Technical Paper No. 18.

Fan, S. and Agcaoili–Sombilla, M. (1997), 'Why projections on China's future food supply and demand differ', *The Australian Journal of Agricultural and Resource Economics*, **41**(2), pp. 169–190.

Fan, S. and Pardey, P. (1997), 'Research, productivity, and Output Growth in Chinese Agriculture', *Journal of Development Economics* **53**, pp. 115–137.

Francois, J. and Strutt, A. (1999), *Post Uruguay Round Tariff Vectors for GTAP Version 4*, Faculty of Economics, H8–23 Erasmus University Rotterdam and Economics Department, Waikato Management Scholl University of Waikato.

Fuller, F., Beghin, J., De Cara, S., Fabiosa, J., Cheng F. and Matthey, H. (2001), 'China's Accession to the WTO: What Is at Stake for Agricultural Markets?', Working Paper 01–WP 276, Center for Agricultural and Rural Development, Iowa State University.

Hertel, T.W. (1997), *Global Trade Analysis – Modeling application*, Cambridge University Press.

Huang, J. and Chen, C. (1999), 'Effects of Trade Liberalization on Agriculture in China: Institutional and Structural Aspects', Working Paper Series 42 and 43, The CGPRT Center.

Huang, J. and Rozelle, S. (1998), *China's Grain Economy to the Twenty First Century*, China Agriculture Press.

Huff, K., McDougall, R. and Walmsley, T. (1999), 'Contributing Input–Output Tables to the GTAP Data Base', GTAP Technical Paper No. 1.

Jin, S., Huang, J., Hu, R. and Rozelle, S. (2001), 'The Creation and Spread of Technology and Total Factor Productivity in China's Agriculture', unpublished.

Li, N. (2002), 'China's Food Economy and Its Implications for the Rest of the World', Ph.D. Dissertation, School of Economics, University of the Philippines, Diliman.

McMillan, J., Whalley, J. and Zhou, L. (1989), 'The Impact of China's Economic Reforms on Agricultural Productivity Growth', *Journal of Political Economy* **97**, pp. 781–807.

Nyberg, A. and Rozelle, S. (1999), *Accelerating China's Rural Transformation*, The World Bank, Washington, D.C.

Salvatore, D. (1995), *International Economics*, Prentice–Hall International, Inc.

State Statistical Bureau, China (1980 - 2000), *Statistical Yearbook of China*, China Statistics Press.

State Statistical Bureau, China (1985 - 2000), *Statistical Yearbook of China Urban Household Survey in China,* China Statistics Press.

State Statistical Bureau, China (1985 - 2000), *Statistical Yearbook of Rural Household Survey in China.* China Statistics Press.

The World Bank (2001), *Global Economic Prospects and the Developing Countries*, The World Bank

Walmsley, T.L. and Hertel, T.W. (2000), *China's Accession to the WTO: Timing is*

Everything, Center for Global Trade Analysis, Purdue University.
Working Party on the Accession of China (2001), *Draft Report of the Working Party on the Accession of China*, World Trade Organization.

Index

APRE (Asian Pacific Rim Economies)
  exports 110, 120
  members 108–9
  XRCA 112–4, 116–8
  see also EAE
Argentina
  credits 173–5
  currency crisis 133
  export externalities, and GDP 45–6
  exports 134–6
    composition 137
    destinations 141, 157
  international borrowings 185–7
  Mexican/Thai
    devaluation effect 177
    trade competition 179, 180–2, 184
    trade linkage 176
  openness 62
  stock volatilities 197
Asia, exports 134–40
Asian Crisis (1997) 133

Backward linkage, economic growth 62–3
Balassa, Bela 108, 111
'Banker Effect', stock pricing 265–75
Bellman equations 251
Beveridge curve 252
Bin, Guoqiang 265–75
Bolivia
  exports 134–6
  international borrowings 185–7
Brazil
  credits 173–5
  exports 134–6
    composition 137
    destinations 142, 158
  international borrowings 185–7
  Mexican/Thai
    devaluation effect 177
    trade competition 179, 180–2, 184
    trade linkage 176
  stock volatilities 197

Capital accumulation
  and foreign trade, model 76–8
  and product development, model 67–73
CAPSiM (China's Agricultural Policy Simulation Model) 277–300
  GTAP, linkage 278–83
  trade and linkage 297–8
  WTO scenario 284, 290–5
Catching up, economic growth 56–9, 61
Chao, Chi-Chur 83–96
Cheng, Leonard K. 108–30
Cheung, Yin-Wong 201–16
Chile
  credits 173–5
  exports 134–6
    composition 137
    destinations 143, 159
  Japanese international lending 186–7
  Mexican/Thai
    devaluation effect 177
    trade competition 179, 180–2, 184
    trade linkage 176
  stock volatilities 197
  US international lending 185, 187
China
  accounting reforms 33
  banking system 36–7
  catching up 56–9, 61
  coal reserves 43
  export externalities 43–8
  as export platform 59–60
  exports 134–6
    composition 137
    destinations 144, 160
  farm land 43
  FDI 83–96
    from Hong Kong 97–9, 102–3
    from US 97–8, 100, 102–3
  fiscal decentralization 30–3
  food economy, international implications 276–300
  food security 283, 296–7
  GDP 22, 48–9, 276

income, per capita 248
international borrowings 185–7
market reforms 26–7, 51–4
Mexican/Thai
devaluation effect 177
trade competition 179, 180–2, 184
trade linkage 176
migration restrictions 13, 245
natural resources 42–3
openness 41, 46, 54, 60, 62
petroleum reserves 43
policy reforms 33–7
population 42, 276
rural 245–6
urban 245–6
relative per capita real income 50, 51
size, and economic growth 41, 50, 54
stock market, pricing model 266–70
stock volatilities 196
tax structure 25–30
trade 276
TVEs 31–2
urbanization 245, 247
VAT 25, 33–6
China's Agricultural Policy Simulation Model *see* CAPSiM
CHIP (China Household Income Project) 11–2
Choi, I. 87–8
Chou, Win-Lin 83–96
CIs (Certificates of Indebtedness) 218–9
Colombia
credits 173–5
exports 134–6
composition 138
destinations 145, 161
Japanese international lending 186–7
Mexican/Thai
devaluation effect 177
trade competition 179, 180–2, 184
trade linkage 176
stock volatilities 197
US international lending 185, 187
Commodities
classification system 124–7
intra-regional exports 109–11
Contagion
coefficients, GARCH Model 193–4
currency crisis 133–5
definitions 156–9
financial markets 192
CSRC (China Securities Regulatory Commission) 266
Currency boards
characteristics 218
Hong Kong 218–23, 237–8
Currency crises 133–5

DOLS (Dynamic Ordinary Least Squares) method 91–3
Dornbusch overshooting model 203–5, 213–4

EAE (East Asian Economies)
exports 120
members 109
XRCA 112–4, 116–8
East Asians, export externalities, and GDP 45
Economic growth
backward linkage 62–3
catching up 56–9, 61
and FDI 97
and fiscal decentralization 38
and higher education 3–5, 7–11, 16–8
and size 41, 50, 54
and taxation 22–40
Economic and Technological Development Zones *see* ETDZs
Education, and resource allocation
households 12–4
labor market 14–6
see also higher education; schooling
ETDZs (Economic and Technological Development Zones) 100, 104–5
EU (European Union)
exports 110, 120, 134
members 108
XRCA 112–4, 116–8
Exchange Fund, Hong Kong 218–20
Exchange rates, saddle–path dynamics 201–15
Exports
Asian countries 134–6
EU 134–6
externalities 44
Latin American countries 134–6
NAFTA, share 110, 112
share
APRE 110
EU 110, 112
trade linkages 141–72

FDI (Foreign Direct Investment)
  and economic growth 97
  and GDP 92–3, 104
  Hong Kong 97–9, 102–3
  regional competition
    empirical analysis 86–91
    model 83–94
  and tax revenue 83–4
  US 97–88, 100, 102–3
Finance, linkages 164–71
  measures 183–6, 192
Financial markets, contagion 192
Fiscal decentralization 30–3
  and economic growth 38
Fleisher, Belton M. 3–21
Food security, China 283, 296–7
Forbes' Measure of Income Effect 177
Forbes' Trade Competition Index, trade composition 182
Foreign Direct Investment *see* FDI
Fung, K.C. 97–107

GARCH Model 192–3
Gardeazabal, Javier 201–16
GDP (Gross Domestic Product)
  China 22, 48–9, 276
  export externalities 45–6
  and FDI 92–3, 104
  government revenue, as proportion 34–5
  and higher education 5–6, 8–9
  and seignorage, international comparisons 24, 28
Glick and Rose Absolute Trade Competition Index 179
Global Trade Analysis Project *see* GTAP
Gordon, Roger H. 22–40
Government revenue, GDP 34–5
Grossman–Helpman model 66, 78
GRP (Gross Regional Product) 109
  exports 117–9
GTAP (Global Trade Analysis Project) 277–8
  CAPSiM, linkage 278–83

Harris–Todaro model, rural/urban migration 249–63
Higher education
  and economic growth 3, 4–5, 7–11, 16–8
  international comparisons 4
  and GDP 5–6, 8–9
  and income 11–2
  rate of return 7, 10
  and TFP 8
HKMA (Hong Kong Monetary Authority) 220–1
Hong Kong
  currency board 218–23, 237–8
  currency crises 133, 235–7
  currency system 218–9
  exchange rate regimes 220
  Exchange Fund 218–20, 222, 235, 238
  exports 134–6
  FDI, in China 97–9, 102–3
  international borrowings 185–7
  Mexican/Thai
    devaluation effect 177
    trade competition 179, 180–2, 184
    trade linkage 176
  monetary systems 222
  stock volatilities 196
Households, education, and resource allocation 12–4

Iizaka, Hitomi 97–107
Income
  and higher education 11–2
  rural/urban 248
Income tax, rate 25
India
  exports 134–6
    composition 138
    destinations 146, 162
  international borrowings 185–7
  Mexican/Thai
    devaluation effect 177
    trade competition 179, 180–2, 184
    trade linkage 176
  stock volatilities 196
Indonesia
  currency crisis 133
  exports 134–6
    composition 138
    destinations 147, 163
  international borrowings 185–7
  Mexican/Thai
    devaluation effect 177
    trade competition 179, 180–2, 184
    trade linkage 176
  stock volatilities 196

International Commodity Trade
Classification System 124–7
International trade, model 76–8
INTRA (Intra–Regional Exports) 117–21
APRE 118, 120–1
calculation 127–9
EAE 120–1
EU 118, 120–1
NAFTA 118, 120–1
Investment, incentives 28–9

Japan
banks, lending 186
creditors 173–5
export externalities 46, 48
exports 112, 134–6
international lending 187
openness 52–3, 55, 62
Relative per capita real income 52, 56
XRCA 112–4, 116–8
Johansen procedure 202–3, 205, 207–13

Korea (South)
currency crisis 133
exports 43–4, 134–6
composition 138
destinations 148, 164
international borrowings 185–7
Mexican/Thai
devaluation effect 177
trade competition 179, 180–2, 184
trade linkage 176
openness 53, 55–6, 62
Relative per capita real income 53
stock volatilities 196
Kwan, Yum K. 217–41

Labor market, education, and resource
allocation 14–6
Laing, Derek 245–64
Latin America
borrowings
Japan 187, 189
US banks 185, 189
exports 134–40
Lau and Yan's Trade Competition Index
184
Lau, Lawrence J. 133–200
Leung, Siu Fai 108–30
Li, Ninghui 276–300
Li, Wei 22–40

Lin, Chelsea C. 97–107
Lui, Francis T. 217–41

Ma, Zihui 108–30
McKoskey–Kao test 89, 91
Malaysia
currency crisis 133
exports
composition 139
destinations 149, 165
international borrowings 185–7
Mexican/Thai
devaluation effect 177
trade competition 179, 180–2, 184
trade linkage 176
stock volatilities 196
Market reforms, China 26–7, 51–4
Mexico
credits 173–5
devaluation effect 177
direct trade linkage 176
exports 134–6
composition 139
destinations 150, 166
international borrowings 185–7
stock volatilities 195
Thai
devaluation effect 177
trade competition 179, 180, 182
trade linkage 176
Migration model
rural/urban 249–63
basic environment 249–53
comparative statics 260–2
steady state equilibrium 255–60
wage bargaining 253–5
Migration restrictions, China 13, 15, 245
Monetary systems, Hong Kong 222

NAFTA (North American Free Trade
Area)
exports 110, 112, 120
members 108
XRCA 112–4, 116–8
National Tax Bureau 25–6
Natural resources
China 42–3
US 42–3
North–South product–cycle model 73–6

OCCs (Open Coastal Cities) 103, 105

Openness
  Argentina 62
  China 41, 46, 54, 60, 62
  index 47, 54
  Japan 52–3, 55, 62
  Korea 53, 55–6, 62
  Taiwan 62

Panel cointegration 89, 91–2
Panel error correction model 92–3
Panel regression 99, 100–1
Panel unit root tests 87–8
Park, Chuhwan 245–64
Penn World Table 45–6, 54
Petroleum reserves 43
Philippines
  currency crisis 133
  exports 134–6
    composition 139
    destinations 151, 167
  international borrowings 185–7
  Mexican/Thai
    devaluation effect 177
    trade competition 179, 180–2, 184
    trade linkage 176
  stock volatilities 196
Policy reforms 33–7
Population
  China 42, 245–6, 276
  US 42
Product development, and capital accumulation, model 67–73
Product innovation, model 67–73, 79

RCA (Revealed Comparative Advantage) indices 108–9
  see also XRCA
Relative per capita real income
  China 50–1
  Japan 52, 56
  Korea 53
Resource allocation, and education 12–4
  labor market 14–6
Romer model 66–7, 78
RTGS (Real Time Gross Settlement), HKMA 220
Russia, currency crisis 133–4

Saddle-path dynamics 201–15
Schooling
  and resource allocation, labor market 14–16
  and wages 11–12
Seignorage, and GDP, international comparisons 24, 28
SEZs (Special Economic Zones) 97, 100, 103
Shenzen Stock Exchange
  listed companies 271
  pricing mechanism 265–74
Shu, Yuan 265–75
Silver standard 218
Singapore
  currency crisis 133
  exports
    composition 139
    destinations 152, 168
  international borrowings 185–7
  Mexican/Thai
    devaluation effect 177
    trade competition 179, 180–2, 184
    trade linkage 176
  stock volatilities 196
SITC (Standard International Trade Classification) 124–7
Siu, Alan 97–107
South (Korea), US international lending 185
Southeast Asian countries
  international borrowings 185–7
  Mexican funds competition190–1
Sterling, and Hong Kong dollar 219
Stock market, China, pricing model 266–70
Stock pricing, 'Banker Effect' 265–75
Stock volatilities 195–8

Taiwan
  exports 134–6
    composition 140
    destinations 153, 169
  international borrowings 185–7
  Mexican/Thai
    devaluation effect 177
    trade competition 179, 180–2, 184
    trade linkage 176
  openness 62
Taxation
  and economic growth 22–40
  reforms 25–6
  revenue
    FDI 83–4

as proportion of GDP 34–5
sources 22–3
structure 25–30
see also income tax; VAT
Technology transfers, model 73–6
TFP (Total Factor Productivity), and higher education 8
Thailand
currency crisis 133, 192
direct trade linkage 176
exports 134–6
composition 140
destinations 154, 170
international borrowings 185–7
Mexican
devaluation effect 177
trade competition 179, 180–2, 184
trade linkage 176
stock volatilities 195
trade competition 179
Trade
and capital accumulation, model 76–8
competition index 184
intra-regional
commodities 109–10
comparison 108–29
exports 117–21, 127–9
statistics 134–6
XRCA 108, 111–29
linkages 161–3, 171–83
TVEs (Township & Village Enterprises) 31–2

Uruguay
credits 173–5
exports 134–6
composition 140
destinations 155, 171
international borrowings 185–7
Mexican/Thai
devaluation effect 177
trade competition 179, 180–2, 184
trade linkage 176
US
banks, lending 185
coal reserves 43
creditors 173–5
FDI in China 97–8, 100, 102–3
international lending 185, 187
petroleum reserves 43
population 42
trade 116–17

VAR (Vector Autoregressive) model 218, 223–6
VAT (Value-Added Tax) 25, 33–6
Vázquez, Jesús 201–16
Venezuela
credits 173–5
exports 134–6
composition 140
destinations 156, 172
international borrowings 185–7
Mexican/Thai
devaluation effect 177
trade competition 179, 180–2, 184
trade linkage 176
stock volatilities 197

Wages, and schooling 11–2
Wan, Henry 41–65
Wang, Ping 245–64

XRCA (Export Revealed Comparative Advantage)
APRE 112–8
empirical studies 111–2
EU 112–8
intra-regional trade 108, 111–29
Japan 112–4, 116–8
NAFTA 112–8

Yan, Isabel K. 133–200
Yu, Eden S.H. 83–96

Zou, Heng-fu 66–80